# FIRST HANDBOOK OF PSYCHOLOGICAL AND SOCIAL INSTRUMENTS

**CONCEPTS IN COMMUNICATION INFORMATICS & LIBRARIANSHIP (CICIL)**

General Editor: **S.P. AGRAWAL**

For a list of titles in this series, see pp. 420-22 at the end of the book.

**Books Published in the Series:**

1. First Handbook of Psychological and Social Instruments/ **Udai Pareek and T.Venkateswara Rao**

2. Second Handbook of Psychological and Social Instruments/ **D.M. Pestonjee**

3. Third Handbook of Psychological and Social Instruments 2 Vols/ **D.M. Pestonjee**

# PREFACE TO THE SECOND EDITION

THE FIRST **Handbook** was published in 1974, and was out of print in three years. Since then there has been a demand for it. We had seen the need of continuing the series. Our colleague, Professor D.M. Pestonjee, edited the **Second Handbook** two years back and it was equally well received.

Concept Publishing Company now intend to carry on this work under their new series of documentation under the able guidance of Shri S.P. Agrawal. We are very pleased to see the **First Handbook** in print again. Each **Handbook** will have new material, and therefore will not be a revised edition of the previous one. The addresses of quite a few authors of the instruments contained in this **Handbook** are likely to have changed.

We appreciate the initiative taken by Concept in reprinting the **First Handbook**, and the generosity of the original, Samashti Publishers, for their permission to do so.

UDAI PAREEK
T. VENKATESWARA RAO

January 26, 1992

# PREFACE TO THE FIRST EDITION

SEVERAL RESEARCH instruments have been developed and standardised in India. In the absence of information about instruments developed in a particular area, efforts are duplicated to develop instruments, instead of building on the previously standardised ones. The **Handbook** has been prepared to fulfil this important need.

Files of the first ten years of several well known journals were searched, and a list was prepared of instruments reported and cited in the papers. **Mental Measurement Year Book** compiled by NCERT and **Handbook of Research Instruments in Agricultural Extension** prepared by IARI were also searched for selecting instruments. After collecting information about the instruments, the original authors were requested to complete and return a form giving technical details about the instruments, and for providing copies of the original instruments.

The four different sections of the **Handbook** described below grew out of necessity to include even incomplete information to make it comprehensive.

### The Scope and Classification System

The scope of the **Handbook** was limited to instruments in English language and it was decided not to include research instruments in the areas of intelligence, aptitudes and achievement. A large number of questionnaires and interview schedules had to be excluded, unless they were precise and contained enough technical information regarding their reliability and validity.

### Using the Handbook

The coding system used in the **Handbook** will be helpful both in indicating the exact nature of the instrument as well as in continuing the series in the future volumes of the **Handbook.**

The coding system is based on the following 3-tier classification:

**Part** indicates the field. The **Handbook** is divided into four Parts as follows:

1. Personality
2. Education
3. Organisational Behaviour
4. Social Phenomena

**Each Part** is further divided into sections. The first number of the code number of the instrument indicates the Part, and the second number indicates the Section under that part.

Under each Section four categories of instruments are included, as given below:

A Instruments reproduced with information
B Instruments with technical information only
C Citations
D Adaptations

In each category the instruments are serially numbered. Thus, in numbering an instrument the Part number occurs first, followed by the Section number, the Category letter and the Serial number. For example, instrument 12A5 would indicate that the instrument is in Part 1, i.e. Personality, dealing with Adjustment (Section 2), is reproduced here with technical information (Category A) and has a Serial number 5 in that category. Similarly, 31D1 indicates that the instrument falls under Organisational Behaviour (Part 3), dealing with Industrial Organisations (Section 1), is an Indian adaptation of a foreign instrument (Category D) and has a Serial number of 1 under that category. There are three indices provided at the end· instrument index, author index and subject index. The indices use the coded numbers of the instruments, and not page numbers. These may be used by the reader for locating a desired instrument.

A cyclostyled pre-publication copy of the **Handbook** was

prepared and circulated amongst about 100 heads of departments and research institutions. We are very grateful for the comments and suggestions and for some instruments brought to our attention.

This volume of the **Handbook** is the first in a continuing series. As soon as we collect a sufficient number of new instruments we shall publish the next volume. We shall be grateful if the authors of the instruments in the categories B and C send us copies of the instruments, and other missing details. These instruments will then appear in category A in the next volume. The numbering of instruments will be continuous from this volume, and the volumes of the **Handbook** will be cumulative in nature. Authors and publishers of instruments not included in this volume are requested to bring them to our notice.

We are extremely grateful to the Indian Council of Social Science Research for the grant without which the preparation of this **Handbook** would not have been possible. We should particularly like to express our gratefulness to Shri J.P. Naik for his personal keen interest and encouragement. We are grateful to various Research Assistants who worked on this project: Mohan Advani, Shashi Sood, and R.K. Dashora. We would also like to thank D.S. Saruparia, Narendra Dixit, M.P. Jain, C.P. Joshi, and R.K. Singhvi, students of the Department of Psychology, University of Udaipur for their help. In the end we would like to thank M.C. Sharma for the secretarial help he provided.

Our greatest obligation is to the authors and publishers who sent us their instruments and technical information. As stated on the second inside cover page, the copyright of the instruments vests in the authors and/or the publishers, as the case may be, and no instrument, or its part, may be reproduced without their specific permission.

*Indian Institute of Management*
*Ahmedabad*
*August 15, 1974*

UDAI PAREEK
T. VENKATESWARA RAO

# CONTENTS

## PART 4: SOCIAL PHENOMENA

# PART I

# PERSONALITY

# Introduction

THIS PART of the Handbook reports instruments dealing with personality dimensions. These instruments are reported under five sections : general, adjustment and problems, anxiety, self concept, and motivation. This classification system is a pragmatic one reflecting the number of instruments reported, and not a rigorous conceptual one based on theoretical distinctions. When instruments to measure a particular personality dimension were found to be sufficient in number to make to warrant special attention, the dimension was treated separately. Thus self-concept, anxiety, adjustment and motivation emerged as distinct categories. However, the sections on self concept, and anxiety include instruments dealing exclusively with these dimensions, whereas the sections on adjustment and motivation report instruments dealing with several types of adjustment and motivation respectively. Even in these two sections the instruments on one aspect are more frequent than on others. For example, the section on motivation is heavily loaded with instruments to measure achievement motive. By the rule of exclusion, the instruments dealing with the rest of the personality dimensions have been grouped under the title of general instruments of personality. These include instruments dealing with several other personality dimensions like extraversion, introversion, authoritarianism, rigidity, conformity, aggression, etc. The details are described under that title below.

There are in all 218 instruments reported in this part of the Handbook. Of these 73 are adaptations. There are 37 instruments reproduced here half of them being in the general category. Information is provided for another 77 instruments. Titles for another 31 have been cited and the information for these is not available. The detailed break up of the instruments on personality appears in Table 1.

**General Instruments**

There are in all 134 instruments listed under this title. These are general personality inventories and cover different personality dimensions. Most of these instruments are multi-trait personality tests and cover more than a single personality dimension each. Some are exclusively meant to cover a single or a selected few dimensions like extraversion, introversion, neuroticism etc. The different dimensions covered by these instruments include : intolerance of ambiguity, neuroticism, authoritarianism, rigidity-flexibility, dependency, trust, initiative, activity level, insecurity, inferiority, aggression, conformity, extraversion, introversion, fear, cognitive imbalance, sex role preference, time appreciation, achievement press, conservatism, ascendance, submission, ego strength, dogmatism, ethical discrimination, hostility, and emotional maturity. A few instruments for clinical diagnosis measuring schizophrenic, manic-depressive, paranoid tendencies etc. are also reported here. Of these

134 instruments 51 are adaptations. From the remaining 83 developed in India, 18 instruments are reproduced here along with information, only information is given for another 44, and 20 titles are cited for which information and instruments could not be procured. An analysis of the 83 instruments developed in India (original) reveals the following trends :

TABLE 1: Break up of Personality Instruments

| Classification | Originals reproduced | Information only provided | Citations | Adaptations | Total |
|---|---|---|---|---|---|
| General | 18 | 44 | 21 | 51 | 134 |
| Adjustment | 5 | 20 | 4 | 11 | 40 |
| Anxiety | 2 | 2 | 1 | 5 | 10 |
| Self concept | 4 | 3 | 2 | — | 9 |
| Motivation | 8 | 8 | 3 | 6 | 25 |
| Total | 37 | 77 | 31 | 73 | 218 |

Instruments are available for all levels including rating scales for pre-school children, scales for pre-adolescents and other instruments for high school students, college students and adults. A few instruments are also reported for special groups like farmers, teachers, block officers, and executives.

Instrumentators in this area seem to have concentrated more on high school and college students. A little more than 50 per cent of the instruments are meant for school going population. A little over 30 per cent of them are for adults or for all age groups.

Different techniques have been used in measuring the personality dimensions mentioned above. About a third of them are scales, a fourth of them inventories and questionnaires, about a sixth of them projective tests, another one sixth are tests, and the rest are rating scales and checklist.

Reliabilities and validities have been reported only in some of these instruments. In the reliabilities, split-half and test-retest are the most reported forms of reliability. In spite of the fact that there are quite a few projective tests other forms of reliability like inter-scorer reliability are not reported. About 45 per cent of the instruments have not reported any kind of reliabilities. About one sixth of the instruments make a mention that reliabilities have been calculated without giving any details or report just reliability coefficients. Among those establishing reliability, split-half and test-retest reliabilities seem to have been the most preferred types. About a quarter of them report test-retest reliability coefficients, while about one sixth of them report split-half. The size of the sample on which these reliability coefficients are based is reported only in a few cases and hence no significant conclusions can be drawn on this. However, in view of the high order reliability coefficients reported in most of the cases these instruments can be considered fairly well standardised.

An examination of these instruments indicates that validity has been grossly neglected by most of the authors. A little more than half of these instruments do not seem to have been validated. Another quarter of them simply report as having been validated without giving the details of the validity coefficients. Known-group validity, validity by ratings and concurrent validity seem to be somewhat popular types. For concurrent validities borrowed instruments from other countries have been used, the cross-cultural validities of which are questionable in some cases. Wherever reported, the validity coefficients are fairly high and encouraging. Authors should concentrate on using systematic validational techniques while developing personality instruments.

There are 51 adaptations of some of the standard instruments in this area. Most of these original instruments were developed for American subjects. This great number of adaptations indicate a tendency to borrow among the Indian authors, especially psychologists.

Adorno's F scale, Bernreuter's Personality Inventory, Eysenck's Personality Inventory, Junior Personality Inventory, Allport's A—S Reaction study, Guilford-Zimmerman Temperament Survey, Maudsley Personality Inventory and Apperception Tests seem to be the most popular for adaptations by Indian scientists. There are cases where some of these instruments have been adapted for the same language group by more than one author. It is not known whether this duplication was necessary, i.e. whether such duplication in adaptation to same language was intended to take care of the cultural differences in the same language groups. If such is the case, the author may do well in indicating the geographical areas of application of these instruments. Instruments have been adapted into several languages. English, Hindi, Bengali, Telugu, Tamil, Malayalam, Urdu and Oriya are the main languages for adaptations. Reliability and validity have been reported for most of these instruments. However, in a few cases it is not clear whether the reliability reported is for the original instrument or for the adapted version.

Among the 18 original instruments reproduced here, Motion Picture Group Test of Personality by Dass is a projective test and has sequence motion pictures. The pictures are described here and could be used to measure the different personality qualities described by Guilford Zimmerman Temperament survey. The intolerance of ambiguity scale although is meant for students, it could also be used with educated adults with certain precautions. Kundu's Neurotic Personality Inventory requires the scoring key and manual which are commercially available. This is another popular inventory and quite a few researches have been reported in this inventory. The F scale by Prayag Mehta is still in the process of standardisation. This scale measures several dimensions like authoritarian aggression, submission, stereotypes etc. This scale is also being used in several researches conducted by Prayag Mehta and his team. The rigidity-flexibility scale is a short scale for farmers. Being a Guttman scale the scoring is easy.

The next set of four instruments are meant for pre-adolescents. These constitute a personality battery for pre-adolescents developed in connection with a project financed by the Indian Council of Medical Research. Data were collected from Delhi, Calcutta, Coimbatore, Udaipur and Anand samples. Different researchers have used it and the battery is in the process of being commercialised through Manasayan. Further work on standardising these instruments is suggested. It has to be used cautiously with adolescents. Dependency, initiative, classroom trust and activity level could be measured through this battery, the last being a rating scale for teachers to rate the pre-adolescents. The pre-adolescent Adjustment Scale reported in the section on Adjustment and Problems also forms a part of this battery.

The items of the insecurity aggression and inferiority questionnaires by Pati are weighted and the scoring keys are necessary for the use of these inventories. These are fairly well standardised. The primary school pupils personality traits rating scale is another addition to the pre-adolescent personality assessment. There are several dimensions included in this scale. This may be used as a good supplement to pre-adolescent personality battery. However, the advantage of this rating scale is that is could be used even with lower age groups, as it is a rating scale and the dimensions seem to be more meaningful to the lower age groups.

The generalised conformity test by Narayana Rao is meant for adults and measures conformity tendencies. The test could be used as such if the investigator can identify the conformity, non-conformity and neutral responses. Extroversion-introversion inventory by Shanthamani and Hafeez is also for adults and could be used by identifying the items under each of these dimensions. Fear checklist by Usha Rani Sidana could be used in the studies of Children's fears and surveying the fear arousing stimuli. The Dependence Proneness Scale by Sinha for college students can be used as reproduced and could probably also be converted into a Likert type scale.

Most of the inventories reproduced here are fairly well standardised. Although some need more information for use by an interested researcher, some could be used by trained psychologists possessing conceptual clarity about the personality traits they intend to measure.

**Adjustment and Problems**

There are in all 40 instruments measuring adjustment and problems. Of these 29 deal exclusively with adjustment *per se* and the other 11 deal with problems. Eleven out of the 40 are adaptations. Five of the instruments measuring adjustment are reproduced here. Information for another 15 is given and for another two only the sources where they were located are mentioned. Information for five of the problem instruments is given and another two are cited. Information is also given about the 11 adaptations.

The adjustment inventories checklists and scales available seem to measure several areas of adjustment, including adjustment to school, home, peers, teachers, sex, and so on, besides measuring general adjustment neurotic tendencies, emotional problems etc. Instruments are available to measure the adjustment of pre-adolescents, adolescents, adults and old people.

Reliabilities have been reported by 19 of the 22 instruments dealing with adjustment. Both split-half and test-retest reliability coefficients have been worked out for these instruments. The reliabilities are quite high and mostly about .70. Only in case of the pre-adolescent adjustment scale by Pareek and associates the reliability coefficients are rather moderate.

Three of the problem checklists inventories report much higher reliability coefficients. There are test-retest reliabilities. One of the checklists does not report any reliability.

As regards the validity, ratings have been often used to validate these instruments. Nine of the 22 instruments have used the ratings. The raters include parents, teachers, hostel superintendents and the investigators themselves through interview assessments. Five of these instruments report concurrent validities with other adjustment inventories (both Indian and American). Among the Indian scales used for concurrent validity Asthana's Adjustment Inventory, and Saxena's adjustment inventory find place. Bell's Adjustment Inventory, Roger's Test of Personal Adjustment, California's Personal and Social Adjustment Inventory and Brown's College inventory have been used. In some cases more than one type of validity has been used and in concurrent validities more than one test has been used. Three of the instruments also have used contrast group validity or known group validity. Delinquents and non-delinquents formed the groups in validating one instrument. Item-validities have been reported by three of the instruments, construct validity by one and fact validity by anothers. Five instruments have not reported any validities. On the whole, validity coefficients reported by these instruments seem to be at an acceptable level. Validity reported for two of the problems inventories have used correlations with adjustment scores.

Some of the instruments reported here are available in languages like Bengali, Hindi, Gujarati, Telugu and Tamil. They use different scoring systems like simple counting of items checked and weighted scores for items/responses checked etc.

Adjustment Inventory and Money Problem check-list are the two popular instruments having quite a few adaptations. These have been adapted to Hindi, Bengali, Malayalam and English languages for Indian samples. There appears to be some amount of duplication in these adaptations as same inventory has been adapted in the same language separately by different instrumentators. Reliability and validities are reported only in a few cases. There is a high need to increase the standardisation standards of these tests.

The first of those reproduced here is by Bhattacharya and colleagues at Baroda and is available in Gujarati. The scoring system is not given here but simple counting of items checked like in the Adjustment Inventory by Pasricha and associates seem to be applicable to this inventory also.

The Pre-Adolescent Adjustment Scale by Pareek and associates seem to be the only scale available to measure the adjustment at pre-adolescent level. However, this is limited to pre-adolescents of 8-12 years. Scoring key for this is not reproduced here and the manual is commercially available.

The Adjustment Inventory by Pasricha and associates is not well standardised and is reproduced here mainly for the number of statements it contains. These statements may be useful to interested researchers and counsellors for further work.

Adolescent Adjustment Inventory by Reddy is another fairly well standardised inventory for adolescents. P A inventory by Shanthamani and Hafeez can be used with adults. On the whole, the Adjustment Inventories reported here give a fairly satisfactory view of instrumentation in this area. However, there seems to be enough scope for sophistication in the techniques used in order to go deeper into the personality adjustment patterns of individuals.

Inventories to measure adjustment patterns of special groups like military personnel, industrial workers, researchers, teachers etc. are very much missing. While the instruments reported here cover by and large general adjustment,

adjustment problems arising out of certain occupational situations etc. have not been covered. There is a need to develop such occupational adjustment indices.

### Anxiety

There are in all 10 instruments located that measure anxiety. Five of these are adaptations and the rest originals. However, even the few originals seem to take quite a bit from foreign instruments. Only two instruments could be reproduced in this Handbook. This inventory by Dutt is mainly meant for measuring anxiety although it is titled as Personality Inventory. Complete information is not available for one of the anxiety tests reported by Mukerjee and Sinha.

These instruments measuring anxiety seem to have been fairly well standardised. All of them report high reliability coefficients, either test-retest or split-half. Among the originals, except the one by Patel, the rest of the three have been validated against Taylor's Manifest Anxiety Scale and report fairly high validity coefficients. Norms are available for all the scales.

A particular mention should be made here about the popular Sinha's Anxiety Scale. This has been used in several studies on anxiety. Only the major references are cited under this scale. This scale has been used to validate Dutt's Personality Inventory. The Anxiety Scale by Patel, and Sinha's Anxiety Scale could be used on adults as well as students. Although Dutt's scale mentions that it is meant for students, an examination of the items suggests that it could also be used with adults.

Using these inventories requires the manuals and norms which are either commercially available or available from the authors. These inventories in general could be used for conselling purposes and for clinical diagnosis. Unlike in the areas, there is less of duplication as different scales of anxiety find place in adaptations. The adaptations are mostly in Hindi. Much information on the standardisation of these adaptations is not available. Adaptations of Taylor's Manifest Anxiety Scale seem to have been fairly well standardised.

### Self Concept

Although 9 inventories to measure self concept could be located, of these four are reproduced here. One of these by Kakkar deals with self-acceptance, measuring the extent to which the individual can accept self-disparaging statements. The techniques used in these inventories seem to be either semantic differential type or simple checking of the statements and adjectives. One of these by Ramakumar has used Q sorting technique to study self concept.

Reliabilities have been reported by instruments. Split-half and test-retest reliabilities reported are fairly high.

A problem that often arises with self concept inventories is regarding their validity. One approach is that Self Concept Inventories being self-ratings, validity is built in the instrument and the instrument becomes valid as long as the respondent follows the instructions properly. Probably with this contention most of the investigators do not bother to validate the instruments and content validity is reported. From the instruments reported here, one has used content validity (Sharma), one item validity (Basanna) and another two concurrent validities (Bhatt as well as Sharma). The Hindi Personality Differential by Agrawal seems to go a little deeper into different aspects of personality than the adjectives used in the inventory suggest. As the author reports that factor scales consist of conformity, tough mindedness, normalcy and tenseness, the inventory could also probably be used as a general personality inventory for studying these dimensions. More information from the author may be required for using this inventory.

Basavanna's S-C Inventory is more a measure of self-confidence than general self-concept. Some of the items are positively worded towards this dimension and some are negatively worded. Hence any one intending to use this inventory will have to sort out these for purposes of scoring. Norms are available but not reported here. Hence the user may find it useful to get more information on the scoring procedure and norms from the author.

The self-acceptance inventory by Kakkar measures another dimension of self-concept. The scoring is simple but the inventory needs to be validated or used with care as the inventory is on a sensitive aspect of personality. A question that arises with this instrument is with regard to the social desirability weightages of the different items. This seem to have been assumed to be about equal for all statements which may not actually be the case. The statements should have been weighted.

The self-concept inventory by Sagar Sharma is a broad one in assessing several dimensions of self-concept. It needs a scoring key. The respondent could be studied using this inventory for his actual self as well as the ideal self. Self-ideal discrepancies could be drawn from this.

**Motivation**

There are 25 instruments listed under this area. Full details along with the instruments are provided for 8 of them and only information is given for another 8 and three have been only listed. Six are adaptations. Broadly the instruments (originals) under this area fall under four categories: those dealing with achievement motivation only (7); those measuring a set of needs or different motivational dimensions (5); those dealing with aspirations (3); and those dealing with individual needs like need satisfaction and need security (2). Most of these instruments are projective tests or semi-projective tests as is demanded by the nature of this personality dimension. However, there are a few structured questionnaires also. While a number of them are meant for high school level, a few others are for other levels also. A few on achievement motivation and level of aspiration are exclusively for farmers.

These instruments on motivation seem to be on a sound footing as far as their standardisation is concerned. Fourteen of the 16 instruments (for which information is available) report reliability of one kind on the other 8 report test-retest reliabilities. These coefficients are either moderate or fairly high. The moderate reliabilities are apparent mostly in projective techniques where they are excepted due to the intervening problems like scorer reliabilities and so on. Surprisingly, only of the six projective tests has reported inter-scorer reliability coefficients. This dimension has been badly neglected. Seven of the instruments also report split-half reliability coefficients and these appear to be fairly high in almost all the cases reporting them. Judges ratings have been used in one and internal consistency has also been used in another. More than one type of reliability has been reported in two of the instruments.

There are six adaptations reported here: Aberdeen Academic Motivation Inventory, Atkinson's *n* Ach Test, EPPS, Kogan and Wallach's choice dilemma test, Life Satisfaction indices and Symond's Picture test. Validities and reliabilities have been reported in four of the six adaptations. The Life Satisfaction Indices are in Telugu while the others are in Hindi.

For validating these instruments on motivation the instrumentators seem to have been limited by the theoretical considerations of the concept. Construct and predictive validity have been reported simultaneously for three instruments measuring *n* achievement. These coefficients range from very low to fairly high. Ratings by teachers, parents, judges and self-ratings have also been used for 4 instruments. Details of these are not reported in most cases. Some instruments have been validated against some standard foreign tests like Maslow's S-I Inventory, A-S Reaction Study etc. In all there seems to be enough scope for improving the validational components of the motivation instruments. In spite of the difficulties involved in measuring motivational dimension, there is ample scope to validate them. For example observation could be used for validating achievement motivation tests by selecting extreme groups through the test. Concurrent validities could be worked out with tests that have already been standardised. More imaginative work is probably needed in this area.

The first of these instruments reproduced here is the TAT instrument to measure *n* achievement. The pictures used in this are only described here (like a few other cases as reproducing the pictures here is beyond the scope of this Handbook). This test is developed for South Indian high school boys. For those interested in using these pictures with South Indians the manual with norms and the pictures are available from the authors. This appears to be fairly well standardised instrument. The next two tests by Prayag Mehta are also meant for measuring the achievement motivation of high school boys. The first is a projective instrument with a set of six pictures The second one is a parallel inventory (more a semi-projective scale) based on the same pictures These are among the well standardised and very popular instruments to measure *n* achievement. The references cited are an indication of the same. The achievement motivation inventory could be used by an interested researcher straight as the scoring key is reproduced here. The next two instruments are again on achievement motivation and are semi-projective instruments. The sentence completion test by Shanthamani and Hafeez is meant for adults and could also be used with college students. Three instruments have been developed for farmers to measure the levels of aspiration and change proneness.

# 1. General Instruments

## Complete instruments A

### *11A1 PERSONALITY WORD LIST

*Author* : Pratibha Deo.

*Availability* : Author, Department of Education, Panjab University, Chandigarh.

*Uses* : For measuring aspects of self concept.

*Time required* : No time limit but usually takes 40-50 minutes.

*Levels* : High School, Colleges, University students, adult male and female, and professional college students.

*Main features* : The check-list is a two-step type self-rating scale consisting of various adjectives which can generally describe personality. These are divided not positive and negative as well as into 5 different dimensions of personality like intellectual, emotional, social, character and aesthetic traits. The Rating Scale is of Likert-type using 5-point scale. While in the check-list antonyms are used, the rating scale utilises only one out of a pair. Both are standardised.

*Scoring* : In check-list, the number of words marked on positive and negative dimensions give separately positive-negative scores and these are further subdivided into 5 dimensions. The Rating Scale has 1 to 5 points on each word.

*Reliability* : Test-retest reliability for check-list was found to be .89. Reliability for rating scale being worked out.

*Validity* : Discriminant and convergent validity for the check-list was worked out. For rating scale it is being worked out.

*References* :


1. Deo, Pratibha, A study of self-concepts of University students in Punjab. *Psychological Studies*, 1964, 9(2), 74-90.
2. Deo, Pratibha, Sex-differences in self-concepts of Panjab University students. *Psychological Studies*, 1965, 10(2), 80-94.
3. Deo, Pratibha and Bangia, Vimla, Sex-differences in self-acceptance of Panjab University students *Psychological Studies*, 1966, 11(2), 99-109.
4. Deo, Pratibha, Omissions and contradictions in the self-concepts of Panjab University engineering students. *Psychological Studies*, 1966, 11(2), 99-109.


* See Preface for the meaning of the numbers of the instruments.

5. Deo, Pratibha and Singh, Harbhajan, Establishing validity of self concept measures, *Indian Educational Review*, 1971, 6(1), 92-100.
6. Bhalla, S.K., A comparative study of the self-concepts of disciplined and indisciplined students. Ph.D. Thesis, Panjab University, 1970.

## 11A1 PERSONALITY WORD LIST

(The following words have to be checked on a 5-point scale ranging from "very much like this" to "not at all like this").

graceful
cheerful
intelligent
aggressive
kind
harsh
artistic
confident
fair-minded
impatient
wicked
clean
formal
talkative
lazy
affectionate
reliable
alert
resourceful
modest
fussy
obstinate
delicate
vague
friendly
adventurous
unsteady
anxious
social
superior

brave
likable
happy
systematic
miser
irresponsible
attractive
curious
frank
impressive
quiet
optimistic
energetic
foolish
active
insincere
excitable
clever
shy
argumentative
greedy
jealous
disciplined
ambitious
quarrelsome
independent
tense
willing
efficient
thoughtful

nervous
irritable
enthusiastic
careless
critical
boastful
simple
serious
suspicious
sympathetic
inventive
weak
contented
tolerant
idealistic
strict
obedient
shirker
humorous

mischievous
restless
bossy
selfish
rude
determined
punctual
broad-minded
bluffer
smart

## 11A2 MOTION PICTURE GROUP TEST (MPGT) OF PERSONALITY

*Author*: S.L. Dass.
*Availability* : Commercially available. Manasayan, 32-Netaji Subhash Marg, Delhi.
*Time required*: About 1 hour.

*Level* : Adolescent boys.

*Main features* : MPGT is based on 10 silent, black-and-white movie picture sequences finalised from the rankings of experts. Each sequence depicts only mid-portion of a situation taken from the day-to-day life of Indian adolescents, but is also related to personality quality of Guilford-Zimmerman (GZ) Temperament Survey. However, the test situations provides adequate scope to subject not only for formulating its preceding and concluding portions, but also for subjectively interpreting the activities presented.

*Scoring* : Each sequence of the MPGT is meant for assessing only one personality quality of the G-Z Temperament Survey. The story is scored in the form of checking three 5-point linear scale.

*Reliability* : Inter-assessor reliabilities on 500 stories ranged between .01 and .70, with a median of .39. Test-retest reliabilities (N=30) ranged between .43 and .85, with a median of .74.

*Validity* : MPGT when correlated against the G-Z Temperament Survey (N=222) gave low coefficients. But when the MPGT assessment of 137 boys of the Residential Public Schools was correlated with their Teachers' assessment, the coefficients ranged between .18 and .51 with a median coefficient of .37. These coefficient values when correlated for attenuation, improved and ranged between .25 and .71, with a median of .66. MPGT was also correlated against the Sociometric assessment of the Residential Public Schools boys (N=214). Coefficients of correlation between these two assessments range between .22 and .41, with a median of .30.

*Norms* : Separate norms for each of the ten picture sequences of the test are available.

*Reference* : Dass, S.L. Developing a motion picture group test of personality for adolescents on the lines of Thematic Apperception Test. Doctoral thesis in Psychology, Panjab University, 1960.

11A2 MOTION PICTURE GROUP TEST OF PERSONALITY

(Particulars of situations which from the movie pictures group test of personality).

| Personality Quality | | Short Description | Length in footage | Projection Time in in Seconds |
|---|---|---|---|---|
| Gen. Activity | : | A boy is getting ready to proceed on a journey. Suddenly, he realises that a certain thing of his is missing. Starts searching the things. | 11.5 | 25 |
| Sociability | : | A group of boys is going for a picnic. Two boys on a bicycle are ahead of others. On the way they hide themselves behind a mound. | 18 | 39 |

| | | | | |
|---|---|---|---|---|
| Restraint | : | A boy comes home running carrying a small packet in his right hand. Entering a room he waves the packet in the air. In the room, a person covered with a bed sheet, is lying on a cot. | 10 | 21 |
| Ascendance | : | A man is pacing up and down in a room where a lady is sitting on a chair with her head rested on a table. After a while the man goes and looks out of a window. | 11 | 24 |
| Emotional Stability | : : | Three persons are holding a conference. At a distance, a young man is seem approaching where the conference is being held. | 11 | 24 |
| Friendliness | : | Two boys coming on bicycles from opposite directions, collide with each other on a turning. Both fall on the ground. One boy was carrying something in a bucket in one hand. | 10 | 22 |
| Thoughtfulness | : | A boy is sitting in a room on first floor and is looking towards the ceiling in a reflective manner. A small boy comes running up the stairs leading to the room. | 10 | 22 |
| Objectivity | : | A boy comes out of his house and is about to go on a bicycle. A cat crosses his way. | 13 | 29 |
| Personal Relations | : | Four boys are collecting funds from a middle aged persons. After giving him a receipt they go to the next house and knock at the door. | 12 | 27 |
| Masculinity | : | Two boys and a girl reach a river bank for beating. One boy and the girl jump in the water near the bank. The other boy shows reluct-ance. | 14 | 30 |

11A3 INTOLERANCE OF AMBIGUITY SCALE

*Author*: Department of Psychology, Aligarh Muslim University.
*Availability*: Authors.
*Level*: University students.
*Main features*: It contains 24 items to be checked with 'true' or 'false' response alternatives.
*Reliability*: Split-half reliability was found to be .70.
*Validity*: Item validities were established.
*Reference*: Hasan, Q. A study of relationship between dogmatism, social attitudes and certain personality characteristics. Ph.D. Thesis in

Psychology, Aligarh Muslim University, 1972.

## 11A3 INTOLERANCE OF AMBIGUITY SCALE

1. I always make up an ending for a story when the authors leave me in doubt as to the fate of the hero.
2. Most women/men are either good or bad.
3. If I have the choice of two alternatives and I cannot decide, I find it better to choose either one to get the decision over with.
4. I dislike working puzzles to which there seems to be no solution.
5. There is only one true religion.
6. It makes me uncomfortable when someone is speaking about something which I do not understand.
7. I change my mind easily when someone puts forth a convincing argument.
8. I take a philosophical view of life most of the time.
9. I make up my mind very rapidly.
10. It makes me uncomfortable to do any thing unconventional.
11. I dislike learning things about which I know absolutely nothing.
12. It is always desirable to do the socially acceptable thing.
13. It is better to love or hate a person fully instead of loving and hating him simultaneously.
14. What is in a man's nature will come out in his actions, and human nature does not change.
15. People who keep changing their opinions cannot be trusted.
16. Modern artists are fakes trying to put something over on the public.
17. In this world definite choices must be made all the times.
18. Everything is best in this best possible worlds.
19. I hate leaving things in an unsettled state.
20. It upsets me when a person does not know the correct behaviour for every occasion.
21. Children should be given every possible opportunity to express themselves freely.
22. It does not bother me in the least to wait for the outcome of a pending situation.
23. A person who is certain about everything is certain to be wrong.
24. If there is some evidence that a person does not bear good character I prefer to severe my relation with him instead of bothering to collect more information about him.

## 11A4 KUNDU'S NEUROTIC PERSONALITY INVENTORY (KNPI)

*Author*: Ramanath Kundu.

*Availability* : Commercially available, author, Department of Psychology, University of Calcutta.

*Uses* : Diagnosis, selection and guidance.

*Level*: Adults.

*Main features* : It is a 66-item inventory using 5-point forced choice response system.

*Scoring* : Key available along with the manual.

*Reliability* : Split-half reliability coefficients range from .72 to .89 for male (N=692), female (N=308) and neurotic (N=50) groups.

*Validity* : Criterion validity coefficients using neurotic group were found to be .86 and .87 respectively for males and females.

*Norms* : Given in the manual.

*Reference* :

1. Kundu, R. Development of Personality Inventory. *Indian Journal of Psychology*, 1962, 37, 171-174.
2. Kundu, R. Item analysis of a new Neurotic Personality Inventory. *Journal of Psychological Researches*, 1963,7, 103-108.
3. Kundu, R. A brief study of reliability and validity of the Neurotic Personality Inventory, *Psychological Studies*, 1963, 8, 98-101.
4. Kundu, R. Standardisation of the Kundu's Neurotic Personality Inventory, *Psychological Studies*, 1964, 9, 69-72.
5. Kundu, R. A new Psychoneurotic Inventory for adults. *Indian Journal of Psychology*, 1966, 41, 17-22.
6. Kundu, R. A comparison of Bernreuter Personality Inventory and Kundu Neurotic Personality Inventory. *Psychological Studies*, 1968, 13, 101-104.


## 11A4 KUNDU'S NEUROTIC PERSONALITY INVENTORY

(The following items have to be checked on a 5-point scale of frequency).

1. As ideas run through head it is difficult to sleep.
2. Day-dreaming about improvable occurrences.
3. Being easily affected by praising and/or blaming.
4. Being hurt by criticism.
5. Having strong desire to meet the most important person present at a gathering (social, political, etc.)
6. Difficulty in starting conversation with a stranger (unknown person).
7. Having feelings of happiness and sadness alternately.
8. Being worried about possible misfortunes.
9. Slow in making decisions.
10. Feeling uneasy due to shyness.
11. Feeling nervous to initiate an idea to start discussion among a group of unknown people.
12. Troubled with feelings of inferiority.
13. Difficulty in taking decision for yourself.
14. Feeling easily hurt.
15. Being bothered by some particular useless thought.
16. Difficulty in doing many things confidently.
17. Experiencing change of moods from pleasant to unpleasant or from unpleasant to pleasant.
18. Being easily gratified (pleased) by admiration.
19. Becoming unduly angry, sulky (morose), or excited in disagreements over trivial matters with friends, or co-workers.
20. Feel inconvenience due to uncontrollable blushing (becoming red),

trembling (shaking with fear) or blanching (growing pale with fear).

21. Having sensation of falling (a) when you are about to sleep, (b) during walking.
22. Suffer from disinclination to sleep and or periods of wakefulness at nights.
23. Feel mentally tired in absence of any physical tiredness.
24. Unable to concentrate as mind wanders due to slightest distraction.
25. Becoming tired (or feeling lack of interest) of friends, amusements, etc. quickly.
26. Jump (make sudden movement) badly at sudden (a) lights, (b) sounds, (c) touches, (d) sights.
27. Troubled with fear of being suffocates and/or crushed in crowd.
28. Things seem to swim (dizzy) or get misty (hazy) or blurred (confused) before eyes.
29. Being afraid that you may fall down when you are looking down from the top of a high place, like high bridge, roof of a high building etc.
30. Wake up frightened in the middle of night without any apparent reason.
31. Troubled by the idea that you may become insane (mad).
32. Troubled by moods of 'fedupness' (i.e. lowness of spirits, feelings of despair).
33. Feeling very restless or unable to concentrate on anything.
34. Having fears and worries about things and/or ideas.
35. Troubled by thoughts about what others are thinking of you.
36. Being compelled to do some useless acts like :

    (a) Counting windows, people, etc.
    (b) Uttering rhymes or phrases,
    (c) Repeatedly washing hands or clothes,
    (d) Tapping lamp posts,
    (e) Reading notices, figures, etc.

37. Feeling inwardly disturbed or uneasy for some time due to difference of opinion with people.
38. Having fear of death about your parents, friends, or other persons whom you love.
39. Being bothered by self-conscious shyness in social situations.
40. Becoming easily over-excited.
41. Like to enjoy jokes concerning yourself.
42. Having complaints of vague ill-health, like obscure pains, digestive disorders, rapid beating of the heart, etc.
43. Having or had (if parents are not living) disagreeable feelings toward parent.
44. Becoming tense or anxious in order to catch a train or bus in time.
45. Thinking yourself as nervous.
46. Becoming unmindful to sit still during a long meeting.
47. Being afraid to remain alone at night in a house.
48. Feeling that life is a great burden.
49. Like to limit friendships mostly to your own sex.
50. Getting shocked by sexual topics.

51. Remaining cheerful.
52. Feeling tired after waking up in the morning without apparent physical cause.
53. Being worried by thoughts of ill-health.
54. Thinking that you are usually unlucky.
55. Thinking to have satisfactory adjustment in life.
56. Taking an active part in giving help in case of an accident before you.
57. Having conflicting moods of love and hate for members of the family.
58. Feeling happy about home environment.
59. Like to enjoy indoor life.
60. Being worried about undecided matters.
61. Feeling unhappy or uneasy to have an unfinished job on your hand.
62. Becoming nervous to face quarrelsome situations.
63. Feeling unhappy.
64. Suffering from bad headache not due to any apparent physical cause.
65. Being easily upsetted or touched by any remark that concerns yourself.
66. Highly sensitive to unpleasant smell.

11A5 F-SCALE

*Authors* : Prayag Mehta in collaboration with B.P. Sinha and P.P. Gokulnathan.
*Availability* : Author, Department of Psychology, University of Udaipur.
*Time required* : 20 minutes.
*Level* : Adults.
*Main features* : The scale is based on Adornoretial. The Authoritarian Personality (1950). Following dimensions are included : Conservatism, authoritarian aggression and submission, superstitions and stereotypes, power and toughness, and destructiveness and synicism. It consists of 19 items.
*Scoring* : Scoring is done on a 5-point scale.
*Reliability* : In process.
*Validity* : In process.
*Norms* : In process.

11A5 F-SCALE

(The following items have to be checked on a 5-point scale of agreement).

1. Science may progress to any extent, still many things will remain which can not be understood by human brain.
2. God has divided society into two parts that is rich and poor.
3. Family planning is not going to be beneficial in any way to the country.
4. It is useless to hope from bad persons that they will work with good persons.
5. There is some supreme power above us and we should accept his decisions without any doubt and suspicion.
6. Natural calamities only will bring an end to the social evils and personal quarrels.
7. We should not be mixed up so much since it produces the feeling of

scorn.
8. It is indispensable to use force for the offenders.
9. Businessmen are more important than poets and writers for the society.
10. Nationalisation of large scale industries will bring deficit in them.
11. If we think deeply, we shall realise that man does every work because of self-interest.
12. One day people will accept it that palmistry (Jyotish-shastr) can predict future events.
13. Western dress might appear exciting, but I would not like that my family members wear it.
14. Military education should be essential for every citizen of India.
15. It is necessary to believe in religion for happy life.
16. The paramount cause of most of the problems of our country is our low moral character.
17. We should believe in religion without any suspicion.
18. It is difficult to work together for the persons belonging to varied religious groups.
19. It is the duty of the Government not to stop privy purses of princes.

11A6 RIGIDITY-FLEXIBILITY SCALE

*Authors* : A.S. Murthy and S.N. Singh.
*Availability* : Authors, Indian Agricultural Research Institute, New Delhi.
*Level* : Farmers.
*Main features* : A Guttman scale in which the respondent only indicates agreement or disagreement.

*Reliability* : Coefficient of Reproducibility was .92 and Minimum Marginal Coefficient of Reproducibility .86.
*Validity* : Correlations of scores with independent judgement on rigidity flexibility and conservatism-liberalism were .894 and .05 respectively, showing high validity.
*Reference* : Singh, K.N.; Singh, S.N. & Lokhande, M.R. *Measurement in extension research : Instruments developed at I.A.R.I.* New Delhi: Division of Agricultural Research, IARI, 1972, pp. 171-177.

11A6 RIGIDITY-FLEXIBILITY SCALE

1. It is unjustifiable burden on the farmer to levy betterment taxes as no such collections are made from urban population (as for example construction of schools or hospitals in cities).
2. Land reforms must be aimed to allow farmers to increase their size of farm to the maximum extent.
3. Family planning is not suitable to intensive cultivation of land as we need more hands for more intensive cultivation.
4. There are enough cases of failures of high yielding varieties of paddy like IR-8 not to justify optimism in farming.
5. Close contact with extension personnel makes a difference in farming.

## 11A7 PRE-ADOLESCENT DEPENDENCY SCALE

*Authors* : Udai Pareek, T.V. Rao, Prabha Ramlingaswamy and Balram Sharma.

*Availability* : Available from first two authors. Indian Institute of Management, Ahmedabad.

*Uses* : For counselling.

*Time required*: About 10-15 minutes. No time limit is fixed.

*Level* : Pre-adolescents of age range 8 to 12 years, could also be used with adolescents.

*Main features* : The scale is available in two forms, A and B. Both the forms are scales consisting of 10 items in each, 5 of the items measuring dependency tendencies and 5 of the item measuring independence. Hindi, Tamil and Bengali versions available.

*Scoring* : Form A is scored on a 3-point scale summated ratings. In Form B scale values of the items are added to give total score. In Form B dependency items are scored positive and independence items negative. Both are added for final score, but two separate scores are possible in each of the forms for dependency and independence.

*Reliability* : Test-retest reliabilities and parallel form reliabilities were worked out. Two of the seven coefficients were not significant. The significant coefficients range from .36 to .84.

*Validity* : Items were selected on the basis of ratings by judges.

*Norms* : Available on Delhi, Coimbatore, Calcutta samples.

*References* :

1. Pareek, U., Rao, T.V., Ramalingaswamy P. and Sharma, B. R. Developing a battery of pre-adolescent personality tests. *Indian Educational Review,* 1970, 5(2), 1-20.
2. Pareek, U. and Rao, T.V. *Motivation Training for Mental Health : a study of teacher behaviour and student mental health,* ICMR Project Reports, NIHAE, New Delhi, 1971.
3. Pareek, U. and Rao, T.V. Motivation Training for Mental Health. *NIHAE Bulletin,* October, 1971, 26-32.
4. Rao, T.V. A study of the patterns of dependency, class trust and initiative of fifth grade children from Delhi, Calcutta and Coimbatore. *Indian Educational Review,* 1972, 7(2).

## 11A7 PRE-ADOLESCENTS DEPENDENCY SCALE (PADS—FORM A)

(The following items have to be checked on a 3-point scale).

1. I blindly follow everything the teacher tells me.
2. I can't do anything without the permission of my parents.
3. I have got full self-confidence.
4. My parents take care of things for me.
5. I do everything by myself without any dictation from others.
6. I do whatever I like.
7. I alone of face the situation in case there is a quarrel and don't prefer help from others.
8. I am easily persuaded by others.
9. I don't accept anything blindly.

10. It is all right if I do any thing along with others, otherwise it is not possible for me to do anything independently.

11A7 PRE-ADOLESCENT DEPENDENCY SCALE (PADS—FROM B)

(The following items have to be checked on 'yes' alternatives).

1. I do everything after consulting others.
2. I need more help from my teacher.
3. I do everything without being asked.
4. I can do everything by myself.
5. I can't do my work by myself.
6. I hesitate to take help from others.
7. I don't indulge in discussion with my parents.
8. I myself take care of my things.
9. I do whatever I like.
10. I like to study with those class fellows who are superior to me.

11A8 PRE-ADOLESCENT CLASS-ROOM TRUST SCALE (PACTS)

*Authors* : Udai Pareek, T. Venkateswara Rao, Prabha Ramalinga- swamy, and B.R. Sharma.
*Availability* : Authors, Indian Institute of Management, Ahmedabad.
*Uses* : To measure classroom trust of students. For counselling purposes.
*Time required* : No time limit. Takes about 20 to 35 minutes.
*Levels* : Pre-adolescents, Age 8 to 12 years.
*Main features* : It is a four alternative scale with 8 items. Hindi, Tamil and Bengali versions available.
*Scoring* : Each item has score values varying with the amount of trust expressed in the responses. Item scores are summated.
*Reliability* : Split-half reliability (odd-even method on an N=219) was found to be 0.814. Test-retest reliabilities in 3 schools range from .33 to .77.
*Validity* : Validated with judges' ratings.
*Norms* : Available on Calcutta, Delhi, Coimbatore and Jodhpur samples.
*References* :

1. Pareek, U. and Rao, T.V. *Motivation Training for Mental Health. ICMR Project Report*, National Institute of Health Administration and Education, New Delhi, 1971.
2. Pareek, U., Rao, T.V., Ramalingaswamy P., and Sharma, B.R. Developing a battery of pre-adolescent personality tests. *Indian Educational Review*, 1970, 5(2), 1-20.
3. Pareek, U. and Rao, T.V. Motivation Training for Mental Health. *NIHAE Bulletin*, October, 1971, 26-32.
4. Rao, T.V. A study of the patterns of dependency, class trust and initiative of fifth grade children from Delhi, Calcutta, and Coimbatore. *Indian Educational Review*, 1972, 7(2).

11A8 PRE-ADOLESCENT CLASSROOM TRUST SCALE (PACTS)

(The student has to choose one of the response alternatives given after the description of each situation).

1. The teacher praised Raman as a very good student and pointed out that he got the highest percentage of marks in mathematics. Venu also got the same percentage of marks, but the teacher forgot to mention his name. What does Venu think? Mark any one of the statements :
   - The teacher is partial towards Raman.
   - I should see the teacher after class and show him my marks.
   - The teacher should have praised me too.
   - I hope some other day the teacher will praise me.
2. Pran was dozing in the class. He had gone to a late film show the previous evening. The teacher warned him for sleeping. What will Pran do? Check one of the following statements :
   - He will tell his friends that the lesson was boring and so he was sleeping
   - He will feel ashamed and cry.
   - He will explain to the teacher why he was feeling sleepy.
   - He will feel that he should not have slept in class.
3. Subash lost his pen. So he was not taking down the notes dictated by the teacher. The teacher scolded Subash. What will Subash do? Check one of the following statements :
   - He will feel that the teacher should have found out why he was not taking the notes.
   - Will grumble against the teacher for dictating notes.
   - Will think that the teacher scolded him because the teacher does not know why he is not writing.
   - Will try to explain his predicament to the teacher and will request him to lend a pen.
4. There was a function in the school. An outside speaker was addressing the children. The children could not follow the speech and were feeling bored. They were whispering among themselves. The class teacher scolded the children. Vineet was one among the children. What will Vineet do? Check one of the following statements :
   - He will join others and make noise whenever the class teacher was not looking at them.
   - Will think that it is his duty to obey the teacher and not bring a bad name to the school.
   - Will tell the teacher afterwards that the speech was boring and uninteresting.
   - Will blame himself and will think that he should not have done so.
5. The teacher praised Ramesh for having solved a difficult sum which was given as a part of home assignment. Ramesh has actually taken help of his elder brother in solving that sum and felt that the teacher should know this. What will Ramesh do? Check one of the statements :
   - He will go to the teacher and tell him that he had taken the help of his brother.
   - He will like to tell the truth to the teacher, but somehow feels shy.
   - He will feel that as he had completed his homework, he deserves praise.

— The teacher has not realised his trick. There is no reason for him to go and tell him.

6. A team from Mohan's school went to play a match against another school. During the match, there was a quarrel between the two teams and Mohan took a leading part in the fight that ensued. The teacher from other school sent a complaint that one boy from this school had made a row. The teacher enquired about the cause of fight, and wanted to know who had taken the leading part in the fight. What will Mohan do? Check one of the following statements :
   — Mohan will explain to the teacher and will admit that it was he who took the leading part.
   — Will think that the teacher will scold him, so he will keep quiet.
   — He will feel sorry that he participated in the fight and will hope that the teacher will not find out.
   — Will feel that it is teacher's duty to enquire about the happennings to prevent them in future.

11A9 PRE-ADOLESCENT INITIATIVE QUESTIONNAIRE (PAIQ)

*Authors* : Udai Pareek, T. Venkateswara Rao, Prabha Ramalinga- swamy and Balram Sharma.

*Availability* : Authors, Indian Institute of Management, Ahmedabad.

*Uses* : Counselling purposes.

*Time required* : No time limit (take about 20 to 40 minutes).

*Levels* : Mainly meant for pre-adolescents (8 to 12 years) but could be used with adolescents.

*Main features* : An open-ended questionnaire with 6 items involving problem-situations requiring the subject to project his initiative taking behaviour. Hindi, Tamil and Bengali versions available.

*Scoring* : Content analysis categorisation of responses which are assigned numerical initiative scores depending on the category of the response.

*Reliability* : Test-retest reliabilities range from 0.50 to 0.66. Inter-scorer reliabilities range between 0.83 and 0.90.

*Norms* : Available for Delhi, Calcutta and Coimbatore samples.

*References* :
1. Pareek, U., Rao, T.V. Ramalingaswamy, P. and Sharma, B.R. Developing a battery of pre-adolescent personality tests. *Indian Educational Review,* 1970, 5(2), 1-20.
2. Pareek, U., and Rao, T.V. *Motivation Training for Mental Health : a study of teacher behaviour and student mental health.* ICMR Project reports, National Institute of Health Administration and Education, New Delhi, 1971.
3. Pareek, U., and Rao, T.V. Motivation Training for Mental Health. *NIHAE Bulletin,* 1970, 5(2), 1-20.
4. Rao, T.V. A study of the patterns of dependency, class trust and initiative of fifth grade children from Delhi, Calcutta and Coimbatore. *Indian Educational Review,* 1972, 7(2).

## 11A9 PRE-ADOLESCENT INITIATIVE QUESTIONNAIRE (PAIQ)

(Respondents have to write their answers to the open-ended questions given below).

1. David obtained very low scores in his monthly test. He felt sorry for this. He wanted to get highest marks next time. This required him to work hard. He could not study at home because firstly there was lot of noise in the room, and secondly there was not enough space. Under these circumstances what did David do?
2. Abdul was very fond of playing hockey. He wanted to build up a good team. There was no playground in the school. What did he do?
3. Krishna found a child crying on a street. He was crying bitterly and was not able to say anything. What did Krishna do?
4. A football match was going on. Wariyam was watching the game. One player was hurt. The match was stopped. All the players were embarrassed and frightened. What did Wariyam do?
5. There was no chalk and duster on the table of the teacher in Kishore's class. How could the teacher teach without these things? What did Kishore do?
6. Shyam was very fond of toys. But he did not have any. He knows that his parents would not give him money for toys. What did he do?

## 11A10 PRE-ADOLESCENT ACTIVITY LEVEL SCALE (PAALS)

*Authors* : Udai Pareek, T.V. Rao, Prabha Ramlingaswamy and Balram Sharma.
*Availability* : Authors, Indian Institute of Management, Ahmedabad
*Uses* : Group Counselling.
*Time required* : No time limit.
*Main features* : It is a rating scale to be used by the teachers for primary and high school boys.
*Scoring* : A 9-point system.
*Reliability* : Test-retest reliabilities were calculated for 3 classes using Mann-Whitney's values.
*References* :

1. Pareek, U., Rao, T.V., Ramalingaswamy, P. and Sharma, B.R. Developing a battery of pre-adolescent personality tests. *Indian Educational Review,* 1970, 5 (2), 1-20.
2. Pareek, U. and Rao, T.V. *Motivation Training for Mental health : a study of teacher behaviour and student mental health,* ICMR Project Reports, National Institute of Health Administration and Education, New Delhi, 1971.
3. Pareek, U. and Rao, T.V. Motivation Training for Mental Health. *NIHAE Bulletin,* 1971, October, 26-32.

## 11A10 PRE-ADOLESCENT ACTIVITY LEVEL RATING SCALE (PAALS)

(Teachers have to rate their students grouping them into the one of the levels described below).

**PAALS-SHEET 1**

Extraordinarily high level:

Is the first to answer questions asked by the teacher. Always first to interrupt or to ask questions in class. Works very fast, always finishes first in class. Shouts, or always chatters. Always volunteers to do things for the class and tries to do more than he has offered to do. Often is involved in fight or brisk sports.

**PAALS-SHEET 2**

Very high level :

Very eager to answer questions asked by the teacher; can hardly wait for his turn.

Persistently interrupts, or asks questions in class.

Works very fast, and is often among the first few to finish.

Talks loudly or frequently.

Volunteers to do things for the class and does well whatever he has undertaken.

Likes fights or brisk sports.

**PAALS-SHEET 3**

High level :

Usually eager to answer.

Often asks questions.

Works fast.

Speaks clearly but has to be asked.

Volunteers eagerly but slows down after a little while.

Occasionally fights or participates in brisk sports.

**PAALS-SHEET 4**

Neither high nor low level:

Occasionally shows eagerness to answer questions.

Occasionally asks questions or offers comments.

Works at an average speed.

Speaks clearly but has to be asked.

Does not volunteer but if entrusted with a task does well.

Does not initiate fight, but does not avoid one.

**PAALS-SHEET 5**

Low level:

Answers only when asked, does not raise his hand.

Asks questions once in a while, but follows the discussion with lively interests.

Is rather slow.

Feels shy and mumbles.

Does not offer to do things for the class.

Avoids fights and brisks sports.

**PAALS-SHEET 6**

Very low level:

Answer only when repeatedly asked and probed.

Does not ask questions, but shows interest in what others say.

A very slow.
Stammers or mumbles when talked to.
Difficult to get him to do extra things for class.
Likes to play quieter games.

**PAALS-SHEET 7**

Exceptionally low level :
Difficult to get an answer out of him.
Is quite and does not show active interest.
Always last to finish the work.
Never speaks unless he is forced to.
Never does anything for the class. If asked, refuses to take responsibility. Does not participate in any kind of outdoor activity.

11A11 INSECURITY QUESTIONNAIRE

*Author* : G.C. Pati.
*Availability* : Author, Clinical Psychologist, Mental Health Institute, SCB Medical College, Cuttack-7, (Orissa).
*Time required* : 40 minutes.
*Level* : Sum of the weightages of the checked items. Weightages based on the ratings of Judges.
*Reliability* : Reliability coefficient was found to be 0.936.
*Validity* : Validity coefficient was found to be 0.713.
*Reference* : Pati, G.C. *A comparative study of socio-cultural and personality factors of delinquents, criminals and juveniles of Orissa.* Doctoral Dissertation in Psychology Utkal University (Published).

11A11 INSECURITY QUESTIONNAIRE

1. Do parents love you less (than your brothers and sisters)?
2. Were you getting food and clothings alright in your childhood?
3. Were you scolded or beaten at home?
4. Were you feeling helpless to stay with the person who scolded or beat you at home?
5. Were your parents, quarrelling frequently regarding the disciplinary measures for you?
6. Do your friends put confidence in your words?
7. Do they say most of the time that you do not play well?
8. If defeated in the game do you accept it easily and mildly?
9. Do you like to shift from work to work?
10. Do you sometimes take oath to justify your words?
11. Do you take oath not to expose your wrongs?
12. Do you usually doubt others authenticity?
13. Do you feel awkward to talk to strangers?
14. Do you like to argue very often?
15. Do you feel bold enough to carryout a responsibility with your social standard?
16. Do you feel insulted if people make fun of you?

17. Do you sometimes feel that it is better to die?
18. Do you feel insulted if people make fun of you?
19. Do you feel discourrged if hindered while doing a work?
20. Do you like sometimes to play truant from home?

## 11A12 INFERIORITY QUESTIONNAIRE

*Author* : G.C. Pati

*Availability* : Author, Clinical Psychologist, Mental Health Institute, SCB Medical College Hospital, Cuttack-7, (Orissa).

*Time required* : 40 minutes.

*Levels* : At all educational levels.

*Scoring* : Sum of the scale values of the items checked by the respondent.

*Reliability* : Reliability coefficient was found to be 0.920.

*Validity* : Validity coefficient was found to be 0.717.

*Reference* : Pati, G.C. *A comparative study of socio-cultural and personality factors of delinquents, criminals and juveniles of Orissa.* Doctoral Dissertation in Psychology, Utkal University (Published).

## 11A12 INFERIORITY QUESTIONNAIRE

1. Do you feel that you are the best from among your brothers and sisters?
2. Does it become unbearable to obey your superiors?
3. Did you get easily the play things etc. You wanted in childhood?
4. Were you obstinate in food and clothing etc.?
5. Do you make friendship with others easily?
6. Were you usually invited by your playmates to play with?
7. Do your friends obey you?
8. Do you get angry with very little provocation?
9. Do you love to get praise from others by doing good or sensational work.
10. Do you like to talk to your friends about the work you do?
11. Do you dislike to go to elders or big people?
12. Do you like to find fault with others?
13. Do you like to contradict others in talk or work?
14. Do you mostly blame yourself if you become unsuccessful in any work?
15. Do people (home or outside) tell you that you are worth nothing?
16. Do you attempt to win him who has proved himself better than you?
17. Do you pray and evoke God's mercy when you begin a work or end it successfully or while doing the work?
18. Do you work hard to improve yourself?
19. Do you feel that whatever way try to help others they do not appreciate?
20. Do you feel that even your smallest faults are greatly exaggerated by others?

## 11A13 AGGRESSION QUESTIONNAIRE

*Author* : G.C. Pati

*Availability* : Author, Clinical Psychologist, Mental Health Institute, SCB Medical

College, Cuttack-7 (Orissa).

*Time required*: 30 minutes.

*Level*: At all educational levels.

*Scoring* : Response alternatives in each item has weighted scores. Sigma deviate weighting method is used in scoring.

*Reliability*: Reliability coefficient was found to be .717.

*Validity*: Validity coefficient was found to be .828.

*Reference* : Pati, G.C. *A comparative study of socio-cultural and personality factors of delinquents, criminals and juveniles of Orissa*, Ph.D. Thesis in Psychology, Utkal University (Published).

11A13 AGGRESSION QUESTIONNAIRE

1. Ram once stole eight annas from his father. When it was known at home, (1) Mother did not care it, telling that it was a childish prank, (2) His elder brother beat him, (3) Father drove him out of home. Whose treatment of this situation can be judged as good?
2. A boy was mischieveous enough to beat other boys of the village always. They became angry and tried to see him jointly. Various suggestions were offered, (1) one of them told that we will threaten him, (2) another put in that we will beat him to our satisfaction, (3) still another declared that we will kill him. Whose suggestion is better?
3. A cyclist by chance hit a boy on the road. When the boy shrieked and complained a number of people near by gathered there. As it happens in such circumstances, (1) some told what has happened, has happened do not abuse the gentlemen, leave him, (2) others insisted to beat him, (3) some others suggested to hand over the cyclist to the police. Which group gave better suggestion?
4. A fast running car occasioned the patches of water deposits on the road to fall upon the passersby. Naturally they were irritated, (1) one of them vented his anger by scolding, (2) another threw a stone which resulted in damaging the glass plate of the car. The car so stopped. (3) a third man ran and slapped the occupant. Who did well?
5. A boy while picking a pocket was caught. A crowd gathered there, amusing over the discomfiture of the boy, (1) some sympathised with him and told to leave him, (2) a 2nd batch of men suggested to give him some lessons, i.e. beat him and leave him, (3) a 3rd batch advised to hand over him to police. Whose advice is better?
6. Shyam without giving any heed to elder's advice, continued roaming about at forbidden places, during mid-day. All were worried over it, (1) mother just did not tell anything, pardoned him for his insolence, (2) uncle gave him two hard slaps. (3) father beat him with a stick. Whose act is appreciable?
7. For some reason Police stopped the march of a procession, (1) some so left the procession and went back, (2) some threw stones at the police, (3) some others clashed with police with knife and lathi. Who did well?
8. A man's landed property was usurped by his rich neighbour. He sought advice as to what to do from his villagers, (1) some advised to file a

case, (2) some advised him to bent the rich man, (3) some others advised him to kill the man, and do away with it. Who gave better advice?

9. A group of men were travelling without ticket in one compartment of the train. T.T.I came in to check, (1) some of the group told to pay him the due charges, (2) some told to bribe him, (3) some told to push him of the running train. Who told right?
10. Once 3 beggars together entered a compound to beg. They were denied alms, (1) one of them whispered an abuse and left, (2) another went away scolding loudly, (3) the last one picked up a stray utensil from the verandah and ran away with it. Who did just?
11. Some magistrates were found as to not working properly. A decision was to be made to punish them, (1) some advised to fine them, (2) some told to discharge them from service, (3) some others opined to imprison them. Whose opinion is preferable?
12. While a loose woman was passing the street, (1) a group of young men gave her obscene songs, (2) a second group talked of her in obscene language, (3) a 3rd group passed her so closely as to give her a contact of their body. Which group's act can be judged as good?
13. Big Officers — Magistrates, Police, Legal Authorities were found taking bribes. To punish them, (1) some told to dismiss them from service, (2) some spoke of imprisoning them, (3) some preferred to hang them. Whose plan is better?
14. A group of men broke entered into a house. A policemen by chance came to the spot, (1) some of the men told to submit themselves to the police, (2) some told of bribing the police and get away, (3) some others thought of attacking the police and he was alone and get out of the scene. Whose way of action is preferred?
15. A man persistently gave false witness against his villagers (in law courts). Villagers met to do something with him, (1) some observed to oust him out of the village, (2) some spoke of giving him a hard beating, (3) some opined to kill him. Whose opinion is better?
16. A man could not get any food for 3 or 4 days. He entered into a hotel and attempted to take forcibly something. He was caught and brought thought, among the ways of action, (1) either to acquit him or (2) to put before the Magistrate. After taking account of the case, Magistrate punish him with a nominal fine or (3) to sentence him for few days. Which is better form of action.

## 11A14 PRIMARY SCHOOL PUPILS PERSONALITY TRAITS RATING SCALE

*Authors* : Marni T. Ramji, P. Das Gupta and N.P. Rastogi.

*Availability* : Authors, National Council of Educational Research and Training, Sri Aurobindo Marg, New Delhi-16.

*Level*: Primary school pupils (age 6-11 years) to be rated by their teachers.

*Main features* : It consists of 10 rating scales and 10 observational schedules to rate 10 traits of the students: cleanliness, punctuality, regularity, cooperation, leadership, honesty, helpfulness, curiosity, obedience, and self-confidence. In the rating scales each trait is described followed by three statements on each of which the student has to be rated on a 3-point scale. Observational schedules contain a number of statements on each trait to be rated by the teacher and are meant to help him to use the rating scales objectively.

*Scoring* : Three-point summated rating on each trait. A trait score on each trait is derived by dividing the total score obtained by three (3=no. of items on which the student is rated for each trait).

*Reference* : Ramji, M.T., Das Gupta, P. and Rastogi, M.P. *Rating Scales of Personality Traits of Primary School Pupils: A Handbook for Teachers.* National Council of Educational Research and Training, New Delhi, 1970.

11A14 PRIMARY SCHOOL PUPILS PERSONALITY TRAITS RATING SCALE

(Definition of each trait is given following by three statements related to the trait on which the teacher has to rate each student on a 3-point scale of frequency. High frequency of occurrence of the trait gets a score of 3 and low a score of 1. Sum of the scores on the three statements divided by 3 gives the trait score for each trait).

1. **Trait : Cleanliness**
   **Definition** : It is the consistent behaviour pattern which shows that one keeps his body, belongings and surroundings free from dirt.
   I. Keeps his body clean. II. Keeps his belongings clean. III. Keeps the surroundings clean.

2. **Trait : Punctuality**
   **Definition** : It is the consistent behaviour pattern which manifests itself in attending concerned programmes on right time irrespective of inconvenience.
   I. Attends the school on time. II. Attends the classes on time. III. Attends the different co-curricular programmes on time.

3. **Trait : Regularity**
   **Definition** : It is the consistent behaviour pattern which shows that one is continuing to do things at even intervals.
   I. Completes class work. II. Submits the home assignment. III. Attends the co-curricular programmes.

4. **Trait : Co-operation**
   **Definition** : It is the consistent behaviour pattern which manifests itself in working towards common objectives in group situations.
   I. Participates in group activities, when required. II. Works towards the common objectives in group situation when required.

5. **Trait : Leadership**
   **Definition** : It is the consistent behaviour pattern which shows that one is showing initiative in planning, organising and completing an activity in a group or community and which also shows that one has persuasive power and is endowed with foresight.

I. Shows initiative in planning group activities. II. Organises group activities by involving others, when required. III. Leads the class or a group when required.

6. **Trait : Honesty**
   **Definition** : It is the consistent behaviour pattern which shows that one is acting with keenness to be straight-forward and with deceiving or cheating and that one is telling or reporting accurately or correctly.
   I. Avoids foul methods while playing. II. Avoids copying from the notebooks of fellow pupils when asked by teachers not to copy. III. Gives correct information regarding an incident or an assignment, when asked by teachers.

7. **Trait : Helpfulness**
   **Definition** : It is the consistent behaviour pattern which shows that one is ready to give aid or assistance to others without expecting any personal gain.
   I. Takes note of the needs of others. II. Shares his things with fellow pupils. III. Assists fellow pupils.

8. **Trait : Curiosity**
   **Definition** : It is the consistent behaviour pattern which reveals one's desire to know new things.
   I. Shows interest in knowing about new and unfamiliar things or aspects in one's environment. II. Asks probing questions. III. Observes keenly one's surroundings.

9. **Trait : Obedience**
   **Definition** : It is the consistent behaviour pattern which shows that one acts in accordance with the established rules and regulations and according to group decisions.
   I. Acts according to the announcements of the teachers. II. Observes the rules and regulations of the school. III. Acts according to the instructions of the group leaders.

10. **Trait : Self-Confidence**
    **Definition** : It is the consistent behaviour pattern which reveals that one has faith in one's own abilities.
    I. Speaks and reads confidently. II. Works confidently, even when alone. III. Plays boldly.

11A15 GENERALISED CONFORMITY TENDENCY TEST

*Author* : T. Narayan Rao

*Availability* : Author, Department of Psychology, Venkateswara University, Tirupati.

*Time required* : No time limit.

*Main features* : A situational test consisting of 14 items. For every situation three alternative responses were provided one indicating conformity, another non-conformity and a third showing neutrality.

*Scoring* : For each conformity response (C) +1, for non-conformity response (NC) −1, and for neutral response 0. Final score=$\Sigma$ C-$\Sigma$ NC.

*Reliability* : Spilt-half reliability based on 100 Ss was found to be +.50 (significant beyond .01 level).

*Reference* : Rao, T.N. Development of generalised conformity tendency test. *Research Bulletin,* 1968, 4, 21-31.

11A15 GENERALISED CONFORMITY TENDENCY TEST

(The respondent has to indicate his decisions on the following items by checking one of the three alternatives in each situation).

1. AB is an young man working in an office. One evening his colleagues come to his house and solicit his company to a movie. But he is not interested in the movie. Then what do you think he should do?
   A. He should simply follow his colleagues to the movie because a number of them would like him to go.
   B. May show some excuse and stay back.
   C. Should express his disinterest and send the colleagues away.
2. A football team is playing a match game. One of the players, DJ is given a place which is not fitting to his ability and skill. He can do more justice to the game if given a different position. But the captain is not prepared to make any change. Do you think the player, DJ should,
   A. Protest against the injustice done to him and ask for redressal of it.
   B. Simply obey the captain's orders.
   C. Withdraw from the game showing some other reason.
3. A group of young men go on a picnic to a place where there is a famous temple. All, the boys excepting one, Mr. Ven are keen on visiting the temple to pray. Ven, however, is a strong atheist. Under the circumstances, what do you think Ven should do?
   A. He can accompany the others up to the temple and do some shopping while others offer the prayer and come back.
   B. Should stick to his principle and stay back without going to the temple.
   C. Simply accompany the others to the temple to pray.
4. GTK, a postgraduate student is a resident of a hostel. He is preparing for forthcoming examination and studying seriously even during the evening hours. His hostel friends decide to attend a test match one evening. But GTK won't like to go to the match. What do you think he should do?
   A. Express his disinterest and refuse to follow the hostelmates.
   B. Simple oblige and follow them because they would like him so much to go with them.
   C. Avoid meeting the hostelmates and not attend the match.
5. There was a seminar organised on the nutrition value of certain species of oil seeds. Regarding some points, all the dieticians participating in the seminar held a unanimous opinion except one of them who doubted the validity of the group opinion. He had a different view. What do you

think he should do?

A. He can informally consult a few others and then decide.

B. The unanimous majority opinion is most likely to be correct and he should agree with majority.

C. If he had a different view he should express it openly.

6. A group of students are travelling in a city bus. They are refusing to pay the fare and buy tickets. The conductor is almost helpless. One student, Roy, however, feels bad about the behaviour of the fellow students. In such a situation what should Roy do?

A. Join his friends and not to buy ticket himself.

B. Condemn his friends behaviour and ask them to buy tickets.

C. Buy his ticket whether others buy or not.

7. A girl student, PRM, coming from a district college took admission in an urban college. Here, styles and social habits of girl students, in dressing, speech manners, mixing with boys, etc. are quite different from her previous social atmosphere. Should PRM

A. Start dressing, speaking and mixing with boys in the same way as other girls do?

B. Behave now and then as other girls do but not always?

C. Behave according to her likes and not care for others' reactions?

8. Students of a college are going on strike demanding reduction of tuition and examination fees which, they think, are very high and unreasonable. CTK, a student of the same college, though in sympathy with the cause of the strike, is afraid of possible violence. Do you think CTK should

A. Raise objection to and condemn violent activities and refuse to join the strike.

B. Avoid other's attention quietly keeping away from the strike.

C. Simply join the striking students and follow them.

9. A teacher was enquiring a class of girl students about their future plans. All girls except one, TVM, reported that they would study further or take up a job but would not get married. TVM had planned to get married and live as a housewife. But she was afraid of being ridiculed by others if she expressed this. What do you think she should do?

A. State fearlessly her independent opinion that she would like to marry.

B. State the same way as others that she would not marry.

C. She could say she had not thought about the matter.

10. In a spinning mill workers fixed limits to the maximum work output. No worker was expected to produce more. MG, a worker of the mill felt he could work and produce more and that the limits imposed were unjust and unreasonable. What should he do under the circumstances?

A. Try to persuade other workers explaining the need for maintaining the production at the maximum level.

B. Behave in accordance with the decision of all.

C. Should work and produce more not caring for others' reaction.

11. A lady is very much tempted to use lipstick. But other ladies in her company who dislike such a practice may not approve of this. If she paints her lips they may avoid her company. What do you think is the

best for her to do?

A. Suppress her desire and behave as ner companions do.
B. She can use it occasionally and not always.
C. If she is very keen she can go ahead and use lipstick.

12. Farmers in villages require to employ workers on daily wages for a part of their field work. In any village all the farmers are expected to follow uniform rate of wages in paying the workers. A farmer, NR, in a village finds it necessary and also reasonable to pay more than the usual wages to get the workers for his work. But this may evoke the anger and disapproval of other farmers. What do you think he should do?
    A. Respect the feelings of other farmers and not raise the wages.
    B. Be true to his feelings and raise the wages as he feels.
    C. Informally and unofficially give the workers some other per cent and not raise the wages openly.
13. An association was celebrating its inaugural function. After the function was over, tea was served to the participants. There was a gentleman, K, whose principle was not to take tea. He found all others on the occasion taking tea. Then what do you think he should do?
    A. Tell others about his principle and not take tea.
    B. He should also take tea along with others.
    C. Should keep away from others' attention moving to some other place.
14. Students of a class have planned to tease and trouble a teacher who is not teaching properly. To one student GTK, of his class the plan of the students seems indecent and unmannerly. Under the circumstances, what should GTK do?
    A. He should simply join his classmates in the plan.
    B. Should refuse to join the others and inform the teacher about the students' plan.
    C. Should dissociate himself from the play by absenting himself from the School.

## 11A16 EXTRAVERSION-INTROVERSION INVENTORY

*Authors* : V.S. Shanthamani and A. Hafeez

*Availability* : Authors, Department of Industrial Management, Indian Institute of Social Science, Bangalore-12.

*Time required* : No time limit. It takes about 10 minutes.

*Level* : English knowing adults.

*Main features* : This inventory has 20 items of which 10 items each relate to Extraversion and Introversion.

*Scoring* : The total number of items answered in the direction of the trait for each scale separately is the score.

*Reliability* : Split-half reliability was found to be .35 for extroversion, significant at .01 level and .29 for introversion, significant at .05 level.

*Validity* : Construct validity for Extraversion was found to be .72 and for Introversion it was .68.

*Norms* : Percentile norms have been developed on 200 employed engineers.

11A16 EXTRAVERSION-INTROVERSION INVENTORY

(The following items have to be checked on 'yes' or 'no').

1. I enjoy social gathering or parties.
2. My feelings change from happy to sad and sad to happy for no reason.
3. I do not like to be a leader at social functions.
4. I can do good work even while people are looking on.
5. I like to change from one type of work to another very often.
6. I become conscious of being observed in the presence of superiors.
7. I am not afraid of being punished.
8. I like to have excitement (i.e. rousing or stimulation) in life.
9. My memory is good.
10. I am unhappy most of the time.
11. I worry over possible misfortune.
12. I blush (become red in the face) very often in the presence of others.
13. I do not have a wide circle of friends.
14. One should act on suggestions quickly rather than stopping to think.
15. I do not like to keep quiet when out in a group.
16. Life is for getting pleasure.
17. I am not usually calm and collected most of the time.
18. I do not easily get tired of meeting people and talking to them.
19. I would prefer to stay at home rather than attend a social function or party.
20. I do not like public speaking.

11A17 FEAR CHECKLIST

*Author* : Usha Rani Sidana.
*Time* : About 10 minutes.
*Level* : 6 to 10 year old children.
*Main features* : It covers 7 areas of fears: Animals, Supernatural Agents, Environmental Situations, Natural Phenomena, Death, Disease and Injury, Other Persons, and Interpersonal Situations.
*Reliability* : Test-retest reliability for the three age groups 1,4,6,8 and 10 years were found to be 0.85, 0.91 and 0.91 respectively (rhos).
*Validity* : Validity, coefficients (rho) with teachers' ratings were found to be 0.51, 0.60 and 0.53 respectively.

11A17 FEAR CHECKLIST

(Fear arousing stimuli from the following items have to be checked).

1. Cat; 2. Tiger, Leopard, Bear; 3. Elephant; 4. Snake, Scorpion; 5. Dog; 6. Cow, Buffalow, Ox; 7. Monkey; 8. Lion; 9. Lizard; 10. Worm; 11. Camel; 12. Deer; 13. Storm; 14. Scooter, Car; 15. Rickshaw; 16. Truck, Bus; 17. Rain; 18. Cloud; 19. Doctor; 20. Police man; 21. Sadhu (Mendicant); 22. Peeping into the well; 23. Shadow; 24. Stranger; 25. Corpse; 26. Dead animal; 27. Ghost, Witch; 28. Darkness; 29. Loud sound; 30. Sickness; 31. Hospital; 32. Old man; 33.

Sleeping alone; 34. Thief, Robber; 35. Looking down from a terrace; 36. Fire; 37. Heaven; 38. Hell; 39. Fairy; 40. Circus, Cinema; 41. God; 42. Being scolded; 43. Beating; 44. Elder brother; 45. Elder sister; 46. Class teacher; 47. School principal; 48. River, Tank; 49. Mother; 50. Father.

## 11A18 DEPENDENCE PRONENESS SCALE

*Author* : Jai B.P. Sinha.
*Availability* : ANS Institute of Social Studies, Patna-1.
*Level* : College Students.
*Main features* : It is a Likert types 5-point scale. Available in Hindi also.
*Scoring* : Simple addition of response numbers.
*Reliability* : Reliability coefficients vary from .70 to .95. Reliability scores were found to be better when the scale is administered individually.
*Validity* : Validity coefficient was found to be .55.
*References* :

1. Sinha, J.B.P. A test of dependence proneness. *Journal of Psychological Researches,* 1968, 12, 66-70.
2. Sinha, J.B.P. The construct of dependence proneness. *Journal of Social Psychology,* 1968, 76, 123-124.
3. Sinha, J.B.P. Dependence proneness and some of its concomitant and background variables. *Journal of General and Applied Psychology,* 1968, 1, 44-49.
4. Sinha, J.B.P. and Lakshmi, Asha. Learning as a function of demand characteristics and dependency. *Psychological Studies,* 1968, 13, 55-59.

## 11A18 DEPENDENCE PRONENESS SCALE

(The following items have to be checked on a five-point scale).

1. I hesitate to take help from others (N).
2. I enjoy doing things that others think are crazy (N).
3. I take my friends to help me in shopping.
4. Before taking a serious decision, one should consult one's good friends or an experienced person.
5. Bright students should help the weak ones.
6. I never disobey my parents.
7. A good man will seek advice from his elders and will provide the same to the younger ones.
8. I don't do things just to please my parents (N).
9. I can't be forced to do anything unless I myself want that way (N).
10. I generally don't go for others' suggestions (N).
11. A good friend will never disagree with me.
12. If a book is difficult to understand, instead of trying on one's own, it is better to ask a class friend or a teacher.
13. My parents unnecessarily impose themselves upon me (N).
14. I want to take my own decisions (N).
15. I want to share both — joys and sorrows — with my friends.
16. I would like to avoid a fight than to have my own way.

17. Leaders are responsible for the slow rate of development of the country.
18. Teachers should explain in detail as to what the students should read.
19. I want to behave according to the wishes of the teachers.
20. In class, it is better to go along with the majority than to have one's own way.

**Note** : (N) at the end of some items indicates that the items are negatively keyed.

## Instruments with technical information B

### 11B1 TACTUAL AUDITORY PROJECTIVE TEST

*Author* : S. Bhattacharya.
*Availability* : Author.
*Level* : Adults of both sex.
*Reliability* : Test-retest reliability coefficients was found to be .78 (an interval of 6 months).
*Validity* : Validation of the test battery rested on the assumption that the test will discriminate between the various criterion groups formed for the purpose of comparison.
*Reference* : Bhattacharya, S. Development a new type of tactual and auditory projective test. *Journal of Psychological Researches*, 1968, 12(2), 95-97.

### 11B2 PERSONALITY INVENTORY

*Author* : Bureau of Educational and Psychological Research, David Hare Training College, Calcutta.
*Availability* : Authors.
*Main features* : Inventory consisting of 49 statements.
*Scoring* : Key available.
*Validity* : .29 to .70 with teachers rating on the traits concerned.

### 11B3 VAKYA PURTI

*Authors* : Central Bureau of Educational and Vocational Guidance, Delhi.
*Availability* : Authors.
*Time required* : No time limit.
*Level* : High school students.
*Main features* : Projective test consisting of 60 items.

### 11B4 PERSONALITY TRAITS QUESTIONNAIRE

*Author* : Maya Deb.
*Availability* : Author, Calcutta University.
*Main features* : A 100 item questionnaire.
*Reference* : Deb, Maya. Personality traits of successful engineers. *Indian*

*Journal of Psychology*, 1968, 43(1-4), 6-10.

### 11B5 SEX ROLE PREFERENCE TEST

*Author* : R.C. Dixit.
*Availability* : Author, Department of Psychology, Jodhpur University, Jodhpur.
*Time required* : Approximately 45 minutes.
*Level* : Below the age of 6 years.
*Main features* : Projective pictures.
*Scoring* : Quantitative scoring.
*Reliability* : Test-retest reliability was .67 for boys .72 for girls.
*Reference* : Dixit, R.C. Sex role consciousness among village children of upper and lower caste groups. *Journal of the Indian Academy of Applied Psychology*, 1968, 4, 32-36.

### 11B6 COGNITIVE IMBALANCE QUESTIONNAIRE

*Author* : H.S. Eswara.
*Availability* : Author, Department of Psychology, University of Mysore, Mysore-6.
*Uses* : To study the choice of response in resolving cognitive imbalance.
*Time* : About 3 to 5 minutes.
*Level* : For high school and college students, and also for adults.
*Main features* : Involves three hypothetical situations presumably producing cognitive imbalance in the subjects. In situation 1, the subject is met with a friend who challenges one of his pet political notions; in situation 2, the subject is confronted with a professor (an expert) who criticises one of his projects; and in situation 3, the subject is opposed by an elderly member of the family (an authority) on an important personal decision. Between the subject and the other person in question, and at the same time, the subject is being opposed by the other person on a certain issue. At the end of each of these situations five alternative modes of reaction to such a situation are presented. These modes of reaction are: (1) Derogate or belittle the other person; (2) Conform or yield to the other person resulting in the modification of one's own behaviour or thinking; (3) Seek the support of others in favour of one's own behaviour or thinking; (4) Make an attempt to change the other person through persuasion and discussion; and (5) Tolerate imbalance by not doing anything about the situation.
*Scoring* : Analysing in terms of the choice of mode of response in resolving the cognitive imbalance.
*Reference* : Eswara, H.S. Resolving cognitive imbalances some personal and situational determinants, *Psychological Studies*, 1969, 14(2), 111-116.

### 11B7 PERSONALITY INVENTORY

*Authors* : E.I. George, V. George Mathew and V. Ramchandran Nair.
*Availability* Authors, Department of Psychology, Kariavattom, Trivendrum, Kerala.
*Uses* : To measure five major factors of temperament: Social Activity, Extraversion, Tolerance, Maladjustment and Masculinity.

*Time required*: 30 minutes.

*Level*: Test developed on high school pupils in Kerala, but with some caution it can be used with all Malayalam knowing adults.

*Main features*: It has 125 items.

*Scoring*: Separate answer sheet and a single scoring stencil.

*Reliability*: Re-test reliabilities ranged from 0.44 to 0.74 and odd-even reliabilities from 0.47 to 0.77.

*Validity*: Significant correlations with self-rating and scores on a Malayalam adaptation of the MPI and an adaptation (English) of the GZTS.

*Norms*: Percentile norms are available.

## 11B8 FEAR, AGGRESSION AND ANXIETY TEST

*Author*: G.L. Julka.

*Availability*: Author.

*Level*: Children.

*Main features*: It is a projective test.

*Reference*: Julka, G.L. Aggression, Fear and Anxiety in Children (Their Educational Implications), Ph.D. Thesis in Education, University of Rajasthan, 1963.

## 11B9 A MEASURE OF AUTHORITARIANISM IN HINDI

*Author*: V.K. Kool.

*Availability*: Author, Department of Psychology, Banaras Hindu University, Varanasi-221005. U.P.

*Time required*: No limit. Approximately 25 mts.

*Level*: Adults/Graduates.

*Main features*: It has 40 items — 22 positively worded and 18 negatively worded representing various areas of life — political, economic, religious, educational, cultural etc.

*Scoring*: The items are scored on a five-point (Likert type) scale ranging from 1 to 5.

*Reliability*: Test-retest = .90 Spilt-half (corrected with S-B formula) —.83.

*Validity*: Correlation Coefficients with California F-scale = .73.

*Reference*: Kool, V.K. A study on the difference in perception of authoritarians and non-authoritarians. Ph.D. Thesis. Banaras Hindu University, Varanasi-221005, U.P., 1969.

*Time required*: No fixed time limit, however, on an average it takes about 15 minutes.

## 11B10 TIME APPRECIATION TEST

*Author*: S.P. Kulshrestha.

*Availability*: Commercially available. M/s. National Psychological Corporation, Labh Chand Market, Raja-ki-Mandi, Agra-2, U.P.

*Uses*: Serves the purpose of emergency test and psychometric tool. It could be used as initial screening device and as a follow up check upon the patients progress in clinics.

*Time required* : 5 to 10 minutes.

*Level* : For the age group of 10 years and above.

*Scoring* : Assign two marks for each correct and one mark for each partially correct response.

*Reliability* : Test-retest reliability for individual was .93 and for group .90.

*Validity* : Validity coefficients with J.N. Buck's test were found to be .91 and .87 respectively for individual and group. With Wechsler-Belleue test validity coefficient was found to be .80.

*Reference* : Kulshrestha, S.P. Some uses of emergency tests in mental clinics. *Manika,* 1968, 1 (2).

## 11B11 SELF-REPORTING INVENTORY OF EXTRAVERSION AND INTROVERSION

*Author* : S.P. Kulshrestha.

*Availability* : Commercially available. M/s. Indian Psychological Corporation, 'Shanti' Sadan, Rai Behari Lal Road, Lucknow-7 (U.P.).

*Uses* : Used as a large scale screening device for extroversion and introversion. And also for guidance and counselling work.

*Level* : School boys, college students and adults.

*Main features* : It is a self-administered, verbal, group as well as individual Inventory in which Hindi phrases are used with high discriminating values in one section. It has a total of six parts with 100 items, emphasising positive and negative sides.

*Scoring* : Scoring stencils are available separately for extraversion and introversion scores.

*Reliability* : Test-retest reliability coefficient, was found to be .85 split-half reliability, coefficient was found to be .89 after Spearman-Brown's correction.

*Validity* : Validity coefficient with the Neymann Kohlstedt Diagnostic Test was .89 and with teachers rating it was 0.92. Content and construct validity were also established.

*Norms* : Cutting scores are given for girls and boys.

*References* : Kulshrestha, S.P. A study of self-reporting test for extraversion and introversion in Hindi. *Journal of Psychology of Education and Guidance.* 1(1).

## 11B12 PERSONALITY INVENTORY

*Authors* : A.K. Majumdar and P.K. Majumdar.

*Availability* : Author.

*Uses* : To study the personality of farmers.

*Time required* : No time limit.

*Level* : Could be used with farmers and other adult groups.

*Main features* : It contains eight personality traits viz. initiative, emotional control, adaptability and flexibility, foresight and good judgement, cooperativeness, enthusiasm and personality.

*Scoring* : Five-point scoring system each item score could range from –2 to +2.

*Reliability* : Test-retest reliability (interval of 15 days) was found to be 0.76.

*Reference* : Majumdar, A.K. and Majumdar, P.K. Adoption and some psychological characteristics of farmers; *Indian Journal of Extension Education,* 1967, 3(3), 138-142.

11B13 WORD ASSOCIATION TEST

*Author* : Manovigyanshala, Allahabad.
*Availability* : Authors.
*Time required* : No time limit.
*Level* : All.
*Main features* : It contains 55 Hindi words.

11B14 PERSONALITY INVENTORY

*Author* : Manovigyanshala, Allahabad.
*Availability* : Authors.
*Time required* : About 30 minutes.
*Level* : For higher secondary students of age group 4 to 20 years.
*Main features* : Inventory divided into four parts referring to different areas of life (1) Home, (2) School, (3) Health, (4) Interpersonal relationship. It is in Hindi.
*Scoring* : By key.

11B15 PERSONALITY ASSESSMENT FROM CHILDREN'S PAINTINGS

*Author* : C.B.L. Mathur.
*Availability* : Author, c/o. Vidya Bhavan Teachers Training College, Udaipur.
*Main features* : For analysis the point of view of factors like form, place-animal figures, inanimate objects, scenery, geometrical designs, maps, movement, perspective, column etc. have been considered from human figures, blue prints—diagrams and aspects.
*Scoring* : Scoring blank for paintings for analysis in above mentioned components.
*Reference* : Mathur, C.B.L. An analytical study of children's paintings as indication of their personality patterns, Ph.D. Thesis in Education, University of Udaipur, 1972.

11B16 SENTENCE COMPLETION TEST

*Authors* : S.K. Mitra, M.M. Trivedi, Saroj Parekh, Leela Pustake, Sudha Parekh and Sybil David.
*Availability* : B.M. Institute, Ashram Road, Ahmedabad-9.
*Time required* : 45 minutes to 1 hour.
*Level* : 12 to 35 years.
*Main features* : It consists of 214 sub-tests and items and 3 forms (male, female and adult).

11B17 CHILDREN'S SENTENCE COMPLETION TEST, 361A, 362B.

*Authors* : S.K. Mitra, Sybil David and Lolla Girdhar Lal.

*Availability* : B.M. Institute, Ashram Road, Ahmedabad-9.
*Time required* : About 20 minutes.
*Level* : 8 to 15 years.
*Main features* : It contains two forms—361A consisting of 40 items and 362B consisting of 37 items.

11B18 WORD ASSOCIATION TEST

*Author* : S.K. Mitra, M.M. Trivedi, Saroj Parekh, Leela Pustake, Sudha Parekh, and Sybil David.
*Availability* : B.M. Institute, Ashram Road, Ahmedabad-9.
*Time required* : 1 to 1.50 hours.
*Level* : Adults.
*Main features* : Verbal Tests consists of 75 sub-tests and items.

11B19 CHILDREN'S WORLD CHAIN ASSOCIATION TEST, 362

*Authors* : S.K. Mitra, Sybil David and Lolla Girdhari Lal.
*Availability* : B.M. Institute, Ashram Road, Ahmedabad-9.
*Time required* : 30 minutes to 40 minutes.
*Level* : 8 to 15 years students.
*Main features* : Projective verbal test, consists of 20 items.

11B20 SCHIZOPHRENIC SCALE

*Author* : H. Narayan Murthy.
*Availability* : Author, All India Institute of Mental Health, Bangalore.
*Uses* : To sort out schizophrenics.
*Main features* : It has 20 items. Available in Hindi and Bengali.
*Validity* : Validated using matched, normal and schizophrenic groups.
*Forms* : T-score norms available.
*Reference* : Murthy, H.N. Development and validation of schizophrenic scale. *Transactions of All India Institute of Mental Health,* 1964, 4, 1-9.

11B21 DEPRESSIVE ANXIETY SCALE

*Author* : H.N. Murthy.
*Availability* : Authors, All India Institute of Mental Health, Bangalore.
*Main features* : It has 26 items.
*Validity* : Validated on known groups of psychiatric diagnosis.
*Reference* : Murthy, H.N. Development of the paranoid depressive, manic and anxiety scales. *Transactions of A.I.I.M.H.,* 1965, 50-59.

11B22 MANIC SCALE

*Author* : H.N. Murthy.
*Availability* : Author, All India Institute of Mental Health, Bangalore.
*Uses* : To diagnose manic patients.
*Main features* : It has 16 items.

*Validity* : Validated on known groups of psychiatric diagnosis.

*Reference* : Murthy, H.N. Development of the paranoid depressive, manic and anxiety scales. *Transactions of the All India Institute of Mental Health,* 1965, 50-59.

11B23 DEPRESSIVE SCALE

*Author* : H.N. Murthy.

*Availability* : Author, All India Institute of Mental Health, Bangalore.

*Uses* : To diagnose depressive patients.

*Main features* : It has 14 items.

*Validity* : Validated using known groups.

*Reference* : Murthy, H.N. Development of the paranoid depressive, manic and anxiety scales. *Transactions of All India Institute of Mental Health,* 1965, 50-59.

11B24 PARANOID SCALE

*Author* : H.N. Murthy.

*Availability* : Author, All India Institute of Mental Health, Bangalore.

*Uses* : To diagnose paranoids.

*Main features* : It has 18 items.

*Validity* : Validated with known groups of psychiatric diagnosis.

*Reference* : Murthy, H.N. Development of the paranoid depressive, manic and anxiety scales. *Transactions of All India Institute of Mental Health,* 1965, 50-59.

11B25 PERSONALITY INVENTORY

*Authors* : Uma Krishna Murthy and Y. Swarajya Lakshmi.

*Availability* : Authors, Department of Psychology, Osmania University, Hyderabad.

*Uses* : To measure the personality on the basis of the 3 gunas (Sattvic, Tamas and Rajas).

*Validity* : Established.

*Reference* : Murthy, U.K., Lakshmi, Y.S. and Parameswaran, E.G. Construction of a personality inventory based on doctrine of 3 Gunas. *Research Bulletin,* 1971, 6, 49-58.

11B26 MOTIVATION PERSONALITY INVENTORY

*Author* : B.C. Muthayya.

*Availability* : Author, Director of Psychology, National Institute of Community Development, Rajendranagar, Hyderabad.

*Uses* : To assess personality—introversion, neuroticism, empathy, ego-ideal, need-achievement, dogmatism, dominance, pessimism and self-confidence.

*Time required* : About half an hour.

*Level* : Block officials.

*Main features* : Contains 50 items, a scale each item to be answered in terms of yes/no. The items in each of the variable varies from 5 to 7.

*Scoring* : As per the scoring key where 1 mark is given for the presence of particular tendency.

*Norms* : Available for B.D.Os., Shikya Sevikas, Gram-Sevaks, and Grama Sevikas of southern States, Mysore, Kerala, Tamil Nadu.

### 11B27 PICTURE-FRUSTRATION TEST

*Author* : B.C. Muthayya

*Time required* : 20 minutes.

*Level* : High school students.

*Main features* : Contains 15 cartoon-like pictures with captions indicating a frustration-stimulus.

*Scoring* : Through a scoring scheme adopted from that of Rosenzweig.

*Reliability* : Test-retest reliability has been worked out.

*Validity* : Based on experimental trend analysis and comparison of delinquents and normals.

*Norms* : Available for boys and girls separately.

*References* :

1. Muthayya, B.C. The picture-frustration test: its development. *Manas*, 1961, 29-35.
2. Muthayya, B.C. Reliability of a new picture frustration study. *Journal of psychological Researches*, 1960 4(3).
3. Muthayya, B.C. An experimental validation of picture-frustration study. *Psychological Studies*, 1962, 7(1).

### 11B28 HUMOUR TEST

*Authors* : B.C. Muthayya and M. Mallikarjunan

*Availability* : Author, Director of Psychology, N.I.C.D., Rajendranagar Hyderabad.

*Uses* : To assess the sense of humour among the students.

*Time required* : 20 minutes.

*Level* : Students—high school and college—and adults.

*Main features* : It contains 25 cartoon strips in the final test.

*Scoring* : A 5-point rating scale is provided for rating each cartoon from not funny to extremely funny, where the higher the score, the higher the sense of humour.

*Reference* : Muthayya, B.C. and Mallikarjunan, M. A measure of humour and its relation to intelligence. *Journal of Psychological Researches,* 1969, 13(2), 101-105.

### 11B29 MOTHER CARE SCALE

*Author* : Kamal Patel.

*Uses* : For measuring the degrees of mother care received by children.

*Time required* : No time limit.

*Level* : Mothers.

*Main features* : The elements of child rearing universe were included which consist of feeding, putting the baby to bed, picking up or attending to the child when he works, elimination, bathing and dressing and play to see the differential impact.

*Reliability* : Split-half reliability was found to be .72.

*Reference* : Patel, K. A mother care scale and comparison of children receiving extreme scores on the scale. *Indian Journal of Psychology,* 1965, 39(4), 179-189.

11B30 CONSERVATIVE REFORMIST SCALE

*Author* : A.S. Patel.

*Availability* : Author, Department of Psychology, M.S. University, Baroda.

*Level* : Common educated man.

*Main features* : It contains 50 items, 25 on conservatism and 25 on reformists.

*Reliability* : Reliability coefficients for the conservatistic and reformistic groups were found to be .88 and .83 respectively.

*Validity* : Validated against self-ratings of known groups.

*Norms* : Available.

*Reference* : Patel, A.S. A rational, construction and try-out of test scales measuring some personality traits. *Advances in Education,* 1965, 1(2), 11-27.

11B31 PERSONALITY INVENTORY FOR EXECUTIVES IN INDUSTRY

*Author* : P.M. Patel.

*Availability* : Author, National Institute of Education.

*Time required* : 15 minutes.

*Scoring* : Objective key.

11B32 ACHIEVEMENT PRESS INVENTORY

*Author* : P.M. Patel.

*Availability* : Author, National Institute of Education, Sri Aurobindo Marg, New Delhi-16.

*Time required* : 15 minutes.

*Level* : High school pupils.

*Main features* : Standardised forced-choice inventory, available in Hindi.

*Scoring* : Objective scoring.

*Reliability* : Established.

*Validity* : Established.

*Reference* : Patel, P.M. Measurement of Achievement Press. Ph.D. Thesis in Psychology, Delhi University, 1971.

11B33 CONSERVATIVE-RADICAL ATTITUDE SCALE

*Authors* : P.M. Patel, M.M. Patel, D.S. Parikh, M.N. Palsane, M.B. Buch, Jamnaji Parikh.

*Availability* : P.M. Patel, National Institute of Education, Sri Aurobindo Marg, New Delhi-16.

*Level* : 13+ to 18+ minutes (Adolescents).

*Main features* : Standardised inventory, available in Gujarati only.
*Scoring* : Objective.
*Norms* : Available.
*References* : Bhatt, L.J., Patel, P.M., Patel, M.M., Parikh, D.S. *Inquiry into Psychological Factors Related to Adolescent Adjustment.* Report of the Indian Council of Medical Research Project. Baroda : Faculty of Education and Psychology, 1960.

11B34 ADOLESCENT PICTURE FANTASY TEST

*Author* : Jai Parakash.
*Availability* : Author, Department of Psychology, University of Sagar, Saugar.
*Time required* : 1 hour 20 minutes.
*Scoring* : Key available.
*Reliability* : Test-retest reliability established.
*Validity* : Validated against TAT and picture story test of P.M. Symonds.

11B35 QUESTIONNAIRE FOR MEASURING EGO-IDEALS

*Author* : P. Pratap.
*Availability* : Author.
*Main features* : Questionnaire containing the names of six heroes and six heroines and list of corresponding masculine and feminine qualities.
*Reference* : Pratap, P. The development of ego-ideal in Indian children: A survey. Ph. D. Thesis in Education, Banaras Hindu University, 1969.

11B36 EMOTIONAL MATURITY SCALE

*Authors* : A.J. Qadri, S. Sultan Akhtar and F. Jafri.
*Availability* : Authors, C/o. Department of Psychology, Aligarh Muslim University, Aligarh.
*Time required* : About 20 minutes.
*Level* : University and college students.
*Main features* : It is in two parts.
*Scoring* : Scored by a key.
*Reliability* : Split-half reliability coefficients (N=50) were found to be .73 and .62 respectively for parts 1 and 2.
*Validity* : Statements representing emotional maturity-immaturity were sent to 53 psychologist. Scale values for statements of part I were calculated and statements having low quartile deviation were selected. Discriminative value of statements of part II were found out and statements having high discriminative value were selected. The scale has also been validated against Aligarh Adjustment Inventory.
*Norms* : Normative sample consists of 300 men students of Aligarh Muslim University.

11B37 EMOTIONAL MATURITY SCALE

*Author* : P.V. Ramamurthi.

*Availability* : 20 minutes.
*Level* : Adult males and older people.
*Main features* : It gives separate scores for death and future.
*Scoring* : Simple 1-0 scoring.
*Reference* : Ramamurthi, P.V. A study of certain factors related to adjustment of urban aged men. Ph.D. Thesis in Psychology, S.V. University, Tirupati, 1968.

11B38 S.V.U. PERSONALITY SCALE

*Author* : S. Narayana Rao.
*Availability* : Author, Department of Psychology, Shri Venkateswara University, Tirupati, A.P.
*Uses* : Assessment of neurotic difficulties of subject and screening students for counselling assistance.
*Time required* : About 30-40 minutes.
*Level* : College students and adults (knowledge of English necessary).
*Main features* : It is a scale with 72 items each with 5 response categories of the Likert type.
*Scoring* : Hand scoring only. Total score obtained by numerical addition of weights for each response.
*Reliability* : Split-half reliability by Odd-Even method was found to be .98; First half-Second half it was .96* and retest reliability (4-5 weeks) was *.88 (N=85) and 8-10 weeks it was .84 (N=64).
(*corrected by S-B formula).
*Validity* : r with Bernreuter Personality Inventory (B 1-N) was .72 (N=115) and with achievement at graduation r was –.352.
*Norms* : Developed with 2648 college students of all faculties.
*Reference* :
1. Rao, S.N. The S.V.U. Personality Scale. *Psychological Research,* 1962.
2. Rao. S.N. The revised S.V.U. Personality Scale. *Psychological Studies,* 1965.
3. Rao S.N. Student Performance and Adjustment, 1967, Tirupati, S.V. University.

11B39 COLOUR SCALES TO EMOTIONAL SITUATIONS

*Author* : Mirza S. Saiyadain.
*Availability* : Author, Indian Institute of Management, Ahmedabad, India.
*Level* : College students and adults.
*Uses* : To measure the degree of emotions associated with different colours.
*Main Features* : There are eight statements representing emotional situations of different degrees.
*Validity* : Validity of statements was established by judges, ratings.
*Scoring* : The statement chosen for each colour gives the strength of emotion aroused by that colour.
*Reference* : Saiyadain, Mirza and Siddiqui, B.B. Sex difference in colour scales to emotional situations. *Indian Journal of Applied Psychology,* 1969, 6(2), 62-68.

11B40 VERBAL PROJECTION TEST

*Author* : T.E. Shanmugam.
*Availability* : Author, Department of Psychology, University of Madras, Madras.
*Time required* : About 45 minutes.
*Level* : 12 to 18 years students.
*Reliability* : Split-half and parallel form reliabilities have been established.
*Validity* : Validated against parental and teacher's ratings.
*Norms* : Available on 1000 students.

11B41 PERSONALITY INVENTORY

*Author* : T.E. Shanmugam.
*Availability* : Author, Head, Department of Psychology, University of Madras, Madras (Tamil Nadu).
*Uses* : Guidance.
*Time required* : About 45 minutes.
*Level* : 12 to 18 years students.
*Norms* : Available on 100 students.

11B42 MARITAL PREFERENCE CHECKLIST

*Author* : B.N. Singh.
*Availability* : Author.
*Level* : College students.
*Reference* : Singh, B.N. A study of certain personal qualities as preferred by college students in their marital partners. *Journal of Psychological Researches*, 1964, 8(1), 37-48.

11B43 TEST OF TEMPERAMENT AND CHARACTER

*Author* : B.K. Sohoni.
*Availability* : Author, 1957, Sadashiv Peth, Poona-2.
*Time required* : About 20 minutes.
*Level* : 14 to 16 years old boys.
*Main features* : Consists of 36 sub-tests.
*Reliability* : Test-retest reliability was established.
*Validity* : Validated against teachers' opinions.

11B44 SEVEN-POINT PERSONALITY RATING SCALE

*Authors* : Shashi Lata Verma and R.M. Verma.
*Uses* : To find our personality traits of students.
*Main features* : The personality traits covered are: smart, receding, self-confidence, realistic-unrealistic, optimistic-pessimistic, emotionally mature, immature, responsive-easy going, cooperative-individualistic.
*Reliability* : The reliability coefficients for different traits range from .57 to .85.
*Reference* : Verma, S. and Verma, R.M. Some Personality traits under different socio-cultural status groups. *Journal of Psychological Researches*, 1969, 13(1), 28-31.

## Citations

11C1 ANANT'S BELONGINGNESS QUESTIONNAIRE

*Author* : S.S. Anant.
*Reference* : Anant, S.S. A cross-cultural study of belongingness, anxiety neuroticism, and extraversion. *ICSSR Research Abstracts,* 1972, 1(2), 42-48.

11C2 BOSE'S NEUROTIC QUESTIONNAIRE

*Reference* : Kundu, R. Some suggestions for the improvement of Bose's Neurotic Questionnaire. *Indian Journal of Psychology,* 1958, 33(2), 112-120.

11C3 NEUROTIC QUESTIONNAIRE

*Author* : N.C. Das, Department of Applied Psychology, Calcutta University.
*Reference* : Das, N.C. Psychological study of unemployment. *Indian Journal of Psychology,* 1966, 41(2), 89-91.

11C4 INTROVERSION-EXTROVERSION TEST

*Author* : N.C. Das, Department of Applied Psychology, Calcutta University.
*Reference* : Das, N.C. Psychological study of unemployment. *Indian Journal of Psychology,* 1966, 41(2), 89-91.

11C5 NUMERICAL RATING SCALE FOR EXTROVERSION

*Author* : K. Devadasan.
*Reference* : Devadasan, K. Validity of personality rating as a function of information about the rating technique. *Journal of the Indian Academy of Applied Psychology,* 1966, 3(2), 47-49.

11C6 EMOTIONAL STABILITY QUESTIONNAIRE

*Author* : B.R. Devi.
*Reference* : Devi, B.R. Adjustment problems of married and unmarried women teachers. *Journal of Psychological Researches,* 1960, 4(2), 65-68.

11C7 FRUSTRATION REACTION SCHEDULE

*Author* : G. Devi.
*Reference* : Devi, G.A. A study of sex difference in reaction to frustrating situation. *Psychological Studies,* 1967, 12(1), 17-27.

11C8 SENTENCE APPERCEPTION TEST

*Author* : R. Dixit.

*Reference* : Srivastava, D.N. Performance as a function of drive in regressive and fixative girls with special reference to interactions. *Indian Journal of Psychology,* 1971, 46(4), 385-395.

11C9 PERSONALITY INVENTORY

*Author* : J.C. Gaur.

*Availability* : Author, Department of Education, Agra University, Agra (U.P.).

*Reference* : Gaur, J.C. Personality profiles of Isolates. Ph.D. Thesis in Education, Agra University.

11C10 QUESTIONNAIRE TO STUDY GUILT FEELING

*Author* : N. Khalique

*Reference* : Khalique, N. A study of reaction of guilt feeling. *Journal of Psychological Researches,* 1961, 5(2), 80-72.

11C11 PERSONALITY TYPES QUESTIONNAIRE (CYCLOTHYMES AND SCHIZOTHYMES)

*Author* : B. Krishnan

*Reference* : Krishnan, B. Order of birth and treatment. *Indian Journal of Psychology,* 1954, 26, 85-87.

11C12 MAJUMDAR PERSONALITY INVENTORY

*Author* : P.K. Majumdar.

*Reference* : Mukherji, K. and Majumdar, P.K. A comparison of direct and projective method of personality assessment. *Manas,* 1968, 15(1), 19-24.

11C13 INTROVERSION-EXTROVERSION QUESTIONNAIRE

*Author* : C.R. Parmesh

*Reference* : Parmesh, C.R. Introversion-Extroversion and figural after effects. *Indian Journal of Psychology,* 1963, 38(2), 93-97.

11C14 BEHAVIOUR RATING SCALE

*Author* : S.K. Paul

*Reference* : Murthy, H.M. and Satyavati, K. Group-theory and behaviour change in chromic schizophrenics. *Transactions of All India Institute of Mental Health,* 1966, 6, 60-68.

11C15 EMOTIONAL RESPONSE TEST

*Author* : S. Rajangam

*Reference* : Rajangam, S. Personality structure of some inmates of the Madras vigilance and reserve homes. *Journal of Psychological Researches,* 1967, 1(1), 47-58.

11C16 NEUROTIC INVENTORY

*Author*: E.J. Raman

*Reference*: Raman, E.J. A neurotic inventory. *Journal of the indian Academy of Applied Psychology,* 1967, 4(2), 48-53.

11C17 SECURITY INDEX

*Authors*: N.S.N. Sastry, R.S.K. Rao and M.C. Satyanarayan.

*Reference*: Sastry, N.S.N., Rao, R.S.K., Satyanarayan, M.C., Security Index. *Indian Journal of Psychology,* 1950, 25(1-4), 33-38.

11C18 DEPENDENCE INVENTORY

*Author* : H.K. Shivadasani

*Reference* : Shivadasani, H.K. Dependence proneness in work organisation. *Indian Journal of Industrial Relations,* 1971, 7(1), 53-58.

11C19 PERSONALITY RATING INVENTORY

*Author* : J.P. Srivastava

*Reference* : Srivastava, J.P. A synthetic approach to the problems of personality. Ph.D. Thesis in Education, Allahabad University, 1953.

11C20 PERSONALITY TRAIT QUESTIONNAIRE

*Author* : Usha Uppal

*Reference* : Uppal, U. Personality traits of adolescent girls in Meerut district. Ph.D. Thesis in Education, Agra University, 1971.

11C21 RIGIDITY PICTURE TEST

*Author* : L.D. Rabindradas

*Reference* : Rabindradas, L.D. Rigidity picture test. *Journal of Psychological Researches,* 1969, 13(2), 77-84.

## Adaptations D

11D1 ADORNO'S F-SCALE

*Authors* : T.N. Guha and G.S. Mohanty.

*Main features* : Final form consisting of 34 items.

*Reference* : Guha, T.N., and Mohanty, G.S. A comparative study of authoritarianism among service officers and higher secondary school teachers. *Psychological Researches,* 1966, 1(1 and 2), 9-11.

11D2 ADORNO'S F-SCALE

*Author* : C.S. Prasad.
*Availability* : Author, Patna University.
*Reference* : Prasad, S.C. Attitude of authoritarian and democratic subjects towards nationalisation. *Monovaigyanik,* 1970, 1(1), 44-47.

11D3 ALLPORT'S A-S REACTION TEST

*Authors* : Dharmendriah and A. Hafeez.
*Language* : English.
*Availability* : Authors, Department of Industrial Management, Indian Institute of Social Sciences, Bangalore-12.
*Reliability* : Repeat reliability and split-half reliabilities were found to be 0.782 0.044 and 0.895 0.021 respectively.
*Validity* : Rating of associates with scores on test gave a validity coefficient of 0.459 0.28.
*Norms* : Means and S.D. on 336 college students.
*Reference* :
1. Hafeez, A., Dharmendriah. Distribution of ascendance-submission scores among college students. *Manas,* 1966, 13, 29-23.
2. Hafeez, A. A study of ascendance-submission among engineering, humanities and science students, employed engineers and supervisors. *Indian Journal of Social Work,* 1971, 32(1), 95-98.

11D4 ALLPORT'S A-S REACTION TEST FOR ADOLESCENTS

*Authors* : E.G. Parameswaran and B. Govardhan Reddy.
*Language* : English and Telugu.
*Availability* : Authors, Department of Psychology, Osmania University Hyderabad.
*Main features* : 33 items were selected after item analysis.
*Reliability* : Test-retest reliability with an interval of 6 weeks was .77 (N=62) and split-half reliability was .73 (1961 study). Test-retest reliability coefficients were .79 and .77 respectively for English and Telugu versions (1924 study) and split-half reliabilities were .86 and .92 for English and Telugu (N=100).
*Validity* : Item validation as only validated items on extreme group criterion basis were retained.
*Reference* : Parameswaran, B.G. and Reddy, B.G. A-S Reaction test for adolescents. *Psychological Studies,* 1964, 9(2), 119-123.

11D5 ALLPORT'S ASCENDANCE-SUBMISSION REACTION TEST

*Authors* : K. Raychoudhury and P.S. Hundal.

*Reference* : Raychoudhury, K. and Hundal, P.S. Allport's Ascendance- submission reaction study in Indian situation-1. *Indian Psychological Bulletin,* 1958, 3, 11-22.

11D6 BARRON'S EGO-STRENGTH SCALE

*Author*: Qamar Hasan.
*Language* : Hindi and Urdu.
*Availability*: Author, Department of Psychology, Aligarh Muslim University.
*Reliability* : Split-half reliability was found to be .78. The test-retest reliabilities were found to be .86 and .82 respectively for Hindi and Urdu versions.

11D7 BERNBERG'S HUMAN RELATIONS INVENTORY

*Author*: R. Bhushan.
*Language* : Hindi
*Availability*: Author
*Reliability* : Split-half reliability was found to be .59 (N=100 corrected by S-B formula). Internal consistency coefficient was found to be .81 (N=100) and temporal stability coefficient was .74 (4 weeks).
*Reference* : Bhushan, R. Intolerance of ambiguity in conformists and non-conformists. *Manas,* 1970, 17(1), 35-39.

11D8 BERNREUTER PERSONALITY INVENTORY

*Author*: Dr. Ramanath Kundu.
*Language* : Bengali
*Availability* : Author, Department of Psychology, University of Calcutta, 92, Acharya Prafulla Chandra Road, Calcutta-1.
*Reliability*:

| Scale | B1-N | B2-S | B-31 | B4-D | F1-C | F2-S |
|---|---|---|---|---|---|---|
| Split-half reliability | .58 | .85 | .76 | .76 | .67 | .56 |

*Reference* : Kundu, R. Adaptation of Bernreuter personality inventory to Bengali language. *Psychological Studies,* 1967, 12(2), 107-112.

11D9 BERNREUTER'S PERSONALITY INVENTORY

*Author*: D. Mohanta.
*Reference* : Mohanta, D. Assessment of personality. *Research Bulletin of the Council of Social and Psychological Research,* 1(11), 17-22.

11D10 BERNREUTER'S PERSONALITY INVENTORY

*Authors* : S.K. Pal and P.C. Saxena.
*Language* : Hindi.
*Availability*: Commercially available, Rupa Psychological Corporation, Varanasi.
*Reliability*: Split-half reliabilities range from .73 to .84 for different measures.
*Validity* : Only four scales have been validated against Indian adaptation of Maudsley Personality Inventory and Cattell's 16 PF. The validity coefficients

range between .69 to .76.
*Norms* : Available on undergraduate level only.

11D11 BERNREUTER'S PERSONALITY INVENTORY

*Author* : Gopi B. Saha.
*Language* : Bengali.
*Main features* : It has 30 items.
*Reliability* : Reliability coefficient .87.
*Reference* : Saha, G.B. An investigation into the school maturity of high school students. *Indian Journal of Psychology,* 1960, 35, 47-54.

11D12 BROWN-HOLTZMAN

*Authors* : M.C. Joshi and J. Pandey.
*Availability* : Rupa Psychological Corporation, Varanasi
*Reliability* : Test-retest reliabilities range between .795 to .854 and split-half reliability coefficient was found to be .685.
*Validity* : Established.
*Norms* : Under process.
*Reference* : Pandey, J. A psychological study of the adjustment problems of adolescents in relation to their personality variables. Ph.D. Thesis, Banaras Hindu University.

11D13 CALIFORNIA F-SCALE

*Author* : L.I. Bhushan.
*Language* : Hindi.
*Availability* : Author.
*Reliability* : Split-half reliability coefficient of the scale was found to be .69 (N=100) and the test-retest reliability (after an interval of 4 weeks) was found to be .73 (N=50).
*Validity* : Data in process.
*Norms* : In process.
*Reference* :
1. Bhushan, L.I. Personal factors in authoritarianism. *Journal of Psychological Researches,* 1967, 2(3), 119-125.
2. Bhushan, L.I. Comparison of four political groups on a measure of authoritarianism. *Journal of Social Psychology,* 1969, 79, 141-162.

11D14 CALIFORNIA F-SCALE

*Author* : G.C. Gupta.
*Main features* : Only 20 items are used.
*Reference* : Gupta, G.C. A study of authoritarianism in its relation with tolerance of ambiguity and tolerance of frustration in four groups. *Journal of Psychological Researches,* 1963, 6(1), 21-27.

11D15 CALIFORNIA F-SCALE BY ADORNO

*Author* : Qamar Hasan.
*Language*: Hindi and Urdu (20 items).
*Availability* : Split-half reliability coefficients were found to be .70 and .71 respectively for Hindi and Urdu versions.

11D16 CATTELL'S 16 P-F TEST

*Author*: S.D. Kapoor.
*Availability* : Commercially available, Psychocenter.
*Reference* : Kapoor, S. D. Norms on the 16 P-F Test : Forms A & B (VKKJ : KA & KHA). *Indian Journal of Psychology*, 1965, 40(1)

11D17 CHILDREN'S APPERCEPTION TEST (BELLACK'S)

*Author* : Uma Chowdhury.
*Availability* : Commercially available from Manasayan, 32, Netaji Subhash Marg, Delhi-6.
*Scoring* : A culture based scoring system is developed.
*Reliability*: Established.
*Validity* : Established .
*Norms* : Available.

11D18 CHILDREN'S APPERCEPTION TEST (BELLACK'S)

*Author* : Manovigyanshala.
*Availability* : Authors, Allahabad, U.P.

11D19 COOPER'S PARENT EVALUATION SCALE

*Author* : Awadhesh H. Singh.
*Language* : Hindi.
*Main features* : Final adapted version contains 20 items (mother scale) and 24 items (father scale).
*Reliability* : Test-retest and split-half reliabilities of the scales ranged from .81 to .92
*Reference* : Singh, A.K. A cross-validation of Cooper's Parent Evaluation Scales on an Indian Sample. *Indian Psychological Review*, 1970, 6(2), 118-122.

11D20 DOGMATISM SCALE FORM D BY ROKEACH

*Author* : Qamar Hasan.
*Language* : Hindi and Urdu.
*Availability* : Author, Department of Psychology, Aligarh Muslim University.
*Reliability* : Split-half reliabilities were found to be .71 and .62 respectively for Hindi and Urdu versions.

11D21 ETHICAL DISCRIMINATION TEST (KOH'S)

*Author* : Rajalakshmi P. Varma.
*Availability* : Author
*Uses* : To study ethical discrimination.
*Level* : Nursery and lower primary children.
*Reference* : Varma, R.P. Ethical discrimination as related to intelligence, age and sex. *Journal of Psychological Researches,* 1962, 6(1), 44-51.

11D22 EYSENCK'S NEUROTICISM SCALE

*Author* : A.K. Sinha.
*Reliability* : Test-retest and split-half coefficients were found to be .86 and .84 respectively.
*Reference* : Sinha, A.K. Psychology and non-psychology College women: a comparison on some personality traits. *Psychological Studies,* 1968, 13(1), 94-97.

11D23 EYSENCK'S PERSONALITY INVENTORY (FORM A)

*Author* : L.I. Bhushan.
*Language* : Hindi and English.
*Reliability* : Split-half and test-retest reliabilities for E and N scales respectively were found to be 0.78, 0.69, 0.73 and 0.76.
*Validity* : Validity coefficients for both English and Hindi versions were found to be .89 and .84 respectively.
*Norms* : Norms are reported in terms of Means and SDs for different age groups and political party members.
*Reference* : Bhushan L.I. A Hindi version of Eysenck's Personality Inventory (Form A). *Psychology Annual,* 1969, 3, 27-30.

11D24 EYSENCK'S PERSONALITY INVENTORY (FORMS A&B)

*Author* : B. De.
*Language* : Author.
*Reliability* : Established.
*Validity* : Worked out.
*Norms* : Available

11D25 GREEN AND STAEY'S HOSTILITY AGGRESSION QUESTIONNAIRE

*Author* : G.G. Prabhu.
*Availability* : Available from the author. As also from *Acta Psychologica,* Vol. 26, pp. 265-85 wherein the free instruments is provided.
*Uses* : The principal component measured by this questionnaire is the low threshold for anger, with the accompanying sub-clusters that can be described as "revenge", "contempt", "domination", "verbal aggression".
*Level* : (Originally used on normals and psychiatric cases) could be used with adults having knowledge of English upto Matriculation level.

*Reliability* : Test-retest reliability coefficient was .77 (N=90/with a gap of 45 to 60 days).

*Validity* : Validity by extreme group was established. Paranoed patients differed from normals at .01 level.

*Norms* : Men (260) Score 28.8 ± 6.45, Women (80) 25.6 ± 5.80.Cut off point for indicating clinically aggressive personalities: Indian Men score 36 or above. Women score 32 or above.

*Reference* : Prabhu, G.G., A questionnaire measures of hostility and aggression. *Journal of Psychological Researches,* 1968, 12(3), 156-157.

11D26 GUILFORD-ZIMMERMAN TEMPERAMENT SURVEY

*Author*: M.P. Jaiswal.

*Language* : Hindi.

*Availability*: Author, Department of Psychology. R.D.S. College, Bihar University, Muzaffarpur.

11D27 GUILFORD-ZIMMERMAN TEMPERAMENT SURVEY

*Author*: V. George Mathew.

*Language* : English.

*Availability* : Author, Department of Psychology.

*Uses* : To measure the temperament pattern of college students who have completed two years of college education in Kerala.

*Level*: Applicable with caution to English knowing persons all over India.

*Scoring*: Separate answer sheet and a single stencil key.

*Reliability*: Odd-even reliabilities range from 0.47 to 0.84 (only one is lower than 0.6).

*Validity* : Large correlations (upto 0.69) with scales of a personality Inventory in Malayalam and a Malayalam adaptation of the MPI. Nine out of the ten scales should significant differences among college students specialising in nine fields of study.

*Norms* : T score norms are available.

11D28 JUNIOR EYSENCK PERSONALITY INVENTORY (BENGAL)

*Author*: Ramnath Kundu.

*Language* : Bengali.

*Availability* : Author.

11D29 JUNIOR PERSONALITY INVENTORY

*Authors* : V. Mohan and P. Purang.

*Language* : Hindi.

*Availability* Authors.

*Main features* : It has 68 items in Hindi to measure neuroticism and extroversion with 17 items for each variable and each item having a parallel form.

*Reference* : Mohan, V. and Purang, P. A study of scores on JPI, *Journal of Psychological Researches*, 1969, 13(1), 37-42.

11D30 LUCKIE-WITHERS TEST FOR LIABILITY FOR DEPRESSION

*Author* : G.G. Prabhu.

*Availability* : Author, Department of Psychiatry, AIIMS, New Delhi-16.

*Reference* : Prabhu, G.G. A questionnaire measure for the evaluation of depression. *Journal of Psychological Research,* 1971, 15(3), 114-115.

11D31 MASLOW'S SECURITY-INSECURITY SCALE

*Author* : A.K. Sinha.

*Language* : Hindi.

*Availability* : Author.

*Reliability* : Test-retest and split-half reliability coefficients were found to be .88 and .90 respectively.

*Reference* : Sinha, A.K. Psychology and non-psychology personality traits. *Psychological Studies*, 1968, 13(1), 94-97.

11D32 MAUDSLEY PERSONALITY INVENTORY

*Authors* : P.A. Abraham and E.T. George.

*Language* : Malayalam.

*Availability* : Department of Psychology, Kerala University, Trivendrum.

*Reliability*: Reliability coefficients for the introversion-extroversion and neuroticism scales were found to be 0.60 and 0.85 respectively.

*Reference* : Abraham, P.A. and George, E.I. A comparative study of leaders and non-leaders among pupils in secondary schools. *Journal of Psychological Researches,* 1966, 10(3) 116-120.

11D33 MAUDSLEY PERSONALITY INVENTORY

*Author* : Gita Das.

*Language* : Oria.

*Availability* : Author.

*Scoring* : The responses are scored according to a prepared key taken from Eysenck.

*Reliability* : Test-retest reliability of the N scale is .76 (significant at .01 level) and of E scale .49 (N=35).

*Validity* : Correlation of the scores of its N scale with the scores of insecurity test .51 (N=67).

*Norms* : Decile norms.

*Reference* : Das, Gita. Standardisation of Maudsley Personality Inventory (M.P.I.) on an Indian Population. *Journal of Psychological Researches,* 1961, 5(1), 7-9.

11D34 MAUDSLEY PERSONALITY INVENTORY

*Author* : B. De.

*Language* : Hindi.

*Availability* : Author.

*Reliability* : Inter-test reliabilities for MPI and EPI Hindi versions was found to be .82 for E-1 dimension and .90 for N.
*Validity* : Concurrent validity.
*Norms* : Available.

11D35 MAUDSLEY PERSONALITY INVENTORY (MPI)

*Author* : N.K. Dutta.
*Availability* : Author, Central Institute of Education 33, Chhatra Marg, Delhi-7.
*Reliability* : N-Scale is more reliable than E-Scale. Odd-even reliability for E-scale = 0.70 and for N-Scale = 0.96. KR-21 reliability for E-Scale = 0.71 and for N-Scale = 0.97.
*Reference* : Dutta, N.K. Adaptation of MPI on Indian Population. *Psychological Studies*, 1967, 12(1), 65-69.

11D36 MAUDSLEY PERSONALITY INVENTORY

*Author* : T.E. Shanmugam.
*Languages* : English and Tamil.
*Availability* : Author, Department of Psychology, University of Madras, Madras.
*Reliability*, Split-half reliability using Spearman-Brown Prophecy formula was found to be .64.
*Validity* : English and Tamil versions have been in use in Madras since 1960. It has been used on varied samples. Including delinquents and criminals was found to be valid test to measure traits proposed to study in the investigation.
*Reference* : Shanmugam, T.E. Personality traits of pupils who had their education through the medium of their mother tongue and English. *Journal of Educational Research and Extension*, 1965, 11(2), 51-57.

11D37 MIDDLESEX HOSPITAL QUESTIONNAIRE

*Author* : G.G. Prabhu.
*Availability*, Author, All India Institute of Medical Sciences, New Delhi-16.
*Time required* : 15 to 20 minutes.
*Reliability* : Test-retest reliability of the different scales were: FFA=.71, PHO=64, OBS=.79, SOM=.65, DEP=.59 and HYS=.67.
*Validity* : Found to discriminate.
*Norms* : Available on Indian sample.
*Reference* : Prabhu, G.G. Clinical utility of the Middlesex hospital questionnaire in India. *Indian Journal of Psychiatry*, 1972, 14(2), 127-129.

11D38 MURRAY'S THEMATIC APPERCEPTION TEST

*Author* : Manovigyanshala, Allahabad.
*Language* : Instructions for administration in Hindi.

11D39 MURRAY'S THEMATIC APPERCEPTION TEST

*Author*: Uma Chaudhary.
*Availability*: Manasayan, 32, Netaji Subhash Marg, Delhi-6.
*Scoring* : Scoring system is developed which is partly cultural and partly based on clinical techniques. Full scoring scheme has not yet been published. Manual of Indian Modification of TAT can be consulted.

11D40 NEUROTICISM SCALE QUESTIONNAIRE

*Author*: Kamlesh Kapoor.
*Language* : Hindi.
*Availability* : Author.
*Reference* : Kapoor, K. Hindi version of the Neuroticism Scale Questionnaire (N.S.Q.). *Indian Journal of Psychology,* 1965, 40(2), 93-98.

11D41 PARENT ATTITUDE SURVEY

*Authors* : L.K.N. Sinha and K.P. Krishna.
*Language* : Hindi.
*Availability* : Patna University.
*Reference* : L.K.N. and Krishna, K.P. Child rearing practices in young and old adults. *Indian Journal of Georontology,* 1971, 33(3&4), 72-75.

11D42 PERSONALITY QUESTIONNAIRE

*Author*: J.N. Lal.
*Language* : Hindi.
*Availability*: Author, Department of Psychology, University of Gorakhpur, (U.P.).
*Reliability*: Coefficients of stability from .47 to .78 for the various scales.
*Validity* : Validity coefficients with teachers; ratings ranged upto .68 for the various scale.
*Norms* : T-Score norms have been drawn separately for males, females and the total standardisation sample.
*Reference* : Lal, J.N. Development of Hindi form of elementary school personality questionnaire. *Indian Psychological Review,* 1968, 5(1), 76-80.

11D43 RANKING RORSHACH TEST

*Author*: G.B. Saha.
*Language* : Bengali.
*Availability* : Author, Department of Psychology, University Science College, Calcutta-9.

11D44 RORSCHACH INK BLOT TEST

*Author*: Manovigyanshala, Allahabad.
*Language* : Instructions in Hindi.
*Scoring* : List, manual, tabulation sheet, psychogram etc. are available.

11D45 ROSENZWEIG PICTURE-FRUSTRATION STUDY FOR CHILDREN

*Author* : Udai Pareek.
*Language* : Hindi.
*Availability* : Author, Commercially available, Manasayan, 32, Netaji Subhash Marg, Delhi-6.
*Scoring* : Manual available for the Indian version.
*Reliability* : Scoring reliability = 98% agreement. Stability coefficients range from .51 to .78.
*Validity* : Validated using teacher's ratings, delinquent groups and by artificially induced frustration.

11D46 ROSENZWEIG PICTURE-FRUSTRATION STUDY (ADULT FORM)

*Authors* : Udai Pareek, R.S. Devi and Saul Rosenzweig.
*Availability* : Commercially available from Rupa Psychological Corporation, 15/23, Sora Kuan, Varanasi.
*Main features* : Minor changes were made in almost all the original picture situations and major changes were made in 9 situations.
*Scoring* : Manual available.
*Reliability* : Inter-scorer agreement = 98% after discussion. Reliability coefficients were high for both matrix and item reliabilities. Stability coefficients ranged from .27 to .82 and consistency values from .46 to .74.
*Norms* : Standardised on 800 adults.
*Reference* : Pareek, U., Devi, R.S. and Rosenzweig, S. *Manual of the Indian Adaptation of the Rosenzweig Picture-Frustration Study: Adult Form*, Rupa Psychological Corporation, 1968, 135 pp.

11D47 TORRANCE'S INTOLERANCE OF AMBIGUITY TEST

*Author* : S.Q. Hasan.
*Language* : Hindi.
*Availability* : Author.
*Reliability* : Split-half reliability was found to be 0.70.

11D48 VANELAND SOCIAL MATURITY SCALE (SSMS OF E.A. DOLL)

*Author* : Gopi B. Saha.
*Language* : Bengali.
*Main features* : It has 33 selected items.
*Validity* : It has correlation of .66 with modified Bernreuter's Personality Inventory.
*Reference* : Saha, G.B. An investigation into the school maturity of high school students. *Indian Journal of Psychology*, 1960, 35, 47-54.

11D49 VEROFF'S TAT

*Authors* : N.P. Singh and Karan Singh
*Language* : Hindi.

*Reference* : Singh, K. Motivational components of agricultural business entrepreneurs in India. *Indian Journal of Industrial Relations*, 1971, 7(1), 81-92.

11D50 VETTER'S ATTITUDE SCALE (RADICALISM- CONSERVATISM)

*Author* : M. Rajamanickam.
*Availability* : Author, Annamalai University.
*Reliability* : 0.82, Level .001.

11D51 WESLEY RIGIDITY SCALE

*Language* : Hindi.
*Reference* : Ojha, Hardeo. The relation of prestige suggestion to rigidity and dependence proneness. *Journal of Psychological Researches*, 1972, 16(2), 70-73.

# 2. Adjustment and Problems

## Complete instruments A

12A1 ADJUSTMENT INVENTORY

*Authors* : S. Bhattacharya, M.M. Shah and J.C. Parikh.
*Availability* : Author, CASE, M.S. University, Baroda.
*Level* : Adolescent School Students.
*Main features* : The Inventory is in Gujarati and English and consists of 55 items.
*Reliability* : Test-retest reliability (after an interval of 3 months) was found to be .88.
*Validity* : Expert opinion was collected for determining face validity of the inventory. Correlation coefficients between the ratings and scores obtained came upto .63.
*Reference* : Bhattacharya, S., Shah, M.M. and Parikh, J.C. *Construction and validation of an adjustment inventory for the study of maladjustment particularly among adolescents*, Baroda: Centre of Advanced Study in Education Research Monograph, 1967.

12A1 ADJUSTMENT INVENTORY

(The following items have to be rated on a three-point scale).

1. I do not like physical exercises.
2. I am worrying about my diet and its effects on my physical strength.
3. I am always worry about my weak health.
4. I am worried when I cannot get sound sleep.
5. I constantly feel that my height is not normal.
6. I am constantly conscious that my weight is not normal.
7. I feel ashamed of myself being too much thin.
8. I am anxious to know about various diseases.
9. I like to play outdoor games very much.
10. I do not understand whether I am bright enough to join a college.
11. I feel uneasy in the presence of others.
12. I am over sensitive.
13. I feel I am much superior to others.
14. I feel extremely bad when I am not able to do the work with which I am entrusted.
15. I feel very miserable when I make a poor show before others.
16. I lose self-confidence when I am required to compete with others.

17. I get easily misled by smart people.
18. I am afraid by new atmosphere.
19. I cannot be at home with other person.
20. I cannot take my decision on any matter.
21. I am not sure of my ability to achieve success even in my own field.
22. I feel that I am useless.
23. I wish I can speak fluently.
24. I feel I have not enough clothes.
25. I like to live alone.
26. I always like to play second fiddle.
27. I have not much of self-confidence.
28. I get frightened when I am alone at night in my house.
29. I constantly feel I am miserable.
30. I have to suffer much due to unfavourable conditions at home.
31. I suffer from inferiority complex because of my unattractive appearance.
32. I do not feel it necessary to learn social activities that I need to perform when $ grow up.
33. I feel I have too many social responsibilities.
34. I feel I do not know much of etiquette.
35. Even the idea of failure dreads me much.
36. I do not understand what I read.
37. I have no interest in studies.
38. I constantly feel that some of my subjects are weak.
39. I wish I would know how to collect information about various subjects without anybody's help.
40. I am very much weak in written expression.
41. I need to know about different careers that are open after S.S.C. examination.
42. I would like much to quit the school.
43. I feel depressed when I am asked to go to school.
44. I feel that my progress is hindered because there are play ground and auditorium in the school.
45. I feel that my parents sacrifice too much for me.
46. I very often argue with my parents even on trivial questions.
47. I find it very difficult to adjust to my home environment.
48. My progress is hindered because of unordial relations of my parents with our neighbours.
49. Generally a teacher is unpractical.
50. I cannot attend to my lessons in the class because of the presence of the necessary opposite sex.
51. I am strongly disturbed when I find my friend (of opposite sex) in a company of the persons of my sex.
52. I find it very difficult to adjust with members of the opposite sex.
53. I hate the members of the opposite sex.
54. I feel embarrassed when I am required to deal with the members of opposite sex.
55. I like to see only the pictures wherein there is much of sex.

12A2 PRE-ADOLESCENT ADJUSTMENT SCALE (PAAS)

*Authors* : Udai Pareek, T.V. Rao, P. Ramalingaswamy and B.R. Sharma.
*Languages* : Hindi, Tamil and Bengali.
*Availability* : Available from the first two authors. Indian Institute of Management, Ahmedabad or Manasayan, 32, Netaji Subhash Marg, Delhi-6.
*Uses* : Counselling the students. Identifying areas of maladjustment.
*Time required* : 15 to 20 minutes.
*Levels* : Pre-adolescents 8 to 12 years.
*Main features* : It is a scale developed by Thurstone's method of Equal Appearing Intervals using 190 judges. Contains 40 items, measuring adjustment towards home, school, peers, teacher and general.
*Scoring* : Scale values of the items checked are added. Negative scores indicate maladjustment and positive scores adjustment. Scoring key available which gives 5 scores and 5 areas and an overall adjustment score.
*Reliability* : Test-retest reliability coefficients range from 0.22 to .60 for different areas.
*Validity* : Validated against teachers' ratings. Mann-Whitney's U Values show acceptable level of validity.
*Norms* : Available for Delhi, Calcutta and Coimbatore sample. *Educational Review*, 1970, 5(2), 1—20.
*References* :

1. Pareek, U., Rao. T.V., Ramalingaswamy, P. and Sharma,
2. Pareek, U. and Rao, T.V. Motivation training for mental health; A study of teacher behaviour and student mental health, ICMR Project Report, National Institute of Health Administration and Education, New Delhi, 1971.
3. Pareek, U. and Rao, T.V. Motivation training for mental health, *NIHAE Bulletin*, October, 1971, 26-32.
4. Rao, T.V., Pareek, U. Purushothaman, S. and Gangzee, Z. A comparative study of the patterns of adjustment of fifth grade children from Delhi, Calcutta and Coimbatore. *Indian Educational Review*, 1972, 6(1), 1-113.

12A2 PRE-ADOLESCENT ADJUSTMENT SCALE

(Responses have to be given by checking the items that are true with the respondent).

1. My parents get annoyed with me easily.
2. The school is a burden for me.
3. My neighbours are not good people.
4. My parents give me full freedom to play.
5. My teacher encourages me very much in my studies.
6. I do not want to make many friends.
7. My friends don't allow me to do my school work.
8. I don't get frightened in the presence of my teacher.
9. The teacher takes lot of work from us in the school.
10. I hesitate to speak before others in the class.
11. My friends in the school tease me.

12. My teacher listens to me.
13. My parents take care of my amusements.
14. I live very happily with my brothers and sisters at my house.
15. My parents interfere with me in every affair.
16. I feel inferior to others.
17. I am very happy in the company of my friends.
18. I am not friendly with my companions.
19. I want more holidays.
20. Very few friends help me.
21. I Don't like my friends at all.
22. I go to school daily.
23. I don't feel hesitant in asking questions to the teachers.
24. We have got sufficient freedom in the class.
25. Everybody pays attention to whatever I say.
26. My teacher does not make me understand anything properly.
27. I shall be happy if my teacher is transferred.
28. The rules of the school seem to be senseless to me.
29. I do not get angry easily.
30. I like my parents very much.
31. My parents don't allow me to go out alone.
32. Nobody at home helps me in my school work.
33. I like to study very much.
34. I don't have the habit of quarrelling with others.
35. I don't like frivolous jokes.
36. Some of my friends are good.
37. I can't express myself properly.
38. I trust my friends.
39. I remember everything at home, but forget in the teacher's presence.
40. My teacher is very strict.

12A3 ADJUSTMENT INVENTORY

*Authors* : Prem Pasricha, R.M. Pagedar and J.J. Gajjar.
*Availability* : Faculty of Education and Psychology, CASE, M.S. University, Baroda.
*Level* : College students.
*Main features* : It is a check-list containing 232 items covering 11 areas of adjustment : health and physical, sensitivity and confidence, economic and lack of facilities, self-schedule and independence, mild neurosis, self and self-image, sex and marriage, social family, studies, school and teachers, work career and future.
*Scoring* : Number of problems checked in each area.
*Norms* : Available on 1,424 university students of Baroda.
*Reference* : Pasricha, Prem, Pagedar, R.M. and Gajjar, J.J. *Adjustment Inventory for College Students*. Baroda : Centre for Advanced Studies in Education, 1964.

12A3 ADJUSTMENT INVENTORY

(Items that are true with the respondent have to be checked).

1. I always feel inferior due to my personal appearance.
2. I feel my progress is held up due to a physical defect.
3. I cannot speak some words correctly.
4. I am always worried about my weak health.
5. I have got weak eyesight.
6. My choice is unattractive.
7. I feel I have got excess perspiration.
8. My height is not normal.
9. I cannot get sound sleep.
10. I cannot take part in sports due to physical handicap.
11. I cannot take part in sports due to weak health.
12. I am over-sensitive.
13. I feel inferior to others.
14. I feel I am much superior to others.
15. I am very self-conscious.
16. I feel extremely bad when I am not able to do the work which I have decided.
17. I feel guilty too long after doing something that I think is wrong.
18. I have no self-confidence.
19. I feel very bad to lose in games.
20. If I make a poor show before others, I feel it for long time.
21. I lose self-confidence when I compete with others.
22. I find it difficult to express myself effectively.
23. I need information regarding all sorts of necessities.
24. I have to suffer due to lack of hostel accommodation.
25. I have to suffer a lot due to irregularity of buses.
26. I cannot get newspaper to read.
27. I do not get healthy food.
28. I cannot participate in sports and games.
29. I do not know different sources of enjoyment.
30. I have to suffer due to poor study conditions at home.
31. I have no books for reading at home.
32. The financial conditions of my family is not good.
33. I am worried about the maintenance of the family in future.
34. The financial difficulties in my family make me unhappy.
35. I do not get enough pocket money.
36. It is very difficult to attend the morning lectures as I am coming from a village.
37. I cannot afford medicine for my family.
38. I cannot afford education for my family.
39. I am not able to solve my own difficulties.
40. I find it impossible to live away from my family.
41. I cannot concentrate.
42. I always misplace my things.
43. I cannot take decision on any matter.

44. I am very careless.
45. I do not know how to divide my time for different activities.
46. I have to suffer due to lack of independence.
47. I feel helpless when in trouble.
48. Irrelevant ideas keep on disturbing my thinking.
49. I am not allowed to choose my own clothes.
50. I am over anxious to make a success of my life.
51. I am very anxious to become famous.
52. I am scared of accidents.
53. I think of murdering somebody.
54. I work under a great deal of tension.
55. I have fits of laughing and crying that I cannot control.
56. I am over anxious about my ability to achieve success.
57. I cannot stop worrying.
58. I have nightmares every few nights.
59. I become very nervous when my abilities are being tested.
60. I have a fear that somebody is going to attack me.
61. I get frightened when I am alone at home at night.
62. I have a very strong fear of failure.
63. I feel I am not intelligent.
64. I am unhappy.
65. Most of the time I am not in a good mood.
66. I feel that I have not got good memory.
67. I often think of committing suicide.
68. I wish I was not born.
69. I need to be a bit more aggressive.
70. No one seems to understand me.
71. I feel that I am a failure in my work.
72. I feel that I am useless.
73. I think I am miserable.
74. I feel that nobody loves me.
75. I am too afraid to love, romance and marriage.
76. I cannot adjust with the students of the opposite sex.
77. I am engaged to a girl whom I dislike.
78. I am engaged to a boy whom I dislike.
79. Most of my time is spent in thinking about sexual matters.
80. I am very much worried whether my married life will be happy or not.
81. I am anxious to know about secret diseases.
82. I feel very much that I am dominated by girls.
83. I feel very much that I am dominated by boys.
84. I fear to have members of the opposite sex as friends.
85. I dislike members of the same sex as friends.
86. I hate members of the opposite sex.
87. I think of things too bad to talk about.
88. I strongly dislike the custom of marriage.
89. I fail to make friends with the members of opposite sex.
90. I feel shy while talking to girls.
91. I feel shy while talking to boys.
92. I feel that marriage is an unnecessary burden.

93. I do not like restriction on friendship with opposite sex.
94. I cannot talk freely with others.
95. I dislike fat people.
96. I get easily misled by smart people.
97. I always quarrel on small matters.
98. I do not like to talk with others.
99. I have got no sympathy for others.
100. I like to live alone.
101. I cannot stand criticism.
102. I am afraid of talking with a man of position.
103. I am afraid of new atmosphere.
104. I do not know how to behave in certain situations.
105. I always like to rebel against authority.
106. I cannot tolerate others' beliefs and opinions.
107. I feel very embarrassed when I have to speak before a group of people.
108. I cannot mix with people.
109. I cannot make friends easily.
110. I feel I do not know much of etiquette.
111. I have too many social responsibilities.
112. I do not like social restrictions.
113. I am disturbed in studies because of too many friends.
114. I find it hard to get along with friends.
115. My friends do not co-operate with me.
116. My friends do not help me.
117. My friends cheat me.
118. I feel that I am getting spoiled by bad company.
119. I am very much worried about my friends.
120. I fail to win friends.
121. I cannot maintain friends for a long time.
122. I have no friends.
123. I cannot face a group.
124. I cannot take part in social activities.
125. I feel that my friends have no moral standards.
126. I feel that my friends have no manners.
127. I do not like to accept responsibility as a leader.
128. I cannot participate freely in the conversations among the people around me.
129. I find it difficult to ask permission to leave the group.
130. I am afraid of criticism of others.
131. My parents do not agree with my views.
132. I have differences of opinion with my parents because they are conservative.
133. My parents do not allow me to go to cinemas.
134. My parents criticise my behaviour very often by giving examples of my brothers, sisters and friends.
135. Often it so happens that my father does not agree to a decision of mine, while my mother agrees to it.
136. I very often feel that my parents do not understand me.
137. I constantly feel that my parents dominate me too much.

138. I become nervous by peculiar behaviour of my parents.
139. My parents often find faults with my appearance.
140. I find my parents always confused or nervous.
141. Sometimes I feel that my brothers and sisters are getting what they need while I do not.
142. At home I am not allowed to use the radio.
143. I feel that I am not getting enough liberty at home.
144. I feel the loss of my mother very much.
145. I feel the loss of my father very much.
146. I do not get freedom as I am the youngest child in the family.
147. The atmosphere of my home is very tense.
148. My parents have no feelings for me.
149. There are many conflicts in my family.
150. There are no modern things in my house.
151. My parents are always sick.
152. My parents are very orthodox.
153. My parents are suspicious.
154. My parents worry too much when I fail.
155. I am very much worried about the future of my parents.
156. I am worried about the health of my parents.
157. I am ashamed of my father's occupation.
158. I am afraid of my father.
159. I am not allowed to argue with my parents.
160. My parents cannot understand me.
161. My parents neglect me.
162. My parents do not agree with my social activities.
163. I quarrel with my brothers and sisters.
164. At home nobody trusts me.
165. My grand-parents do not agree when my parents have given me permission to visit to a picture or a drama.
166. I feel that my home life is not happy and satisfactory like that of my friends.
167. I feel like running away from my home.
168. My brothers and sisters are jealous of me.
169. I feel that my parents are disappointed in me.
170. There are frequent quarrels in my family.
171. I feel there is too much interference from my family in my personal affairs.
172. I feel ashamed of my parents.
173. I cannot talk of my experiences to my parents.
174. I feel that I am the unfortunate one in my family
175. I miss my home so much that it affects my studies.
176. My parents do not exercise enough discipline on me.
177. I have too many responsibilities at home.
178. I have to suffer due to extreme religious attitudes of parents.
179. My parents insist on my choosing a vocation which I dislike.
180. While studying I get disturbed very easily.
181. I dislike certain teachers.
182. My teacher hates me.

183. I have no interest in studies.
184. I have ineffective studying habits.
185. I want information regarding monetary help, freeships and books.
186. I have no interest in certain subjects.
187. I cannot understand certain subjects.
188. I feel my teachers are not teaching properly.
189. I think my teacher is a problem to the students.
190. I feel that examination papers are not valued properly.
191. I need to know about different post-graduate studies.
192. Expressing myself in English is very difficult for me.
193. I cannot cope up with studies.
194. I cannot understand lectures in English.
195. I need very much to know a better method of studying.
196. I cannot concentrate on studies.
197. I could not join the course in which I was interested.
198. I become very difficult when text books change too frequently.
199. I want to improve my memory.
200. I am not able to follow the lectures.
201. I need information regarding library.
202. I want to take aptitude test.
203. I do not know about extra-curricular activities.
204. I do not know the method of answering questions.
205. I need proper help in selecting subjects.
206. I think I am a dull student.
207. I do not find suitable atmosphere for studying in the college.
208. I am over burdened with academic work.
209. I cannot progress in learning.
210. I cannot devote enough time to studies.
211. I am too much worried about examination.
212. I need to know whether I should study or not.
213. I do not know in which subject I am interested.
214. I have a strong dislike for certain subjects.
215. I feel my choice of a college course is not proper.
216. I need guidance for the choice of a college.
217. I am not satisfied with the marks I am getting in college.
218. I am very much worried about my future.
219. I want to run away from work.
220. I need specific help in getting part-time work.
221. I need to know about different careers that are open after S.S.C.
222. I want to know about different careers that are open after graduation.
223. I do not like to work.
224. I worry that I have no experience of work.
225. I need to know which career will fit me the best.
226. I need to know different vocations that are open for girls.
227. I need to know about the special training that is necessary for different vocations.
228. My choice of a vocation is unwise.
229. I do not know how to be prepared for an interview.
230. I do not know how to choose from different vocations.

231. I do not have the means for the preparation necessary for the vocation chosen.
232. I have difficulty in finding a job.

## 12A4 ADOLESCENT ADJUSTMENT INVENTORY

*Author*: N.Y. Reddy.

*Availability* : Author, Department of Psychology, Osmania University, Hyderabad-7.

*Level*: Adolescents.

*Main features* : It measures personal and social adjustment. Items on personal adjustment measure neurotic tendencies, feelings of inferiority, guilt, personal worth and attitude towards future, social adjustment items measure the adjustment towards home and school as well as sex adjustment.

*Scoring*: Three-point scoring system. Key available.

*Reliability* : Odd-even reliability coefficients were .84 and .95 for personal and social adjustment respectively after applying Spearman Brown correction. Scores on both the parts were also found to be correlated significantly.

*Validity* : The inventory has been validated against teachers' ratings. Bell's adjustment inventory, California personal and social adjustment inventory, parents' ratings and by comparing the adjustment scores of delinquent and non-delinquent groups.

*Norms*: Available for Hyderabad area.

*Reference* : Reddy, N.Y. Development of an adjustment inventory for use with adolescents. *Journal of Psychological Researches*, 1964, 8(1), 68-76.

## 12A4 ADOLESCENT ADJUSTMENT INVENTORY

(The following items have to be checked on a 3-point scale of always, sometimes and never).

1. Do you like to live for many years?
2. Do you like to mix freely with girls?
3. Are you generally interested in all the subjects taught in your class?
4. Do you worry unnecessarily?
5. Do you find many persons younger to you are brighter and more capable than you?
6. Do you feel uneasy if you happen to be in a gathering of girls?
7. Do you feel that you are not the 'Studious' type?
8. When the teacher asks you questions do you feel nervous and upset?
9. Do you get the feeling that you are not competent to do many of the jobs you are asked to do?
10. Do you find it easy to carry on conversion with girls who are strange to you?
11. Do you feel your parents should allow you more freedom?
12. Do you think that the subjects taught in the school should be made more interesting?
13. Do you feel difficulty in making quick decisions?

14. Do you get the feeling that you are not attractive to the girls?
15. Do you feel your parents still treat you as baby not showing respect for your individuality?
16. Do you feel that success in life does not depend on school marks?
17. Are you annoyed and disturbed when you hear a sudden noise?
18. Do you hesitate to meet important and highly placed persons?
19. Do you feel very much nervous when you happen to be along with a strange girl?
20. Do you feel your parents do not take adequate interest in your future?
21. Do you get excited very quickly?
22. Do you feel bad for having mixed in bad company?
23. In the class if you get any good idea do you volunteer to speak it out?
24. Whenever you get ideas about girls do you try to suppress them?
25. Do your parents oppose your deciding your own affairs?
26. Do you feel that there should be more of extra-curricular activities at the school/college?
27. Do you have strong dislike for certain kinds of food?
28. Do you feel that life is full of difficulties and problems?
29. Do you get enough chances for mixing with girls?
30. Do you feel your parents are backward in many of their ideas and customs?
31. Do you feel that your teachers are not good at teaching?
32. When you walk through the streets, do you get the feeling that others are watching you?
33. Do you think that if a person fails in an examination two or three times he would do well to stop trying further?
34. After seeing film do you think about them for a long time?
35. Do you feel that people who commit suicide, are in many instances doing the right things?
36. In your conversation with friends do you talk mostly about sex matters?
37. Do you feel that your teachers show partiality to some students?
38. Do you like to take responsible jobs and do them?
39. Do you very much enjoy day-dreaming and thinking yourself doing various things?
40. Do you feel that on the whole you are unlucky in many respects?
41. Do you feel it is not right for a boy and a girl to go about alone?
42. Do your brothers or sisters fight with you?
43. Do your teachers take interest in your studies?
44. Do you feel shy when people look at you?
45. Do you like to meet people even if they are strangers?
46. If you fail in achieving success in a job do you continue to do it till you succeed?
47. Do you feel that girls are puzzling and disturbing?
48. Do you consider yourself equal to you brothers and sisters in all respects?
49. Do you think that your teachers understand your difficulties?
50. Are you confident that your family will support you if you get in any trouble?
51. Do you find many girls respecting only boys who are rich?

52. Do you feel your brothers and sisters have been morally better than you?
53. Are you satisfied with the study facilities you have?
54. When people scold you, do you feel very sad?
55. Are you very much afraid of not getting a job when you finish your studies?
56. Do you find many girls respecting only boys who are physically wellbuilt?
57. Do you feel that the appearance and surroundings of your home are not as good as you would like them to be?
58. Do you meet your teachers in connection with your personal problems?
59. Do you get the feeling that you have committed many sins?
60. Do you feel you were happier when you were a child?
61. Are you disturbed by sexdreams?
62. Do you feel ashamed to bring your friends to your house because your house is not clean and well-furnished?
63. Do you feel that many of your classmates do not understand you?
64. Do you get discouraged easily?
65. Do you feel that you are not using properly the love and facilities provided by your father and mother?
66. Are you satisfied with the teaching in your class?
67. Do your brothers and sisters quarrel with you unnecessarily?
68. Do you feel that many of your classmates are proud and showy?
69. Do you find difficulty in sitting still without moving your hands and legs?
70. Do you feel you are not doing justice to your studies?
71. Do your parents put too many restrictions on you?
72. Do you discuss your personal problems with friends?
73. Are you afraid of thunder, lightning, a narrow passage etc?
74. Do you get the feeling that your future will be dark and gloomy?
75. Are you disturbed by useless thoughts?
76. Do Your parents oppose your mixing with some of your friends?
77. Do you take active part in organising debates, picnics, parties etc?
78. Do you find life full of sorrow and difficulty?
79. Do you begin many hobbies and leave them easily?
80. Do you feel that others are happier than you?
81. Do you feel that your brothers and sisters are given more privileges than you?
82. Whenever you hear rumour concerning you, are you worried till you know the truth?
83. Do you feel that you are neglected by your father/mother?
84. Do you dislike meeting strangers?
85. Do you get along well with your classmates?
86. Do you feel that your parents are responsible for many of your difficulties?
87. Do you get the feeling that you are not equal to your classmates: in (a) Physical Appearance; (b) Strength; (c) Athletic Abilities?

12A5 P. A. INVENTORY

*Authors* : V.S. Shanthamani and A. Hafeez.

*Availability* : Author, Department of Industrial Management, Indian Institute of Science, Bangalore-12.

*Uses* : To identify the personality maladjustment of an individual.

*Time required*: No time limit, takes about 10 minutes.

*Levels* : English knowing adult males.

*Main features* : This is a personality inventory with 20 items related to neuroticism.

*Scoring* : The total number of items answered Yes or No (as the case may be) is the score of each individual.

*Reliability* : Split-half reliability of the test was found to be .64.

*Validity* : Construct validity was worked out.

*Norms* : Percentile norms have been developed for 200 employed engineers.

12A5 P.A. INVENTORY

(The following statements have to be answered on an yes = no scale)

1. I get up rested most of the mornings.
2. My interests change again and again.
3. I have been off work/classes a good deal because of sickness.
4. Sometimes I walk in sleep.
5. I am anxious (worried) about something or someone almost all the time.
6. I work under a great deal of tension (mental strain).
7. I can sit quiet without fidgetting (without making movements).
8. I feel rather poorly adjusted to people as I do not seem to get on as well as I should.
9. Now and then I have dreams about my work.
10. I like to be very correct in manners and social obligations.
11. Criticisms or scoldings do not hurt me very much.
12. I have no confidence in others.
13. I do not feel inferior to other people.
14. I cannot sleep because ideas run through my mind.
15. Sometimes I get short of breath without having done heavy work.
16. I am not worried and upset very often.
17. I have the habit of twitching (jerking moving my face, neck and shoulders).
18. I get palpitations or thumping (loud beating) in my heart.
19. Usually I sleep well.
20. I feel many people do not care for me.

# B Instruments with technical information

## 12B1 ADJUSTMENT INVENTORY

*Author* : H.S. Asthana

*Availability* : Author, Head, Department of Psychology, Sagar University, Saugar (M.P.) or Rupa Psychological Corporation, Sora Kuan, Varanasi.

*Uses* : Counselling.

*Time required* : About 30 minutes.

*Level* : Hindi knowing school and college students.

*Main features* : It contains 42 'yes'/'no' type questions in Hindi.

*Scoring* : Key available.

*Reliability* : Split-half reliability coefficient with Spearman Brown's correction was found to be .97.

*Validity* : Item-validities established.

*Norms* : Percentile norms available on 200 high school and college students, of 14 to 18 years age range and also on 205 boys and 206 girls of 14 to 21 years.

*References* :

1. Asthana, H.S. Psychoneurotic tendencies among University students, *Indian Journal of Psychology*, 1945, 20, 94-95.
2. Asthana, H.S. Hindustani adjustment inventory. *Education*, 1950, 29, 17-20.
3. Asthana, H.S. *Manual of Direction and norms for Adjustment Inventory in Hindi*, Varanasi. Rupa Psychological Corporation, 1968.

## 12B2 FAMILY ADJUSTMENT INVENTORY

*Author* : H.D. Badami.

*Availability* : Author, Department of Psychology, School of Psychology, Education, and Philosophy, Gujarat University, Ahmedabad-9.

*Uses* : Guidance and Counselling.

*Time required* : About 15 minutes.

*Level* : High school and college students.

*Main features* : Self-administered inventory. Available in Gujarati.

*Scoring* : Counting adjustment responses to the questionnaire.

*Reliability* : Test-retest reliability was found to be .82. Split half reliability was found to be .87.

*Validity* : Validated against interview data, teacher's estimate of adjustment, Validated with other test and contrasted groups.

*Norms* : Available in T scores. Standardised on a sample of 3,273 males and females selected from several districts of Gujarat.

*References* : Badami, H.D. Development of the family and social adjustment inventories. *Vidya Journal of Gujarat University*, 1970, 13(1).

12B3 INCOMPLETE SENTENCES BLANK (ISB)

*Author* : Kusum K. Bhatt.

*Availability* : Author, Department of Psychology, University School of Psychology, Education and Philosophy, Gujarat University, Ahmedabad-9.

*Uses* : Diagnosis of the area and degree of conflict among upper high school level and college students, and Guidance and Counselling.

*Time required* : About 30 to 35 minutes.

*Level* : Upper high school and college students.

*Main features* : A Semi-projective test based on Rotter's (1950) ISB. The subject is required to complete 40 incomplete sentences in his own words. Available in Gujarati.

*Scoring* : Responses analysed into various degrees of conflict and positive adjustment by content analysis. Those responses which cannot be included here are regarded as neutral.

*Reliability* : Test-retest reliability was found to be .75. Split-half reliability was found to be .71.

*Validity* : Validated against teacher's ratings and interview data.

*Norms* : In progress.

*References* :
1. Bhatt, K.K. Validation of the ISB for the use of Gujarati speaking Adolescents. *Vidya*, 1971, 14(1).
2. Bhatt, K.K. Adjustment problems of the underachieving with the help of ISB. Ahmedabad: Gujarat University, Department of Psychology, 1971.

12B4 STORY COMPLETION TEST

*Author* : Bureau of Education and Psychological Research, David Hare Training College, Calcutta.

*Availability* : Authors.

*Level* : 11 to 14 years students (class VI to VII).

*Main features* : It is projective test, consists of (a) Family relationship: 22 items (b) School relationship: 16 items (c) Heterosexual relationships: 3 items.

*Scoring* : Key available.

*Validity* : Validity coefficient with Roger's Test of Personality adjustment as the criterion (N=100)=.46.

12B5 PERSONALITY INVENTORY

*Author* : Bureau of Psychology, Allahabad.

*Availability* : The Bureau.

*Uses* : To Study the adjustment of adults of home, school health and society.

*Level* : Adolescents.

*Main features* : Consists of 145 items.

*Reliability* : Kakkar, A. A study of relationship among certain adolescents' area of adjustment. *Journal of Psychological Researches*, 1967, 11(3), 93-96.

## 12B6 REVISED ADJUSTMENT INVENTORY (RAI)

*Author*: Promod Kumar.

*Availability*: Author, Department of Psychology, Jodhpur University, Jodhpur.

*Uses* : Developed to spot poorly adjusted college going students who need psychodiagnostic probing and counselling.

*Level*: Adult college going female students.

*Reliability*: Test-retest reliability is .74 with an index of reliability of 0.86 with two week's interval time.

*Norms* : Percentile norms are available.

*Reference* : Kumar, Promod. Standardisation of revised adjustment inventory. *Journal of Psychological Researches*, 1963, 7(3), 126-129.

## 12B7 FAMILY ADJUSTMENT INVENTORY

*Authors* : P.M. Patel, M.M. Patel, D.S. Parikh, M.N. Palsane, M.B. Buch, Jamnaji Parikh.

*Availability* : P.M. Patel, National Institute of Education, Sri Aurobindo Marg, New Delhi-16.

*Time required*: 10 minutes.

*Level*: 13+ to 18+ (adolescents).

*Main features*: Standardised inventory. Available in Gujarati only.

*Scoring*: Objective.

*Norms*: Available.

*Reference* : Bhatt, L.J., Patel, P.M., Patel, M.M., and Parikh, D.S. *Inquiry into Psychological factors related to adolescent adjustment*, Baroda: Faculty of Education and Psychology, 1960.

## 12B8 EMOTIONAL ADJUSTMENT INVENTORY

*Authors* : P.M. Patel, M.M. Patel, D.S. Parikh, M.N. Palsane, M.B. Buch, Jamnaji Parikh.

*Availability* : P.M. Patel, National Institute of Education, Sri Aurobindo Marg, New Delhi-16.

*Time required*: 10 minutes.

*Level*: 13+ to 18+ (adolescents).

*Main features*: Standardised inventory. Available in Gujarati only.

*Scoring*: Objective.

*Norms*: Available.

*Reference* : Bhatt, L.J., Patel, P.A., Patel, M.M. and Parikh, D.S. *Inquiry into psychological factors related to adolescent adjustment*, Baroda: Faculty of Education and Psychology, 1960.

## 12B9 KISHOR ABHIYOJAN PRASHNAVALI (Adolescent Adjustment Inventory)

*Author*: Jai Prakash.

*Availability*: Author, Department of Psychology, Sagar University, Saugar.

*Time required*: About 75 minutes.

*Level* : 12 to 18 years students.
*Main features* : It is in Hindi.
*Reliability* : Test-retest coefficient was found to be .90 and split-half reliability coefficient was found to be .896.
*Validity* : Concurrent validity coefficient with Saxena's adjustment inventory was found to be .601.
*Norms* : Available on 2000 students.

### 12B10 ALIGARH ADJUSTMENT INVENTORY

*Authors* : A. Jamil Qadri and Guidance Unit.
*Availability* : Authors, Department of Psychology, Aligarh Muslim University, Aligarh.
*Time required* : About 20 minutes.
*Level* : For college and university students.
*Main feature* : It has the following areas: Social, Emotional, Health, Family and Financial. Total number of items are 90; each area has 20 items except the financial which has 10 items.
*Reliability* : Split-half reliabilities were found to be: for Social=.77, Emotional=.87, Health=.85, Family=.89, Financial=.87.
*Validity* : With ratings based on clinical interviews .73.
*Norms* : Available.

### 12B11 ADJUSTMENT INVENTORY FOR OLDER PEOPLE

*Author* : P.V. Ramamurti.
*Availability* : Author, Department of Psychology, S.V. University, Tirupati.
*Uses* : To study general adjustment of middle aged and older people in the area of health, home, social, emotional and self.
*Time required* : 30 minutes.
*Level* : Older people.
*Scoring* : Simple 1, 0 scores. Score indicates maladjustment.
*Reliability* : Test-retest reliability coefficient was found to be 0.88 with a gap of 10 days.
*Validity* : Item analysis was done. Discriminates well between well adjusted and maladjusted in each area.
*Norms* : Available for a sample of 300 adults.
*Reference* : Ramamurti, P.V. Adjustment inventory for the aged. *Indian Journal of Psychology*, 1968, 43, 27-29.

### 12B12 INDIRECT ACADEMIC ADJUSTMENT INVENTORY

*Author* : S. Narayan Rao.
*Availability* : Author, Head of the Department of Psychology, S.V. University, Tirupati, A.P.
*Uses* : For counselling and guidance.
*Time required* : About 50-60 minutes.
*Level* : College students.
*Main features* : Is a sentence completion device. Has 100 incomplete sentence

stubs. The instrument is in Telugu.

*Scoring* : Manual, numerical weights 0-4 are assigned to each response.

*Reliability* : Inter-score r=0.84, self score r=0.86, re-test r=0.83.

*Validity* : Validity coefficients were 0.788 with academic achievement, 0.672 with teacher's ratings, 0.410 with Borow's College Inventory of academic adjustment.

*Norms* : Available on college (men) student N=424.

*Reference* : Rao, S.N. *Student Performance and Adjustment*, S.V. University, Tirupati, A.P. 1967.

12B13 ADJUSTMENT INVENTORY

*Author* : T.S. Rao.

*Availability* : Author, National Institute of Education, NCERT, Sri Aurobindo Marg, New Delhi.

*Level* : This inventory is for teachers and parents who rate their students and children of 6 to 10 years.

*Main features* : Two inventories consisting of 66 and 79 items including some check items for teachers and for parents respectively.

*Scoring* : Three-point summated ratings method. Combined maladjustment scores using the ratings of teachers and parents could be derived by weighted scores method suggested by the author.

*Reliability* : Split-half reliabilities for the inventories were found to be 0.37 and 0.47 respectively for parents and teachers.

*Validity* : Correlation coefficient between the ratings of teachers and parents was found to be 0.22. The instruments were found to discriminate between well adjusted and maladjusted groups of students when the groups were based on unanimous judgements of three teachers.

*References* :
1. Rao, T.S. Adjustment inventory for children of age group 6-10. *Psychological Studies*, 1964, 9(2), 99-108.
2. Rao, T.S. Balingualism and adjustment difficulties. *Indian Educational Review*, 1969, 4(1), 37-63.

12B14 VYAKTITVA PRAKASH PRASHNAVALI

*Author* : M.S.L. Saxena.

*Availability* : Author, Department of Psychology, Banaras Hindu University, Varanasi

*Time required* : No time limit.

*Level* : 11 years to adulthood. School and college students.

*Main features* : This Verbal test in Hindi has 5 separate measures of adjustment — home, health, social, emotional and school or college. 90 items in all.

*Reliability* : Test-retest reliability is .87. Split-half reliability corrected by Spearman Brown formula is .89, by rational equivalence is .80.

*Validity* : With Asthana's adjustment inventory .80.

*Norms* : T-scores for males and females for whole test and sub-tests are available.

*References* :
1. Saxena, M.S.L. Vyaktitva Parakha Prashnavali. *Shiksha*, July 1962, 123-127.

2. Saxena, M.S.L. Factorial Study of a Personality inventory. *Indian Journal of Psychology*, 1963, 33(3), 115-120.

12B15 ADJUSTMENT INVENTORY FOR COLLEGE STUDENTS

*Authors* : A.K.P. Sinha, and R.P. Singh.

*Availability* : National Psychological Corporation, Labh Chand Market, Raja Mandi, Agra-2 (U.P.).

*Time required* : No time limit.

*Level* : College students.

*Main features* : Inventory, consists of 102 items on five areas of adjustment (home, health, social, emotional and educational).

*Scoring* : Scored by hand or by scoring stencil.

*Reliability* : Reliability coefficients obtained by various methods are (1) Split-half reliability=0.94, (2) test-retest=0.93, (3) Hoyt's method=0.94, (4) K-R Formula=0.92. Reliability on various areas of adjustment was also found to be high.

*Validity* : Item analysis validity coefficients were significant at .001 level. Correlation between inventory scores and hostel superintendent ratings was 0.58.

*Norms* : Percentile norms for males and for females separately.

12B16 PERSONALITY INVENTORY

*Author* : Krishnakant Mehrotra.

*Availability* : Authors, Bureau of Psychology, Allahabad.

*Uses* : To explore the major personality problems of the students in four major areas of life (a) home, (b) school, (c) social and (d) health.

*Level* : Students.

*Main features* : This inventory includes four broad areas of social life viz. home, school, social and health represented by 30, 40, 35 and 40 problems respectively. All items have been related to specific needs. The items are in problem from and show either the presence of negative needs or the frustration of positive needs.

*Reference* : Mehrotra, Krishnakant. A study of adolescent problems. *Psychological Researches*, 1966, 1(1-2), 33-35.

12B17 BEHAVIOUR PROBLEMS INVENTORY

*Author* : R. Murlidharan.

*Availability* : Author, DPFE, National Institute of Education, Sri Aurobindo Marg, New Delhi-16.

*Uses* : For the measurement of behaviour disorders.

*Time required* : Approximately half an hour.

*Level* : Pre-school and school age children 3 to 8 years.

*Main features* : The Inventory consists of 130 items which were classified into 8 different categories such as sleeping difficulties, eating difficulties, other difficult habits, a sense of self-adequacy — inadequacy, aggressive behaviour, unsocial behaviour, non-compliant behaviour and some specific behaviour difficulties (delinquent related behaviour). These consisted of statements of problem behaviour in children to which the parents could respond by indicating the frequency with which the prevalent behaviour was shown by the children.' A personal data sheet intended to provided information with reference to the background of the child is also a part of the inventory. It elicited information about (1) the biological factors, (2) the personal historic factors and (3) The social factors.

*Scoring* : The parents were instructed to underline the word that best told how often the child showed that behaviour. Points were given in proportion to the frequency of behaviour — 'never' was given a score of zero, 'sometimes' a score of one and 'often' a score of 2. The total score for each category indicated the problem score for that particular type of difficulty and the total score for all the categories put together indicated the total behaviour problem score of the child.

*Reliability* : Test-retest reliability coefficient was found to be .94.

*Norms* : The norms are available only for the sample from the city of Madras.

*Reference* : Murlidharan, R. Size of family and its relationship with the behaviour difficulties of children. *Journal of Psychological Researches*, 1969, 13(2), 94-100.

## 12B18 PROBLEM CHECKLIST

*Availability* : College of Educational Psychology and Guidance, Jabalpur.

*Uses* : To be used as a diagnostic tool for guidance.

*Time required* : 30 minutes.

*Level* : Higher secondary classes (Hindi).

*Main features* : The checklist consists of 160 items, regarding needs and problems in four areas; school, self, home and adjustment with others. The student has to check whether each statement ascertains his need or problem. The checklist is in Hindi.

*Scoring* : Number of needs and problems in each area.

## 12B19 PROBLEM INVENTORY FOR OLDER PEOPLE

*Author* : P.V. Ramamurti.

*Availability* : Author, Department of Psychology, S.V. University, Tirupati, A.P.

*Time required* : 30 minutes.

*Level* : Adults and older people.

*Main features* : It is a checklist measuring problems in the areas: health, home, economic and social status, personal betterment, social relations, personality and occupation, and religion and leisure utilisation.

*Scoring* : Total problems in each of the areas are counted.

*Reliability* : Test-retest reliability was found to be 0.94 (10 days).

*Validity* : Discriminated highly between a well adjusted and poorly adjusted group.

*Norms* : Available on a sample of 1350 (35+).

*References* :
1. Ramamurti, P.V. Problem inventory for older people. *Journal of Psychological Researches*, 1969, 13(3), 162-163.
2. Ramamurti, P.V. Problems of older people: An analysis of age

trends. *Psychological Studies*, 1970, July, 128-130.

12B20 PROBLEM INVENTORY

*Authors* : P.V. Ramamurti and B. Konda Reddy.
*Availability* : Authors, Department of Psychology, S.V. University, Tirupati, A.P.
*Time required* : 30 minutes.
*Level* : School students of VIth to Xth standards.
*Main features* : It is a checklist covering the major areas of home, school, personal and social relationships. Available in Telugu.
*Scoring* : Total number of problems in each area checked.
*Reliability* : Test-retest reliability was found to be 0.92 with 10 days gap.
*Validity* : It discriminated between well adjusted and poorly adjusted group (parents and teachers ratings).
*Norms* : Available on a sample of 500.

## C Citations

12C1 ADJUSTMENT INVENTORY

*Author* : E.G. Parameswaran.
*Reference* : Parameswaran, E.G. Social adjustment of group of early adolescent boys. *Journal of Psychological Researches*, 1957, 1(3), 29-45.

12C2 PERSONAL-SOCIAL MALADJUSTMENT INVENTORY

*Author* : S. Rajangam.
*Reference* : Rajangam, S. Personality structure of some inmates of the Madras Vigilance & Rescue Homes. *Journal of Psychological Researches*, 1957, 1(1), 47-58.

12C3 BEHAVIOUR PROBLEMS QUESTIONNAIRE

*Author* : Maqsood Ali.
*Reference* : Ali, M. A study of behaviour problems among dull and bright children. *Research Bulletin*, 1967, 3, 27-30.

12C4 BEHAVIOURAL PROBLEMS INVENTORY

*Authors* : A.R. Faizunnisa and E.G. Parameswaran.
*Reference* : Faizunnisa, A.R. and Parameswaran, E.G. Maternal behaviour and problem in children II. *Research Bulletin of the Department of Psychology, Osmania University*, 1967, 3, 57-59.

# D Adaptations

12D1 BELL'S ADJUSTMENT INVENTORY

*Authors* : P.A. Abraham and D.I. George.
*Language* : Malayalam.
*Availability* : Authors, Department of Psychology, Kerala University, Trivendrum.
*Reliability* : Coefficient was found to be 0.91.
*Reference* : Abraham, P.A. and George, E.I. A comparative study of leaders and non-leaders among pupils in secondary schools. *Journal of Psychological Researches*, 1966, 10(3), 116-119.

12D2 BELL'S ADJUSTMENT INVENTORY

*Author* : Bureau of Educational and Vocational Guidance, Bihar.
*Language* : Hindi.

12D3 BELL'S ADJUSTMENT INVENTORY

*Authors* : B.G. Karkare and B.C. Keskar.
*Language* : Hindi.
*Availability* : Authors, c/o Institute of Vocational Guidance, 3, Cruickshank Road, Bombay-1.
*Time required* : No time limit. Usually it takes two school periods.

12D4 BELL'S ADJUSTMENT INVENTORY (STUDENT FORM)

*Author* : R.S. Nair.
*Language* : Malayalam.
*Availability* : Author, Department of Education, Kerala University.
*Reference* : Nair, R.S. Study of the effect of N.C.C. training on physical growth, adjustment, academic achievement and certain personality traits of high school pupils in Kerala. Ph.D. Thesis in Education, Kerala University, 1972.

12D5 BELL'S ADJUSTMENT INVENTORY

*Authors* : J. Pandey and J.B.P. Sinha.
*Availability* : Authors.

12D6 BELL'S ADJUSTMENT INVENTORY

*Authors* : J. G. Tewari and J.N. Tewari.
*Availability* : Authors, Department of Psychology, Aligarh Muslim University, Aligarh, (U.P.).
*Main features* : Its 100 items cover five area of adjustment—social, home and

family, emotional, health and financial.

*Reliability* : Reliability coefficients for different areas vary from .77 to .89.

*Validity* : Validity was established against rating by clinical interviews.

*Reference* : Tewari, J.G. and Tewari, J.N. On extremes of personality adjustment as measured by adjustment inventory. *Journal of Psychological Researches*, 1968, 12(2), 75-81.

12D7 BRUNSCHWIG'S ADJUSTMENT INVENTORY

*Author* : K. Majumdar.

*Language* : Bengali.

*Availability* : Author.

*Reference* : Majumdar, K. A study of the personality adjustment of Bengalis. *Indian Journal of Psychology*, 1963, 38(2), 69-73.

12D8 MOONEY PROBLEM CHECKLIST

*Authors* : M.C. Joshi and J. Pandey.

*Availability* : Rupa Psychological Corporation, Varanasi.

*Reliability* : Reliability coefficients range between .71 to .90.

*Validity* : Satisfactory validity has been found using different criteria.

*Reference* : Pandey, J. Psychological study of the adjustment problems of adolescents in relation to their personality variables. Unpublished Ph.D. Thesis in Psychology, Banaras Hindu University.

12D9 MOONEY PROBLEM CHECKLIST

*Authors* : Kamal Mukherji and Manas Raychaudhari.

*Language* : Bengali.

*Availability* : Authors.

*Reference* : Mukherji, Kamal and Raychaudhari, Manas. Assessment of equivalence of clinical ratings, structured and projective measures of personality. *Manas*, 1970, 17(2), 67-76.

12D10 CHECKLIST (COLLEGE FORM)

*Authors* : S.K. Pal and P.A. Saxena.

*Language* : Hindi.

*Availability* : Authors, Department of Education, University of Allahabad, Allahabad-2 (U.P.).

*Reliability* : Test-retest for total areas was found to be .874 and for different areas varying from .561 to .884.

*Validity* : Validity has been established using testees' ratings of the items. The mean number of items for eleven separate problem areas of the checklist ranged from 1.40 to 7.13. Nearly 87 per cent of the students of the present study responded in 'yes' on the question "Do you feel that the items you have marked on the list give a well rounded picture of your problems".

*Norms* : Available for undergraduate science students only.

*Reference* : Pal, S.K. and Saxena, P.A. The problem of over, under and normal achieving college students. Research project financed by the NCERT, Department of Education, University of Allahabad, Allahabad.

12D11 MOONEY PROBLEM CHECKLIST

*Author*: S. Narayan Rao.
*Language* : English.
*Availability* : Author, Department of Psychology, S.V. University, Tirupati, A.P.
*Main features* : It is a shorter list containing 225 items.
*Norms* : Available on 2,358 college students.
*Reference* : Rao, S.N. Student performance and adjustment. Sri Venkateswara University, Tirupati, 1967.

# 3. Anxiety

## Complete instruments

A

13A1 DUTT PERSONALITY INVENTORY (DPI)

*Author* : N.K. Dutt.
*Availability* : Author, Central Institute of Education, Delhi-7.
*Uses* : For clinical diagnosis and for measuring anxiety.
*Time required* : No time limit is fixed. Subjects take about 20-25 minutes.
*Level* : From high school boys to university students. Students above 15 years of age are suited better.
*Main features* : It is a questionnaire with 3 response categories. Available both in Hindi and English.
*Scoring* : Keyed response=2; Non-keyed response=0; ?=1. Total scores are obtained by summing.
*Reliability* : Ranging between .87 to .95.
*Validity* : Validated against TMAS and Sinha Anxiety Scale and found to be satisfactory.
*Norms* : Available.
*Reference* : Dutt, N.K. Psychological and Educational implication of the concepts of mental health in Indian thought. Ph.D. Thesis in Psychology, 1966, unpublished, Panjab University.

13A1 DUTT PERSONALITY INVENTORY (DPI)

(The following items have to be checked on a 3-point scale of frequency: often, sometimes and never).

1. Do you want someone to look after you or advise you?
2. Do you feel uneasy if you have to sit long in a small room with the door shut?
3. Does your attention wander so badly that you lose the thread of what you are doing?
4. Do you find it difficult to go to sleep due to excitement?
5. Have you been afraid of going mad?
6. Do you find it difficult to concentrate your mind when you need doing so?
7. Do you think you are much more cautious, tense and strung-up than need be?
8. Do you bother about pains in your heart or in chest?
9. Do you worry about your health?

10. Do you wish that you should be as happy as others seem to be?
11. Do you have periods of such great restlessness that you cannot sit long in a chair?
12. Do you definitely admit that you have been worried beyond reason over something that did not really matter?
13. Do you think you are careless about what happens to you?
14. Is life a strain for you?
15. Does your heart beat too quickly or thumb in your ears so that you cannot sleep?
16. Have you feared that you are a victim to heart-trouble or to some disease like cancer or tuberculosis?
17. Do you try to avoid going to a strange shop or talking to a strange man?
18. Do you feel yourself a happier person than many others?
19. Do you get mentally tired easily?
20. Do you get a dragging sense of pressure on the top of your head or the back of your neck?
21. Do you find yourself getting irritated and aggressive without cause, bursting at people over trifles?
22. Do you have much trouble in making up your mind as to what you will do next?
23. Are you troubled by the sweating of the skin and palms?
24. Do you suffer from frequent urination?
25. Have you tremors of hands and feet?
26. Do you suffer from indigestion and impaired apetite?
27. Do you have feelings of fulness in the stomach?
28. Do you have feelings of dizziness and sickness without any apparent cause?
29. Do you have feelings of suffocation, of inability to get sufficient air and choking of breath?
30. Do you jump badly at sudden lights, sounds or touches?
31. Are you bothered by cold feet and hands going blue even in moderate cold?
32. Does the power go out of your limbs so that you have to lean against something?
33. Do things swim before your eyes, go blurred or mistry?
34. Is your sleep fitful and disturbed?
35. Did you have period when you lost sleep over worry?
36. Do you feel that you are going to blush?
37. Do you have nightmares?
38. Do you worry as to what will happen to your family members after your death?
39. Do you find yourself much bored and irritated when waiting for something?
40. Do you feel you are a relaxing and happy-go-luck sort of person?

13A2 SINHA'S ANXIETY SCALE (W-A Self-Analysis Form).

*Author*: Durganand Sinha.

*Availability*: Rupa Psychological Corporation Sorakuan, Varanasi.

*Level* : Adults, college and school students.

*Uses* : It provides a measure of anxiety, useful instrument for a quick estimate of manifest anxiety and also for locating the forms and dimensions in which anxiety may express itself.

*Time required* : About 30 minutes.

*Main features* : Self-administered. May be administered in group also. Available both in English and Hindi.

*Scoring* : Each item which is checked 'yes' is awarded score of one. The score of every individual would be the total number of items checked positively.

*Reliability* : Split half reliability = .92 (N=88).

*Validity* : Correlation with Taylor's Manifest Anxiety Scale = .69 (N=70).

*Norms* : Percentile norms based on 310 boys and 475 girls (college and university) are available.

*References* :

1. Sinha, Durganand. *Manual for Sinha W-A self-Analysis Form in Hindi*,. Varanasi: Roopa Psychological Corporation, 1968.
2. Sinha, D. Development of two anxiety scales. *Manas*, 1961, 8, 1-10.
3. Sinha, D. Validation of anxiety scales. *Journal of Psychological Researches*, 1965, 9 (2), 55-62.


13A2 SINHA'S ANXIETY SCALE

(The respondent has to check the following items as true or false).

1. I feel uncomfortable on a conveyance which is driven at a fast speed.
2. I am often upset even by the slightest noise.
3. When I meet a member of the opposite sex (girl or boy, as the case may be), I feel somewhat uneasy.
4. When I go out of my house, I sometimes suspect that I have not locked my door or my trunk.
5. I often feel uneasy that others may makes fun of me.
6. I sometimes suspect that some friends of mine may reveal my secrets.
7. Often I experience a sense of guilt without any cause.
8. I sometimes bite my nails.
9. I often have the foreboding that some misfortune or bad luck may befall me.
10. I sweat easily even on cool days.
11. I always have bad and fearful dreams.
12. I am sometimes sorry that I may become important.
13. I am sometimes disturbed by the thought that I may not be able to make good progress in my work.
14. Criticism upsets me greatly.
15. Sometimes I get such an intense feeling of shame that I feel like getting far away from society.
16. I feel uncomfortable if some one talks of my mistakes in the presence of others.
17. I rarely drink water outside for fear that it may contain disease germs.
18. Sometimes I feel unhappy without any apparent cause.
19. I often feel that I am being ignored by others.

20. I am easily embarrassed.
21. I often find it hard to concentrate or keep my mind on one job or work.
22. I often feel sick in my stomach.
23. My hands tremble or shake when I try to do some work.
24. I sometimes fear that I may look awkward in my new dress.
25. I often feel disturbed that I am going to blush.
26. I often feel my heart beating fast.
27. I am a little more nervous than others.
28. I feel like crying quite easily.
29. At times I lose sleep over worry.
30. I feel uneasy when I have to meet my superiors (teachers, boss etc.).
31. At times I get very restless.
32. Often I feel ashamed even at the faults of others.
33. I am often short of breath when engaged in quick work.
34. It is under great deal of strain that I do my work.
35. I often feel that I am not wanted at all by anyone.
36. I tend to tremble or perspire when I face a difficult task ahead.
37. Sometimes I dream that I have been taken ill seriously.
38. I often dream about things I do not like to tell other people.
39. If I have to wait for something, I feel uneasy.
40. My feelings get hurt quite easily.
41. I often worry about something or other.
42. I have great deal of stomach trouble.
43. I have good deal of difficulty in coming to a decision.
44. I have at times been very worried about things which did not really matter.
45. I often fear that I may lose my friends.
46. Sometimes I get so excited that I cannot speak clearly.
47. I am more self-conscious than others.
48. I often find life to be something of a strain.
49. I am not at all confident about myself.
50. It is at times difficult for me to maintain mental balance.
51. When I wake up due to a bad dream, I find it difficult to sleep again.
52. Sometimes I get feelings of shame or remorse even no small matters.
53. I feel nervous when I have to meet a person I have not known before.
54. My sleep is usually restless and disturbed.
55. Sometimes I have the feeling that I cannot face the society.
56. When two or more people are talking in whispers I often have the feeling that they are talking about me.
57. If I make an awkward social mistake, I find difficult to forget it.
58. I often feel somewhat ashamed when I think of past events of my life.
59. Sometimes I feel disturbed that my children will not respect me when I grow old.
60. I feel a little worried when I have to start on a journey.
61. I dislike facing situations where I am required to make quick decisions.
62. I often worry that my appearance is not attractive.
63. I sometimes feel that I am getting old too soon.
64. I feel uneasy when I have to consult a doctor or a surgeon.
65. I sometimes suspect that my friends may let me down.

66. When I do something new, I feel disturbed whether others would approve of it or not.
67. I have often been worried about my health.
68. Even when I am in a group I often get the feelings of being lonely.
69. When I am waiting for someone who has promised to come at a particular time I often feel that he may not turn up.
70. Sometimes I feel anxious due to causes I am not clearly aware of.
71. Many a time I have a feeling of being confused.
72. Quite often I am unable to decide what course of action is good for me.
73. I am frequently uncertain about myself.
74. Sometimes I get the feeling that I am worthless as a person.
75. I often get the feeling that this world and human existence is meaningless.
76. I seldom can begin any work because of the thought that I may fail in it.
77. I often dream of death of some near and dear ones.
78. I feel tired very quickly.
79. I get sweat in my palm frequently.
80. I dislike talking before a group of people for fear that they may mock at what I say.
81. I often have the feeling that some calamity will befall me.
82. I sometimes get the feeling that people do not like me.
83. I often worry as to what my fate has in store for me.
84. I am often blamed for the doings of others.
85. I often worry over petty things.
86. I often get perturbed at the thought that I may not fulfil my promise.
87. I get over-excited in a difficult situation.
88. I feel hungry almost all the time.
89. I often worry that I may get involved in some troubles in future.
90. I feel disturbed at the thought that in old age my health may breakdown.
91. The thought that some death or tragedy may befall my family disturbed me.
92. I often feel worried that I may be discharged from my job.
93. At times I get so excited that it is hard to get any sleep.
94. I feel disturbed at the thought that one day I shall also grow old.
95. I can seldom hide my excitement.
96. I tend to stammer when I have talk to members of the opposite sex.
97. I often wonder if my friends will respect me when I am old.
98. I feel disturbed that I may loose my physical capacities in old age.
99. I often worry that in my anger I may one day kill someone or harm him grievously.
100. I often worry as to what will happen to my family after I die.

# B Instruments with technical information

## 13B1 ANXIETY INDEX SCALE

*Author*: A.S. Patel.
*Availability*: Author, Department of Psychology, M.S. University Baroda.
*Level*: Educated common man or students.
*Main features*: It contains 40 items (25 anxious and 15 non-anxious statements).
*Reliability*: Test-retest coefficient was .87.
*Validity*: Validity coefficient against self-ratings was .76.
*Norms*: Available.
*Reference*: Patel, A.S. A rationale, construction and tryout of test scales measuring some personality traits. *Advances in Education*, 1956, 1(2) 11-27.

## 13B2 SHARMA MANIFEST ANXIETY SCALE (SMAS)

*Author*: Sagar Sharma.
*Availability*: Author, Department of Psychology, Panjab University, Chandigarh.
*Time required*: 10 to 15 minutes.
*Level*: High School boys (11th grade) or Adolescents of about 16 years.
*Main features*: It is a scale in Hindi consisting of 46 items. Fully standardised.
*Scoring*: The responses on each item have been assigned differential weights and the scale is scored as a whole by using scoring key.
*Reliability*: Reliability coefficients using KR-21 was .90.
*Validity*: Content validity using 10 psychologists was worked out. Concurrent validity with TMAS (Adaptation by Krishnan) was .72 (N=100). Correlation with Cattel's IPAT Anxiety questionnaire was .91 (N=100). Correlation with Spilberger's State-Trait Anxiety Inventory was .80 (N=100).
*Norms*: C-Scale norms are available.
*References*:
1. Sharma, Sagar. Manifest anxiety and school achievement of adolescents. *Journal of Consulting and Clinical Psychology*, 1970, 34, 403-407.
2. Sharma, Sagar. Anxiety among higher secondary students in relation to their sex and caste affiliations. *Haryana Journal of Education*, 1970, 46-49.
3. Sharma, Sagar. Standardisation of an anxiety scale. *Recent Trends in Education*, 1970, 1, 14-16.
4. Sharma, Sagar. Parental occupation and anxiety. *New Trends in Education*, 1971, 2, 21-24.
5. Deo P. and Sharma, Sagar. Relationship of self-acceptance and anxiety. *Journal of Psychological Researches*, 1971, 15, 63-65.

## Citations C

### 13C1 CHILDREN'S MANIFEST ANXIETY SCALE

*Author* : M.A. Durett.

*Reference* : Durett, M.A. Normative data on the children's manifest anxiety scale for Marathi speaking children of different income levels. *Indian Journal of Psychology*, 1965, 40, 1-6.

## Adaptations D

### 13D1 FREEMAN ANXIETY TEST

*Authors* : B.N. Mukerjee and B.N. Sinha.

*Reference* : Mukerjee, B.N. and Sinha, B.N. Some relationship between anxiety level and need for achievement. *Journal of the Indian Academy of Applied Psychology*, 1967, 4(1), 11-20.

### 13D2 IPAT ANXIETY SCALE

*Author* : Mukerjee, B.N.

*Language* : Hindi.

*Validity* : Concurrent validity using a psychiatric criterion ranged from 0.3 to 0.4 which after attennuation is expected to reach almost 0.5. The author reports that anxiety scale distinguish very sharply between normals and high anxiety cases and thus the scale has been found valid against clinical psychiatric judgement also.

*Reference* : Mukerjee, B.N. and Menon, A.S. Personality characteristics and intra-individual variability in industrial out put. *Indian Journal of Industrial Relations*, 1969, 4(4), 462-481.

### 13D3 PITTSBERG REVISION OF MANIEST ANXIETY SCALE

*Authors* : N.P. Singh and Karan Singh.

*Reference* : Singh, N.P. and Singh, K. Motivational components of agricultural and business entrepreneurs in India. *Journal of Industrial Relations*, 1971, 7(1), 81-92.

### 13D4 TAYLOR'S MANIFEST ANXIETY SCALE

*Author* : N.P. Singh

*Availability* : Author.

*Reliability* : Split-half and test-retest reliability coefficients were found to be 0.92 and .87 respectively.

*Validity* : Validity coefficient against the original MAS was .83.

*Reference* : Singh, N.P. Anxiety, a potent sensitiser to industrial accidents. *Psychological Researches*, 1969, 4(1-2), 45-49.

## 13D5 TAYLOR'S MANIFEST ANXIETY SCALE

*Author* : A.K. Sinha.

*Availability* : Author.

*Reliability* : Test-retest reliability coefficient was found to be .83.

*Reference* : Sinha, A.K. Psychology and non-psychology college women: a comparison of some personality traits. *Psychological Studies*, 1968, 13(1), 94-97.

# 4. Self Concept

## Complete instruments A

14A1 HINDI PERSONALITY DIFFERENTIAL (HPD)

*Author* : K.G. Agrawal.
*Availability* : Author, NIHAE, E-16, Greater Kailash-1, New Delhi-48.
*Uses*: HPD can be used for making meaning profiles of personality related concepts like, I, myself.
*Time required* : Depends on number of concepts used. On an average it takes one minute per concept.
*Level* : Age 15 and above.
*Main features* : Meaning profiles can be prepared for concepts related with person perception. The factor scales consists of conformity, tough mindedness, normalcy and tenseness.
*Scoring* : Semantic differential type. +3, +2, +1, 0, —1, —2, —3.
*Reference* : Agrawal, K.G. Personality dimensions as revealed by the Hindi Personality Differential. *Indian Journal of Psychology*, 1970, 23-37.

14A1 HINDI PERSONALITY DIFFERENTIAL

(Hindi equivalents of the following words have to be rated on a semantic differential scale).

| | |
|---|---|
| Light | — Heavy |
| Thin | — Thick |
| Easy | — Difficult |
| Hard | — Soft |
| Nectarlike | — Poisonous |
| Happy | — Angry |
| Superior | — Inferior |
| Glorious | — Dull |
| Typical | — Unique |
| Usual | — Unusual |
| Relaxed | — Tense |
| Religious | — Corrupt, atheist |
| Fickle | — Serious |
| Impermanent, weak | — Strong |
| Clean | — Dirty |
| Dishonest | — Honest |
| Deligent | — Shirker |
| Pleasure-seeking | — Self-restrained |
| Humourous | — Serious |
| Efficient | — Inefficient |
| Kind | — Cruel |
| Bitter | — Sweet |
| Intelligent | — Dull |
| Reputable | — Disreputable |
| Active | — Passive |
| Calm | — Excitable |

## 14A2 S-C INVENTORY

*Author* : M. Basavanna.

*Availability* : Author, Department of Psychology, S.V. University, Tirupati.

*Uses* : To assess the level of self-confidence.

*Time required* : 20 to 30 minutes.

*Level* : College students or wards.

*Main features* : It is an inventory of 100 items, to be answered either true or false. Can be scored easily, the higher the score lower is the level of self-confidence and vice-versa.

*Scoring* : Key is available.

*Reliability* : Split-half reliability was found to be 0.91.

*Validity* : Item validities for all the items are at or above 0.90.

*Norms* : Percentile norms for a sample of 800 college students is available.

*Reference* : Basavanna, M. A study of self-confidence as an attitude of self-concept. Unpublished Doctoral Dissertation, 1971, Sri Venkateswara University, Tirupati.

## 14A2 S-C INVENTORY

(The following items have to be checked for whether they are true or false with regard to the respondent).

1. It is rather difficult for me to make new friends.
2. I can be natural while at a party.
3. I am never at conflict with myself.
4. I enjoy mixing with people.
5. In social conversation I am usually a listener than a talker.
6. I can usually find a ready answer for remarks made to me.
7. When things go wrong I pity or blame myself.
8. I have a horror of failing in anything I want to accomplish.
9. I often cross the street to avoid meeting some people known to me.
10. I find it very difficult to speak in public.
11. I feel insecure within myself.
12. I find it hard to do my best when people are watching.
13. I can recover easily and quickly from social blunders.
14. I do not care much for what others think of me.
15. I have difficulty in talking to most people.
16. I stay in the background in social gatherings.
17. I feel embarrassed to enter into assembly when all are already seated.
18. I have difficulty in saying the right thing at the right time.
19. I tend to worry over possible troubles.
20. I frequently feel thwarted because I am unable to do as I desire.
21. I think of myself as a successful person.
22. I am much affected by the praise or blame of many people.
23. My feelings are rather easily hurt.
24. I can face a difficult situation without worry.
25. I am hesitant about forming decisions.
26. I feel bored much of the time.

27. I can tackle new situations with a reasonable degree of assurance.
28. I am often unable to decide until it is too late for action.
29. I tend to be quick and certain in my actions.
30. I always feel that I can achieve the things I wish.
31. I feel no obstacle can stop me from achieving my final goal.
32. I am generally confident of my own ability.
33. I often feel that in life's competition I am generally the loser.
34. I frequently feel unworthy.
35. I worry over humiliating situation more than most persons.
36. I feel physically inferior to my friends.
37. I find it hard to continue work when I do not get enough encouragement.
38. I am bothered by inferiority feelings.
39. My people believe that I am as much a success as I could be.
40. I can play my best in a game or contest against an opponent who is much superior to me.
41. I am always ready to decide what my next step should be.
42. I can adjust readily to new situations.
43. I often feel rather awkward.
44. I am afraid that other people will dislike me.
45. My friends have made better life adjustments than myself.
46. I am happy go lucky person.
47. I can relax myself easily.
48. I blush very often.
49. When upset emotionally. I take much time to recover.
50. I day dream very often.
51. I am readily moved to tears.
52. When a critical situation is past, I often think what I should have done but didn't.
53. I often feel that my movements are clumsy.
54. I don't have initiative.
55. I usually work things out for myself rather than get someone to show me.
56. I am a dominant person.
57. I am usually discouraged when the opinions of others differ from my own.
58. I am often confused.
59. People frequently blame me for things unjustly.
60. I feel that my parents are disappointed in me.
61. I envy the happiness that others seem to enjoy.
62. Criticism disturbs me greatly.
63. I get discouraged easily.
64. I can get a job any day.
65. I seem to make friends about as quickly as others do.
66. I shrink from facing a crisis or difficulty.
67. If given a chance I could do something that would be of great benefit to the world.
68. If given a chance I would make a good leader of people.
69. I have several times given up doing a thing because I thought too little of my ability.

70. No one seems to understand me.
71. I need someone to push me through things.
72. Life is a strain for me much of the time.
73. I have had blank spells in which my activities were interrupted and did not know what was going around me.
74. I am worried about sex matters.
75. I have periods of such great restlessness that I cannot sit long in a chair.
76. I refuse to play some games because I am not good at them.
77. I find it hard to keep my mind on a task or job.
78. I seem to be about as smart as most others around me.
79. I usually feel well and strong.
80. I think too much over everything.
81. My daily life is full of things that keep me interested.
82. I am certainly lacking in self-confidence.
83. Almost always I find myself worrying about something or the other.
84. I have often lost good chances because I would not make up my mind soon enough.
85. I spend much of the time worrying over the future.
86. I do not get tired quickly.
87. I think I have an attractive personality.
88. I don't think too long over my problems.
89. I have feeling of hopelessness.
90. I cannot express my emotions freely.
91. When my friends criticise me I take it well.
92. I am a responsible person.
93. Generally I am quite sure of myself.
94. Usually I am dissatisfied with myself.
95. I have the feeling that I am just not facing things.
96. I have enough faith in myself.
97. I am often in low spirits.
98. I often feel helpless.
99. I am often disorganised.
100. I can usually make up my mind and stick to it.

## 14A3 SELF-ACCEPTANCE INVENTORY

*Author*: S.B. Kakkar.
*Availability*: Author, State College of Education, Patiala.
*Uses*: To measure the ability to accept the self-disparaging statements.
*Times*: About 10 minutes.
*Level*: High school and college students.
*Scoring*: Simple counting of items checked.
*Reference*: Kakkar, S.B. Adjustment and self-acceptance. *Manas*, 1967, 14(1), 31-35.

## 14A3 SELF-ACCEPTANCE INVENTORY

(The following items have to be checked for acceptance).

1. At times I abuse may parents.
2. Sometimes I copy from the notes of my classmates.
3. When I know I shall not be caught, I steal or tell lies.
4. At times I disobey my teachers.
5. At times I indulge in false excuses to get out of things I dislike.
6. At times I say indecent words or things.
7. Sometimes I am fussy over trifles.
8. Sometimes I shirk work that I am supposed to do.
9. At times I have been mischievous with my classmates.
10. At times I am uncharitable to those who love me.
11. Sometimes I am unsportsman like in my behaviour.
12. At times I brag about my qualities before others.
13. At times I do not keep tidy.
14. At times I am unkind to the young of little birds, and animals.

14A4 SELF CONCEPT INVENTORY

*Author* : Sagar Sharma.
*Availability* : Author, Department of Psychology, Panjab University, Chandigarh.
*Time required* : No time limit.
*Level* : High School Students (X and XI Standards).
*Main features* : Available in both Hindi and English.
*Scoring* : Scoring keys are used.
*Reliability* : Test-retest reliability coefficient on self-concept scores was found to be .81 and test-retest reliability on self-ideal discrepancies was found to be .72.
*Validity* : Content validity was established. Convergent validity with Deo's Personality test was also worked out.
*References* :

1. Sharma, Sagar, and Deo, Pratibha. Self Concept and School achievement. *Indian Educational Review*, 1970, 5, 101-105.
2. Sharma Sagar, and Deo, Pratibha. Self-Ideal discrepancy and school achievement. *Adolescence*, 1970, 5, 353-360.
3. Sharma, Sagar. Standardisation of self concept inventory. *Psychological Studies*, 1960, 14, 84-87.
4. Sharma, Sagar and Deo, Pratibha. Relationship of self-acceptance and anxiety. *Journal of Psychological Researches*, 1971, 15, 63-65.
5. Sharma, Sagar. Caste affiliation and sex as source of variation in self-acceptance of adolescents. *Manas*, 1969, 87-93.
6. Sharma, Sagar. Inter-relationship between two dimensions of assessing self-concept. *Journal of Psychological Researches*, 1970, 14, 103-106.
7. Sharma, Sagar. A comparative study of two techniques of obtaining self-ideal discrepancy scores. *Recent Trends in Education*, 1970, 1, 36-37.

### 14A4 SELF CONCEPT INVENTORY

[The student has to rate himself on the following characteristics on a 5-point scale of frequency (very often, often about 50 per cent of the times, rarely and very rarely) separately for what he thinks he is at present and for what he would like to be.]

1. Coward
2. Sympathetic
3. Inventive
4. Honest
5. Wicked
6. Obedient
7. Shirker
8. Humourous
9. Restless
10. Bossy
11. Rude
12. Wavering
13. Inferior
14. Hostile
15. Bluffer
16. Democratic
17. Harmful
18. Adventurous
19. Anxious
20. Social
21. Superior
22. Determined
23. Brave
24. Snobbish
25. Quiet
26. Hateful
27. Impatient
28. Stern
29. Jealous
30. Disciplined
31. Cautious
32. Quarrelsome
33. Confused
34. Superficial
35. Simple
36. Awkward
37. Self-controlled
38. Sarcastic
39. Noble
40. Affectionate
41. Frank
42. Alert
43. Resourceful
44. Charitable
45. Obstinate
46. Religious
47. Expressive
48. Reasonable
49. Friendly
50. Suspicious
51. Cheerful
52. Well-mannered
53. Intelligent
54. Kind
55. Conservative
56. Sensitive
57. Artistic
58. Unselfish
59. Irritable
60. Enthusiastic
61. Dependent
62. Escapist
63. Tardy
64. Modest
65. Boastful
66. Cooperative
67. Shy

## B Instruments with technical information

### 14B1 SVATA SAMBODH SOOCHI

*Author*: Central Bureau of Educational and Vocational Guidance.
*Availability* : Authors, DPFE, National Institute of Education, Mehrauli Road, New Delhi-16.
*Uses* : Guidance and counselling.
*Time required*: About 30 minutes.
*Level*: Mainly for high school students. Could be used with all.
*Main features* : Available in Hindi only. It contains three forms—real self, social self and ideal self—each containing 54 items.

14B2 SELF-PERCEPTION INVENTORY

*Author*: Kusum Bhatt.
*Availability*: Author, Department of Psychology, Gujarat University, Ahmedabad.
*Uses*: To measure attitude towards self.
*Level*: Adolescents.
*Main features*: A self-checking inventory consisting of 173 items to be checked on a 3-point scale.
*Scoring*: 0, 1 and 2 scores for each item.
*Reliability*: Test-retest reliability was .48 and split-half reliability was .91.
*Validity*: Correlation between SPI and incomplete sentence blank was .58 and between SPI and questionnaire .48, both significant at .01 level.

14B3 SELF-PERCEPTION QUESTIONNAIRE

*Author*: B.N. Mukherjee.
*Reliability*: Split-half reliabilities of the order .81 were observed.
*Reference*: Mukherjee, B.N. A multivariate study of the relationship between manifest anxiety, test performance and self-ratings. *Journal of Indian Academy of Applied Psychology*, 1969, 6(1), 8-21.

## Citations C

14C1 A-Q TECHNIQUE MEASURE OF SELF CONCEPT

*Author*: Vasantha Ramkumar.
*Reference*: Ramkumar, Vasantha. Ordinal position in family self concept and achievement of college students. *Journal of Educational Research and Extension*, 1972, 8(4), 211-216.

14C2 SELF-RATING INVENTORY

*Author*: U.P. Singh.
*Reference*: Singh, U.P. The self concept of the criminals. *Psychological Studies*, 1968, 13(2), 118-126.

# 5. Motivation

## A Complete instruments

15A1 TAT INSTRUMENT TO MEASURE ACHIEVEMENT

*Authors* : P.G. Aaron, V.G. Marihal and R.N. Maltesha.
*Availability* : Authors, Department of Education, Karnatak University, Dharwar.
*Level* : High school boys of South India.
*Main features* : The set consists of five pictures depicting scenes that are common in life of a high school boy from South India. These were drawn from leading Indian journals and redrawn. The pictures are mono-chromatic, structured, are printed on thick, white cards of 8 × 6 inches size.
*Reliability* : Test-retest reliabilities were found to be 0.511; 0.52; 0.53; 0.49; 0.42 and 0.74 (N=35) for the 5 pictures and for the total set.
*Validity* : Construct and predictive validities were established. The validity coefficients of 5 different pictures and for the total set were as follows:- Construct: 0.50; 0.45; 0.45; 0.30; 0.44; 0.65; Predictive: 0.59; 0.75; 0.01; 0.23; 0.12; 0.59.
*Norms* : T-Score norms are available.
*Reference* : Aaron, P.G., Marihal, V.G. and Maltesha, R.N. *A TAT Instrument to measure n-achievement of high school boys in South India*, Department of Education, Karnatak University, Research Monograph No. 2, March, 1969.

15A1 TAT INSTRUMENT TO MEASURE *N*-ACHIEVEMENT

(The following are the descriptions of the 5 pictures used).

**Picture No. 1 :** A young boy is sitting on the floor holding a book in his hands. In the foreground is shown a woman.

**Picture No. 2 :** An adolescent boy is seated in reclining posture with his eyes closed. An older man is sitting near by with an open book in his hands.

**Picture No. 3 :** A boy is standing with a handkerchief in his hands. He appears to be wiping off the sweat from his forehead. In the background is a table on which a number of books are strewn.

**Picture No. 4 :** Three figures are shown in this picture. A motherly looking woman. A fatherly looking man, and a young boy in between them. The man appears to be warning the boy who is standing with a down cast head.

**Picture No. 5:** In what appears to be a balcony, a boy is seated on a chair. He has one book open in his hand. His attention, however, is fixed on something else and not the book.

## 15A2 THEMATIC APPERCEPTIVE MEASURE OF NEED ACHIEVEMENT

*Author* : Prayag Mehta.

*Availability* : Author, Department of Psychology, University of Udaipur, Udaipur.

*Uses* : To measure the level of need achievement.

*Time required* : 30 minutes.

*Level* : High school students.

*Main features* : It is a projective test containing six cards: 1. A boy with a note-book, an ink-pot and a pen, 2. A boy reading a book sitting on a cot, 3. A boy painting, 4. A doctor and a patient, 5. A group of boys playing cricket, 6. A boy learning table from his teacher.

*Scoring* : McClelland's scoring system "C" for *n* Ach. is followed.

*Reliability* : Coefficient of split-half reliability=.73 (N=22), and test-retest reliability coefficient was found to be .39 (N=41) and .56 (N=42).

*Validity* : Construct and predictive validity were calculated.

*References* :

1. Mehta, P. *The achievement motive in high school boys*, New Delhi: National Council of Educational Research and Training, 1969, 282 p.
2. Chaudhry, N. The relationship between achievement motivation and anxiety, intelligence, sex, social class and vocational aspirations. Ph.D. Thesis Psychology, Panjab University, 1971.
3. Desai, D.B. and Trivedi, R.S. *Achievement Motivation Development in High School Pupils*, Baroda: Centre of Advance Study in Education, 1971.
4. Desai, D.B. Incentives as a basis for motivating pupils in classroom learning. *Journal of Education and Psychology*, 1970, 28(3), 101-121.
5. Gokulnathan, P.P. A study of achievement related motivation (n-ach. and anxiety) and educational achievement among higher secondary school pupils. Ph.D. Thesis in Education, Dibrugarh University, 1971, 168 p.
6. Namdeo, Gajanan. Need achievement and socio-economic status of adolescents. *Indian Academy of Applied Psychology, Research Abstracts*, 1972.
7. Pandharipande, P.S. Interrelationship among four measures of achievement motivation. *Journal of Psychology Researches*, 1972, 16(1). 17-20.
8. Desai, D.B. and Trivedi, R.S. Achievement motivation developed in high school students. Baroda: Centre of Advanced Study in Education and M.B. Patel College of Education, Vallabh Vidyanagar, Gujarat, 1971.
9. Desai, D.B. Achievement motivation development through specially designed curricula in high school pupils. U.G.C. Report. M.B. Patel College of Education, Vallabh Vidyanagar, 1972.
10. Mehta, P., Kumar, K. and Sharma, B.R. Level of n-Ach. in high school boys, NCERT, New Delhi, 1969.
11. Desai, D.B. Achievement motivation in high school pupils of

Kaira district of Gujarat, NCERT Project Report, Sardar Patel University, 1970.

12. Sinha, B.P. and Mehta, P. Farmer's n-Ach. and change-proneness in a farm telecast. New Delhi: Indian Institute of Mass Communication.
13. Nijhawan, H.K. and Chaudhry, N. Anxiety, n-Ach., and vocational aspiration. *Indian Journal of Psychology*, 1970, 45(3), 211-218.
14. Mehta, P. and Kanade, H.M. Motivation development for educational growth: A follow-up study. *Indian Journal of Psychology*, 1969, 46, 1-23.
15. Mehta, P. Achievement motivation training for educational development. *Indian Educational Review*, 1968, 3(1).
16. Gokulnathan, P.P. and Mehta, P. Achievement motive in tribal and non-tribal Assamese secondary school adolescents. *Indian Educational Review*, 1972, 17(1), 67-90.

## 15A2 INSTRUMENT

(Description of the pictures is given under main features).

## 15A3 ACHIEVEMENT MOTIVATION INVENTORY

*Author* : Prayag Mehta.

*Availability* : Author, Department of Psychology, University of Udaipur.

*Time required* : 30 minutes.

*Level* : The inventory is meant for high school students.

*Main features* : The inventory contains 22 items with 6 alternatives of which, the respondents are required to check one.

*Scoring* : Key reproduced.

*Reliability* : K-R 20 reliability was .67 and split-half reliability was found .55.

*Validity* : Theoretical validation of the achievement motivation inventory has been presented by the author.

*Reference* : Mehta, P. *The Achievement Motive in High School Boys.* National Council of Educational Research and Training, New Delhi, 1969, pp. 202.

## 15A3 ACHIEVEMENT MOTIVATION INVENTORY

1. A boy is sitting on a cot. He has a book in his hand. An almirah full of books is lying nearby.
   (i) He is preparing questions suggested by his teacher for the forthcoming examination.
   (ii) He is trying to find out the meaning of that word which no one in the class could explain.
   (iii) He is looking at the coloured picture given in a book.
   (iv) He is quickly doing the home task given by the teacher.
   (v) He is thinking about a new application of the principles given in a book.
   (vi) He is reading a story.

2. A boy is reading a picture.
   (i) He is thinking whether to complete the picture or to leave it unfinished.
   (ii) He is practising to make pictures.
   (iii) He is making a picture to participate in the annual art competition to be held in the school.
   (iv) He is thinking whether he should colour the picture.
   (v) He is learning the art of making pictures.
   (vi) He is thinking that when he will have learned drawing well, then he would make beautiful pictures.

3. A boy is holding a model of an aeroplane and is looking at it.
   (i) He is thinking of becoming an engineer.
   (ii) He is guessing the price of the aeroplane.
   (iii) He is observing as to how the aeroplane has been made.
   (iv) He is carefully checking the aeroplane before demonstrating his flying skill.
   (v) He is waiting for his friend so that he can get the aeroplane started by him.

4. Two boys are standing, facing the mountains.
   (i) They are enjoying the beauty of nature.
   (ii) They are planning to climb up to the highest peak of the mountain.
   (iii) They are studying the herbs available on the mountain.
   (iv) They have become tired after a lot of walking and are just relaxing.
   (v) They are thinking about the new techniques of mountaineering.
   (vi) They are thinking of writing a report after having inspected the mountainous region.

5. A farmer's son is ploughing the field.
   (i) He is contributing his share to make up the deficit of food in the country.
   (ii) He is thinking of sowing after he has ploughed the land.
   (iii) He is trying to get the maximum possible yield from his field.
   (iv) He is ploughing the land to get sufficient food for himself and his family.
   (v) He is ploughing the field to sow seeds.
   (vi) He is using chemical fertilisers to make the land more productive.

6. A boy is doing something in the laboratory.
   (i) He is thinking that he should discover some new thing.
   (ii) He is practising an experiment for the examination.
   (iii) He is clearing the instruments kept in the laboratory.
   (iv) He is busy in discovering new things.
   (v) He is doing an experiment in science.
   (vi) He is looking at instruments placed in the laboratory.

7. A man and a boy are sitting with a tabla.
   (i) The boy is learning to play on the tabla.
   (ii) The boy is learning the tricks of the trade from his teacher in order to become a good artist or a good musician.
   (iii) They are wondering as to why other persons have not turned up so far.
   (iv) The boy is preparing for the examination in music.
   (v) The boy is absorbed in learning new music compositions from that man.
   (vi) They are playing on the tabla to entertain themselves.

8. Two boys are playing hockey.
   (i) They are playing hockey to pass the evening.
   (ii) They are learning hockey from the instructor.
   (iii) They are practising hockey to regain the trophy lost by them in the last competition.
   (iv) They are playing for their amusement.
   (v) They are playing hockey to check whether the ground is suitable for playing a hockey match.
   (vi) They are preparing for the final hockey match.

9. A teacher and some boys are in the class.
   (i) They are participating in a discussion competition on 'How to check the growing indiscipline in schools'.
   (ii) They are learning a new lesson from the teacher.
   (iii) They are getting a complicated problem solved by the teacher.
   (iv) They are taking part in a group discussion to evolve indigenous methods to solve the food problem.
   (v) They are talking with the teacher.
   (vi) They are learning a new formula in mathematics from their teacher.

10. A teacher is sitting in a chair. A boy is standing by his side.
   (i) The boy is informing the teacher about the truants.
   (ii) That boy has just now developed a new thing and he is eager to show it to the teacher.
   (iii) The boy is standing beside the teacher to recite his lesson.
   (iv) The boy is standing there to hand over a letter from his father to the teacher.
   (v) He is standing there to show the teacher the essay that he has prepared to submit for the essay competition.
   (vi) He is standing there to understand a problem from his teacher.

11. A boy is reading something.
   (i) He is looking for the meaning of that word which nobody could tell in the class.
   (ii) He is reading a book of stories to pass the time.
   (iii) He is reading about new discoveries made in the different fields.
   (iv) He is preparing the lesson assigned to him by his teacher.

(v) He is enjoying a book of film songs.
(vi) He is preparing for some competitive examination.

12. The principal is giving something to a boy.
    (i) He is presenting a certificate to that boy for keeping up the name of the school in the last competition.
    (ii) He is praising that boy for maintaining discipline in the class.
    (iii) He is giving some important instructions to that boy.
    (iv) He is giving a prize to the boy for his courageous act.
    (v) He is giving a booklet of rules and regulations to the boy for forthcoming regional competition.
    (vi) He is giving the attendance register to the boy for taking attendance of the class in the absence of the class teacher.

13. Some boys are playing cricket.
    (i) They are learning to play cricket.
    (ii) They are trying to improve their game.
    (iii) They are playing to pass their recess.
    (iv) They are practising the game.
    (v) They are preparing to take part in the annual school competition.
    (vi) They are playing an exhibition match to collect funds.

14. A boy is holding some arrows in his hand. There is a target board placed at some distance.
    (i) That boy is waiting for the end of the P.T. period, so that he can go home.
    (ii) He is learning the art of arrow-shooting.
    (iii) He is practising arrow-shooting to become a good arrow-shooter.
    (iv) He is trying to finish this game quickly so that he can play some other game.
    (v) He is thinking of different techniques of shooting.
    (vi) He is practising in order to get the first position in the arrow-shooting competition.

15. A doctor is sitting with a patient.
    (i) He is talking to the patient.
    (ii) He is carefully examining the patient.
    (iii) The doctor has given an injection to the patient and now he is waiting for his fee.
    (iv) The doctor is prescribing the diet for him.
    (v) The doctor is carefully listening to the patient so that he can diagnose his disease properly.

16. A boy is sitting under a lamp. He has a book in his hand.
    (i) He is thinking of doing some great work after completing his studies.
    (ii) He is thinking that now he should start preparing for the examination.
    (iii) He is trying to write something in the book.

(iv) He is preparing all the possible questions which can be asked in the examination, so that he may score the highest marks in the class.
(v) He is turning the pages of the book and trying to find out that page on which the questions to be asked by the teacher on the following day is given.
(vi) He is checking whether there is any name written on the book that he found on way back from school.

17. A boy is doing something with the help of a hammer and a chisel.
(i) He is making a model.
(ii) He is trying to improve his skill in the craft.
(iii) He is checking whether the hammer and chisel work properly.
(iv) He is repairing the broken model.
(v) He is trying to become a sculptor.
(vi) By doing this he is getting physical exercise.

18. A boy is standing with a pen in his hand. He has a notebook.
(i) He will fill in the ink and write something on the notebook.
(ii) He is thinking of writing an interesting story.
(iii) He is imagining that he will become a writer.
(iv) He is checking whether the pen writes properly.
(v) He is thinking of the outlines for an essay for a competition.
(vi) He is solving assigned questions on the notebook with the help of that pen.

19. Some persons are doing various types of work.
(i) They are discussing as to what they would do so that they can progress.
(ii) They are busy in their respective tasks.
(iii) They are working to earn money.
(iv) They are thinking about various ways to march ahead on the path of progress.
(v) They are doing their work.
(vi) A man has to do something to earn his livelihood. These people are also doing some such work.

20. A boy is flying a kite.
(i) He is amusing himself.
(ii) He is thinking as to how he should fly the kite so that he may win the kite-flying competition.
(iii) He is wondering whether he should participate in the kite-flying competition on the following day.
(iv) He has just bought the kite out of the money that he got from his mother and is now trying to fly it.
(v) He is thinking of becoming a good kite-flier so that he may compete with his companions.
(vi) He is thinking whether he should compete with the other kite-flier.

21. The teacher is teaching in the class.
    (i) The teacher is trying to complete the course.
    (ii) He is teaching to earn his salary.
    (iii) He is making a study of the effective methods of teaching.
    (iv) He is answering the questions put to him by the students.
    (v) He is punishing those students who have not done their work.
    (vi) He is making a difficult lesson easier by giving new examples.

22. Three boys are running a relay race.
    (i) They are practising in order to improve their performance.
    (ii) They are learning the relay race during the games period.
    (iii) They are carrying out instructions.
    (iv) They are trying to surpass each other in the race.
    (v) They are demonstrating their skill.
    (vi) They are observing Sports Day.

**SCORING KEY FOR THE INVENTORY**

| *Item No.* | *AR* | *TR* | *UK* |
|---|---|---|---|
| 1 | 2,5 | 1,4 | 3,6 |
| 2 | 3,6 | 2,5 | 1,4 |
| 3 | 1,4 | 3,6 | 2,5 |
| 4 | 2,5 | 3,6 | 1,4 |
| 5 | 3,6 | 1,4 | 2,5 |
| 6 | 1,4 | 2,5 | 3,6 |
| 7 | 2,5 | 1,4 | 3,6 |
| 8 | 3,6 | 2,5 | 1,4 |
| 9 | 1,4 | 3,6 | 2,5 |
| 10 | 2,5 | 3,6 | 1,4 |
| 11 | 1,6 | 3,4 | 2,5 |
| 12 | 1,4 | 2,5 | 3,6 |
| 13 | 2,5 | 1,4 | 3,6 |
| 14 | 3,6 | 2,5 | 1,4 |
| 15 | 2,5 | 3,6 | 1,4 |
| 16 | 1,4 | 2,5 | 3,6 |
| 17 | 2,5 | 1,4 | 3,6 |
| 18 | 3,5 | 2,6 | 1,4 |
| 19 | 1,4 | 2,5 | 3,6 |
| 20 | 2,5 | 3,6 | 1,4 |
| 21 | 3,6 | 1,4 | 2,5 |
| 22 | 1,4 | 2,5 | 3,6 |

**Note:** The AMI consists of 22 items. Each item is followed by six responses of which two are achievement-related (AR), two are task-related (TR) and the rest are unrelated to achievement (UR). The numbers given against each item under AR, TR and UR in the scoring key show the nature of the numbered responses. For example, responses nos. 2 and 5 out of six responses under Item 1 are AR responses to Item 1, and responses no. 1 and 4 are TR responses and responses 3 and 6 are UR responses. The response to any one item can be either AR or TR or UR.

## 15A4 FARMER'S LEVEL OF ASPIRATION TEST

*Authors* : Udai Pareek and S.N. Chattopadhyay.
*Availability* : First Author, Indian Institute of Management, Ahmedabad.
*Uses* : To measure level of aspiration of farmers.
*Level* : Farmers.
*Main features* : Semi-projective test.
*Scoring* : Responses are scored in terms of standard scores shown below:

| *Education Level* | *Standard* | *Land holding Level in bighas* | *Standard Score* |
|---|---|---|---|
| Primary | 33 | 0 | 38 |
| Middle | 43 | 1 | 48 |
| Hr. Sec. | 53 | 2 | 55 |
| College | 61 | 3-4 | 60 |
| University | 69 | More than 4 | 68 |

| *Income Level in Rs.* | *Standard Score* | *Housing Level* | *Standard Score* |
|---|---|---|---|
| 100 & less | 34 | 0 | 31 |
| above 100 to 200 | 43 | the same house | |
| " 200 to 300 | 50 | with pucca walls | 41 |
| " 300 to 400 | 56 | | |
| More than 400 | 65 | 1 pucca house | 52 |
| | | 2 pucca houses | 64 |

| *Production Increase Level (In md/acre)* | *Standard Score* | *Stock Level (in no.)* | *Standard Scores* |
|---|---|---|---|
| 0-1 | 35 | 0 | 42 |
| 2 | 46 | 1 | 55 |
| 3 | 54 | 2 | 66 |
| More than 3 | 64 | 3 | 74 |

| *Furniture (in number of items) Level (in no.)* | *Standard Scores* | *Possessions (in number of items). Level (in no.)* | *Standard Scores* |
|---|---|---|---|
| 0 | 43 | 0 | 41 |
| 1 | 55 | 1 | 51 |
| 2 | 59 | 2 | 56 |
| 3 | 63 | 3 | 60 |
| 4 | 69 | 4 | 66 |
| 5 | 77 | 5 | 73 |

*Norms* : Percentage distribution in different areas of aspirations (for N=173).

*Reference* : Pareek, Udai and Chattopadhyay, S.N. Measuring level of aspiration of farmers through a projective technique. *Indian Journal of Social Work*, 1965, 15(4), 363-373.

15A4 FARMER'S LEVEL OF ASPIRATION TEST

Sriram is a farmer of some other village. The village is 10 miles away from Delhi and has been included in the Delhi Master Plan. There are also bus services both private as well as of Delhi Transport Undertaking. There are a school, a charitable dispensary-cum-hospital and other usual facilities. In the village proper, the houses are both types 'pucca' and 'kutcha'. There are a few rich persons as well as some very poor men in that village.

Sriram owns a 'kutcha' house. The compound of the house, you may say, is fairly spacious. The walls of the compound are also 'kutcha'.

Sriram's family is not too big not too small. After the death of his father, he and his brother have separated. His family consists of 7 members his old mother, he himself, his wife and his four children — 2 sons, and 2 daughters. His first child, a son, is 8 years old.

His land holding is of average type: 20 bighas. Farming is his principal occupation. He labours hard in his farm. His family members also help him in his farming. He takes each year the usual crops of this area. Wheat is the main crop, you know. You can well imagine his income, say it is Rs. 600 to Rs.700 per year.

He is neither extravagant nor miserly. Of course he has to spend money for all the necessary requirements of his family.

Sriram has all those worries and anxieties that a man in every village has to face in his daily life. But he is a man of honesty, sincerity and integrity.

**General Instruction**

This much information about Sriram has been given to me. "I don't know anything more. But I've been asked to depict a few features of Sriram's future. As an outsider; it is extremely difficult for me. On the other hand, being a man of this locality you can well conceive of a man—this Sriram. You can even think of him in your own personal plane. You can well imagine all other aspects which have not been covered above. I solicit your help in framing the following aspects of Sriram's future. But before I ask you those, I repeat the story once again."

1. *Area of Education* :

Can you guess how far Sriram will educate his eldest son?

Upto Primary School

Upto Middle School

Upto Higher Secondary School

Upto College

Upto University.

2. *Area of Landholding* :
Would you guess how far Sriram will increase his land holding in the next 5 years?
more than 5 bighas
only 5 bighas
only 4 bighas
only 3 bighas
only 2 bighas
only 1 bigha

3. *Income* :
How much his income do you think will increase in the next five years?
Rs. per year.

4. *Housing* :
Would you guess what improvements he will bring in his housing during the next 5 years?
He would own 2 pucca houses
He would own 1 pucca house
He would own the same house with pucca compound walls
No change.

5. *Wheat Production* :
Will you guess, during the next 3 years how far Sriram will increase his production of wheat per bigha?
10 mounds
9 mounds
8 mounds
7 mounds
6 mounds
5 mounds
4 mounds
3 mounds
2 mounds
Upto 1 mound
No increase.

6. *Livestock* :
Please guess how many livestock he will have in the next 5 years.
1 | 2 | 3 | 4 | 5 | - |

7. *Furniture* :
Out of the following list of furniture which are the things Sriram will keep in his house during the next 5 years?
Bench
Chairs
Table
Almirah
Mirror
Ulna

8. *Other material possession* :
Please guess, out of the following list of articles which ones he will be above to possess during the next 5 years:
Watch
Clock
Timepiece
Petromax
Radio
Cycle
Cart
Sewing machine.

15A5 RAO ACHIEVEMENT MOTIVATION TEST

*Author* : D. Gopal Rao.
*Availability* : Author, Regional College of Education, Shymala Hills, Bhopal-13 (M.P.).
*Time required* : There is no time limit, but it takes about 10 minutes.
*Level* : VIII to XI standard.
*Main features* : There are 20 incomplete sentences, each of which is followed by two possible alternatives A and B. The student has to indicate the alternative he generally prefers.
*Scoring* : The total number of responses to the achievement related items, as provided in the key forms the Achievement Motivation Score of the individual.
*Reliability* : Test-retest reliability of the test was found to be 0.79.
*Validity* : Correlation coefficient between test scores and teachers' ratings was found to be 0.73, and between test scores and parents' rating was found to be 0.71.

15A5 RAO ACHIEVEMENT MOTIVATION TEST

(For High School Students).

The respondent has to check one of the alternatives he prefers for each of the statements given below:

1. I enjoy reading ...
   - A. a comic book
   - B. a book of adventure
2. As a student I like to be called ...
   - A. a well dressed student in my class
   - B. an intelligent student in my class
3. When I grow up, I want ...
   - A. to do something which other have not done
   - B. to lead a comfortable life
4. As a doctor, I want ...
   - A. to be a well known surgeon
   - B. to make a lot of money
5. During the holidays, I want ...
   - A. to visit my friends and relatives
   - B. to point or write a story or a poem
6. While answering in the examination, I aim ...
   - A. at finishing before time
   - B. at answering better than my classmates
7. I want to become rich ...
   - A. by earning money by hard work
   - B. by earning a prize in the lottery
8. I take pride ...
   - A. in standing first in my class
   - B. in helping poor students
9. It is my nature ...
   - A. to take life easily
   - B. to undertake difficult tasks
10. I have a tendency ...
    - A. to work on a task till it is completed
    - B. to change the task if I get bored
11. I want to study well ...
    - A. to avoid blame from my parents
    - B. to excel others in my class
12. As an Engineer, I would like ...
    - A. to construct a model building in my town
    - B. to grow rich and buy a car
13. After 10 years, I will be ...
    - A. earning a lot of money
    - B. a well known person in my job
14. As a student, I would like ...
    - A. to study for my future career
    - B. to visit different places in the world
15. I feel very unhappy ...
    - A. when some one knocks away my purse
    - B. when I fail to do my best in the examination.
16. I want to do something ...
    - A. which will make me wealthy
    - B. which others can hardly do.
17. Generally I make friends ...
    - A. with those who are intelligent
    - B. with those who are clean and neat
18. I feel upset ...
    - A. when I am blamed
    - B. when I fail to succeed

| | |
|---|---|
| 19. I feel my success depends ... | A. upon my hard work<br>B. upon my parents and relatives |
| 20. I want to practice hockey everyday ... | A. so that I may be selected for the Olympic game<br>B. so that I may keep myself fit and healthy. |

15A6 SENTENCE COMPLETION TEST FOR ACHIEVEMENT MOTIVATION

*Authors* : V.S. Shanthamani and A. Hafeez.

*Availability* : Authors, Department of Industrial Management, Indian Institute of Science, Bangalore-12.

*Time required* : No time limit. Usually it needs 20 minutes to complete the test items.

*Level*: Adult men who know English.

*Main features* : There are 50 sentences each of which has three alternatives A, B, C and the subject has to indicate the alternative he generally prefers.

*Scoring* : By totalling the number of achievement related items that have been indicated in the keyed direction. Each triad has one achievement related item.

*Reliability*: Split-half reliability of the test was found to be 0.77.

*Validity*: Coefficient of concurrent validity was found to be 0.88.

*Norms* : Percentile norms for SCT based on the scores of 150 engineering graduates and 233 engineering diploma holders are available.

*Reference* : Shanthamani, V.S. and Hafeez, A. Need for achievement among engineering arts and commerce students. *Manas*, 1968, 15(2).

15A6 SENTENCE COMPLETION TEST OF ACHIEVEMENT MOTIVATION

| | |
|---|---|
| 1. I like ... | A. to be faithful to my friends and colleagues<br>B. to be very systematic in my work<br>C. to do my best in whatever work I undertake. |
| 2. In accomplishing a task I like ... | A. to be neat and clean<br>B. to do it much better than others<br>C. to finish it before time. |
| 3. I wish I could have always been ... | A. successful in doing difficult things<br>B. generous with my friends<br>C. sympathetic to the sick and poor. |
| 4. When working in groups I desire ... | A. to take the lead<br>B. to excel others in similar tasks<br>C. to do every thing in an orderly fashion. |
| 5. My aim of life is ... | A. to make a long record of successful achievements |

B. to serve my nation
C. to attain high status in the society.

6. I often desire to be ...
A. a silent worker in uplifting the poor
B. successful in doing something very significant
C. a true devotee of God.

7. I am of the opinion that for pleasure and happiness one must ...
A. support charities
B. get the basic amenities of life
C. enrich the record of one's achievements.

8. I want to know ...
A. the easiest path to achieve salvation
B. how I can be successful in whatever I undertake
C. the honest means of accumulating wealth.

9. I like ...
A. reading fiction, adventure, travel etc.
B. visiting different places in the world
C. to think of my future career.

10. I believe that it is possible for me ...
A. to be a recognised authority
B. to achieve social status
C. to get sufficient power in my hands.

11. I frequently desire ...
A. to be a popular social reformer
B. to be a great political leader
C. to do something of great significance.

12. I am very serious ...
A. about being truthful
B. about helping those who really deserve help
C. about being a great man in my own profession.

13. I consider my self better than those ...
A. who do not have any aim in life
B. who are unsociable in nature
C. who are irresponsible.

14. I will be very happy if ...
A. I can do something very valuable
B. I can earn a lot
C. I can be my own boss.

15. I like to praise those who ...
A. have devoted their life to social service
B. have earned a reputation in their own field
C. have some principles of life.

16. In whatever work I undertake ...
A. I like to make advance plans
B. I like to do my very best
C. I like to assume full responsibility for it.

17. It is my nature ...
A. to keep things neat and orderly
B. to do things for my friends
C. to undertake tasks which require great skill.

18. I like to be ...
A. friendly and sympathetic with those in trouble
B. a great authority in some job or profession
C. very systematic in all my activities.

19. I am always keen ...
A. to fight for a noble cause
B. to remove untouchability and other social evils
C. to develop my qualifications.

20. I feel best when ...
A. I tell others about my personal experience
B. I am assigned a difficult job
C. I am requested to give advice to others.

21. I frequently aspire to be ...
A. a man with wonderful achievements
B. a very rich man
C. the centre of others' attention.

22. I am happiest when ...
A. making others happy
B. successful in my work
C. I become the centre of other's attention.

23. I often think of ...
A. accomplishing something great
B. helping those who are hurt or sick.
C. being respected as a leader.

24. I like to be able ...
A. to forgive those who have hurt me
B. to use words that others do not know the meaning of
C. to do things better than others.

25. I feel ...
A. unhappy when I fail to do my best in the examination
B. depressed when I hear about somebody's death
C. angry when I see injustice done to my friends.

26. My secret ambition in life is ...
A. to enjoy a happy married life
B. to obtain a highly paid job

C. to establish a glorious record of achievements.

27. I like to do something which ...
A. others can hardly do
B. will make me wealthy
C. others regard as a manifestation of leadership.

28. It gives me great satisfaction ...
A. to supervise and direct others
B. to be in the company of distinguished persons.
C. to undertake very difficult tasks

29. In most social situations ...
A. I try to follow the customs
B. I do not always accept and follow the usual religious practices
C. I try to impress others.

30. What I want most in my life is ...
A. to get an ideal home life
B. to do something requiring effort
C. to be a popular man in society.

31. I like others to think of me as ...
A. very intelligent
B. very industrious

32. In judging my merit, I believe that ...
A. my grades were justified.
B. my grades were not a fair index of my work
C. my teachers were partial to others.

33. I wish the atmosphere ...
A. in my home was more congenial to study
B. in my school would really help me to achieve something
C. in my city was more peaceful and healthy.

34. I am ...
A. quite punctual and I am never late for work, school, appointment etc.
B. quite neat and organised in what I do
C. courageous, but avoid unnecessary danger and risk.

35. I am always careful ...
A. to please everybody with my manners
B. to do my best in whatever I undertake
C. to perform my activities in my own way.

36. I have a general tendency ...
A. to continue a work till it is finished
B. to analyse others judgement critically
C. to be polished in my manners.

37. Before starting a difficult task ...
    A. I would take other's suggestion
    B. I would plan its details so as to lead to success
    C. I would imagine the difficulty that might arise.

38. I am anxious ...
    A. to know my own defects so as to overcome them
    B. to do something of great significance
    C. to be the object of attraction in the group.

39. In general I might be described as ...
    A. optimistic (believing that everything is ordered forth best)
    B. tolerant
    C. polite.

40. I take pains ...
    A. not to hurt other's feelings
    B. to overcome obstacles and attain a high standard
    C. to avoid blame from others.

41. I am often tempted ...
    A. to undertake very difficult tasks
    B. to see new places, new people and new things
    C. to be sympathetic with those who are unhappy.

42. I am sure that after ten years ...
    A. I will be achieving true freedom
    B. I will be earning a lot
    C. I will be a recognised authority in my field.

43. I am ...
    A. tolerant about people who hurt
    B. a morally upright person
    C. determined to work towards a high goal.

44. I enjoy ...
    A. a long spell of continuous activity to solve a difficult problem
    B. the company of fun-loving people
    C. the company of children.

45. I feel happy ...
    A. If I get an opportunity to do someone a favour
    B. If I get an opportunity to entertain others with some jokes
    C. When I have finished successfully a difficult task.

46. I avoid ...
    A. gay and irresponsible pleasure
    B. mental confusion and disorder, seekers

C. those situations which are not competitive.

47. I prefer ...
A. getting encouragement from my friends and elders
B. difficult tasks to easy ones
C. the company of elders and experienced persons.

48. I feel upset whenever ...
A. I am blamed
B. I fail to reach my desired goal
C. I am neglected or not loved.

49. I believe that ...
A. It is better to be faithful than famous.
B. love is more just than justice.
C. my future depends upon my doing some notable work.

50. I would like to solve ...
A. the socio-economic problems of my country.
B. very difficult puzzles and quizzes
C. those problems which will give me novel experiments.

## 15A7 LEVEL OF ASPIRATION SCALE

*Authors* : Ranjit Singh and T.S. Sohal.
*Availability* : Authors, Punjab Agricultural University, Ludhiana.
*Time required* : 1 hour.
*Level* : Farmers.
*Scoring* : Total spread of the scale has been kept 100 points. $2^1/_2$ points are deducted for every negative response.
*Reliability* : Test-retest reliability coefficient was found to be .91.
*Validity* : Jury opinion and known group techniques were used to establish the validity of the scale.

## 15A7 LEVEL OF ASPIRATION SCALE

(The respondent has to check the first 35 items on 'yes'/'no' responses, and the rest on the response alternatives provided under each item).

1. Do you feel that a peasant can lead prosperous life even in the profession of farming if he does hard work?
2. Suppose you have been offered a double piece of land than what you already have at some other place but which requires a little reclamation, would you move to the new place leaving behind your community and native place?
3. You are being provided an opportunity to attend a tour for familiarising you with the new techniques of farming. Will you be prepared to spend some money to attend the tour?
4. Your V.L.W. has offered you the free use of an improved implement

which could be obtained from his headquarter at a distance of 8 miles from your village. Will you go and bring this for your use and then return it there?

5. Your son wants to attend young farmers training course at Punjab Agricultural University, Ludhiana for three months. Would you allow him to attend the course when you know that you would have to work more in his absence?
6. Do you feel satisfied with your present method of farming?
7. If you do not have sufficient finances, would you like to borrow them for making permanent improvements on your farm?
8. Good crops can only be obtained from improved seed. Suppose improved seed has been provided to you at some higher rate than the local seed, will you purchase it?
9. It has been said that seed rate should be adjusted according to the percentage of germination. Will you get your seed tested for germination in future, if you have the facilities?
10. Uniform size of seed is essential. Will you try to get your seed graded before sowing?
11. Seed treatment with chemicals is done against certain diseases, but it sometimes create trouble when it comes in contact with skin at the sowing time. Will you in spite of this danger treat your seed keeping in view its effectiveness?
12. Crops should be sown at proper time but sometimes it becomes difficult to get labour at peak season. Will you sow your crops at proper time even if you have to pay high wages to labourers?
13. In case of late sowing will you try to compensate it with sowing late variety and by applying higher doze of fertiliser?
14. Experts are of the opinion that you should sow your crops in lines. Will you adopt this method when you know that it is the costly method?
15. Proper placement of seed and fertiliser is very essential to get good harvest. Will you engage a skilled person for this operation even if you have to pay high wages?
16. Interculture is essential to control weeds and facilitates air and water movement in soil. Will you do it even when you know that labour is very costly during these days?
17. A chemical (2-4 D) is very effective to control weeds of wheat crop. Will you use it even when you know that it can some time give reverse results with slight negligence at the time of using it?
18. Experts are of the opinion that green manuring is essential to maintain the fertility of the soil and its effect lasts for several years. Will you do green manuring knowingly that you have to sacrifice your crops for one season?
19. Chemical fertilisers are essential to get good yields. Suppose you have no money to purchase these will you get taccavi without being sure that your crop will be successful?
20. It is being said that soil should be got tested in order to know exact fertiliser requirements. Will you put some efforts to get your soil tested?
21. "Compost should be kept in spite even if it involves more labour and care". Will you adopt this practice?

22. It is a fact that animal excreta is a very good manure. Will you convert it into manure instead of making cakes even when you know that you will face acute shortage of fuel?
23. Suppose you have no money to instal a tube-well, Government provides you the facilities of loan for this purpose. Will you get it fully knowing that to take loan is not considered good in your society?
24. Defective irrigation water can render soil unfit for cultivation, so it must be tested. Will you put some efforts to do the same?
25. Suppose you have no facility for irrigation, and the canal is at a distance of two furlongs from your farm. Canal authorities informed you that you will be provided water if you dig the channel yourself. Will you do it?
26. Do you think that one should spray his crops in order to save them from pests, knowingly that insecticides sometimes may endanger man's life due to carelessness?
27. Spraying means killing the insects. Will you spray your crops knowingly that it is a sin to kill living beings?
28. Scientists at Agricultural University, Ludhiana have obtained wheat yield about 87 mds. per acre. Do you think that farmers can also do the same?
29. "Nature plays a vital role in successful harvest of the crops so it is useless to put extra efforts". Say a few farmers. Do you agree?
30. Will you raise your yields if more facilities are provided to you or have you reached the climax and it is not possible to increase it?
31. Are you satisfied with the implements you use?
32. Are you going to purchase some improved implements in the near future?
33. Some farmers are of the opinion that 'muna plough' is sufficient for ploughing. Will you admit it?
34. It is not possible for individual cultivator to purchase a power thrasher, then?

    Suppose a few farmers want to purchase it collectively, will you join (a) to become a member of the village panchayat.
35. You want to purchase some implements for your farm and at the same time you have to purchase certain articles for your home. But you have not enough money to purchase all. Will you forego some of your comforts and give first priority to purchase farm implements.
36. A farmer gets a lottery of Rs. 3,000 what will you suggest him to do from the following?

    a) Start some business and leave farming.

    b) Use to purchase luxuries of life.

    c) Use it to make improvement on the farm.
37. What you want to achieve from the following:

    a) To become an official of the village institutions.

    b) To become best farmer of the village.
38. How do you feel about farming?

    a) A traditional way of life.

    b) A commercial undertaking.
39. What will you suggest to a farmer if some one consults you from the following?

a) Use his own seed.
b) Purchase improved seed from Government or any other reliable agency.

40. How do you think your average yields compare with those of your neighbours?
(a) Less, (b) Equal, (c) Higher.

15A8 ACHIEVEMENT MOTIVATION SCALE

*Author* : S.N. Singh.
*Availability* : Author, Training Officer Bayer (India) Limited, Express Tower, 19th floor Bombay-400001.
*Level* : Originally used on Farmers. Could also be used with adults and college students.
*Main features* : It is a 6 item scale with 5 alternative responses to each item. The respondent has to check one of the alternatives to each item.
*Scoring* : Summated ratings.
*Reliability* : Split-half reliability coefficient=0.79 Test-retest reliability coefficient=0.84.

15A8 ACHIEVEMENT MOTIVATION SCALE
Questionnaire Method of Measuring Achievement Motivation of Farmers

(The respondent has to check one of the alternatives to each item).

| | | | | | |
|---|---|---|---|---|---|
| 1. Success brings relief or further determination and not just pleasant feeling. | Strongly agree | Agree | Undecided | Disagree | Strongly disagree |
| 2. How true it is to say that your efforts are directed towards | Quite natural | Not very true | Not sure | Fairly | Quite true |
| 3. How often do you seek opportunity to excell? | Hardly ever | Seldom | About half the time | Frequently | Nearly always |
| 4. Would you hesitate to undertake something | " | " | " | " | " |
| 5. In how may sphere that might lead to your failing? | Most | Many | Some | Few | Very few |
| 6. How many situations do you think you will succeed in doing as well as you can? Do you avoid in which you may by exposed to evaluation. | Most | Many | Some | Few | Very few |

# B Instruments with technical information

## 15B1 INVENTORY OF MOTIVATIONAL TRAITS

*Authors* : E.I. George and V. George Mathew.
*Availability* : Authors, Department of Psychology, Kariavattom, Trivendrum, Kerala.
*Uses* : To measure four motivational traits (academic interest, general ambition, persistence and endurance) of high school pupils.
*Time required* : About thirty minutes.
*Level* : High school pupils of Kerala.
*Main features* : An inventory consisting of 92 items.
*Scoring* : Separate answer sheets are used and scoring is by stencil.
*Reliability* : Odd-even reliability coefficients were found to be .76, .56, .78 and .64 respectively for academic interest, general ambition, persistence and endurance. Retest reliability coefficients were .49, .50, .51 and .71 respectively for the four dimensions.
*Validity* : AI had a correlation of .23 with the n-Achievement test. GA had a correlation of .16 with self-ratings on general ambition. P had a correlation of 0.17 with self-ratings on persistence F had a correlation of 0.23 with self-ratings on endurance. P correlated 0.68 with scores on a different persistence inventory.
*Norms* : Percentile norms are available for pupils of standard X.

## 15B2 NEED HIERARCHY QUESTIONNAIRE

*Author* : T.N. Govindarajan.
*Availability* : Author, Indian Institute of Technology, Madras.
*Uses* : To measure the need satisfaction of industrial personnel.
*Level* : Industrial personnel.
*Main features* : A 49-item questionnaire.
*Validity* : Items were selected after judges' ratings.
*Reference* : Govindarajan, T.N. Executive leadership and need satisfaction. *Journal of Indian Academy of Applied Psychology*, 1972, 9(1), 14-17.

## 15B3 KUMAR NEEDS RATING SCALE

*Author* : K. Kumar.
*Availability* : Author, Professor of Psychology, Banasthali Vidyapith, Rajasthan.
*Uses* : For studying the manifest needs of students.
*Time required* : About 40 minutes.
*Level* : From class VII to XI (both boys and girls).
*Main features* : The rating scale studies the twelve manifest needs selected from the list of twenty manifest needs of Murray. The needs rated include: abasement, aggression, affiliation, deference, dependence, dominance,

achievement, nurturance, sex, autonomy, succorance and exhibition.

*Scoring* : Scoring key is given in the rating scale.

*Reliability* : Split-half reliability coefficients range from .85 to .92 for the different needs.

*Validity* : Item validity has been established through biserial correlations and *t* values. Correlation coefficients range from .31 to .89 and *t* values from 2.59 to 12.66. Against teachers' rating correlation coefficients range from .52 to .62.

*Norms* : Norms are available for both boys and girls from classes VII to XI. These are in the form of stanines and mean performances.

*Reference* : Kumar, K. Influence of intelligence on the needs of school children. *Indian Educational Review*, 1969 4(2), 133-136.

15B4 SECURITY MOTIVE TEST

*Author* : Afzal Kureshi.

*Availability* : Author, Department of Psychology, Aligarh Muslim University.

*Uses* : To measure security-insecurity feelings.

*Main features* : It is a TAT set to test security imagery. A scoring manual is available prepared by the author in the reference cited below.

*Scoring* : For scoring a story for security motive there should be at least one character having desire to attain an atmosphere in which he would feel contented, satisfied and free of insecurity, or conversely he should be dissatisfied with insecure and unfavourable atmosphere.

*Reliability* : Inter-scorer reliability=.784.

*Validity* : Gave a correlation coefficient of .63 with Maslow's S-I inventory.

*Reference* : Kureshi, A. A scoring manual for the security motive. *Indian Journal of Psychology*, 1972, 47(1), 97-103.

15B5 AAPAS MOTIVE TEST

*Author* : Afzal Kureshi.

*Availability* : Commercially available, Rupa Psychological Corporation, Sora Kuan, Varanasi.

*Uses* : The test can be employed for measuring five important human motives i.e. achievement, affiliation, power, aggression and security.

*Time required* : Administration time comes to about an hour.

*Level* : Mainly for adolescent students, both male and female.

*Main features* : It consists of ten pictures, designed for studying achievement, affiliation, power, aggression and security motives.

*Scoring* : The method of scoring is given in the manual of directions for the test.

*Reliability* : Split-half reliability coefficients for the five motives are: Ach : 85; Aff : .81; Agg : .88; and Secur : .78. The inter-score reliability coefficients are Ach : .820; Aff : .779; Pow : 850; Agg : .990 and Score : .784.

*Validity* : Validity of scores of achievement, affiliation and Power motives has been reported to be fairly high by the authors of schemes for these motives. (McClelland, 1953; Heyns, *et al.* 1958; Veroff, 1958). A.S. Reaction study has been used as an external criterion to determine the validity of scores for aggression motive, the *r*-value being .55. The validity of security motive scores has been determined by using security-insecurity inventory as an external criterion. Here the *r*-value is .63.

*References* : The AAPAS Motive Test which was known by a different title before its final publication has been used in the following studies:

1. Siddiqui, M.M. and Akhtar, S. Quantitative study of n-achievement, n-affiliation and n-power among disciplined and indisciplined students. *Journal of Psychological Researches*, 1969, 13(2), 85-89.
2. Beno, H. A study of affiliation and security motives of highly secure and highly insecure adolescents. Unpublished Master's dissertation in Psychology, Aligarh Muslim University, 1966.
3. Akhta, I. A study of achievement motive in relation to level of aspiration. Unpublished Master's dissertation in Psychology, Aligarh Muslim University, 1968.
4. Jan, F. A study achievement motive of the academically bright and dull college students. Unpublished Master's dissertation in Psychology, Aligarh Muslim University, 1969.
5. Bhatnagar, Anila. A cross-cultural study of achievement motive of Indian and African students. Master's dissertation in Psychology, Aligarh Muslim University, 1970.

## 15B6 ACHIEVEMENT MOTIVATION SCALE

*Authors* : Uma Dutta Pandey and Ranjit Prasad Singh.

*Availability* : First author, Senior Scientific Officer, Directorate of Psychological Researches, Ministry of Defence, 'M' Block, New Delhi-1.

*Time required* : No time limit. Roughly it takes 30 minutes.

*Level* : College students.

*Main features* : It is a Likert type scale consisting of 20 items related to social and academic problems.

*Scoring* : As in Likert type scale.

*Reliability* : Test-retest reliability was found to be .52.

*Validity* : Items were judged by 10 psychologists, and 80 per cent agreement on each item was the criterion to select the items.

*Reference* : Pandey, U.D., and Singh, R.P. The effect of sex and culture on achievement motivation religious beliefs and religious practices. *Journal of Psychological Researches*, 1971, 15(2), 49-52.

## 15B7 PRE-ADOLESCENT LEVEL OF ASPIRATION TEST

*Authors* : Udai Pareek, T.V. Rao, Prabha Ramlingaswamy, Bala Ram Sharma.

*Availability* : Indian Institute of Management, Ahmedabad.

*Uses* : To study the aspiration patterns of students. For counselling purposes.

*Time required* : About 20 minute each. Four forms are available.

*Level* : Pre-adolescents and adolescents who can read and write Hindi letters.

*Main features* : Four forms are available with four experimental conditions: normal condition, reward, punishment, and reward and punishment combined. A digit symbol type test. Can be used for group administration with adolescents only. It is in Hindi.

*Scoring* : Subjects could be classified into different personality types with regard to their aspirations.

*Reference* : Pareek, U., and Rao, T.V. Motivation training for mental health. New Delhi: National Institute of Health Administration and Education, New Delhi, 1971.

15B8 TRIPATHI PERSONAL PREFERENCE SCHEDULE

*Author* : R.R. Tripathi.

*Availability* : Author, Department of Psychology, Banaras Hindu University, Varanasi-3.

*Uses* : Counselling, guidance, selection and research.

*Time required* : 40 to 50 minutes.

*Level* : College students.

*Main features* : A measure of 15 normal personality variables (manifest needs) as suggested by Murray (1938) and adopted by Edwards (1959). The personality statements have been modified by the present author in accordance with the cultural conditions of the college going population of the Hindi speaking areas in the North. Items are of the forced-choice format. The 135 personality statements have been scaled on the undesirability-desirability continuum by the method of successive categories. Then, pairs of statements matched on the basis of equality of their social desirability scale values (SDSVs) have been prepared. Each pair constitutes as item of the scale. Thus, the social desirability variable has been adequately controlled. Items in the scale are entirely different from those of the EPPS. The variables include : achievement, deference, order, exhibition, autonomy, affiliation, interception, succorance, dominance, abasement, nurturance, change, endurance, heterosexuality, and aggression. Available in Hindi language.

*Scoring* : Separate answer-sheets are provided which can be scored with the help of a template.

*Reliability* : Internal consistency coefficients (corrected by the S-B formula) and test-retest reliabilities for different variables are as follows:

*Internal Consistency* :

.99 .92 .94 .97 .97 .99 .96 .98 .96 .99 .99 .88 .82 .86

*Stability* : .66 .73 .65 .65 .64 .66 .76 .81 .71 .67 .65 .67 .74 .72 .66

*Validity* : Convergent validity coefficients as against the TAT. protocols are as follows:

| Ach | Def | Ord | Exh | Aut | Aff | Int | Suc | Dom | Aba | Nur | Chg | End | Het | Agg |
|---|---|---|---|---|---|---|---|---|---|---|---|---|---|---|
| .82 | .76 | .53 | .56 | .83 | .65 | .90 | .82 | .93 | .92 | .82 | .88 | .90 | .91 | .86 |

Discriminant validity coefficients as against the Sinha Anxiety scale are as follows:

| Ach | Def | Ord | Exh | Aut | Aff | Int | Suc | Dom | Aba | Nur | Chg | End | Het | Agg |
|---|---|---|---|---|---|---|---|---|---|---|---|---|---|---|
| -.14 | -.18 | -.24 | .15 | .02 | .00 | .04 | .05 | -.10 | .15 | .18 | .06 | -.11 | .22 | .06 |

*Norms* : Norms available for the college boys and girls, separately.

*Reference* : Tripathi, R.R. Construction of a personality test with the SR variable controlled, Doctoral Thesis, Patna University.

## C Citations

15C1 FRUSTRATIONS AND ASPIRATIONS QUESTIONNAIRE

*Author*: T.B. Mathur.
*Reference* : Mathur, T.B. Causes of frustration in adolescents and its relation with the level of aspiration. Ph.D. Thesis in Education, Agra University, 1970.

15C2 MOTIVATION TEST

*Authors* : Robert, D. Meade and Labh Singh.
*Reference* : Meade, Robert D. and Singh, Labh. Motivation and progress effects on psychological time in sub-cultures of India. *Journal of Social Psychology*, 1970, 80(1), 3-10.

15C3 BEHAVIOUR DETERMINANTS SCALE

*Author*: S. Singh.
*Reference* : Singh, S. A study of some personality and background variables related to the use of unfair means a testing situation. Ph.D. Thesis in Education, Patna University, 1970.

## D Adaptations

15D1 ABERDEEN ACADEMIC MOTIVATION INVENTORY

*Authors* : Bimaleswar De and R. Singh.
*Language* : Hindi.
*Availability* : Senior Author.
*Reliability* : Split-half and test-retest reliabilities were found to be .34 and .31. The coefficient of stability of .82 was obtained from the performance of 80 students after an interval of a month.
*Validity* : Validity was determined by the rankings of hostel superintendents. The coefficient was found to be .62. Concurrent validity was also established by comparing the overachievers and underachievers.
*References* :
1. De, Bimaleswar and Singh, R. A Hindi adaptation of the Aberdeen academic motivation inventory, *Indian Education Review*, 1970, 5(1), 71-74.
2. De, Bimaleswar and Singh, R. Home adjustment and academic motivation. *Indian Educational Review*, 1970, 5(2), 52-58.

15D2 ATKINSON'S N ACH TEST

*Authors* : N.P. Singh and Karan Singh.
*Reference* : Singh, N.P. and Singh, K. Motivational components of agricultural and business entrepreneurs in India. *Indian Journal of Industrial Relations*, 1971, 7(1), 71-92.

15D3 EDWARD'S PERSONAL PREFERENCE SCHEDULE

*Author* : R.P. Bhatnagar.
*Language* : Hindi
*Availability* : Author.
*Reliability* : Split-half reliabilities corrected by Spearman-Brown prophecy formula range from .73 to .91 for the 15 scales.
*Reference* : Bhatnagar, R.P. Development of the Edwards personal preference schedule in Hindi. *Indian Psychological Review*, 1966, 2(2), 103-108.

15D4 KAGAN AND WALLACH'S CHOICE DILEMMA TEST

*Authors* : N.P. Singh and K. Singh.
*Language* : Hindi.
*Availability* : Author, Bhagalpur University.
*Reference* : Singh, N.P. and Singh, K. Motivational components of agricultural entrepreneurs in India. *Indian Journal of Industrial Relations*, 1971, 7(1), 81-92.

15D5 LIFE SATISFACTION INDICES (NAUGARTEN AND TOBIN'S)

*Author* : P.V. Ramamurti.
*Language* : Telugu.
*Availability* : Author, Department of Psychology, S.V. University, Tirupati.
*Reliability* : Test-retest reliabilities (15 days) were found to be 0.88 and 0.84.
*Validity* : Discriminated at 1 per cent level between a well adjusted and poorly adjusted group.
*Norms* : Available on a sample of 300 older people.
*Reference* : Ramamurti, P.V. Life satisfaction in the older years. *Indian Journal of Gerontology*, 1970, 2(3&4), 3, 68-70.

15D6 SYMOND'S PICTURE TEST

*Author* : M.A. Kureshi.
*Availability* : Author.
*Reliability* : Inter-scorer reliability coefficients were .82, .77 and .85 and reliability coefficients were .85, .81 and .98 respectively for achievement, affiliation and power motives.
*Validity* : Validated with disciplined and indisciplined students.
*Reference* : Kureshi, M.A. Quantitative study of n-achievement, n-affiliation and n-power among disciplined and indisciplined students. *Journal of Psychological Researches*, 1969, 13(2), 85-89.

# PART II

# EDUCATION

# Introduction

THIS PART of the Handbook reports instruments dealing with different dimensions of education. These instruments are reported under five sections: general instruments, student problems and adjustment, interests and preferences, attitudes, and institutions. As in the previous part, this classification is a pragmatic one based on the number of instruments reported on each area rather than a rigorous conceptual one based on theoretical distinctions. Several dimensions in education have been left untouched by investigators. For example, several of the organisational aspects like job satisfaction, teaching practices, administration styles etc. have not been covered. Areas like vocational interests and preferences, student adjustment and so on have been very popular. The instrumentators seem to have been guided more by tradition, simplicity of the problem and the easy availability of the samples, rather than the theoretical and practical requirements of the area of education. The different sections reported here represent only a broad classification of the instruments. However, same instruments which would not be clearly classified have been included in the general section.

There are in all 84 instruments reported in this area. Of these 22 instruments have been reproduced here : only technical information is given for 46 instruments; 8 are adaptations; and another 8 are only citations. The detailed break up of the instruments on education appears in Table 2.

TABLE 2: Break up of Instruments in Education

| *Classification* | *Originals reproduced* | *Information only provided* | *Citation* | *Adaptation* | *Total* |
|---|---|---|---|---|---|
| 1 | 2 | 3 | 4 | 5 | 6 |
| 1. General | 8 | 10 | 0 | 0 | 18 |
| 2. Student problems and adjustment | 3 | 8 | 0 | 0 | 11 |
| 3. Interests and preferences | 0 | 16 | 5 | 4 | 25 |
| 4. Attitudes | 9 | 10 | 3 | 2 | 24 |
| 5. Institutions | 2 | 2 | 0 | 2 | 6 |
| Total | 22 | 46 | 8 | 8 | 84 |

An overview of these instruments indicates a complete lack of sophistication and methodological concern. One good feature of several of these instruments is their concern for reliability. Most of the instruments have reported split-half and test-retest reliability coefficients, and most of them are convincingly high. Validity seems to have been grossly neglected. In an area like education which is highly indigenous, borrowing from other countries is likely to be limited. This is reflected in the limited set of instruments available as adaptations. Norms are also likely to be of limited value in an area of this kind where the main population dealt with, viz. the students, are a transient group. The intrinsic characteristics of the students change from year to year in the same college and from college to college in the same year. In view of this, norms established at a particular point of time are likely to have only limited value. Some instruments report the norms on limited samples, but a great caution is warranted in using these. The reader interested in the personality aspects of the teachers and students will do well in referring to the earlier part, as several instruments reported there are meant particularly for students. Although the target population there is not cited as students in all cases, the classification of pre-adolescents, etc., might suit the student samples.

**General Instruments**

There are in all 18 instruments reported here under this category. These instruments cover several dimensions related to teachers personality, effectiveness, styles, student aspirations and interactions. Of the 18 instruments eight are reproduced here along with information about them and only information is provided for another 10. The dimensions covered by these instruments include cosmopoliteness, role conflict, teaching quality, leadership styles, role perceptions, teacher expectations, job satisfaction, parent-child interactions, educational aspirations, student traits for academic success, environment for academic success, and human relationships. Of the instruments reported here six are meant for teachers, three for heads of institutions, one for children, two for college students, five for high school students, and three for parents. There are two common scales, one between headmasters and teachers and the other for parents and teachers. Nine of the instruments are scales (including two rating scales) five questionnaires and inventories and the rest are tests, check lists, interview schedules and study forms (one each).

The Standardisation of these instruments is rather disappointing. Only five of them have reported reliability coefficients. If absence of such information is a broad indication of the lack of concern of the researchers in education for quality of instruments, it is high time that we did something about this. It is, however, gratifying to note that the reliability coefficients reported by instruments are fairly high. Both split-half and test-retest methods have been used. Coming to validity, again only six instruments have reported some kind of validation. Three used face and content validity methods, one instrument was validated against another standard instrument, another instrument has used item criterion correlation and another convergent discriminant validities. In all, the trend is disappointing from a methodological point of view.

Since most of the instruments are simple ones, scoring does not seem to be an issue. They use simple scoring techniques like summated ratings and also qualitative analysis.

Among the instruments reported here, the leadership styles questionnaire, cosmopoliteness scale, and the role conflict questionnaires by Bhogle seem to be good contributions to the measurement of some interesting dimensions. Indirasen's job-satisfaction scale is another contribution. From the methodological point of view it is a unique instrument. The parent-child interaction scale has been developed as a part of the development norms project of the National Institute of Education and is likely to generate good amount of data from different parts of the country. The other two are rating scales providing some useful dimensions for teacher evaluation.

From this brief review it appears that there is great scope in development of instruments to study various dimensions, of standardisation of the instruments available, and of introduction of sophistication in instrumentation.

**Student Problems and Adjustment**

Instruments on student problems adjustment and other factors that have a direct bearing on student campus behaviour like student morale etc. are included under this section.

There are 11 instruments reported in this section. Of these only three are reproduced along with information about them and only information is provided for the others.

Instruments under this category have paid more attention to standardisation as compared to these reported under the general section. Five of them have worked out reliability coefficients and another four report validity. Both internal consistency and test-retest reliability coefficients have been worked out. The reliability coefficients whenever reported are fairly high. Two instruments have been validated against teachers ratings, one reports item validity, and another construct validity.

Among these instruments some are student problem checklists/ inventories, to measure discipline versus indiscipline, another to measure student morale, one to measure school adjustment and one to measure personality and environmental factors leading to unrest. While these instruments reported here are exclusively for high school and college students, a few more instruments reported in the adjustment section of the first part (Personality) of this book may also be useful for investigators interested in studying student adjustment problems. While most of the adjustment problems instruments reported in this section are checklists and inventories, instruments reported under the adjustment section are more systematically developed scales.

Nine of the instruments here have the target population of college students and two high school students. However, some of them could be used for both the levels.

The first of those reproduced here is a student problem inventory (actually a checklist) by Badami containing a list of 293 problems to be checked. This is divided into nine parts. Scoring is as simple as a mere counting of the total number of problems checked. This is an exhaustive list of problems and shorter versions depending on the necessity of the user are possible to prepare from this. The second one is a discipline-indiscipline inventory by Deo and Bhalla. Although the authors group it as a projective instrument, not much of projection is involved as the response system is direct indication of preferences in pairs.

This is a very useful instrument for educational researchers. The last of those reproduced here is by Hafeez, and appears to be a specific instrument developed for the students of Indian Institute of Science. Users can borrow some of the items relevant but the instrument is not advised to be used as such unless the user also has similar problems for his sample, one example is the problem of single rooms of the hostel converted into double rooms (item 3).

In general, instruments reported here have high action value. Feedback of responses on these instruments to the concerned educational administrators are likely to be useful in creating proper learning environment. While such feedback might be done at the individual item level, the total score could be used for research studies using correlational and associative methodologies.

**Interests and Preferences**

Instruments relating to curricular interests, preferences, reading interests, vocational and occupational interests and preferences are reported here. Information is provided here for 14 such instruments. None could be reproduced. Some instruments using pictures etc. have been received but could be reproduced here. These instruments include questionnaires, inventories, scales and tests. The terminology has been used rather loosely, and most of these use some kind of scaling method. Instruments are available for both high school and college students. About eight of them cater to high school students and the rest to college students. Some of these meant for college students could also be used with high school students. The instruments reported here would be of great use for the guidance and counselling purposes.

Eleven of the instruments report reliabilities. Eight of them have worked out split-half reliabilities and three stability coefficients. The reliability coefficients wherever reported are fairly high. Different techniques have been used for validational purposes. Ratings and external criteria like discriminant scores of persons in different occupations have been commonly used. Four of the actual occupational groups, two have used both content and construct validities, and another three have used parent, teacher or self ratings.

Some instruments reported in the last part of this book in the section on values may also be of relevance to this section. As quite a few of the dimensions measured by the value instruments have direct bearing on the occupational preferences, an interested user may refer to that section for additional references.

**Attitudes**

Instruments dealing with teacher and student attitudes to various issues are reported in this section. Areas like teaching and other educational processes, teaching profession, punishment, coeducation, school, extension education, cocurricular activities modern educational trends, NCC, compulsory primary education, teaching English in secondary schools etc. are covered by the instruments reported in this section. In all 24 instruments have been reported in this section of which nine are reproduced, information is provided for another ten, and three originals and two adaptations are cited.

All except two of the instruments included here are scales. Two are called as inventories. Most of them are Likert scales.

Only three of the inventories reproduced here report reliability coefficients and only two of the nine report validities, factorial and content. All of the other ten for which information is presented here report reliability coefficients. Six of them have reported validities — mostly content and construct. Nine of the 19 instruments have worked out split-half reliability coefficients and two test-retest reliability coefficients. Wherever reliability coefficients are reported they are of a very high order indicating a general pattern of high reliability estimates of instruments in educational attitudes.

Scoring system used in all these inventories is simple; most of them use Likert's summated ratings. The different target groups covered include; high school students, medical students, university students, teacher trainees and teachers. A few of them could be used with even the general population.

The first of the instruments reproduced under this section is a Teacher Attitude Inventory by Ahluwalia. This is in the process of standardisation. It attempts to measure attitudes towards teaching profession, classroom teaching, child centered policies, educational processes, pupils and teachers. There are 150 questions grouped into these six scales. The final standardised version is likely to be shorter. There are four more scales reproduced here, dealing with attitudes towards teaching profession. Three of them are Likert scales varying in length.

Although all these scales are called as attitude scales towards teaching professions, the content and orientations differ from scale to scale. For example the orientation of Bhogle's scale is more towards measuring attitudes to school and administration than the teaching profession per se. Katti and Baunur's scale has a different orientation; it measures the general orientation of the teachers. Unbrocks is still broader in orientation covering the general orientation to the profession as such than to the school as a system or teachers as persons. Users need to go through the scales carefully before they select one for research etc. Factor analytic studies on these scales are likely to be very useful, delineating different dimensions covered by them.

An interesting instrument reported here is to study the attitudes towards punishment by Pratibha Deo. This is a situational test. While most of the physical punishment situations described there are not likely to hold good to the present day school systems, the others may still be relevant in the study of several schools. With modification the scale could be used in undergraduate colleges where social and economic punishments still exist.

Vidhu Mohan's scale is constructed using Thurstone's technique and measures attitude towards coeducation. Gopal Rao's School Attitude Inventory is useful for studying the student reactions to the school. This is a kind of school climate inventory and pooling of data gathered from each of the schools is likely to be useful in developing descriptions for school. Professional perceptions inventory by Rao is just a set of adjectives on which the respondent has to rate his profession. This could be used for any professional body of students like those in technology, management, agriculture, medicine, education, social work etc. Inter-professional attitude differences may be taken up by researchers.

An over all trend of simplicity, superficiality and limited concern for standardisation is revealed by the investigators in developing instruments under this section. While the other areas of study on attitudes are progressing with methodological sophistication and are going deeper into the structural and dynamic aspects of the attitudes, several areas in education remain untouched. While there are sufficient instruments on teaching profession, instruments are needed to measure attitudes of the public, students, teachers and administrators towards emerging educational concepts like autonomous institutions programmed instruction, student participation in decision-making, decision-making strategies, revised examination systems of UGC etc. These might be helpful in exploring practical problems.

**Institutions**

There are six instruments reported under this section dealing with the institutional environment. Only two are reproduced here, information about other two are provided and the last two are adaptations. Four of these are meant for teachers, one for students and one for both. One is for teachers in the engineering and technology college and another for students of medical colleges. The others are general instruments for all college and school teachers. Two of them have been developed with student teachers in mind.

The two instruments reproduced here are fairly well standardised as they report both reliability and validity coefficients. Factor analysis is reported to have been done for both these instruments and scores are based on scales, using factor analysis data. Reliability and validity have not been reported for the other three instruments.

A good amount of work has recently been initiated at the Centre for Advanced Study in Education, MS University, Baroda for studying the institutions at primary and high school level. The Indian Institute of Management has also started working on institutions of higher education and research. A few projects are underway and some more instrumentation is likely to emerge in the coming years at both these places. There is an increasing awareness about the need for systematic researches on educational institutions as organisations. Such awareness is likely to result in increased attempts to bring out well standardised instruments in this area.

# 1. General Instruments

## Complete instruments A

### 21A1 LEADERSHIP STYLES QUESTIONNAIRE

*Author*: Shalini Bhogle.
*Availability* : Author, Department of Psychology, Osmania University, Hyderabad-7.
*Time required*: 7 to 10 minutes.
*Level* : Originally developed for School Head Masters and Head Mistresses. Can be adapted for any head of the teaching institution.
*Main features* : There are 13 different situations posed to the head, in the form of an event. Three different choices are presented in the form of a possible solution to each of the event. The headmaster chooses one. Each denotes a fixed style of leadership, Autocratic, democratic and laissez faire. The test is self administered.
*Scoring* : One unit score for a response of any style : democratic, autocratic and laissez faire. Each response alternative indicates one of these styles.
*Validity* : Items were selected on the recommendation of 30 psychologists and educationists in India. 75 per cent compatibility with the approved definitions of the three styles determined the criterion for selection. The criterion for validation are face validity and content validity.
*Reference* : Bhogle, S. Development of a test to measure the leadership style of Headmasters. *Indian Educational Review*, 1969, 4(2), 73-83.

### 21A1 LEADERSHIP STYLE QUESTIONNAIRE

(One response alternative has to be chosen from the three given after each of the following situational descriptions).

1. In order to attend a workshop meant for headmasters, you are to be away from the school for four months. The annual examination of the school and new admissions would be conducted during this period. It is not compulsory for you to attend the workshop.
   A. I shall ask the school management to make suitable arrangements in my absence and attend the workshop.
   B. I shall attend the workshop. Our teachers are well experienced. They can run the school quite efficiently even in my absence. I shall distribute the charges amongst the teachers and the assistant headmaster will be in over all charge.
   C. An headmaster worth his salt cannot be away from the school for a

long period of four months especially at the time of examination and admissions. If it were shorter period, the assistant headmaster would have managed it. In this case I will not attend it.

2. The Director of Public Instruction has written to you, to undertake the responsibility of housing and organising a camp with participants from 10 school, during the December vacation. Your teachers are very reluctant to have it in your school. You are expected to reply to D.P.I.
   A. I shall write to the D.P.I. that the School will undertake the responsibility, and shall tell the teachers that they have to organise the camp whether they like it or not.
   B. If the teachers are not willing then headmaster cannot do any thing. I shall have to write to the D.P.I. that the school cannot organise the camp because the teachers are not wanting it.
   C. The organisation or a camp is a creative activity. The school and the staff are likely to get some opportunity to learn how to organise a camp. So, I shall discuss with the teachers to make it possible as good as they can.
3. One of the assistant teachers has suggested a new way of scheduling the work-load of teachers through a committee of teachers.
   A. If the teachers come forward to manage their own work through a joint co-operative system, I shall join them in the enterprise and shall welcome such an initiative as it provides sharing of experience and ideas.
   B. I consider, it will make things difficult for me to maintain discipline amongst the teachers. After all scheduling the work-load is headmaster's duty and, I do not want others to do it for me. I cannot accept such a proposal.
   C. Scheduling is not so important as to require my attention. If the teachers want to decide what should be done let them decide. I shall approve the plan.
4. The governing body of the school is of the opinion that you as a headmaster did not use sufficient tact in handling students strike, and consequently the school was put to considerable loss and damage. They have asked you to send your explanation if any.
   A. I will explain that in meeting the situation I have been continuously in touch with my colleagues for adopting a suitable course of action. And I think it was the best under the circumstances of which I assume the full responsibility.
   B. I considered it was futile to meet the agitated students, they were in a violent mood. Nothing better was possible in the situation.
   C. With all the power that I have as a headmaster, I tried to suppress the students, but apparently the students were out of control. Of course I feel that deterrent punishment should have been given.
5. You receive a request from some brilliant students of the final year class that they want some extra coaching for the coming Public Examination in order to secure higher ranks.
   A. It is difficult to arrange such classes, as I cannot impose additional burden on the teachers under the existing rules. So let the students make their own arrangements.

B. I shall encourage the students for this initiative, but tell them I like to discuss the matter with the other teachers and possibly the teachers' committee may find a way out.
C. Since, rank holders are a matter of prestige to the school I shall send a circular to the teachers assigning some of them for the extra coaching class.

6. A lady teacher had a delivery early in the summer vacation. She has applied for maternity leave from the date of re-opening of the school after the summer vacation. The rule governing the maternity leave is rather vague, (as to when this period of two months should commence) and much depends on your discretion.
   A. The teacher has had enough rest when she needed it, and she should join the school on completion of two months from the date of delivery.
   B. I have to find out from her how many days of leave she thinks she would need, after the reopening, and if it is reasonable shall help her to have it.
   C. I do not think I have much to do in this case. I shall simply recommend the application for two months of maternity leave.
7. A very influential member of the school management asks you to admit his below normal child in your school. His admission is to affect the discipline of the class and so the class teacher has advised you against this admission. You know the admission would help the school in getting more grants.
   A. I think it would be in the interest of the school to admit the child, one dull child in the class will not effect the class materially. But the grants will surely be helpful for the school and could even be used to improve many such children.
   B. I shall circulate the letter among other teachers for their opinion and shall ask the assistant headmaster to decide in the matter.
   C. I shall ask a competent teacher to study the child carefully. On the merit of report the class teacher and I shall jointly take the decision, if the child should be admitted or not.
8. You get a letter from a parent that his son was beaten up by bigger and stronger classmate for refusing to do the home work for him. On inquiries you find that the complaint was valid.
   A. Quarrels among the students are numerous and so often that a single headmaster of such a big institution cannot afford to waste time in investigating them. However, I shall try to speak to the miscreant and inform the father accordingly.
   B. I shall meet out severe punishment to the bigger boy and warn him that in case he misbehaves again, he would be rusticated.
   C. I shall discuss the incident with the class as a whole and also discuss with the teacher for finding ways such that the two boys are able to do their home work themselves.
9. You receive an application from your assistant teacher requesting you to relieve him of his job as he has secured a better one elsewhere. You did not know that the teacher had applied elsewhere. Rules require, that application for any job should be sent through you. If the teacher is

relieved now, teaching would greatly suffer.

A. I shall call for the explanation of the teacher and tell him that he cannot be relieved, as he did not apply through proper channel. I do not want the school work to suffer and shall warn him, that in future applications should be sent through the headmaster.

B. The teacher is to be relieved as it is a better job. I cannot ask him to continue when he is not willing. I shall explore what alternative arrangements could be made to relieve him.

C. The teacher should see the Secretary of the Managing Committee and get his clearance. Personally I do not have any objection, after all, no one is indispensible.

10. You have received a note from the Students' Union of your School (obviously under outside inspiration) that they would go on strike if the evaluation of the examination papers is not made more leniently.

A. I shall sit with the students to discuss with them about the suitable action regarding evaluation. To me strike is not the problem, problem is their dissatisfaction about evaluation.

B. I shall inform the Students' Union that if they went on strike or cause any disturbance severe disciplinary action will be taken against them.

C. I shall send the note to the governing body of the school and the Parent Teacher Association as, I consider the decision of what is to be done in such situation is upto them.

11. The governing body of the school considers that some weak students need extra coaching in some subjects beyond the school hours and you should make arrangements for it. You apprehend some resistance to this idea from some teachers.

A. I shall also share the extra work with my teachers, shall find out if they can volunteer to do the work by rotation. I shall also try to impress them that, the teachers credit lies in pulling a backward student up and here is an opportunity for them.

B. Teachers are full time employees of the school and it is a part of their duty to teach the subject well, it affects the school performance. They should attend to these backward children.

C. Shall forward the letter to the assistant headmaster to make suitable arrangements for these children. If there is something that I can do, I shall do so.

12. You heard a rumour that a certain teacher is very communal in his approach towards pupils. On preliminary inquiries, you understand that although there is exaggeration yet there was some truth in it. You also discover that communal tendencies were present in some other teachers also.

A. I think, as a free citizen every person has his own ways of thinking and I cannot go on correcting individual opinions or modes of thinking.

B. I shall convene a meeting of the teachers to discuss about communalism. Shall firmly point out that communalism is not conducive in a school situation. It is an unhealthy feature.

C. I shall call each of the teachers and tell him that there is absolutely no place for communal feeling in my school. If I find any body communal I can become ruthless to outcast such a person.

13. The assistant headmaster of the school who happens to be your colleague and friend over a long period of time suggests you in writing that the school teachers and students would show remarkable progress in their achievements if you reduce your check on them.
    A. I can never trust my assistants and students. The assistant headmaster is too good to be a leader. I think he does not know that school would be a big mess if I do not check constantly.
    B. As a headmaster as I think I was expected to take rounds, I used to go round but if that is a problem I may stop going around.
    C. I have always been thinking for the progress of my school. I think I should try out this suggestion for a fortnight to see the results. If there is a worthwhile progress I shall willingly follow this suggestion.

## 21A2 COSMOPOLITENESS SCALE

*Author* : Shalini Bhogle.

*Availability* : Author, Department of Psychology, Osmania University, Hyderabad-7.

*Level* : Teachers.

*Main features* : It is a 8-item Likert type scale.

*Scoring* : Five-point summated ratings.

## 21A2 COSMOPOLITENESS SCALE

(The following items have to be checked on a 5-point scale of agreement).

1. I read as many journals as I can as I like diversity instead of intensity in the field of my specialisation.
2. It is no use attending the various workshops and seminars in one's field it is much better to study for oneself.
3. Teachers should not participate in students activities. Real relationship between the teachers and students develops only when teachers teach well in the class and not through any thing else.
4. One should not jump from one job to another after a certain age, even if it means increased emoluments and comforts.
5. When a teacher associates with a number of teachers' organisations for exchange of ideas, it creates disturbances in his quiet devotion.
6. I do not think I will read all those useless educational journals even if I am paid for it. They do not help the teacher any way.
7. Although it is a modern trend to accommodate students' views in running the school, it reduces the efficiency of the school.
8. It is an exertion and a bother more than a matter of joy to go out of town these days. I would like to avoid travelling and enjoy my leisure at home.

## 21A3 ROLE CONFLICT SCALE FOR TEACHERS

*Author*: Shalini Bhogle.
*Availability* : Author, Department of Psychology, Osmania University, Hyderabad-7.
*Level*: Teachers.

## 21A3 ROLE CONFLICT SCALE FOR TEACHERS

PART I

(The teacher has to indicate in the following table how, he thinks his headmaster expects him to carry out his assignments. He has to use the following symbols A,B,C,D, and E as the situation requires):

A. If he thinks the headmaster expects him to do the assignment a great deal more than he is doing now.
B. If he thinks the headmaster expects him to do it a little more than he is doing now.
C. If the headmaster expects him to do it to the same extent as he is doing now.
D. If he thinks the headmaster expects him to do it a little less than he is doing now.
E. If the headmaster, he thinks expects him to do it a great deal less than he is doing now.

| **Teaching** | **Organising games and sports** | **Supervising the Library** | **Organising Celebrations** | **Organising Debates** |
|---|---|---|---|---|

PART II

(Similarly the teacher has to indicate the difference in the amount of importance, attached by him and his headmaster to these activities using the following code).

A. The headmaster thinks this activity is a great deal more important than what the teacher thinks it is.
B. The headmaster thinks this activity is a little more important than what the teacher thinks it is.
C. The headmaster thinks this activity is about as important as what the teacher thinks it is.
D. The headmaster thinks this activity is a little less important than what the teacher thinks it is.
E. The headmaster thinks this activity is a great deal less important than what the teacher thinks it is.

| **Teaching** | **Organising games and sports** | **Supervising the Library** | **Organising Celebrations** | **Organising Debates** |
|---|---|---|---|---|

PART III

(The teacher has to indicate the extent to which he would like to carry out the functions if he had things his way, using the following category system).

A. If he would like to do it a great deal more than at present.
B. If he would like to do it a little more than at present.
C. If he would like to do it the same way as now.
D. If he would like to do it a little less than at present.
E. If he would like to do it a great deal less than at present.

| **Teaching** | **Organising games and sports** | **Supervising the Library** | **Organising Celebrations** | **Organising Debates** |
|---|---|---|---|---|

21A4 ROLE CONFLICT SCALE FOR HEADMASTERS

*Author*: Shalini Bhogle.
*Availability:* Author, Department of Psychology, Osmania University, Hyderabad-7.
*Level*: Headmasters.

21A4 ROLE CONFLICT SCALE FOR HEADMASTERS

PART I

(The Headmaster has to indicate in the following table how he thinks different groups of people (students for column 1, assistant teachers for column 2, etc.) expect him to fulfil the function indicated using the following symbols A,B,C,D and E as the situation requires).

A. If he thinks they expect him to do it a great more than he is doing now.
B. If he thinks they expect him to do it a little bit more than what he is doing now.
C. If he thinks they expect him to do it to the same extent as he is doing now.
D. If they expect him to do it a little less than what he is doing now.
E. If they expect him to do it a great deal less than what he is doing now.

| **A teacher to the Students** | **A leader to the Assistant Teachers** | **An administrator to the Managing Committee** | **Head of the Institution** | **Colleagues to other Heads** |
|---|---|---|---|---|

PART II

(The Headmaster has to rate the relative amount of importance he attaches to the different functions against the expectations of other people (indicated in different column heads) using the symbol codes given below).

A. If he thinks they consider this function a great deal more important than what he thinks it is.
B. If he thinks they consider this function a little bit more important than what he thinks it is.
C. If he thinks they consider this function about as important as he thinks it is.
D. If he thinks they consider this function a little less important than what he thinks it is.
E. If he thinks they consider this function a great deal less important than what he thinks it is.

| A teacher to the Students | A leader to the Assistant Teachers | An administrator to the Managing Committee | Head of the Institution | Colleagues to other Heads |
|---|---|---|---|---|

21A5 JOB SATISFACTION INVENTORY

*Author*: Jayalakshmi Indirasen.
*Availability* : Author, Indian Institute of Technology, Mehrauli Road, New Delhi-16.
*Uses* : To measure job satisfaction.
*Level*: Engineering teachers.
*Main features* : This inventory is in three parts, each part containing 30 items representing the factors — pay, opportunity for advancement, supervision, co-workers, organisation policy and management, working conditions, recognition, achievement and independence. It is a 5-point Likert-type scale.
*Reliability*:

| Reliability | Indian sample | English sample |
|---|---|---|
| Part I | .873 | .833 |
| Part II | .948 | .934 |
| Part III | .948 | .955 |

Item correlations has been also reported.
*Validity* : Convergent and discriminant validities.
*Scoring* : Sectional scores and overall scores are possible. Summated ratings.
*Reference* : Indirasen, Jayalakshmi. Multivariate analysis of factors affecting job satisfaction of engineering teachers. Doctoral thesis in Psychology, Indian Institute of Technology, New Delhi, 1973.

21A5 UNIVERSITY TEACHERS JOB SATISFACTION INVENTORY

PART I

(The respondent has to check the following statements on a 5-point scale. The alternatives for the 5 points are: (a) very much less than what it should be, (b) less than what it should be, (c) just what it should be, (d) more than what it should be, (e) very much more than what it should be).

1. Salary I get is
2. The cordiality of relationship with my colleagues is
3. The interest my head of the department shown in my work is
4. The security I have in my job is
5. The cordiality of relationship with my head of the department is
6. The comforts of physical working conditions (like place of work, light, noise, temperature etc.)
7. The liking I have for the nature of my work is
8. The achievement I have attained in my job is
9. The use of my talents in my job is
10. The responsibility I have in my job is
11. The autonomy I have in my job is
12. The technical competence of my head of the department is
13. The level of promotion I have reached in my job is
14. The fairness of authority in my job is
15. The prestige I have in my job is
16. The freedom of expression in my job is
17. The recognition I have in my job is
18. The challenge of my assignment in the job is
19. The fringe benefits (like housing, medical aid, provident fund, etc.) in my job are
20. The possibility for advancement in my job is
21. My involvement in my work is
22. The help from the administration in my job is
23. The status of my job is
24. Opportunity to exercise leadership in my job is
25. Opportunity to participate in decision-making in my job is
26. The ease of procedural formalities in my job is
27. The sense of belonging I have in my job is
28. The respect I have from my colleagues is
29. The technical facilities for my work in my job are
30. The work load I have in my job is

PART II

(The respondent has to check the following statements on a 5-point scale of satisfaction: very dissatisfied, somewhat dissatisfied, neither satisfied nor dissatisfied, somewhat satisfied, very satisfied).

1. Salary I get
2. Cordial relations with my colleagues
3. Interest shown by my head of the department in my work
4. Security of my job
5. Cordial relations with my head of the department
6. Comforts of physical working conditions (like place of work, noise, light, temperature) of my job
7. Liking for the nature of my job
8. Achievement in my work
9. Use of my talents

10. Responsibility in my job
11. Autonomy in my job
12. Technical competence of my head of the department
13. Level of promotion reached in my job
14. Fairness of authority in my job
15. Prestige of my job
16. Freedom of expression in my job
17. Recognition of my work
18. Challenge of my assignment
19. Fringe benefits (like, housing, medical aid, provident fund etc.) in my job
20. Possibility for advancement in my job
21. My involvement in my work
22. Help from administration in my job
23. Status in my job
24. Opportunity to exercise leadership in my job
25. Participation in decision-making in my job
26. Ease of procedural formalities in my job
27. Sense of belongingness in my job
28. Respect from my colleagues in my job
29. Technical facilities for work in my job
30. Workload in my job

PART III

(The respondent has to check the following statements on a 5–point scale of chances: none at all, very little, cannot say, quite good and very good).

1. The chances of my salary going up are
2. The chances of the cordiality of relationship with my colleagues improving are
3. The chances of the interest of my head of the department in my work improving are
4. The chances of my sense of security in my job improving are
5. The chances of the cordiality of relationship with my head of the department improving are
6. The chances of the comforts of physical working conditions (like place of work, noise, light, temperature etc.) of my job improving are
7. The chances of my liking for the nature of my job improving are
8. The chances of my having better achievements in my job are
9. The chances of my talents being better used in my job are
10. The chances of my having more responsibility in my job are
11. The chances of my autonomy in my job improving are
12. The chances of my having a more technically competent head of the department are
13. The chances of my promotion going up are
14. The chances of fairness of authority in my job improving are
15. The chances of the prestige of my job improving are
16. The chances of my having more freedom of expression in my job are
17. The chances of recognition of my work improving are

18. The chances of the challenge of my assignment in my job improving are
19. The chances of the fringe benefits (like medical aid, housing, provident fund etc.) in my job improving are
20. The chances of opportunity for advancement in my job improving are
21. The chances of my involvement in my work improving are
22. The chances of help from administration improving are
23. The chances of my status in my job improving are
24. The chances of my opportunity to exercise leadership in my job improving are
25. The chances of my having more participation in decision-making in my job are
26. The chances of the ease of procedural formalities in my job improving are
27. The chances of my sense of belongingness in my job improving are
28. The chances of respect from colleagues improving are
29. The chances of technical facilities for work improving are
30. The chances of my having better workload in my job are

21A6 TEACHER QUALITY RATING SCALE

*Author* : S.B. Kagkar.

*Availability* : Author, Department of Psychology, Government Training College, Jullundhar.

*Level* : Teachers.

*Main features* : It is a 5-point rating scale containing twelve characteristics on which the teacher has to be rated.

*Reliability* : Mean test-retest reliability for each of twelve characteristics was found to be .87.

*Validity* : Validity coefficients with H.G. Gough's California Psychological Inventory were .81 and .80 respectively for intellectual efficiency and self-acceptance.

21A6 TEACHER QUALITY RATING SCALE

(The teacher has to be rated on a 5-point scale of the degree of possession of each of the following qualities).

1. Self-confidence
2. Capacity for independent thinking and action
3. Persuasive ability
4. Outspokenness
5. Sharp wit
6. Self acceptance (sense of personal worth and satisfaction with self)
7. Clear thinking
8. Intelligence
9. Alertness
10. Thoroughness
11. Resourcefulness
12. Intellectual efficiency (efficiency level at which one utilises intellectual

and personal resources.)

21A7 PARENT-CHILD INTERACTION SCALE

*Authors* : S.V. Kale.

*Availability* : Department of Applied Psychology, University of Bombay, Bombay-29.

*Uses* : To assess the extent of active interaction between parents and children which may help cognitive development and scholastic achievement of children.

*Time required* : No time limit. Time required for parents ranges from 20-40 minutes, depending upon their literacy.

*Scoring* : Method of unsummated ratings (0 to 3).

*Reliability* : Reliability Coefficient = .98 (Spearman-Brown formula).

*Validity* : The item-criterion correlation ranges between .72 and .44.

21A7 PARENT-CHILD INTERACTION SCALE

(The respondent has to check the following items on a 3-point scale of frequency).

1.* I take interest in the child's daily homework and if necessary help him to complete it.
2. My child is fond of magazines and I encourage him to read them.
3. I visit other parents to know what they are doing, for their children so that I can do similar things for my child.
4. I encourage my child to think and act independently.
5. I have no time to take interest in my child's studies, but my other partner/wife/husband does it.
6. I encourage my child to read magazines, newspapers, story books etc. other than study books.
7. I learn new teaching methods for my child.
8. I explain to my child the reasons for doing things.
9. My child discusses with me what he reads in the newspapers.
10. I encourage my child to speak in grammatically correct language.
11. I usually reward my child whenever he shows a good progress in school.
12. I encourage my child to enrich his/her vocabulary by constantly using a dictionary, by asking elders, by keeping word book etc.
13. I provide my child with enough reading material, during his leisure time such as story books, magazines, but I ensure that they do not distract his mind too much.
14. I help my child to learn his lessons in a practical way (e.g. arithmetic by shopping, language by word games, science by seeing a practical demonstration at an exhibition, nature study by going to places of educational interest or through movies etc.).
15.* I encourage my child to study at least for sometime every day.
16. I spend sometime with my child in explaining word meanings and differences in meaning of words.

17. I encourage the child to use compound and complex sentences rather than simple short sentences all the time.
18. If my child understands abstract words like courage, patience, tolerance etc., I encourage the child to use such words.
19. My use of language with my child does not tend to be impulsive but a well-thought out one.
20. I try to make the child see the other child's point of view in quarrels, play etc.
21. I take care that my child does not remain, absent from school.
22.* I am particular that my child should reach school in time.
23. I buy games and toy articles for my child which help in his/her intellectual development.
24. I encourage my child to study alone.
25. I ask my child how the day was in school and what happened.
26. I spend some time reading to my child, or telling stories, or giving interesting puzzles to solve.
27. I encourage my child to have a hobby like stamp collection, coins collection, etc.
28. I make it a point to attend any function in which my child is participating.

* Items (1, 15 and 22) are not to be scored in the final scoring.

## 21A8 TEACHERS' SELF-EVALUATION FORM

*Author:* Y.P. Singh.

*Availability* : Author, Department of Extension, Haryana Agricultural University, Hissar.

*Uses* : For self-evaluation of teachers in Agricultural Universities following credit courses system. Purpose is that teachers know correctly their image as held by the pupils and their (students) opinion suggestion for improvement about the course.

*Time required* : 20 minutes.

*Level* : P.G. and U.G. Agriculture University Students.

*Main features* : A checklist.

*Scoring* : No scoring is done. Teachers see their weak and strong points.

## 21A8 TEACHERS' SELF-EVALUATION FORM

I. Attitude towards teaching (check more than one if applicable):
   1. Always seems to enjoy him teaching.
   2. Encourages discussion.
   3. Hopeful in answering questions.

II. Attitude towards students (check more than one if applicable):
   1. Is easy to talk to both in and out of class.
   2. Seems interested in students.
   3. Gives extra help to students who ask for it.
   4. Courteous and considerate.
   5. Often inconsiderate.

III. Open mindedness:
   1. Welcomes differences of viewpoint on controversial issues.
   2. Tolerant.
   3. Does not encourage difference of opinion.

IV. Ability to arouse interest in the subject:
   1. Stimulates independent study and effort.
   2. Creates only mild interest in the subject.
   3. Does not create interest in the subject.

V. Ability to stimulate thinking:
   1. Thinking encouraged.
   2. Thinking discouraged.
   3. Too much memorisation.

VI. Knowledge of subject matter:
   1. Sound and up-to-date.
   2. Covers major points only.
   3. Shallow.

VII. Ability to present subject matter:
   1. Presentation is clear, definite and forceful.
   2. Usually clear, but sometimes confusing.
   3. Frequently vague.
   4. Fails to point out relative importance of items.
   5. Sometimes mechanical and monotonous.

VIII. Personal appearance:
   1. Always neatly dressed.
   2. Usually neatly dressed.
   3. Often untidy.

IX. Course organisation:
   1. Logical sequence which is easy to understand and follow.
   2. Occasionally confusing.
   3. Difficult to understand and follow.

X. Number of assignments:
   1. Excessive.
   2. Optimum.
   3. Meagre.

XI. Course contents:
   1. Covers too much ground.
   2. Reasonable for the time and credit.
   3. Covers too little ground.

XII. Comprehension difficulties:
   1. Most difficult parts of this course are ______________________
   2. More time should have been spent on covering ______________
   3. In my opinion ______________ course should be pre-requisite for this course.

XIII. Laboratory facilities:
   1. Adequate.
   2. Moderately adequate.
   3. Inadequate.

XIV. Library resources for the course:
   1. Plenty of books on this course.

2. A few books.
3. Number of books not proportionate to the number of readers.
4. Important books not available in the library.

XV. Personal help:
1. Got great deal of personal help.
2. Got quite a bit of personal help.
3. Got some help.
4. Could not get personal help from the instructor, he is always busy.

XVI. Utility perception:
1. Will be extremely valuable to me for my professional activities.
2. Will probably be valuable to me for my professional activities.
3. Will probably be not valuable to me professional activities.

XVII. Examination and quizzes:
1. Too many quizzes.
2. Reasonable number of examinations.
3. Too few examinations.
4. Examinations too long and lengthy.
5. Grading explained when papers are returned.

XVIII. Question papers:
1. Good
2. Moderate
3. Stiff.

XIX. How do you rate your teacher?
1. Outstanding
2. Very good
3. Good
4. Fairly good.
5. Average.

## Instruments with technical information B

21B1 EDUCATIONAL ASPIRATION INVENTORY SCHEDULE

*Author* : S.P. Jain, National Institute of Community Development, Rajendranagar, Hyderabad-30.

*Availability* : Author.

*Uses* : Measuring the educational aspiration of the fathers for their sons and daughters in relation to caste and class background.

*Time required* : About half an hour.

*Level* : Head of the household.

*Main features* : It contains questions related to the socio-economic background of the household head and his aspirations. In addition there were numerous questions on other aspects of the study. In order to measure the educational aspirations of the heads of the household, they were asked to state the level of education which they *intend* to provide to their children irrespective of their capacity.

*Scoring* : Simple frequency counts.

*Reference:* Jain, S.P. Religion, caste, class and parental educational aspiration in a north Indian community. *Indian Educational Review,* 1969, 4(2), 64 72.

## 21B2 PIAGETIAN TASK TEST

*Author* : H.N. Majoo.

*Availability* : Author, Lecturer in Education, Department of Education, Lucknow University.

*Uses* : To study the concept formation in children.

*Main features* : The test situations study the concepts of conservatism, length, mass, weight, correspondence, transitionality, ordinal and cardinal relations, serial correspondence, additive composition etc.

## 21B3 ROLE PERCEPTION INVENTORY

*Authors* : S.S. Mathur and P. Sethi.

*Availability* : Author.

*Level* : School teachers and headmasters.

*Main features* : It contains 100 items representing five different aspects of school administration (a) administration, (b) teaching, (c) supervision and inspection, (d) school administrator and his relations with teachers and pupils, and (e) administrator and community.

*Scoring* : Scale values of items are given.

*Reference* : Mathur, S.S. and Sethi, P. Perceptions of the role of school administrator by the school principals and teachers. *Educational Trends,* 1972, 6(3-4), 12-21.

## 21B4 RATING SCALE

*Authors* : Hemkanta Misra and Durganand Sinha.

*Availability*; From the first author, NCERT, Mehrauli Road, New Delhi-16.

*Uses* : To determine the pattern of traits perceived to be "relevant to success" in engineering profession and education.

*Time required* : About 40 minutes.

*Level* : Originally used on engineering colleges, could be used with adults.

*Main features* : It is in two forms. First form is provided to rate the traits of relevance to success as a student of engineering and another was an 8-point scale. The rating scale was annexed to the traits list. Each trait is defined. The definitions were judged by three Psychologists for communicability and 20 Engineering teachers for preparing relevance.

*Validity* : Face validity was established from a consensus of 20 Engineering teachers.

*References* :

1. Misra, H. and Sinha, D. Qualities desirable for engineering students and professions: Part II. students' sample, *Journal of Psychological Researches,* 1961, 5, No. 2, pp. 53-62.
2. Misra, H. and Sinha, D. Qualities desirable for engineering students and professions: Part III Comparison of the Teachers' and students'

samples. *Journal of Psychological Researches*, 1963, 7, No. 1.

3. Misra, H. and Sinha, D. Non-inellectuaal factors for success in Engineering Education in India, Sinha, Misra, Kanth and Rao (eds.). Contributions to Psychology, Institute for Social and Psychological Research, New Delhi, 1968, 126-132.

21B5 ENVIRONMENTAL STUDY FORM

*Authors* : B.K. Passi and W.S. Waraich.

*Availability* : Authors, Department of Education, Panjab University, Chandigarh.

*Uses* : To study the environmental conditions having bearing upon the scholastic achievement of the students. The contents are from health, socio-economic status, neighbourers and peers, games and other activities, and school environment.

*Time required* : No time limit but ordinarily it takes around 10 minutes.

*Level* : High school boys.

*Main features* : It is a scale.

*Scoring* : Stencil scoring in which positive and negative weightages are given to items.

*Validity* : Content validation.

*Reference* : Passi, B.K. and Waraich, W.S. Comparative study of self-concept of over-achievers and under-achievers at XI Grade level. *New Trends in Education*, 1971, 2(2), 9-15.

21B6 SCALE FOR LEVEL OF EDUCATIONAL ASPIRATION

*Author* : P.M. Patel.

*Availability* : Author, National Institute of Education, Sri Aurobindo Marg, New Delhi-16.

*Time required* : 5 minutes.

*Level* : 13+ to 18+ (adolescents).

*Main features* : It is a rating scale. Available in Gujarati also.

*Scoring* : Objective.

*Norms* : Available.

*Reference:* : Bhatt, L.J., Patel, P.M., Patel, M.M., and Parikh, D.S. *Inquiry into Psychological Factors related to Adolescent Adjustment.* Report of the Indian Council of Medical Research Project, Baroda : Faculty of Education and Psychology, 1960.

21B7 PARENT-TEACHER EXPECTATION INVENTORY

*Author* : P.M. Patel.

*Availability* : Author, National Institute of Education, Sri Aurobindo Marg, New Delhi-16.

*Time required* : 15 minutes.

*Level* : Parents and teachers.

*Main features* : Questionnaire.

*Scoring* : Free-response analysis.

*Reference* : Patel, P.M. Parent-Teacher Expectations Inventory. *Journal of the*

*M.S. University f Baroda*, 7, 1958, 39-52.

21B8 YOUTH INVENTORY

*Author* : P.T. Raval.
*Availability* : Faculty of Education and Psychology, M.S. University, Baroda.
*Level* : 13 to 19 years students.
*Main features* : Verbal test with total number of sub-test 7; total number of items 140.
*Reliability* : Test-retest reliability coefficient was found to be .65.

21B9 SEMANTIC DIFFERENTIAL SCALE

*Authors* : R.P. Singh and S.N. Sharma.
*Availability* : From the authors.
*Uses* : For assessing teaching effectiveness at secondary school level.
*Time required* : 5 minutes.
*Level* : Secondary school students.
*Main features* : Consists of 15 semantic scales (adjectives and anonyms) related to effectiveness in the student learning at the secondary school level.
*Scoring* : Summated ratings technique is applied. Each semantic scale receives a weight from 1 to 7.
*Reliability* : Reliability coefficients range from .92 to .93.
*Reference:* Singh, R.P. and Sharma, S.N. Semantic differential scale for secondary school students, *Indian Journal of Psychometry and Education*, 1971, 2(1-2), 17-20.

21B10 HUMAN RELATIONSHIPS QUESTIONNAIRE

*Author* : R.S. Thakar.
*Availability* : Author, Faculty of Education and Psychology, M.S. University, Baroda.
*Level* : 14 to 18 years boys and girls.
*Main features* : It consists of 4 sub-tests.

# 2. Student Problems

## Complete instruments A

22A1 STUDENT PROBLEMS INVENTORY

*Author* : H.D. Badami
*Availability* Author, Department of Psychology, University School of Psychology, Education and Philosophy, Ahmedabad-9.
*Uses* : Individual and group guidance, research purposes. Available in English and Gujarati, Languages.
*Time required* : 60 minutes.
*Level* : College and post-graduate students.
*Main features* : Checklist type inventory covering nine areas of student adjustment: physical health and fitness, self-image, economic facilities, friendship, family, social, educational vocational, religious etc.
*Scoring* : Total no. of problems checked.
*Norms* : Quartile norms for class-wise and sex-wise groups on 1,364 and 383 males and females from colleges and university departments are available.
*Reference* : Badami, H.D. *Student Problems Inventory: Manual.* Gujarat University Press, Ahmedabad.

22A1 STUDENT PROBLEMS INVENTORY

(The following problems have to be checked).

PART I

1. I am overweight/underweight.
2. I am too tall/short.
3. I have weak eyesight.
4. I have ear trouble.
5. I have tooth trouble.
6. I cannot hear clearly.
7. I have frequent headaches.
8. I catch cold easily.
9. I have stomach trouble.
10. I have heart trouble.
11. I have anemic condition.
12. I have poor digestion.
13. I have weak health.

14. I am loosing hair.
15. I am unable to participate in many activities because of poor health.
16. I need medical care.
17. My muscles always ache.
18. I feel tired even after a good night's rest.
19. I have physical defect.
20. I oversleep.

PART II

21. I am too much emotional.
22. I get nervous while talking with other people.
23. I feel lonely.
24. I am unable to stand criticism.
25. I find difficulty in expressing myself.
26. I am careless.
27. I am very stubborn.
28. I have inferiority complex.
29. I have superiority complex.
30. I do not have self-confidence.
31. I do not have enough courage.
32. I am unable to understand myself.
33. Some people are more active than I.
34. I feel life dull and uninteresting.
35. I hate myself.
36. I feel like committing suicide.
37. I feel like taking revenge.
38. I get excited very easily.
39. I am unable to control my temperament.
40. I am timid.
41. I am unable to bear even the slightest scolding.
42. I am married at an early age.
43. I am unable to adjust to the circumstances.
44. I am betrayed by my friends.
45. I do not get appreciation in any kind of work.
46. I am suspicious by nature.
47. I get easily tired.
48. I have bad complexion.
49. I have poor appearance.
50. I get tired because of many activities.
51. I get easily nervous.
52. I am too much self-conscious.
53. I do not have an intimate friend.
54. I take everything seriously.
55. I do not have interest in any kind of activity.
56. I am afraid of shouldering adult responsibilities.
57. I am afraid of committing mistakes.
58. I am afraid of failure in whatever I undertake.
59. I have many problems at a time.

60. I have fear of accident.
61. I cannot stop worrying.
62. I feel home sick.
63. I am bothered by mechanical city life.
64. I get nervous when I do not get cooperation.
65. I get easily offended.
66. I am unable to go to bed when desired.
67. I am unable to get up when desired.
68. I am unable to get enough sleep.
69. I am unable to do something good as desired.
70. I have no goals in life.
71. I need someone for proper guidance.
72. I want to know how to get rid of bad habits.
73. I want to learn how to depend on myself.
74. I am unable to solve difficulties.
75. I find difficult to select right type of clothes.
76. I do not have a nack for talking with other people.
77. I am unable to plan in advance.
78. I am unable to feel free to talk about personal difficulties to other people.
79. I cannot make day-to-day planning.
80. I cannot forget the past.
81. I am unable to do many things which other persons are able to do.
82. I am unable to do things at the right moment.
83. I cannot decide about my interests.
84. I am unable to complete whatever I undertake.
85. I am unable to improve my temperament.
86. I argue too much.
87. I quarrel on small matters.
88. I do not have different activities.
89. I waste too much time on radio and movies.
90. I waste too much time in day-dreaming.
91. I often tell what I should not tell.
92. I often do what I should not do.
93. I always get late.
94. I get night mares.
95. I have nocturnal discharge.
96. I am worried because of watching several movies.
97. I want to get rid of masturbation.

PART III

98. I do not have enough clothes.
99. I do not know about different types of entertainments.
100. I do not have steady income.
101. Mother has to work for maintaining family.
102. Family runs short of money.
103. I need work to help the family.
104. I do not have a radio set at home.

105. I do not have enough space in the house.
106. I do not have the house in a good locality.
107. I do not have enough space for study at home.
108. I do not have money for entertainment.
109. I do not have enough money.
110. I am unable to purchase educational necessities.
111. I am too extravagant.
112. I want to earn enough money.
113. I do not get proper food.
114. I experience difficulty in fulfilling my basic needs of life.

PART IV

115. I need sex knowledge.
116. I hate opposite sex.
117. I want to be attractive to the opposite sex.
118. I am unable to get along well with the opposite sex.
119. I am much haunted by thoughts of the opposite sex.
120. I get easily excited sexually.
121. I become easily nervous while talking with opposite sex.
122. I have too much attraction for opposite sex.
123. I do not know when to marry.
124. I am worried whether the parents will give consent for love marriage.
125. I am unable to decide whether to marry according to personal choice or parent's choice.
126. I am married against will.
127. I need divorce.
128. I am unhappy in married life.
129. I find difficulty in getting a suitable life partner.
130. I am worried about success in married life.
131. My marriage problem bothers me much.
132. I am in extra-marital love.
133. I am afraid of failure in love.
134. I am in love with one whom I am unable to marry.
135. I am frustrated in love.
136. I am unable to cultivate friendship with opposite sex.
137. I find difficulty in making friends.
138. I do not have many friends.
139. I do not know how to maintain friendship.
140. I am bothered by the fact that heterosexual friendship is looked upon with suspicion.
141. I do not have freedom in selection of my friends.
142. My parents/guardians put too many restrictions on me.
143. I find my parents/guardians confused.
144. My parents/guardians are conservative.
145. My parents/guardians neglect me.
146. My parents/guardians make many false allegations against me.
147. My parents/guardians do not give freedom to select my future career.
148. My parents/guardians are suspicious.

149. My parents/guardians do not allow me to go out of the city for study.
150. My parents/guardians do not allow me to take my own decisions.
151. My husband/wife is always nagging me.
152. My husband/wife is suspicious towards me.
153. My parents/guardians expect too much from me.
154. My parents/guardians do not understand me.
155. My husband/wife does not understand me.
156. My husband/wife inquires too much about all kinds of my activities.
157. My parents/guardians inquire too much about all kinds of my activities.
158. At times I have to tell a lie to my parents/guardians for getting things done.
159. Whenever I do something wrong, I am afraid to tell my parents/guardians.
160. My parents/guardians do not ask my opinion in important family matters.
161. I cannot discuss any matters freely with my parents/guardians.
162. I dislike my parents/guardians.
163. My parents/guardians quarrel with each other.
164. My parents/guardians getting nervous frequently.
165. My parents/guardians are irritable.
166. My husband/wife is irritable.
167. My parents/guardians have to suffer too much for me.
168. I have difference of opinion with my parents/guardians.
169. I am being forced to join business of my parents/guardians.
170. My parents/guardians are illiterate.
171. I feel like running away from home.
172. I find my home atmosphere tense.
173. I have to take care of other children in the family.
174. I have too many family responsibilities.
175. I lack feeling of oneness with my family.
176. I lack feeling of oneness with my husband/wife.
177. I am unhappy at home.
178. I am afraid of going home.
179. I have serious sickness in my family.
180. I do not have enough freedom at home.
181. I am unable to live away from my family.
182. I have to depend upon my parents/guardians in money matters.
183. My siblings always hinder my work.
184. My parents/guardians do not do as much for me as they do for my brother(s) sister(s).
185. I have no brother/sister.

## PART V

186. I am not sociable.
187. People do not like me.
188. I have too narrow a social circle.
189. I want to be liked by others.
190. Everyone is against me.
191. I am considered responsible for that for which I am not at fault.

192. I am being forced into marriage.
193. I want to rebel against authority.
194. I am bothered by people who treat me as a child.
195. I do not like certain things just for the sake of popularity.
196. I want many things which other people have.
197. I cannot participate with enthusiasm in social functions.
198. I do not know how to say 'No' without injuring others feelings.
199. I am unable to get along with others.
200. I do not know to deal with proud people.
201. I do not know how to deal with hypocrites.
202. I do not know how to deal with undependable people.
203. I do not know how to deal with people who take advantage of me.
204. I do not know how to deal with selfish people.
205. I do not know how to deal with people who consider money everything.
206. I do not know how to deal with people who laugh at things they do not understand.
207. I am bothered about people finding fault with me.
208. I am bothered about people who spread gossip about me.
209. I am bothered by people who give their opinion thoughtlessly.

PART VI

210. I want to improve my English.
211. I am unable to understand text books.
212. I find some subjects difficult.
213. I do not know whether I have selected right courses.
214. I am unable to select courses of my choice.
215. I do not have enough books.
216. I find difficulty in getting books from the library.
217. I am slow in reading.
218. I am unable to learn quickly.
219. I am unable to follow lectures in English.
220. I do not get necessary guidance for studies.
221. I am unable to read at night.
222. I find college dull and uninteresting.
223. I find college time table unsuitable.
224. I do not get enough time for study.
225. I am irregular in studies.
226. I am unable to remember what is studied.
227. I do not know how to study.
228. I have a poor memory.
229. I am unable to concentrate on studies.
230. I am unable to speak before the class.
231. I am unable to decide about my studies.
232. I am worried whether I will be able to complete my studies.
233. I am unable to do extra readings.
234. I do not like to study.
235. I am bothered by being forced to study.
236. I am bothered because of peoples' attitude towards Arts education.

237. It is difficult to purse studies due to marriage.
238. I find some teachers with no grasp over their subject matter.
239. I find some teachers having no interest in students.
240. I find some teachers giving importance to their subjects only.
241. Some teachers disappoint me.
242. I find some teachers unable to explain their subject matter properly.
244. I find some teachers making fun of me in the class.
245. I am disliked by some teachers.
246. I do not like some teachers.
247. I find some teachers discriminating between students.
248. I am bothered by the fact that some teachers do not finish their courses.
249. Some teachers are boring.
250. I am worried by the fact that the students are evaluated only on the basis of examination.
251. I am worried about getting class in the examination.
252. I am afraid of examination.
253. I am worried about success in the examination.
254. I am unable to get good grades in spite of hard work.
255. I am bothered by the partiality in the internal marking system.
256. I find too much work in the college.
257. I am unable to make progress in the college.
258. I have to spend much time in college work.
259. I waste too much time in the college.
260. I need more educational activities in college.
261. I do not get proper opportunity to develop my abilities in college.
262. I do not have intellectual freedom in college.
263. I find some college rules and regulations unjust.
264. I am bothered by prevalence of influence in the college.

PART VII

265. I do not get money according to worth of my work.
266. My work hinders the activity of my interest.
267. I want to know how to select right kind of vocation.
268. I need a part time job.
269. I need a job.
270. I do not like present job.
271. I doubt whether I will get a job after completing my studies.
272. I do not know how to get a job.
273. I do not know how far study will help me in my future vocation.
274. I am worried about my future career.
275. I am bothered by the present problem of unemployment.

PART VIII

276. I want to know how to develop my character.
277. I am bothered by customs like dowry in marriage.
278. I am unable to marry outside my caste.
279. I do not like religious ceremonies.

280. I am bothered by unlawful behaviour of my friends.
281. I am bothered by lack of morality in elderly and respectable people.
282. I am bothered by immoral thoughts.
283. My conscience bites.
284. Sometimes I am unable to understand what is right and what is wrong.
285. I have difference of opinion with family in religious matters.
286. I have to perform religious ceremonies because of the family pressures.
287. I doubt the existence of God.
288. I am unable to live according to the dictates of my religion.
289. I am unable to understand what is heaven and what is hell.
290. I find difficult to live morally.
291. I am unable to live according to the ideals of life.
292. I hate mankind.
293. I do not have respect for religion.

## 22A2 D-I INVENTORY

*Authors* : Pratibha Deo and S.K. Bhalla.
*Availability* : Authors, Department of Education, Panjab University, Chandigarh.
*Uses* : For objectively identifying indisciplined and disciplined students.
*Time required* : No time limit but ordinarily takes about 30 to 40 minutes.
*Level:* High school, college and university students of professional colleges. Adult males and females can take this inventory.
*Main features:* It is a projective instrument, inventory type consisting of 25 items. Each item has a pair of statements which are equated on social desirability or undesirability. Forced choice technique is used so that a subject taking the inventory must choose one of the statements in each item. Every statement has been given a weightage on the basis of its capacity of discrimination determined in three pilot studies. Available in Hindi as well as English languages.
*Scoring* : Weightage has been assigned on the basis of power of discriminating between the two groups. Scoring is based on the weightages.
*Reliability* : Test-retest reliability coefficient (45 days interval) was found to be 0.68 on a sample of 150 subjects.
*Validity* : Item-validity was established by point biserial correlation.
*Norms* : Percentile norms are based on 900 students.
*References* :

1. Deo, Pratibha and Bhalla, S.K. Construction of an inventory for identifying indisciplined students. *Educational Series*, 1969, I (1 and 2), 15-24.
2. Bhalla, S.K. A comparative study of the self-concept of disciplined and indisciplined students, Ph.D. Thesis, Panjab University, 1970.

## 22A2 D-I INVENTORY

(Preferences for one in each of the following pairs of items have to be indicated).

1. A. Conflict with the authorities should be resolved by trying to find out

some middle way for settlement.

B. College union should function in consultation with the principal.

2. A. Strict marking on the part of teachers is mainly responsible for poor results.

B. Failures in examinations can be attributed more to the inefficiency and irresponsibility of teachers.

3. A. It is improper to take unnecessary advantage of a teacher who is lenient.

B. Peculiar habits of the teacher in the course of his lecture should not be laughed at.

4. A. Telling lies is also a way of escaping punishment.

B. Besides providing the pleasure of adventure stealing helps one in need.

5. A. When all local colleges observe strike to sympathise with the strikers of one college they should be allowed to do so.

B. College association's elections are in a trial of strength. So, forming parties is essential for this purpose.

6. A. It is improper to laugh in the sleeves after having been scolded by the teacher.

B. In case of grievance against a teacher one should better try to understand the teacher than bear a grudge against him.

7. A. Faltering or stuttering on the part of teacher in the course of the lecture should not be laughed at.

B. Due regards should be paid to a teacher who is ugly but who teaches nicely.

8. A. One should be sympathetic with the handicapped and old persons rather than make fun of them.

B. It is better to wait for one's turn than to push the persons standing ahead in the queue.

9. A. Practice of expelling students should be abandoned altogether as it is the question of their career.

B. Damaging things shows the attitude of opposition. So, it gives the authorities an opportunity to take into consideration the opposite point of view.

10. A. Copying should not be objected to because in some advanced countries books can be consulted in the examination hall.

B. Authorities have not right to take measures against eveteasing, since attraction between the opposite sexes is quite natural.

11. A. Constant criticism of authorities is desirable since it keeps them vigilant.

B. Studentship is a period of allround training. Political training can be had by participating in political demonstrations against government policies.

12. A. When the Principal gives some advice to the students in the college assembly they should hear it patiently.

B. Students should adopt the high ideals of their teachers in their practical life.

13. A. Attendance at the house examination should be made compulsory because it develops regular study habits.

B. Nothing is difficult for the hard-working and painstaking students.

14. A. There is nothing wrong in hooting down a new teachers as it provides a good fun.

    B. Ragging of new-comers is an old practice and should not be given up as it helps them adjust to the new surroundings.

15. A. Authorities should not take a serious view of hooliganism at pubic places by students because youth is an age of adventure and activity.

    B. Police authorities use unjust means to suppress students whenever the latter rise to redress their grievances.

16. A. Talking in the library room is a good entertainer after laborious hours of reading.

    B. Marking of passages in a book drawn from the library saves the bothering of taking down notes.

17. A. Enjoying many leaves goes against the interests of regular study habits.

    B. Late coming should be discouraged if peace is to be maintained in the classroom.

18. A. Going to the night show and entering the hostel from the backdoor is not a fun worth having.

    B. Habit of slipping out of the class after the roll call cannot be appreciated even if there is some urgent work.

19. A. Puncturing the cycles or hiding the belongings of others cannot be regarded as innocent fun.

    B. One should better put up with the quality of meals provided in the hostel than break the crockery as a protest.

20. A. Switching off lights and fans in the college. When they are not needed, is a very unpleasant and unnecessary task.

    B. Calling proxies shows the sense of give and take prevailing in the class.

21. A. Smoking in the educational institutions should not receive encouragement.

    B. Addressing friends and class-fellows in foul language does not behave a student.

22. A. It is better to shout and hoot down the opponent team rather than lose the game.

    B. Judgement of the umpires in the match is influenced by favouritism. So, it should not be binding upon one to accept them.

23. A. One should cartoon the teacher to show one's angry feelings.

    B. Playing foul is justified when one is bent upon winning the match.

24. A. Home work should be made compulsory so that the students follow the subject-matter and become regular in their work.

    B. Habit of sitting on back benches should be avoided for the sake of serious study.

25. A. When authorities are too late to administer justice hunger strikes are the only course left to draw their attention.

    B. In view of soaring prices and government's unscrupulous taxation policy students should hold frequent demonstrations, since all these things go to make education costier.

## 22A3 STUDENT PROBLEMS QUESTIONNAIRE

*Author* : A. Hafeez.
*Availability* : Author, Department of Industrial Management, Indian Institute of Science, Bangalore-12.
*Uses* : Counselling.
*Levels* : Students.

## 22A3 STUDENT PROBLEMS QUESTIONNAIRE

(The following items have to be checked for yes, no responses).

1. Transport to and from the Institute is a serious problem.
2. At night dogs and birds in the Institute premises become a nuisance.
3. The single rooms in the hostel converted into double rooms are narrow and too small for two people.
4. Some of the books prescribed as text-books cannot be bought because they are either too costly or are not available with book sellers.
5. There are no proper outlets for social contacts and social life in this Institute.
6. I do not have the sufficient information about matters of sex.
7. I do not know the proper methods of study.
8. There is no proper guide to direct the new students and their visitors, to them.
9. The services of a tailor for minor repair like patching etc. are needed in the Institute.
10. Double rooms are inconvenient as friends of the room mate come and disturb.
11. Most of the time is spent at the department and no time is available for rest or study.
12. No proper help is being received by the students in the institute from teachers.
13. (a) How much time can you spare for activities like sports and games per day ?
    (b) How much time can you spare per day for cultural activities like social clubs and dramatics, debating societies etc.
14. I do not know how to make friends among the opposite sex.
15. English language is a difficult medium for me to understand the lectures.
16. There is no "centralised time" like a clock tower in the Institute.
17. The climate is not very helpful for people of studious habits, as it makes one lazy and sleepy.
18. Rooms are not swept clean as regularly as they should be.
19. There is no proper supply of copies of syllabi for each subject.
20. (a) Are you receiving help from anybody to solve your problems?
    (b) If 'yes' who is helping you? Mention the person's position?
21. Departments are situated far apart and time is lost due to the improper type of arranging time tables.
22. In the hostel rooms, there is not enough illumination for reading.

23. Mosquitoes are a nuisance in the rooms.
24. The N.C.C. training comes in the way of studies and rest.
25. There is no proper course specialisation in the Institute.
26. I cannot read fast enough to complete my studies on time.
27. There is no banking facility on the premises of the I.I.Sc. due to which a great deal of time is wasted.
28. Some of the laboratory buildings are old and leak in the rainy season.
29. Lavatories are not kept regularly cleaned as they should be.
30. There are far too many submissions and tests, which leave no room for study and rest.
31. There is no frequent use of black boards by the teaching staff to make lectures more clear and understandable.
32. Some of the electrical connections in the laboratories have become old and give shocks.
33. Food is one of the biggest problems in the hostel, as it is
    (a) not tasty
    (b) it does not contain north Indian dishes
    (c) servers are not clean.
    (d) service is not adequate to cope with the rush at meal times
    (e) either all the dishes are good at the same time or none of them is good.
34. There is no proper exchange of thoughts and contacts between teachers and students in the Institute.
35. Library facilities are not adequate.
    (a) As there is only one copy of each book.
    (b) Sometimes very old editions are not replaced by the latest ones.
    (c) Books are not systematically arranged.
36. There are not adequate sports facilities like more tennis courts availability of a net and ball etc.
37. Low speech audibility on the part of the some teachers has come in the way of following properly, the lectures in the class.
38. There is no time available for reading anything except the subjects for tests and submissions.
39. Teachers expect too much from the students in their concerned subjects. This comes in the way of the students' other interests, activities etc.
40. Teachers seem to have developed a preference towards old students as against new students.

# B Instruments with technical information

## 22B1 SCHOOL ADJUSTMENT INVENTORY

*Authors* : P.A. Abraham and E.I George.
*Availability* : Authors, Department of Psychology, Kerala University, Trivendrum.
*Level* : High school students.

*Main features* : It is a 35-item inventory.

*Reliability* : Reliability coefficient was found to be .75.

*Reference* : Abraham, P.A. and George, E.I. A comparative study of leaders and non-leaders among pupils in secondary schools. *Journal of Psychological Researches,* 1966, 10(3), 116-119.

22B2 SOCIAL ADJUSTMENT INVENTORY

*Author* : H.D. Badami.

*Availability* : Author, Department of Psychology, School of Psychology, Education and Philosophy, Gujarat University, Ahmedabad-9.

*Uses* : Guidance and counselling.

*Time required* : 15 minutes.

*Main features* : Self-administered inventory. Available in Gujarati.

*Scoring* : Counting adjustment responses to the questions.

*Reliability* : Test-retest reliability was found to be .85. Split-half reliability was found to be .90.

*Validity* : Validated against interview data and teachers' estimates of adjustment. Validated with other tests and contrasted groups.

*Norms* : Given in T scores, standardised on a sample of 2,912 males and females selected from some districts of Gujarat state.

*Reference* : Badami, H.D. Development of the Family and Social Adjustment Inventories, *Vidya — Journal of Gujarat University,* 1970, 13(1).

22B3 STUDENT PROBLEM CHECKLIST

*Author* : Central Bureau of Educational and Vocational Guidance.

*Uses* : Guidance and counselling.

*Time required* : 20 to 40 minutes.

*Level* : High school students.

*Main features* : Hindi, Malayalam, Telugu, Kannada, Gujarati, Marathi, Bengali and Assamese versions are available.

*Reliability* : Test-retest reliability was found to be .92 (N=97)

22B4 STUDENTS PROBLEM CHECKLIST.

*Authors* : Educational and Vocational Guidance Centre, Aligarh Muslim University.

*Availability* : Authors.

*Level* : College and university students.

*Main features* : It contains 200 problems on ten areas : health, finances, social relations, psychological relations, sex and marriage, home and family, moral and religious aspects academic and curricular aspects, teaching and vocational aspects. Available only in Hindi and Urdu.

22B5 YOUTH PROBLEM INVENTORY

*Author* : S.S. Kulkarni.

*Main features* : It consists of 8 sub-tests : problems related to school (40 items), after high school (29 items), self, getting along with others (48 items), home and family (47 items), boys'-girls' relations, (22 items), health (28 items), and general (28 items).

*Reliability* : Internal consistency coefficients computed by Hoytts. ANOV Technique : For sub-test I=.82; II=.86; III=.87; IV=.89; V=91; VI=.88; VII=.87; VIII=.90.

*Validity* : The test differentiated significantly between mean scores on such variables as socio-economic status, regions, grade, sex, age, caste, fathers' education, and mothers' education. As most of these results were hypothesised on the basis of field theory and previous, empirical research, the instruments can be said to have construct validity.

## 22B6 SOCIAL ADJUSTMENT INVENTORY

*Authors* : P.M. Patel, M.M. Patel, D.S. Parikh, M.N. Palsane, M.B. Buch, Jamanaji Parikh.

*Availability* : P.M. Patel, National Institute of Education, Sri Aurobindo Marg, New Delhi-16.

*Time required* : 10 minutes.

*Level* : 13+ to 18+ (adolescents).

*Main features* : Standardised inventory. Available in Gujarati only.

*Norms* : Available.

*Reference* : Bhatt, L.J., Patel P.M., Patel, M.M. and Parikh, D.S. *Inquiry into Psychological Factors related to Adolescent Adjustment.* Report of the Indian Council of Medical Research Project, Baroda: Faculty of Educational and Psychology, 1960.

## 22B7 STUDENT MORALE (A STUDY OF STUDENT OPINIONS)

*Author* : S. Narayana Rao.

*Availability* : Author, Department of Psychology, S.V. University, Tirupati, A.P.

*Uses* : Counselling.

*Time required* : About 30 minutes.

*Level* : College students.

*Main features* : It is a self-administered 5-point rating scale.

*Scoring* : Key is given in the manual. Numerical weights 0-4 are assigned to each item. Summation of the weights is the final score.

*Reliability* : Split-half reliability coefficient was found to be 0.97 and test-retest coefficient was found to be 0.86.

*Validity* : Validity coefficient of 0.64 was obtained with teachers, ratings and 0.81 with Morale part of the Minnessota Personality Scale.

*Norms* : Available on 435 men college students.

*References* :

1. Rao, S.N. A study of student opinions. *Psychological Studies,* 1967, 12(2)
2. Rao, S.N. *Student Performance and Adjustment,* S.V. University, Tirupati, 1967.

22B8 RATING SCALE

*Availability* : Authors, DPFE, National Institute of Education, Sri Aurobindo Marg, New Delhi-16.

*Uses* : For the assessment of the personality as well as the environmental factors on individual students resulting in the development of unrest in P.G. students.

*Level* : Post-graduate students.

*Main features* : The questionnaire contains seven broad factors with several items in each head. In questionnaire points like physical, intellectual, and temperamental inheritance of the subjects were included; environmental and psychological conditions were also emphasised. The main areas were : (1) Social, educational, and economic background, (2) Health, play, recreation, (3) Attitude towards family politics, (4) Intelligence, (5) Temperamental. Three points on the scale are chosen, according to the gradations of intensity of different factors.

*Scoring* : Three-point summated ratings.

*Reliability* : The measures of the reliability of the questionnaire according to Rulons formula stands as : 0.978.

*Reference* : Roy, Biswanath and Boral Biswanath. Some factors of unrest among post-graduate students. *Psychological Studies,* 1964, 9(1), 44-51.

# 3. Interests and Preferences

## B Instruments with technical information

### 23B1 VOCATIONAL INTEREST INVENTORY

*Author* : H.D. Badami.

*Availability* : Author, Department of Psychology, University School of Psychology, Education and Philosophy, Gujarat University, Ahmedabad-9.

*Uses* : Guidance and counselling.

*Time required* : About 15 minutes.

*Level* : College and senior high school students.

*Main features* : Available in Gujarati. It gives a profile showing relative interests in various occupational areas.

*Reliability* : Reliability coefficients for ten different interest scores range from .78 to .90.

*Validity* : Validated against several professional groups.

*Norms* : Average profile is given for the purpose of comparison.

*References* :

1. Badami, H.D. The development of vocational interest inventory. *Indian Journal of Applied Psychology,* 1968, 5(2).
2. Badami, H.D. The validation of the vocational interest inventory against various groups of workers in different vocational areas. *Indian Journal of Applied Psychology,* 1970, 6(2).

### 23B2 OCCUPATIONAL AND AVOCATIONAL INTEREST RECORD

*Author* : S.B.L. Bharadwaj.

*Availability* : Author, Directorate of Psychological Research, Ministry of Defence, New Delhi.

*Time required* : About 2 hours.

*Level* : Graduates.

*Main features* : It consists of two scales (occupational and avocational) each scale containing 140 items.

*Reliability* : Split-half coefficients using Spearman-Brown correction range from .83 to .94 for the different categories of interests.

*Validity* : Content and construct validities have been worked out.

*Norms* : Available.

### 23B3 VYAVSAYA RUCHI KE JANCH

*Author* : Central Bureau of Educational and Vocational Guidance, New Delhi.

*Availability* : Author.
*Uses* : Guidance and counselling.
*Time required* : About 25 to 35 minutes.
*Level* : 11 to 16 years boys and girls.

23B4 CHATTERJI'S NON-LANGUAGE PREFERENCE RECORD

*Author* : S. Chatterji.
*Availability* : Author, Psychometry Unit, Indian Statistical Institute, 203, B.T. Road, Calcutta-35.
*Uses* : To measure the interest in ten broad areas: fine arts, technical, crafts, outdoor, sports, household work, scientific, literary etc.
*Level* : High school and college students.
*Main features* : Scenes of activity related to one or the other of the above ten areas are presented in triads. The respondent is required to choose from these figures.
*Scoring* : Key is available. Profiles of interests could be made out.
*Reliability* : Reliability coefficients using Kuder-Richardson formula 21 on a sample of 1300 range from .69 to .95 for the ten scales.
*Validity* : Concurrent validity was established indirectly as scales discriminated students in different disciplines in the expected directions. The correlation coefficients with Kuder's Preference Record on four scales (outdoor, scientific, literary and artistic) range from .22 to .45 (rho) and .13 to .29 (Pearsons r).
*Norms* : Norms are provided in the manual.
*References* :

1. Chatterji, S. *Development of a non-verbal interest inventory based on an adaptation of certain aspects of the Kuder Preference Record*, D. Phil Thesis, Calcutta University, 1960.
2. Chatterji, S., and Mukherjee Manjula. Relation between Kuder Preference Record and a non-verbal interest inventory modelled after it to suit Indian condition. *Journal of Psychological Researches*, 1932, 6(3), pp. 115-17.
3. Chatterji, S., & Mukherjee Manjula. Stability of measured interest, *Journal of Vocational and Educational Guidance*, 10(1), pp. 10-14.
4. Chatterji, S., Mukherjee Manjula, Bose Utpala and Sinha S. An investigation into the interest patterns of the students in Science, Humanities and Commerce streams at the higher secondary level, *Journal of Psychological Researches*, 1970, 14(1).
5. Chatterji, S., Mukherjee Manjula, Banerji Chhabi and Dutta, Anath. An investigation into the interest patterns of the deaf children, *Psychological Annual*, 1970, 4, pp. 40-44.

23B5 P.S.M. INTEREST INVENTORY (Hindi)

*Author* : College of Educational Psychology and Guidance, Jabalpur.
*Availability* : College of Educational Psychology and Guidance, Jabalpur.
*Uses* : Measurement of interest in school subjects to be used for allocation.
*Time required* : 20 minutes.

*Level*: Higher secondary classes — 8th to 11th (Hindi).
*Main features* : The inventory consists of 65 items, measures interest in 3 fields — Science, Agriculture and Technical. Responses are given in three categories, like indifference and dislike. The inventory is in Hindi.
*Scoring* : Scoring keys prepared by Garretson and Symond's approach, with weighted score.
*Reliability* : Split-half reliability co-efficients are .63, .66 and .67 for Science, Agriculture and Technical respectively.

23B6 CURRICULAR INTEREST INVENTORY

*Authors* : R.C. Das and K.B. Amanta.
*Availability* : State Bureau of Educational and Vocational Guidance, Cuttack, Orissa.
*Uses* : Guidance and counselling.
*Time required*: About an hour.
*Level*: Students of the age group of 13 to 16 years.
*Main features* : It is a 168-item test in Oriya.
*Reliability* : Split-half reliability coefficients range from .80 to .88 for different interest areas.
*Validity*: Validity coefficients with self-ratings of subjects range from .50 to .64.
*Norms* : Available on 200 students of Cuttack.

23B7 INTEREST TEST

*Author*: A. Hafeez.
*Availability* : Author, Department of Industrial Management, Indian Institute of Science, Bangalore-1, India.
*Uses* : Guidance and counselling.
*Time required*: No time limit.
*Level*: High school boys.
*Main features* : 101 jobs are taken from six job families, such as professional, clerical, agricultural, business and other areas and 'likes' (L), 'dislike' (D), and indifference (I) are computed. One more category (not aware of) is also included.
*Reference* : Hafeez, A. and Shanthamani. Interest patterns of high school leaving students. *Indian Journal of Social Work*, 1970, 30(4), 291-301.

23B8 VYAVASAYIK RUCHI KI JANCH

*Author*: V.G. Jhingran.
*Availability* : Guidance Section, Department of Psychological Foundations of Education, National Institute of Education, Sri Aurobindo Marg, New Delhi-16.
*Uses* : Guidance and counselling.
*Time required*: Approximately 1 hour.
*Level*: All.
*Main features* : It consists of 8 sub-tests in Hindi.
*Reliability*: Split-half reliabilities range from .59 to .95.

*Validity* : Validated against actual occupations entered by 73 subjects after graduation.

*Norms* : Available.

## 23B9 THE INTEREST — PARISUCHI

*Author*: S.P. Kulshrestha.

*Availability* : Commercially available. M/s. Rupa Psychological Corporation, Sora Kuan, Varanasi, (U.P.).

*Uses* : Devised to serve as a quick screening device for use with school and college students and was used for the purpose of guidance in the selection of different diversified courses and placement services.

*Time required* : No fixed time limit, but it takes about 30 to 40 minutes.

*Level* : School and college students.

*Main features* : It contains 350 educational and vocational activities and measures seven interest areas viz. arts and humanities, science, commerce, agriculture, home science, fine arts and technology. It is a half-forced choice and half simple choice parisuchi.

*Scoring* : Separate scoring key stencils are provided for each interest areas.

*Reliability* : Stability coefficients were found to be .78, .88, .81, .85, .77, .83 and .79 for arts and humanities, science, commerce, agriculture, home science and fine arts and technology respectively.

*Validity* : Content and construct validities were established. Correlation coefficient with friends' ratings were found to be .81, .82, .90, .82, .87, .77 and .83 and with teacher's rating .79, .80, .83, .79, .85 and .87 respectively for arts and humanities, science, commerce, agriculture, home science, fine arts and technology.

*Norms* : Norms are given for 900 students of VIII class and 600 students of X class.

*Reference* : Kulshrestha, S.P. Interest pattern of boys of Agra city. *Manika*, 1967, 2(2).

## 23B10 VOCATIONAL AND EDUCATIONAL INTEREST RECORD

*Authors* : S.P. Kulshrestha and O.P. Damle.

*Availability* : Commercially available. M/s. National Psychological Corporation, Labh Chand Market, Raja-ki-Mandi, Agra-2, (U.P.).

*Uses* : Designed as counselling instrument to serve as quick screening device for use with school and college students.

*Time required* : 10 minutes for vocational interests record and 5 minutes for educational interest record.

*Level* : School and college students.

*Main features* : It contains 200 vocational and 98 educational activities, ten areas are covered in vocation and seven in education.

*Scoring* : By counting the answers.

*Reliability* : For educational interest record the test-retest reliabilities were found to vary from 0.79 to 0.90 and for vocational interest record from 0.75 to 0.89.

*Validity* : For vocational record correlation coefficients with parents' rating were found to vary from .79 to .81, with friends opinion from .80 to .85 and with teacher's opinion from .78 to .83. For educational record correlation coefficients with teachers' opinion were found to vary from .75 to .90, and in a follow up study from .68 to .70.

*Norms* : Norms have been developed separately for educational and vocational interest record in the form of sten scores.

*Reference* : Kulshrestha, S.P. and Damle, O.P. Vocational interest of extroverts and introverts. *Journal of Psychology*, 1969, 1(1).

## 23B11 VOCATIONAL PREFERENCE RECORD

*Author* : Manovigyanshala, Allahabad, U.P.

*Availability* : Author.

*Uses* : Guidance and counselling.

*Time required* : About 30 minutes.

*Level* : For students of 10th and 11th standards.

*Main features* : It contains 10 scales in Hindi.

## 23B12 INTEREST INVENTORY

*Author* : J. Mascarenhas.

*Availability* : Author, St. Xavier's Institute of Education, 15 New Marine Lines, Bombay-1.

*Uses* : Guidance and counselling.

*Time required* : About 35 minutes.

*Level* : 14 to 18 years students.

*Main features* : It contains 150 items to measure interest in medicine, engineering, commerce, arts and fine arts. Translated version in Gujarati available.

*Reliability* : Test-retest reliabilities range from .81 to .90 for the five areas.

*Validity* : Validated against external criteria like hobbies etc.

*Norms* : Percentile norms available.

## 23B13 VOCATIONAL INTEREST INVENTORY

*Author* : V. George Mathew.

*Availability* : Author, Department of Psychology, Kerala University, Kariavattom, Kerala.

*Uses* : Originally developed to measure the vocational interest patterns of college students in Kerala who have completed two years of college education. The 7 scales are outdoor, mechanical, clerical, persuasive, aesthetic, social work and scientific.

*Time required* : One hour.

*Level* : English knowing persons in India.

*Main features* : The test has 92 forced choice items of the trial form. The testee has to select from among the three activities the one he likes most and the one he likes best.

*Scoring* : Separate answer sheet and seven stencils.

*Reliability* : Odd-even reliabilities range from 0.78 to 0.90.

*Validity* : Correlations of 0.26 to 0.59 are reported with an adaptation of study of values. Significant differences were obtained between college students specialising in nine fields of study.

*Norms* : T-score norms are available for men and women.

23B14 READING INTERESTS INVENTORY

*Author* : Manohar Priyamvade.

*Availability* : Author, c/o. Indian Institute of Education, Chembur, Bombay-71.

*Level* : Marathi Student of age 10 to 16 years.

23B15 MEDICAL STUDENT'S PROFESSIONAL ASPIRATIONS

*Author* : T. Venkateswara Rao.

*Availability* : Author,Indian Institute of Management, Ahmedabad.

*Time required* : About 12 minutes.

*Level* : Medical students.

*Main features* : It is a self-anchoring technique like that of Cantril and Free's with two open-ended Questions and a ladder by which the level of professional aspiration is measured.

*Scoring* : A category system has been developed to code the professional hopes and fears of medical students. Level of professional aspiration is scored by goal discrepancy scores.

*Norms* : Scores of final year medical students of 7 medical colleges are available.

*Reference* : Rao, T.V. A study of the perceptions of medical college environment and professional socialisation of medical students. Ph.D. Thesis in Psychology, Sardar Patel University, 1972.

23B16 P.S.M. INTEREST INVENTORY

*Author* : Vocational Guidance Bureau, Prantiya Shikshak Maha- vidyalaya, Jabalpur.

*Availability* : Author.

*Uses* : Guidance and counselling.

*Time required* : 30 to 45 minutes.

*Level* : 13 to 18 year students.

*Main features* : It is a 70-item test in Hindi consisting of 245 items related to occupation, school subjects leisure time activities, educational films things like to be owned and books like to be read.

*Reliability* : Split-half reliabilities corrected by Spearman-Brown formula were found to range from .67 to .86 for science, agricultural and technical groups.

*Norms* : Available for science, agriculture and technical groups.

## C Citations

23C1 INTEREST INVENTORY

*Author*: R.G. Chatterjee.

*Reference* : Chatterjee, R. G. Interest pattern of post-graduate and undergraduate students. *Journal of Psychological Researches*, 1961, 5(11), 22-27.

23C2 JAMUAR'S STUDY HABIT INVENTORY

*Author*: C.N. Daftuar.

*Language*: Hindi.

*Availability*: Author.

*Reference* : Daftuar, C.N. Certain correlates of study habits. *Journal of Psychological Researches*, 1967, 11(3), 97-101.

23C3 INTEREST QUESTIONNAIRE

*Author*: T.N. Govindarajan.

*Reference* : Govindarajan, T.N. Vocational interests of leaders and non-leaders among adolescent boys. *Journal of Psychological Researches*, 1964, 8(3), 124-130.

23C4 PSYCHOLOGY INTEREST QUESTIONNAIRE

*Author*: R.M. Loomba.

*Reference* : Loomba, R.M. Motives for the study of psychology as an optional subject among intermediate students. *Indian Journal of Psychology*, 1950, 25(1-4), 117-125.

23C5 INTEREST INVENTORY

*Author*: K.G. Rastogi,

*Reference* : Rastogi, K.G. Interest, intelligence and achievement in high school students. *Guidance Review*, 3(4), 1-8.

## D Adaptations

23D1 HALLER'S VOCATIONAL PREFERENCE INVENTORY (A.O. HALLER'S)

*Author*: J.S. Grewal.

*Languages* : English and Hindi.
*Availability* : Author, Regional College of Education, Bhopal-13.
*Reliability* : In process.
*Validity* : In process.
*Norms* : Available.
*Reference* : Grewal, J.S. Educational choices and vocational preferences of secondary school students in relation to environment process variable. Ph.D. Thesis in Education, Vikram University, 1971.

## 23D2 KUDER PREFERENCE RECORD

*Author* : Bureau of Educational and Vocational Guidance, Bihar.
*Language* : Hindi.
*Availability* : Authors, Patna.

## 23D3 STRONG'S INTEREST TEST

*Authors* : A. Hafeez and K.K. Kuttappa.
*Language* : English.
*Availability* : Authors, Department of Industrial Management, Indian Institute of Science, Bangalore-12, India.
*Norms* : Scores of final year, medical, commerce, law, engineering and pupil teachers, 50 each are available.

## 23D4 WRENN'S STUDY HABITS INVENTORY

*Authors* : Bureau of Educational and Vocational Guidance, Patna.
*Language* : Hindi.

# 4. Attitudes

## A Complete instruments

24A1 TEACHER ATTITUDE INVENTORY

*Author* : S.P. Ahluwalia.

*Availability* : Author, Department of Education, Banaras Hindu University, Varanasi.

*Time* : About 30 minutes.

*Level* : Adult males (student teachers and Practising teachers).

*Main features* : This Teacher Attitude Inventory is constructed in Hindi and English, with two equivalent forms. Both of these forms have six sub-scale viz. attitudes towards: (i) teaching as a profession, (ii) classroom teaching, (iii) child-centred practices, (iv) educational process, (v) pupils, and (vi) teachers.

*Scoring* : As in Minnesota Teacher Attitude Inventory.

*Reference* : Ahluwalia, S.P. Development of a teacher attitude inventory and a study of the change in professional attitudes of student-teachers: Project Reports; NCERT research project. (Varanasi).

24A1 TEACHER ATTITUDE INVENTORY

(The following items have to be checked on a 5 point scale of agreement).

1. If I had a son entering college I would have encouraged him to become a teacher.
2. A classroom should not be as quiet as graveyard.
3. Student's behaviour should be taken into consideration by the teacher.
4. Students work hard if they are not given freedom to ask questions in the class.
5. Students are generally sincere.
6. A teacher respect everybody.
7. I would not prefer my close friends to be from the teaching profession.
8. Mischievous students should be punished by the schools' students council and not by the teacher.
9. Teaching is possible only in the classroom.
10. Individual differences among the students should not be paid much attention to.
11. One should not rely on students of today.
12. Now-a-days teachers don't show favouritism.
13. Teaching develops personality and character.

14. Classroom teaching makes the students disciplined.
15. Freedom should not be given to the students to learn according to their own desire.
16. Students are nct boastful.
17. Pupils should be given freedom to express their views in the class.
18. Teachers are not free to express their views.
19. Those who fail in other fields of work usually become teachers.
20. Teaching work becomes easy in the classroom.
21. Students learn more by love than by punishment.
22. Teachers often talk on ideals.
23. A good many students study only when they are forced to do so.
24. Pupils should not let down before the class.
25. Classroom teaching begets social atmosphere.
26. Students' homework should be corrected with their help.
27. To force students to learn against their wishes handicaps the process of learning.
28. Students do not live together in harmony with one another.
29. When one sees a teacher he feels like laughing at him.
30. No occupation is better than the teaching profession.
31. Generally men of high status do not take up teaching.
32. Classroom teaching develops a feeling of leadership among students.
33. Students learn best by doing.
34. It is not good to keep the students busy.
35. Now-a-days students do not obey their teachers.
36. Everybody pays attention to what a teacher says.
37. Teachers are boastful.
38. Students pay more attention to their clothes than to their studies.
39. Some students know more about some subjects than the experienced teachers.
40. There should be no students' union in school.
41. Teachers do not determine the moral standards of a nation.
42. There are only a few honest people in the teaching profession today.
43. If the teaching profession is not honoured our nation will not progress.
44. There is no alternative to classroom teaching.
45. Students' health is an important responsibility of the school.
46. Just one method of teaching is not suitable for all the students.
47. Students observe discipline only in the school.
48. Most of the teachers are greedy.
49. Due recognition to the work of the students encourages them to learn.
50. Generally teachers do not come to the class well-prepared.
51. Students are generally disinterested in national problems.
52. Group activities do not create a sense of co-operation among the students.
53. Pupils do not develop a feeling of revenge if punished severely.
54. It is not difficult to attend to individual differences in classroom teaching.
55. Teaching profession has a bright future.
56. Teaching profession appears to be interesting only in the beginning.
57. Bright and talented students often suffer in classroom teaching.
58. Students become careless if homework is not given to them.

59. The surroundings of the school have an impact on the learning process.
60. Students should not be given freedom to think.
61. Only trained teachers should have the right to teach.
62. Classroom teaching does not inculcate a feeling of self-confidence in the students.
63. Pupils remain unsatisfied if their doubts are not clarified.
64. Many problems get solved through classroom discussion.
65. Students should be given severe punishment for showing indecent behaviour.
66. People do not look down upon teachers.
67. I take pride in telling that I belong to the teaching profession.
68. Classroom teaching makes students respect each other.
69. It is not reasonable to forgive the rowdyism of students.
70. The talents of students remain hidden if due attention is not paid to their special abilities.
71. Students should enter the class only after getting the permission from the teacher.
72. There are very few good teachers in our country.
73. Teachers do not have a sense of humour.
74. The stammering students are a problem in the class.
75. Student discontent is a sign of short-comings in teaching.
76. Even teachers can learn something from pupils.
77. There are more disadvantages than advantages in the teaching profession.
78. Classroom teaching strengthens the desire to learn.
79. I want to take up the teaching profession only because my parents wish so.
80. The practice of private tuitions is the result of draw-backs of classroom teaching.
81. Books are not all in all for pupils.
82. Students can become good citizens only when teachers are good teachers.
83. I get pleased when mischievous students get a beating.
84. One who does according to what he says, has the qualities of a teacher.
85. It is difficult to lead a luxurious life in the teaching profession.
86. Classroom teaching needs a change.
87. Different activities performed by the students should not have a place in their final evaluation.
88. God relationship between the teacher and the taught is essential for learning.
89. Students should not be allowed to ask questions in the class.
90. Most of the teachers do not show interest in what students say.
91. Teachers cannot satisfy the intellectually superior students.
92. Students can do anything in order to get through the examination.
93. The knowledge that is imparted to the students today is incomplete.
94. Students alone should decide what home work they would do.
95. There is a distance between teacher and students in classroom teaching.
96. Today people do not like to give up teaching to enter other professions.

97. It is a curse to remain in the teaching profession.
98. Back-benchers do not get proper attention in classroom teaching.
99. It is good that now-a-days aptitude of students is given importance.
100. Teaching methods of the past were better than those of today.
101. All the problems of the society cannot be solved by the students.
102. Teachers are often alert.
103. A teacher often thinks himself to be a leader.
104. Very few students study at home.
105. The existing methods of teaching need a radical change.
106. While assigning home task pupils' ability should be taken into consideration.
107. The place of the student should not be supreme in classroom teaching.
108. Persons in the teaching profession always talk about the welfare of the society.
109. Teaching is a very stimulating profession.
110. No student should rebel against authorities.
111. Weak students gain a lot through the revision of the lesson by the teacher in the classroom.
112. The knowledge acquired through classroom teaching is not as lasting as that acquired through excursions.
113. Students are superstitious even today.
114. One who does not inflict corporal punishment on students, is a poor teacher.
115. One should not even dream of becoming a teacher in his life.
116. Students often talk nonsense in the class.
117. Good learning condition is created when the relations between the teacher and the pupil are warm and friendly.
118. It is better to reward a good pupil than to punish a mischievous one.
119. Classroom teaching is not in line with the modern developments in Psychology.
120. Teaching profession makes people lazy.
121. Teaching profession is not as bad as people think is to be.
122. Classroom teaching is book-centred rather than child-centred.
123. Teacher should give special attention to educationally backward pupils.
124. Keeping students informed of their progress has little effect on learning.
125. Increased freedom to the students creates confusion in classroom.
126. Teachers deliberately allot more marks to some students.
127. Today hard work and a sense of dedication are lacking in the teaching profession.
128. In classroom teaching there is too much stress on keeping order in the classroom.
129. The teacher should not make the lesson interesting for children.
130. A good teacher is little need for charts, maps, diagrams and the like.
131. Most students do not respect the teachers.
132. Teaching makes a teacher tired.
133. Teaching profession is not a good medium of serving humanity.
134. In classroom teaching all students do not get an opportunity to work.
135. We should fit the curriculum to the child and not the child to the curriculum.

136. The best way to teach students is to assign them some reading and to tell them that they will be tested in it.
137. Students take pride in the neat and attractive environment of the school.
138. The community neither appreciates teachers nor recognises their worth.
139. A teachers is free to admit his ignorance openly and frankly.
140. Students should have right to express disagreement with what the teacher says.
141. One of the difficulties with modern schools is that discipline is often sacrificed to the interest of students.
142. In classroom teaching the principle of "learning by doing" cannot be implemented.
143. I will not take up any other job except teaching.
144. In classroom teaching one can use the black-board a great deal to emphasise a verbal description.
145. If I do not get any other job, I will join the teaching profession.
146. It is very difficult to generalise about teaching procedures because each pupil responds differently.
147. Teachers should not be strict in their dealing with students.
148. Teachers are the leaders of the nation.
149. If a student does not understand an assignment, it is usually the fault of the teacher.
150. A teacher's job is primarily one of teaching and explaining the subject matter.

## 24A2 ATTITUDE TOWARDS TEACHING PROFESSION SCALE

*Author*: Shalini Bhogle.
*Availability* : Author, Department of Psychology, Osmania University Hyderabad-7.
*Level*: Teachers.
*Main features* : It is a 5-point Likert scale with 18 items.
*Scoring* : Summated ratings.

## 24A2 ATTITUDE TOWARDS TEACHING PROFESSION SCALE

(The following items have to be checked on a 5-point scale of agreement).

1. I get more undesirable time-table than do most teachers.
2. I have seriously considered changing my profession.
3. I do not know of any occupation that I prefer to teaching.
4. It is not proper for a teacher to have outside employment.
5. The administration requires me to spend much of my time sponsoring co-curricular activities.
6. I have all the teaching aids needed for effective teaching.
7. Teachers should not be allowed to earn money by performing non-teaching jobs in the school or outside it.
8. The administration has not assisted me in maintaining outside professional contacts.
9. My classroom is not at all adequate.

10. Subject-matter courses help me more as a teacher than a degree in education.
11. The administration of my school is extremely autocratic.
12. I have never regretted my decision to become a teacher.
13. Teachers should have more to say in the running of this school.
14. Teachers conferences do not accomplish anything professionally.
15. Teachers should be allowed to engage in part-time remunerative activities of all kinds.
16. I prefer to stress the learning of subject-matter more than the acquisition of social skills.
17. I yet have to find anything of value in the professional journals.
18. Petty politics are too prevalent in my school.

24A3 ATTITUDE TOWARDS PUNISHMENT SCALE

*Author* : Pratibha Deo.
*Availability* : Pratibha Deo, Department of Education, Panjab University, Chandigarh.
*Time* : There is no time limit, but the scale can be completed in 30-40 minutes.
*Level* : School children and college students.
*Main features* : This is scale of the Likert type. This has been developed on the basis of four main dimensions; (1) type of the punishment, physical, verbal, social etc., (2) the agent of punishment, e.g. headmaster, teacher, classfellow etc., (3) the situation of the punishment given i.e. while alone or in the presence of others and (4) the condition of punishment being given while guilty or innocent. Five-point scale is used.
*Scoring* : Summated ratings.

24A3 ATTITUDE TOWARDS PUNISHMENT SCALE

(The following items have to be checked one a 5-point scale of feeling whether the punishment in the given situation is fully justified to totally unjustified).

PHYSICAL PUNISHMENT

**By the Headmaster:**

1. When innocent, the headmaster orders me to pull my ears when I am alone then I —
2. When innocent, the headmaster orders me to pull my ears in the presence of others then I —
3. When being at fault, the headmaster commands me to pull my ears when I am alone then I —
4. When being at fault, the headmaster commands me to pull my ears in the presence of others then I —
5. When innocent, the headmaster makes me stand for a long time when I am alone then I —
6. When innocent, the headmaster makes me stand for a long time in the presence of others then I —

7. When being at fault, the headmaster makes me stand for a long time when I am alone then I —
8. When being at fault, the headmaster makes me stand for a long time in the presence of others then I —

**By the Teacher:**

9. When innocent, the teacher pulls my ears when I am alone then I —
10. When innocent, the teacher pulls my ears in the presence of others then I —
11. When being at fault, the teacher pulls my ears when I am alone then I —
12. When being at fault, the teacher pulls my ears in the presence of others then I —
13. When innocent, the teacher makes me stand for a long time when I am alone then I —
14. When innocent, the teacher makes me stand for a long time in the presence of others then I —
15. When being at fault, the teacher makes me stand for a long time when I am alone then I —
16. When being at fault, the teacher makes me stand for a long time in the presence of others then I —

**By the Student:**

17. When innocent, the teacher asks one of my class fellows to pull my ears when I am alone then I —
18. When innocent, the teacher asks one of my class fellows to pull my ears in the presence of others then I —
19. When being at fault, the teacher asks one of my class fellows to pull my ears when I am alone then I —
20. When being at fault, the teacher asks one of my class fellows to pull my ears in the presence of others then I —
21. When innocent, the teacher asks one of my class fellows to beat me when I am alone then I —
22. When innocent, the teacher asks one of my class fellows to beat me in the presence of others then I —
23. When being at fault, the teachers asks one of my class fellows to beat me when I am alone then I —
24. When being at fault, the teacher asks one of my class fellows to beat me in the presence of others then I —

SOCIAL PUNISHMENT

**By the Headmaster:**

1. When innocent, the headmaster complains against me to my parents when I am alone then I —
2. When innocent, the headmaster complains against me to my parents in the presence of others then I —

3. When being at fault, the headmaster complains against me to my parents when I am alone then I —
4. When being at fault, the headmaster complains against me to my parents in the presence of others then I —
5. When innocent, the headmaster asks me not to enter the morning assembly when I am alone then I —
6. When innocent, the headmaster asks me not to enter the morning assembly —

**By the Teacher:**

7. When innocent, the teacher detains me for studying after the school is over when I am alone then I —
8. When innocent, the teacher detains me for studying after the school is over in the presence of others then I —
9. When being at fault, the teacher detains me for studying after the school is over when I am alone then I —
10. When being at fault, the teacher detains me for studying after the school is over in the presence of others then I —
11. When innocent, the teacher gives information against me to the headmaster when I am alone then I —
12. When innocent, the teacher gives information against me to the headmaster in the presence of others then I —
13. When being at fault, the teacher gives information against me to the headmaster when I am alone then I —
14. When being at fault, the teacher gives information against me to the headmaster in the presence of others then I —

**By the Student:**

15. When innocent, one of my class fellows gives information against me to the teacher when I am alone then I —
16. When innocent, one of my class fellows gives information against me to the teacher in the presence of others then I —
17. When being at fault, one of my class fellows gives information against me to the teacher when I am alone then I —
18. When being at fault, one of my class fellows gives information against me to the teacher in the presence of others then I —
19. When innocent, one of my class fellows gives information against me to my parents when I am alone then I —
20. When innocent, one of my class fellow's gives information against me to my parents in the presence of others then I —
21. When being at fault, one of my class fellows gives information against me to my parents when I am alone then I —
22. When being at fault, one of my class fellows gives information against me to my parents in the presence of others then I —

VERBAL PUNISHMENT

**By the Headmaster:**

1. When innocent, the headmaster makes me feel ashamed when I am alone then I —
2. When innocent, the headmaster makes me feel ashamed in the presence of others then I —
3. When being at fault, the headmaster makes me feel ashamed when I am alone then I —
4. When being at fault, the headmaster makes me feel ashamed in the presence of others then I —
5. When innocent, the headmaster gives me warning when I am alone then I —
6. When innocent the headmaster gives me warning in the presence of others then I —
7. When being at fault, the headmaster gives me warning when I am alone then I —
8. When being at fault, the headmaster gives me warning in the presence of others then I —

**By the Teacher:**

9. When innocent, the teacher makes fun of me when I am alone then I —
10. When innocent, the teacher makes fun of me in the presence of others then I —
11. When being at fault, the teacher makes fun of me when I am alone then I —
12. When being at fault, the teacher makes fun of me in the presence of others then I —
13. When innocent, the teacher says to me, "Don't enter my class" When I am alone then I —
14. When innocent, the teacher says to me, "Don't enter my class" in the presence of others then I —
15. When being at fault, the teacher says to me, "Don't enter my class" when I am alone then I —
16. When being at fault, the teacher says to me, "Don't enter my class" in the presence of others then I —

**By the Student:**

17. When innocent, the teacher asks one of my class fellows to scold me when I am alone then I —
18. When innocent, the teacher asks one of my class fellows to scold me in the presence of others then I —
19. When being at fault, the teacher asks one of my class fellows to scold me when I am alone then I —
20. When being at fault, the teacher asks one of my class fellows to scold me in the presence of others then I —

21. When innocent, one of my class fellows rebukes me when I am alone then I —
22. When innocent, one of my class fellows rebukes me in the presence of others then I —
23. When being at fault, one of my class fellows rebukes me when I am alone then I —
24. When being at fault, one of my class fellows rebukes me in the presence of others then I —

ACADEMIC PUNISHMENT

**By the Headmaster:**

1. When innocent, the headmaster punishes me to re-write when I am alone then I —
2. When innocent, the headmaster punishes me to re-write in the presence of others then I —
3. When being at fault, the headmaster punishes me to re-write when I am alone then I —
4. When being at fault, the headmaster punishes me to re-write in the presence of others then I —
5. When innocent, the headmaster gives me extra home work when I am alone then I —
6. When innocent, the headmaster gives me extra home work in the presence of others than I —
7. When being at fault, the headmaster gives me extra home work when I am alone then I —
8. When being at fault, the headmaster gives me extra home work in the presence of others then I —

**By the Teacher:**

9. When innocent, the teacher punishes me to re-write when I am alone then I —
10. When innocent, the teacher punishes me to re-write in the presence of others then I —
11. When being at fault, the teacher punishes me to re-write when I am alone then I —
12. When being at fault, the teacher punishes me to re-write in the presence of others then I —
13. When innocent, the teacher gives me extra home work when I am alone then I —
14. When innocent, the teacher gives me extra home work in the presence of others then I —
15. When being at fault, the teacher gives me extra home work when I am alone then I —
16. When being at fault, the teacher gives me extra home work in the presence of others then I —

ECONOMIC PUNISHMENT

**By the Headmaster:**

1. When innocent, the headmaster fines me when I am alone then I —
2. When innocent, the headmaster fines me in the presence of others then I —
3. When being at fault, the headmaster fines me when I am alone then I —
4. When being at fault, the headmaster fines me in the presence of others then I —

24A4 ATTITUDE TOWARDS TEACHING PROFESSION

*Authors* : V.V. Katti and C.S. Bannur.
*Availability* : Authors.
*Main features* : The final scale consists of 40 statements with 5-point scale.
*Level* : Secondary school teachers.
*Scoring* : Likert type summated ratings.
*Reliability* : Split-half coefficient of correlation was found to be +0.76. Self-correlation of the scale in full length was found to be +0.96.

24A4 ATTITUDE TOWARDS TEACHING PROFESSION

(The following items have to be checked on a 5-point scale of agreement).

1. Teachers are generally well adjusted with their job.
2. Teachers are co-operative with parents.
3. There is nothing new in the so-called modern methods.
4. Teachers always plan their work carefully.
5. Teachers are easily irritated by children.
6. Teachers are well adjusted with their co-workers.
7. Teaching is the sorriest of all the professions.
8. Teaching offers neither monetary benefits nor social status.
9. A teacher helps another teacher in adversity.
10. Teaching profession is a dull profession.
11. A social misfit takes up teaching.
12. Teachers contribute liberally to the teachers welfare fund.
13. A teacher loses his initiative by taking to teaching.
14. A teacher can developed his skill by experience.
15. A teacher is an eminently effective force in the community.
16. The knowledge that a teacher gets for his graduation is enough.
17. A teacher can not make both ends meet without private tuitions.
18. Teachers don't mix with other people.
19. Teachers have very little to contribute towards national development.
20. A teacher has ample opportunity to display his initiatives.
21. Teachers derive more joy and happiness in the company of children while teaching.
22. The best method of teaching is to make the child read again and again.
23. A teacher is man of high moral values.

24. Teachers conserve energy in the classroom so that they can teach better in the private classes.
25. To try to be an ideal teacher is to deceive oneself.
26. A teacher can improve his social status by his honest and hard work.
27. A teacher is more interested in his pupils than in his play.
28. Teachers are sympathetic, kind and helpful to all.
29. Teaching is not a strenuous job.
30. A teacher can influence many generations.
31. Teachers organisations are like trade unions.
32. Teachers worry more about their domestic work than community work.
33. A typical teacher has an abiding faith in the modification of human nature.
34. The professional standards of teaching is far inferior to other professions.
35. Teachers cannot build their status by honest and hard work.
36. All pupils are equal in the eyes of a teachers.
37. Teaching is the noblest of all the professions.
38. Most teachers prepare inadequately for their work.
39. A teacher should be proud of his profession whatever people may say about it.
40. Teachers should have higher moral values and standards than others.

24A5 ATTITUDE TOWARDS CO-EDUCATION

*Author*: Vidhu Mohan.

*Availability* : Author, Department of Psychology, Guru Nanak Dev University, Amritsar.

*Time required*: About 15 minutes.

*Level*: University students (boys and girls).

*Main features* : It is a scale based on the Turstone's technique of attitude scale construction.

*Scoring* : Weighted scores for all the statements.

*Reference* : Mohan, Vidhu, Co-education: A survey of the attitude of post-graduate students. *Psychological Studies*, 1970, 15(2), 81-89.

24A5 ATTITUDE TOWARDS CO-EDUCATION

(From the following statement items with which the respondents agrees have to be checked).

1. Co-education lessen the financial burden on the nation.
2. Co-education help the youth in avoiding post-marital maladjustments.
3. Co-education makes people more romantic and less interested in studies.
4. Co-education helps the boys and girls in understanding each other.
5. There should be co-education in all educational institutions.
6. Too much mixing up of boys and girls in co-education hinders their studies.
7. Co-education makes people broad minded.

8. Co-education provides good opportunity to the students to interact with the opposite sex.
9. Co-education is good for the healthy development of personality.
10. Co-education is economical but it is at the same time less useful for education.
11. Co-education provokes superficiality in dress and leads to national wastage.
12. Co-education helps boys and girls to indulge in healthy competition.
13. Co-education is against our culture.
14. Co-education helps in solving the problems of shortage of highly qualified teachers.
15. Co-education can not be successful in our country because our students don't have a healthy attitude towards the intermingling of two sexes.
16. Co-education inculcates the attitude of equality of sexes.
17. Co-education provides an opportunity for people to indulge in scandal mongering.
18. Too much of intermixture of sexes in co-education leads to wastage of time and energy.
19. The presence of opposite sex in an institution makes students better behaved.
20. Co-education leads youth to develop false values of life.

## 24A6 ATTITUDE TOWARDS TEACHING PROFESSION

*Authors* : P. Ponnambalam and H. Visveswaran.

*Availability* : Authors, Sri Ramakrishna Vidyalay Teachers College, R.K. Vidyalaya, Coimbatore.

*Time required* : No time limit.

*Level* : Teacher trainees of Basic Training College (could be used with general population also).

*Main features* : The scale consists of 50 items.

*Reliability* : Split-half reliability (odd-even) was found to be r=0.94.

*Reference* : Ponnambalam, P. and Visveswaran, H. The influence of socio-economic factors on the attitude of the students in basic training schools towards the teaching profession. *Journal of Educational Research and Extension*, 1966, 3(2), 65-69.

## 24A6 ATTITUDE TOWARDS TEACHING PROFESSION

(The following statements have to be rated on a 5-point scale of agreement).

1. Teacher training builds up a correct attitude towards the profession.
2. A typical teacher is a social misfit.
3. Teachers always plan their work carefully.
4. The training periods is a waste of time.
5. Teaching offers a wide variety of social contact.
6. Teachers are sympathetic and helpful to all.
7. An ideal teacher can exist only in imagination.

8. Teaching is the sorriest of all trades.
9. Teachers are very effective in their work.
10. A good teacher makes his professional life one of continuous growth.
11. Basic education helps to promote the formation of character better than the traditional elementary education.
12. Children in Basic schools are more active than children in any other type of schools.
13. Basic education will help to prevent the villages from decaying.
14. The purpose of basic education is to produce reliable co-operative public spirited citizens.
15. Basic education is unwanted education.
16. In basic school teachers serve not because of their faith but because of non-availability of any other job.
17. Basic school teachers are not enthusiastic about the aim of basic education.
18. Basic education is the best means of preserving our cultural heritage.
19. Basic education is the only means to give training in democracy.
20. All should participate in kitchen work.
21. The teacher must take active part in the community life in order to appreciate its good qualities.
22. In basic schools entrusting children with social responsibilities is dangerous.
23. Students of basic education idle away their time.
24. Manual labour as given in basic training schools exhaust the students.
25. Basic education will create a society based on co-operation.
26. Children acquire good social traits through basic education.
27. The emphasis on simple life in Basic Training Institutions is no sign of progress in this age of civilisation.
28. The teacher should not entangle in power politics.
29. It is impossible for a teacher to deal kindly with each child without prejudice or partiality.
30. Community work deprives the students much of their valuable time of academic work.
31. Basic school is a place of work, experimentation and discovery.
32. Basic education turns its back to the development of science.
33. Proper work experience is necessary for the development of man's personality.
34. Basic education deals with real things and real work.
35. Education through English medium has made the educated people strangers in their own land.
36. Basic trained child can tackle any situation in life.
37. The parents and teachers are utterly distrustful of the soundness of basic education.
38. Basic education will be a great failure than misunderstood traditional relations with students.
39. Craft should be the medium of child's education.
40. Spinning is a pleasing and easy task.
41. Basic education student will be the master of the craft he learns.
42. The charka is the symbol of India's regeneration.

43. Carding is injurious to children's health.
44. Many vital crafts of the village are revised by basic education.
45. Spinning is monotonous.
46. Charka is a symbol of backwardness.
47. Introducing basic craft in a school is a step towards barbarism.
48. Spinning is a craft which cannot be pursued by many in their later life as a life sustaining job.
49. It is sheer waste of time to teach girls weaving instead of sewing.
50. Craft is imposed on children in basic education.

24A7 RAO SCHOOL ATTITUDE INVENTORY

*Author*: D. Gopal Rao.

*Availability* : Author, Regional College of Education, Shyamala Hills, Bhopal (M.P.).

*Uses* : To find out the attitude of a student towards his school.

*Time required*: There is no time limit, but it takes about 15 minutes.

*Level*: VIII to XI standard students.

*Main features* : It consists of 30 questions covering various aspects of the school such as teachers, school subjects, class fellows, home work, cocurricular activities and parental attitude to school as perceived by the pupils. Each question has five category responses such as always, most often, frequently, some times and never, out of which one needs to be checked.

*Scoring* : Summated ratings.

*Reliability*: Test-retest reliability coefficient was found to be 0.81.

*Validity* : Content validity has been established. Also the inventory has high discrimination value between the known groups.

*Reference* : Rao, D. Gopal. A Study of some factors related to scholastic achievement. *Indian Journal of Psychology,* 1970, 45(2), 99-120.

24A7 RAO SCHOOL ATTITUDE INVENTORY

(The respondent has to check each of the following items on a 5-point scale of frequency).

1. Do you think that most of your teachers are kind to you?
2. Do most of your teachers make the lesson interesting?
3. Do you think that your teachers give too much of home work?
4. Do you think that the Principle of this school is too strict with the students?
5. Are you afraid of your teachers?
6. Do you dislike certain teachers in this school?
7. Do most of your teachers command respect from student?
8. Do you feel that your teachers do not understand you?
9. Are you proud to be a student in this school?
10. Do you ever feel like staying away from school?
11. Do you think that your success in life depends upon your success in school?

12. Do you think that there are too many rules and regulations in your school?
13. Do you think that your school prepares you for future occupation?
14. Do you feel that what you learn in the school would be useful even after you leave the school?
15. Do you like all the subjects you are taking in this school?
16. Do you find your studies dull and uninteresting?
17. Do you take pride in achieving well in your studies?
18. Does your school provide good opportunities for sports, games and dramatics?
19. Do you think that participation in sports, games and dramatics is more a hindrance than help to students?
20. Do you think that the 'home work' is a burden on you?
21. Have you found the students in this school friendly?
22. Do you like most of your classmates in this school?
23. Do you help your classmates in their subjects when they seek your help?
24. Do you feel that some of the students in your school do not like you?
25. Do your parents supervise your study at home?
26. Do your parents consider that sending you to school is a waste of money?
27. Do your parents placed high hopes upon your education?
28. Do you feel that your parents send you to school just to get rid of your presence at home?
29. Do you go to the school because of the compulsion of your parents?
30. Do your parents want you to change your school?

24A8 PROFESSIONAL PERCEPTIONS INVENTORY

*Author* : T. Venkateswara Rao.
*Availability* : Author, Indian Institute of Management, Ahmedabad.
*Time required* : About 10 minutes.
*Level* : Medical men. Could also be used with other professions.
*Main features* : Likert type 5-point attitude scale.
*Scoring* : Summated ratings.
*Validity* : Factorial validity worked out.
*Norms* : Scores of final year medical students from 7 colleges available.
*Reference* : Rao, T.V. A Study of the perceptions of medical college environment and professional socialization of medical students, Ph.D. Thesis in Psychology, Sardar Patel University, 1972.

24A8 PROFESSIONAL PERCEPTIONS INVENTORY

(The following characteristics of the medical profession have to be checked by the respondents on a 5-point scale as he sees his profession).

1. Challenging
2. Satisfying
3. Practical

4. Respectable
5. Useful
6. Gives opportunity for (intellectual growth).
7. Easy to be in it
8. Important
9. Interesting
10. Progressive
11. Paying
12. Service oriented
13. Highly developed.

24A9 ATTITUDE TOWARDS TEACHING

*Author*: R.S. Uhrbrock.
*Level*: Teachers.
*Scoring*: Two-point response system.
*Reference*: Uhrbrock, R.S. Attitude of teachers. *Indian Journal of Psychology*, 1962, 37(4), 175-180.

24A9 ATTITUDE TOWARDS TEACHING

(The respondent has to check the items he believes to be true).

1. If I had to live my life again, I would still teach.
2. Retirement provisions for teachers should be liberalised.
3. Teaching is very frustrating.
4. Even I were told that I could not expect a promotion for fifteen years, I would still teach.
5. The main thing I despise in teaching is a clerical work.
6. One of the enjoyable things about teaching is the opportunity for stimulating noon-day conversation during luncheon.
7. Teachers are expected to take part in too many outside activities.
8. There is no sense in trying to 'buck' the professional hierarchy. The sooner I get out of teaching the better.
9. There are many compensations in teaching other than money.
10. Teachers are self-centred in interests.
11. The attitude of students often is discouraging.
12. Teaching is an ideal job, in comparison with those requiring the same level of ability in business and industry.
13. I am convinced that I have gotten more personal satisfaction out of teaching than anything else that I could have done.
14. I would recommend teaching to any intelligent student.
15. The eager faces of the students inspire me to do my best.
16. Honestly, I wish I had not become a teacher.
17. Teaching is for the service minded individual.
18. Monetarily motivated people should not choose teaching as a career.
19. I am more "on my own" in a teaching position than I would be in any other job that I could get.
20. Teachers are recruited from those who are insecure and afraid of the

competition and pace of the business world.
21. I am quite disillusioned about the teaching profession.
22. Despite occasional moments of despair, I generally regard myself as an optimist.
23. Teachers are second class citizens.
24. My teaching load is too heavy.
25. Too many social activities interfere with scholarly interests.
26. I prefer to see the cup of learning half-full rather than half-empty.
27. My classes are too large.
28. Too many teachers leave work on blackboards that someone else has to erase.
29. I have received courteous treatment from administrative officers.
30. I am not really interested in teaching as a career.
31. Teaching is just a job like any other job.
32. Administrators constantly are pressuring us to put "public relations" ahead of teaching.
33. I am criticised unjustly when a student fails in one of my courses.
34. I prize the security that is inherent in a teaching position.
35. The teaching year should be twelve months long, with salary adjusted accordingly.
36. I do not enjoy teaching and feel no loyalty to the profession.
37. No one ever tells me whether I am doing satisfactory work.
38. I hate grading papers.
39. The pay is sufficient for the work I perform.
40. No one consults me when changes that will affect my work are made.
41. There is an "old guard" that runs things.
42. As a teacher I put in more than forty hours per week on my job.
43. The most you can say for teaching as a career is that it offers security.
44. A teacher has professional standing and prestige.
45. I believe I'm less apt to get "knifed in the back" if I remain in teaching.
46. Advancement is rapid because of the marked increase in student enrollment.
47. Long vacations make teaching a desirable vocation.
48. I live to teach; and do not teach to live.
49. Towns people look down on teachers.
50. "He who can does. He, who cannot teaches".

## Instruments with technical information B

### 24B1 ESCAPIST ATTITUDE SCALE

*Author* : N.K. Dutta.
*Uses* : To measure the escapist attitude.
*Level* : Students.
*Main features* : It is a 25-item scale.
*Reliability* : Reliability coefficients using KR-21, Tucker's formula and odd-even

method were .87, .88 and .99 respectively.

*Validity* : Content, construct and congruent validities established.

*Reference* : Dutta, N.K. Anxiety and escapist attitude. *Indian Psychological Review,* 1966, 3(1), 13-20.

24B2 ATTITUDE TOWARDS EXTENSION EDUCATION

*Authors* : P.N. Kaul and T.S. Sohal.

*Availability* : Authors, Himachal Pradesh University.

*Level* : Students.

*Main features* : It is a 105-item Likert-type scale.

*Scoring* : Summated ratings.

*Reliability* : Rank order correlation for consistency was .73, split-half reliability was .91.

*Validity* : Criterion validity established.

*Norms* : Available 142 subjects.

*References* :

1. Kaul, P.N., and Sohal, T.S. Internal consistency, reliability and validity of a scale for measuring attitudes towards extension education. *Indian Journal of Applied Psychology,* 1972, 9(2), 51-54.2.
2. Kaul, P.N. and Sohal, T.S. A technique for measuring students' attitudes towards extension education. *Journal of Psychological Researches,* 1972, 16(1), 10-12.

24B3 ATTITUDE SCALE

*Authors* : D.S. Maduranayagam and M. Feroze.

*Availability* : Authors, S.R.K. Vidyalaya Teacher Training College, Coimbatore.

*Uses* : To study the attitude of primary school teachers, towards organising cocurricular activities and non-academic activities, such as community activities, school improvement scheme and mid-day meals programmes.

*Level* : Teachers.

*Main features* : The scale consist of 142 statements regarding different aspects of a teacher's job collected from various books and journals. They were classified into 'favourable' and 'unfavourable' statements on the opinion of a panel of 18 judges. 24 pairs of statements were selected for the two parallel forms of attitude scale.

*Reliability* : Reliability of the attitude scale was found to be +0.80.

*Reference* : Maduranayagam, D.S. and Feroze, M. Attitude of primary school teachers towards co-curricular activities and non-academic activities. *Journal of Educational Research and Extension*, 1968, V(2), 63-77.

24B4 ATTITUDE TOWARDS MODERN EDUCATION TRENDS SCALE

*Authors* : N.V. Manuel and K.J. Joseph.

*Availability* : Authors.

*Time required* : Takes about 30-45 minutes.

*Level* : Teachers.

*Main features* : It is an attitude scale. The question incorporated were of two types open-ended and limited response question to which a positive or negative answer was required. Out of 96 items in the attitude scale, 25 were selected for the final study on the basis of discriminating index and topics covered.

*Scoring* : The usual arbitrary weighting system used for Likert-type scale 5,4,3,2,1 for favourable and 1,2,3,4,5 for unfavourable items for strongly agree to strongly disagree responses.

*Reliability* : Reliability coefficient of the attitude scale, calculated by Pearson's Product Moment Method and corrected by Spearman-Brown formula was found to be 0.95.

*Validity* : Construct validity is implied and competent judges were used in selecting the trends. The scale was also validated against relevant questionnaire items (treated as independent measures). But validity not expressed terms of an overall coefficient.

*Norms* : Percentile norms available, based on a sample of 230 teachers.

*Reference* : Manuel, N.V. and Joseph, K.J., The attitude of secondary school teachers in Coimbatore district towards some modern trends in Education. *Journal of Educational and Extension,* 1964, 1(1), 26-36.

## 24B5 TEACHER ATTITUDE INVENTORY

*Authors* : E.G. Parameswaran, K. Ravichandra and T.S. Narayana Rao.

*Availability* : Authors, Department of Psychology, Osmania University, Hyderabad-7.

*Uses* : To measure teacher's attitude towards their profession and children.

*Main features* : It has 45 items on Likert scale.

*Scoring* : Summated ratings.

*Reliability* : Split-half and test-retest reliabilities were established.

## 24B6 ATTITUDE TOWARDS COMPULSORY NCC TRAINING

*Authors* : C.K.K. Pillai and M. Feroz.

*Availability* : Authors, Sri Rama Krishna Vidyalaya Teacher Training College, R.K. Vidyalaya, Coimbatore.

*Time required* : No time limit.

*Level* : College students.

*Reliability* : Split-half reliability of the whole test was found to be 0.94.

*Reference* : Pillai, C.K.K. and Feroz, M. Attitude of College students in Coimbatore district towards compulsory N.C.C. training. *Journal of Educational Research and Extension,* 1965, 11(2), 27-34.

## 24B7 ATTITUDE SCALE

*Authors* : C.A. Ramaswamy and H. Visveswaran.

*Availability* : Authors, Ramakrishna Vidyalaya Teachers College, Ramakrishna Vidyalaya, Coimbatore.

*Uses* : To study the attitudes of students towards, education, dress, manners and customs, life and ambitions, religion and politics.

*Time required* : No time limit.

*Level* : Originally used on adolescents. Could be used with any one.

*Scoring* : Five-point system.

*Reliability* : The reliability using Pearson's Product Moment formula corrected by Spearman-Brown Prophecy Formula was found to be 0.90.

*Reference* : Ramaswamy, C.A. and Visveswaran, H. The influence of Commercial films on adolescents in secondary school in Coimbatore town. *Journal of Educational Research and Extension*, 1965, 11(2), 67-74.

24B8 ADOLESCENT SOCIAL ATTITUDE SCALE

*Authors* : N.Y. Reddy, T.N. Rao, V.V. Padmakar and J. Pereira.

*Availability* : Authors, Department of Psychology, Osmania University, Hyderabad.

*Level* : Adolescent students.

*Main features* : It has 64 items covering the areas; home, heterosexual relations, religion and caste system, education and political participation of students.

*Reliability* : Established.

*Validity* : Worked out.

24B9 ATTITUDE TOWARDS COMPULSORY PRIMARY EDUCATION

*Authors* : M.R. Singh and M. Feroz.

*Availability* : Authors, Sri Ramakrishna Vidyalaya Teachers Training College, S.R.K. Vidyalaya, P.O. Coimbatore (Tamil Nadu).

*Main features* : It is a five-point Likert scale.

*Scoring* : Summated ratings.

*Reliability* : Split-half reliability coefficient was found to be 0.89.

*Reference* : Singh, M.R. and Feroz, M. The attitude of primary school teachers and panchayat presidents towards free compulsory elementary education in Perianaickanpalayam panchayat union. *Journal of Educational Research and Extension*, 1964, 1(2), 8-28.

24B10 ATTITUDE TOWARDS TEACHING ENGLISH IN SECONDARY SCHOOLS

*Authors* : R. Sudarshan and H. Visweswaran.

*Availability* : Authors, S.R.K. Vidyalaya Teachers College, Coimbatore.

*Level* : Teachers (could be used with students and adult literates also).

*Main features* : This consists of three parts. Parts I and II are attitude scales consisting of 40 and 10 statements respectively meant to elicit the opinion of teachers. Part III is a questionnaire seeking personal information and details regarding certain aspects of teaching English in secondary schools.

*Reliability* : It has reliability scores ranging from .69 to .83.

*Validity* : Face and content validity have been established.

*Reference* : Sudarshan, R. and Visveswaran, H. A study of the attitude of English teachers in secondary schools in Coimbatore towards teaching English. *Journal of Educational Research and Extension*, January, 1966, 3(3).

## Citations C

24C1 ATTITUDE TOWARDS TECHNICAL EDUCATION (ABS — TE)

*Author* : H.N. Majoo.
*Availability* : Department of Education, Lucknow University, Lucknow.

24C2 ATTITUDE TOWARDS MODERN APPROACH IN TEACHING

*Authors* : S.N. Sharma and R.P. Singh (Patna).
*Reference* : Sharma, S.N. and Singh, R.P. A study of attitudes towards modern approach in teaching. *Indian Journal of Psychometry and Education*, 1972, 3(1), 29-32.

24C3 ATTITUDE SCALE

(Teachers, Parents, Country, Life etc.).

*Author* : T.S. Sodhi.
*Reference* : Sodhi, T.S. A comparative study of the personality patterns of the students of religious and secular institutions. Ph.D. Thesis in Psychology, Agra University, 1972.

## Adaptations D

24D1 MINNESSOTA TEACHER ATTITUDE INVENTORY

*Authors* : M. Mathur.

24D2 MINNESSOTA TEACHER ATTITUDE INVENTORY

*Author* : T.N. Raina.
*Language* : Hindi.
*Availability* : Author, Regional College of Education, Ajmer.
*Reference* : Raina, T.N. Authoritarianism and the professional attitudes of Indian student teachers. *Indian Journal of Psychology*, 1972, 9(1), 24-26.

# 5. Institutions

## A Complete instruments

25A1 ORGANISATIONAL ATMOSPHERE QUESTIONNAIRE

*Author* : Jayalakshmi Indirasen.

*Availability* : Author, Indian Institute of Technology, Mehrauli Road, New Delhi-16.

*Level* : Engineering Colleges (for teachers). Could also be used with other colleges.

*Main features* : It is a 20-item Likert type scale giving organisational atmosphere scores on 5-factors (5-sub-tests): pride or espirit, authority, fairness, hindrance and administration.

*Reliability* : Odd-even reliability coefficient was .934 after S-B formula was used. The sub-test scores were found to be highly intercorrelateable with each other.

*Validity* : The sub-tests were derived by using factor analysis. The factor structure war very much similar to Halpin and Crofts OCDQ dimensions.

*Scoring* : Summated ratings. Five-factor scores are possible for the five dimensions and an overall score by adding the sub-test scores.

*Reference* : Indirasen, J. Multivariate analysis of factors affecting job satisfaction of engineering teachers. Doctoral dissertation in psychology, Indian Institute of Technology, Delhi, 1973.

25A1 ORGANISATIONAL ATMOSPHERE QUESTIONNAIRE

(The following items have to be checked on a 5-point scale of agreement).

**Factor I:**

This Institute is up-to-date
This Institute has a good reputation
The morale in this Institute is high
This Institute turns out a good class of students
This Institute is enterprising
This is a good Institute to work for.

All these items express a high degree of 'pride' about the organisation. Following Halpin (1968) this factor was named 'espirit'.

**Factor II:**

The head of the organisation is respected here because of his competence and judgement.
The head of the organisation is obeyed here because of his

personal qualities and the respect he commands.
In this Institute the faculty has no voice in the administration and policy of the Institute.
This Institute needs fresh people at the top.
The organisation of this Institute is completely muddled.

All these items refer to the quality of leadership in the organisation either directly or indirectly and has been named 'authority'.

**Factor III:** There is no favouritism in this Institute.
The promotion procedures in this Institute are fair.
You have got to have 'pull' with certain people around here to the treatment obtained by the employees and has been identified here as 'fairness'.

**Factor IV:** This Institute treats its employees well.
It is difficult to get on in this Institute.
The working conditions in this Institute are poor.

These items refer to the ease of getting along and has been termed 'hindrance'.

**Factor V:** There is too much of 'red-tapism' in this Institute.
There are too many rules and regulations in this Institute.
In this Institute there are too many people in this offices.

All these items refer to the procedural formalities of the organisation and so has been broadly called 'administration'.

## 25A2 MEDICAL COLLEGE ENVIRONMENT INVENTORY

*Author* : T. Venkateswara Rao.
*Availability* : Author, Indian Institute of Management, Ahmedabad.
*Time required* : About 45 minutes.
*Level* : Medical college students.
*Main features* : It is a 100-item inventory divided into 9 scales: general esteem; academic interest and enthusiasm; extrinsic motivation for academic achievement; Breadth of interest; student scholarship; clear concise and encapsulated instruction; faculty discipline and tolerance; teacher scholarship and academic attitudes, and work facilities and student discipline. The items are rated on a 5-point scale. A total score over all the scales is also used as a general index of the environment.
*Scoring* : Key is available for the direction in which each item has to be scored. Scale-wise score as well as total scores are obtained by the method of summated ratings.
*Reliability* : Test-retest reliabilities with a gap of 3 months ranged from .58 to .96 for the different scales, and .85 for the total scale.
*Validity* : Face and content validities were worked out using judges. Inter-item correlations were statistically significant indicating homogeneity of the scale.

Factors analysis revealed a single general factor running through all the items. Directions of items were validated against medical experts' ratings.

*Norms* : Data from the final year students of 7 medical colleges from different parts of the country are available.

*Reference* : Rao, T.V. A study of the perceptions of medical college environment and professional socialisation of medical students. Ph.D. thesis in Psychology, Sardar Patel University, 1972.

25A2 MEDICAL COLLEGE ENVIRONMENT INVENTORY

(The following items have to be checked on a 5-point scale ranging from definitely true to definitely false).

1. The goals and purpose of the work are clearly defined for the student.
2. This medical college is outstanding for the emphasis it places on student scholarship and research.
3. The faculty here seems more interested in the scientific aspects of a case than in the welfare of the patient.
4. Faculty members are very oriented towards practice application in their approach.
5. Faculty members frequently discuss topics which have no apparent relation to the total course.
6. Very few teachers try to give the student the kind of practical training he will need for the practice of medicine.
7. Departmental heads seems unaware that a well-rounded programme of study includes courses in the behavioural sciences like psychology.
8. The academic atmosphere here is not very helpful to the student who wants to get down to the business of practicing medicine.
9. Faculty members frequently go out of their way to establish friendly.
10. Assignments are usually clear and specific making it easy for students to plan their studies effectively.
11. Teacher really get students interested in their subject.
12. Teachers are always available to help the students with the planning of his medical career.
13. The faculty here stresses the study of the patient as a whole person.
14. There are many facilities and opportunities for individual creative activity.
15. House staff and registrars participate enthusiastically in clinical conferences.
16. Most of the courses stress basic science or scholarship and really probe into the fundamental of their subjects.
17. Faculty members typically exhibit great interest in and enthusiasm for their special fields of interest.
18. Faculty members here really push the students to work to the maximum of their capacities.
19. The faculty here lays great stress on moral behaviour.
20. Examinations here generally provide a good opportunity for the student tc display his knowledge and understanding of the course material.
21. Patient responsibility on the part of the student is closely supervised to

guard against mistakes.

22. Faculty members rarely have parties (tea and dinner) with students.
23. Many of the faculty seem bored with their teaching assignments.
24. The clinical faculty generally expects the students to know a great deal about his patients.
25. In many courses the broad social and historical s[illegible] of the material is not discussed.
26. The faculty rarely encourages a student too read in areas of students' own interest.
27. Many courses stress the speculative or abstract rather than the concrete and tangible.
28. The faculty is very dissatisfied with students who are content just to pass the examination.
29. The college authorities are keen to take really personal, considerable, and extensive care of the students by providing facilities like student health care, student counselling, tutorial etc.
30. It is hard to prepare for examinations because students seldom know what will be expected of them.
31. Very few of the professors here try to get students interested in humanities or in the broad social context of medicine.
32. In many courses where are projects of assignments which encourage students to work in small groups.
33. Very little of the instructions here will be useful to students who go into practice.
34. Students with superior academic ability are admired by other students.
35. Student's competition facilities the acquisition of knowledge here.
36. There is a lot of interest in the philosophy and method of science.
37. The students try to help each other.
38. A lecture by an outstanding behavioural scientist would be poorly attended by the students here.
39. It is hard to find any student in the library on weekends.
40. The environment of medical college stimulates interest in things other than pure medicine.
41. The problem of comprehensive patient care is given little attention here by the students.
42. There is very little group spirit here in the students.
43. Students are concerned only with the physical and not the psychological and social aspect of medicine.
44. Students compete actively among themselves.
45. Students attendance at specially organised extra-curricular programmes related to medicine is good.
46. Students discuss well on the controversial issues in the subject whenever they come up.
47. Most students are concerned with diagnosing the rare and exotic disease rather than eliciting factual data relevant to the diagnosis and treatment of the patient.
48. The student government is active and outspoken.
49. Most students here have strong intellectual commitment.
50. Teasing and practical joking are fairly common.

51. Courses which deal with psychological problems or personal values are resented.
52. The competition for first classes and distinctions is very high.
53. Student elections generate a lot of intense campaigning and strong feeling.
54. Personal hostilities are usually concealed or resolved as quickly as possible.
55. Students who are not ordinarily neat will take extra pains to have a professional bearing when in the presence of patients.
56. Students who work hard for high grades are likely to be regarded as odd.
57. Students are concerned only with the work at hand and have few interests beyond this area.
58. Many students here are content just to get by.
59. Teachers encourage students to express their likes and dislikes.
60. Teachers take individual interest in students.
61. Teachers prepare students to learn than to pass through examinations.
62. Teachers encourage open-mindedness in students.
63. Teachers form impressions about students without verification.
64. Teachers are dedicated scholars in the field.
65. Teachers are hard working.
66. There is no favouritism shown by the teachers.
67. Teachers are busy most of the time.
68. Teachers are mostly concerned with their own advancement.
69. Teachers enjoy good respect from outsiders.
70. Teachers are highly competent in teaching.
71. Teachers have a sympathetic outlook towards the patients.
72. Teachers do not take part in college politics.
73. Teachers conduct the classes regularly.
74. Teachers emphasise specialisation.
75. Teachers give enough attention to the teaching of preventive aspects of medicine.
76. Teachers prepare well before they teach.
77. There is group politics among the teachers.
78. Teachers react to questions in the class as questions meant for criticising them.
79. Teachers give sufficient number of illustrations while teaching.
80. Teachers patiently listen to student's problems.
81. Teachers stress the importance of practical experience.
82. Teachers demonstrate the relevancy of the subjects to the treatment of patients wherever possible.
83. Teachers encourage students to experiment with new ideas.
84. Teachers keep the students informed of the up-to-date knowledge of the subjects.
85. Teachers acknowledge the contributions by the students.
86. Teachers tolerate and encourage the difference of opinion between them and the students.
87. Teachers do not express their likes and dislikes about other teachers openly.

88. Teachers are highly disciplined.
89. Teachers encourage competition among students.
90. In this college there is enough equipment to work in various areas.
91. There are enough books in the library to read on the subjects taught here.
92. Students do not absent themselves usually from the classes.
93. Students work mainly to impress teachers.
94. Students are helpful to each other.
95. Students behave in a highly disciplined way in the classes.
96. Punctuality is maintained by students.
97. The college is generally liked by all students.
98. College politics do not influence the student development in this college.
99. Many students like to do their post-graduation in this college or work here.
100. The college authorities encourage students to take active interest in extra-curricular activities.

## Instruments with technical information B

25B1 ACTIVITIES INDEX

*Authors* : J.N. Joshi and S.B. Chauhan.
*Availability* : Authors, Department of Education, Panjab University, Chandigarh.
*Uses* : To assess the needs of prospective teachers.
*Time required* : About 25 minutes.
*Level* : College of education.
*Scoring* : Responses are tabulated for 'yes' and 'no' system of scoring.
*Reference* : Joshi, J.N. and Chauhan, S.B. Perception of intellectual climate in the colleges of education by residential and non-residential prospective women teachers. *New Trends in Education*. 1971, 11(2), 16-21.

25B2 COLLEGE CHARACTERISTICS INDEX (CCI)

*Authors* : J.N. Joshi and S.B. Chauhan.
*Availability* : Authors, Department of Education, Panjab University, Chandigarh.
*Uses* : CCI is used for analysing the institutional Press of Colleges of Education. AI is used for probing into the needs of prospective teachers.
*Time required* : Around 25 minutes.
*Level* : College of education.
*Scoring* : Responses are tabuled as 'yes' or 'no'.
*Reference* : Joshi, J.N. and Chauhan, S.B. Perception of intellectual climate in the colleges of education by residential and non-residential prospective women teachers. *New Trends in Education*, 1971, 11(2), 16-21.

# D Adaptations

25D1 HAPLIN AND CROFT'S ORGANISATIONAL CLIMATE DESCRIPTIVE QUESTIONNAIRE (OCDQ)

*Author* : J.L. Bayti.
*Language* : Hindi.
*Availability* : Author.
*Uses* : To measure the climate of educational institutions.
*Time required* : 30 to 40 minutes.
*Level* : Employees of educational institutions — teachers, instructors, heads and lecturers.
*Reference* : Bayti, J.L. A comparative study of the organisational climate in Rajasthan schools. *Indian Educational Review*, 1970, 5(2), 107-117.

# ORGANISATIONAL BEHAVIOUR

# Introduction

THIS PART of the Handbook reports instruments dealing with organisational behaviour. These instruments are reported under three sections: (i) industrial organisations, (ii) health organisations, and (iii) military and other organisations. The third section reports instruments related to military, banking, governmental organisations specially in relation to agriculture, and other miscellaneous organisations. Educational organisations have been dealt with in the earlier part and hence any one interested in educational organisations would find the earlier part more useful. Instruments dealing with agricultural practices, diffusion of innovations in agriculture etc. dealt with in the next part under the section of modernisation and social change. Organisational aspects of these systems (except for industry) are reported in this part. The classification scheme here is based on the type of organisations to which the instruments relate rather than the areas of organisational behaviour. We found this classification scheme to be more pragmatic than one based on behaviour area (like instruments relating to job-satisfaction, organisational climate, administrative practices etc.), as these organisations have very different orientations. Secondly, behavioural-area-based classification would have very diffuse categories and the number of instruments under this part are rather too small to warrant such diversification. Instruments in this part deal with various dimensions of organisational behaviour like perception of the organisation by its members, clients and the public at large, job-satisfaction of employees, management attitudes towards administrative practices, unions, job attitudes, employee morale, administrative decentralisation etc.

There are in all 53 instruments reported in this part of the Handbook. There are 22 instruments reproduced here, information is provided for another 14 instruments; 12 are citations and five adaptations. The detailed break-up is presented in Table 3.

TABLE 3: Break-up of Instruments in Organisational Behaviour

| Classification | Originals reproduced | Information | Citations only provided | Adaptations | Total |
|---|---|---|---|---|---|
| 1. Industrial organisations | 10 | 11 | 6 | 5 | 32 |
| 2. Hospitals | 9 | 0 | 0 | 0 | 9 |
| 3. Military, Agriculture and other organisations | 3 | 3 | 6 | 0 | 12 |
| Total: | 22 | 14 | 12 | 5 | 53 |

### Industrial Organisations

There are in all 32 instruments listed under this title. Of these 10 have been reproduced here, information has been provided for another 11; six are citations and five are adopted versions. A review of the general literature in industrial psychology reveals that there have been several instruments developed (perhaps running into hundreds) in the area of selection and aptitudes. However, since the scope of this Handbook excludes instruments on abilities and aptitudes the instruments reported here are mostly attitudinal instruments, inter-personal scales, and so on. There are several rating scales specially relating to job factors etc. Mostly the methodology used has been to present a list of factors like money, status, type of work, security, work conditions etc. and ask the respondent to rate these factors. They have not been included here as it would increase the volume without any additional methodological contributions. The areas covered by the instruments reproduced here include attitudes towards industry, adoption propensity, inter-personal trust, workers' attitude towards supervision, coworkers, management, wages, working hours, cost consciousness, supervisory qualities, job attitudes, adjustment, organisational climate, attitudes towards labour unions, job satisfaction, morale and bureaucratic orientation sales style etc. Most of the instruments reported in this section are scales. Three main types have been developed: Likert type, Thurstone type and simple yes/no checking. The industrial population for whom these instruments are meant vary widely: entrepreneurs, supervisors, managers, industrial workers, union members etc. Most of the instruments have reported either split-half reliabilities or test-retest reliabilities. In this section also reliabilities, wherever are reported, are fairly high. Of the instruments reproduced here, six do not report any reliability coefficients. Validities have been reported only by six instruments out of twenty for which information is provided. Those reporting validity have reported item-total correlation or validities based on supervisory ratings, face validity and so on. Higher order validities have not been reported. One reason may be that most of these instruments deal with variables that are very much apparent and do not involve any deep psychological processes. As the norms of the kind of industrial populations we have keep on changing, and there is high variance according to geography, type of industry, size of the industry etc. they are likely to be of limited use. Although some instruments have reported such type of norms, a great caution is warranted in using such norms for comparative purposes.

Most of the instruments deal with attitudes, job satisfaction and adjustment to the industrial set-up. These probably could be taken to focus on the essential rather than on the creative aspect of an industrial worker. Scales like adoption propensity are rather limited in number. There are several other areas which remain untouched. There is a need for the development of instruments to test some of the methodological issues like hygiene-motivator dimensions of work motivation, role perceptions, role conflict, attitudes towards change etc.

Among the instruments reproduced here, the first three are by Christopher measuring the attitudes towards industry, inter-personal trust and adoption propensity. These are probably among the few developed with great care and standardised well. Different forms of reliabilities and validities have been reported. The first scale measuring the attitudes towards industry could be used with industrial entrepreneurs and is also suggested for use with engineering graduates etc. who intend to become entrepreneurs. These instruments can be used to identify potential entrepreneurs. The interpersonal trust scale has been included here as this was developed in the context of industrial entrepreneurs. A cursory look at the items reveal that most of the items are suitable for the organisational set-up. This could be used profitably in some of the management training programmes and small industry management development programmes, and for identification of entrepreneurs etc. The same is true with the adoption propensity scale. In fact, these sets are currently being tried out in the Indian Institute of Management to validate the identification of entrepreneurs.

The next series is the supervisory qualities questionnaire by Hafeez and Gopal Krishan. This measures the orientation of supervisors in management towards the employees and towards production. Quite a bit of personal touch has been given in the items. An index of orientation is also worked with the help of the responses. This instrument also seems to be fairly well standardised. The workers' attitude questionnaire by Hafeez and Subbaraya measures the attitude of industrial workers to personnel work, work conditions, and employers. Although this is not well standardised, the items seem to cover several areas and might be found useful. Job attitude inventory by Joseph and job questionnaire by Natraj and Hafeez also fall more or less in this category. The sales troika checklist by Pareek is another addition and unique in nature. This categorises the sales personnel into different categories and is very useful in training. The SD Employees Inventory and Employee morale scales by Pestonjee and Akhtar are also good contributions in this area.

Several of the instruments not reproduced here, seem to have better reliabilities and validities than some of these reproduced here. More attention needs to be given by the investigators in this area to the standardisation of the instruments. Five instruments reported here are adaptations. Industrial set-up in India is very much different from the set-up in the developed countries where several instruments have been reported and standardised. Naturally we do not expect many instruments to be borrowed from abroad. However, instruments dealing with interpersonal processes in organisation will be of great utility across cultures. This is probably very much lacking in our adaptations. There is only one inventory, Human Relations Inventory adapted by G.P. Sen. The others are morale and job satisfaction inventories.

### Health Organisations

Nine instruments reproduced here deal with hospitals. These deal with the following dimensions: ward social system, organisational environment, patient satisfaction and several dimensions of patient satisfaction like food, doctors, nurses, treatment etc. community images of the hospital, and internal perceptions in the hospitals. These instruments are reproduced here. Two of them are scales and the test are questionnaires. Even in the questionnaires some method of quantification seem to have been attempted. However, there seems to be still some scope for improvement. One weak area is lack of information on reliabilities and validities. For example, only two of the instruments report reliability coefficients and three instruments report to have worked out validities. One instrument is factorially validated. These instruments are meant for different sectors of population associated with hospitals. Some of them are for employees of hospitals, some are separately meant for doctors, and nurses, some are meant for the patients, and some for visitors in the hospitals. In two of the instruments Semantic Differential scale has been used.

All the instruments reported here have been developed at the National Institute of Health Administration and Education. This being the only institute giving training in health administration with emphasis on social science in the curriculum is naturally involved in developing several research instruments and conducting researches in the area of administration of health services. The instruments have been developed by a team of workers including Thimapayya, Agrawal, Chattopadhyay, Pareek, Advani etc. The first instrument on ward social system is based on the model of Georgopouls. This has been factor analysed and the factor structure appear to fit into Parson's social system model. The questionnaire consists of 30 items with differing number of response alternatives. The next questionnaires on patient satisfaction is meant for studying of nurses' and doctors' perception of patient satisfaction. This a Likert type scale. The hospital food questionnaire is meant to measure satisfaction with food supplied in the hospitals. The organisational environment questionnaire is a fairly well standardised one and currently its factorial validities are being established. Although interview schedules in general are not included in the Handbook the patient satisfaction interview schedule has been reproduced here because of sophisticated standardisation and the scaling components included in its structure. The occupational differential for measuring inter-role perceptions is a Semantic Differential scale and is meant for studying the different roles in the hospital systems. The Semantic Differential has also been used for studying the hospital images.

These scales appear to be very useful for studying different hospital systems mainly because the hospital organisations in India are fairly similar in structure and dynamics. While norms are not reported for several of the questionnaires, they are probably available in ICMR reports published by NIHAE. There are several areas of health organisations which have not been extensively studied. For example, the organisations and management of CGHC dispensaries, private hospitals, family planning clinics etc. require specialised treatment. Some instruments have been reported in the earlier part of this book that relate to the medical college organisations. Some scales related to family planning are reported in the next part of the book. These instruments instead of being included here have been given in the other parts for reasons of their appropriateness in those sections. The interested investigator may consult the index. Some more attention needs to be given to the methodological issues of instrumentation in health organisations. While the principles of instrumentation applicable to industrial organisations will also be applicable for health organisations, there are some unique dimensions that needs to be taken care of in the study of health organisations.

**Other Organisations**

There are in all 12 instruments reported in this section. Of these three are reproduced here and only information is provided for another three.

The instruments reported in this section deal with areas such as military morale, job satisfaction of village level workers, extension officers and block development officers, administrative decentralisations, banking employees' beliefs, leadership behaviour of extension workers and educational administrators, job tension etc. The first three scales reproduced here deal with military organisations and civil administration. In the military set-up several (about 50) aptitude tests and selection tests have been reported. However, only the related scales have been included in this Handbook. Most of the scales relating to agriculture other administrative aspects are reproduced in the next part. A military morale scale is a fairly well standardised scale meant for soldiers. Reliability and validity have been reported and are fairly high. The job satisfaction scale by Rathora is a short Likert type scale meant for different workers in agricultural administration. The administrative decentralisation questionnaire is another standard questionnaire devised by Reddy to study the extent of decentralisation. This could be used with any organisation. Weighted scoring has been reported.

With the continuous administrative reorganisations going on several new areas of enquiry are coming up. Unfortunately behavioural scientists are not using their expertise for the study of these organisations. All the research reported is impression based and do not use quantitative methods. No instruments have been reported in areas like railways, other public sector organisations like Posts and Telegraphs, social welfare departments and research institutions. Very few instruments have been reported for educational organisations. Banking is another area which has been grossly neglected. Role stress and role conflict are the emerging problems of organisational behaviour. This is one area where no instrument has been reported. Attention seems to have been concentrated on job satisfaction but methodological sophistication is lacking. For more instruments dealing with educational organisations the reader is directed to Part 2 on Education.

# 1. Industrial Organisations

## A Complete instruments

### 31A1 ATTITUDE TOWARDS INDUSTRY

*Author* : K.J. Christopher.

*Availability* : Author, SIET Institute, Yousufguda, Hyderabad, A.P.

*Level* : Industrial entrepreneurs of small industries. Could be used with any one thinking to set up an industry.

*Uses* : To measure the attitude towards industry.

*Main features* : It is a 25-item 4-point scale requiring the respondent to check each item on strongly agree, agree, disagree and strongly disagree.

*Scoring* : Summated ratings.

*Reliability* : By rational equivallance method.

*Validity* : The difficulty indices and the validity indices of the 25 items are as follows:

Where K=Coefficient of alienation, E=Coefficient of forecasting efficiency of dependability and 'r'=Correlation coefficient obtained from the conversion of Reliability coefficient, a=Approximate formula, b=Direct formula.

| *Item No.* | *Difficulty Index* | *Validity Index* |
|---|---|---|
| 1. | 0.53 | 0.55 |
| 2. | 0.82 | 0.40 |
| 3. | 0.78 | 0.67 |
| 4. | 0.85 | 0.36 |
| 5. | 0.38 | 0.15 |
| 6. | 0.88 | 0.53 |
| 7. | 0.44 | 0.38 |
| 8. | 0.75 | 0.53 |
| 9. | 0.63 | 0.54 |
| 10. | 0.60 | 0.71 |
| 11. | 0.63 | 0.54 |
| 12. | 0.66 | 0.48 |
| 13. | 0.53 | 0.55 |
| 14. | 0.82 | 0.68 |
| 15. | 0.41 | 0.56 |
| 16. | 0.78 | 0.67 |
| 17. | 0.72 | 0.75 |
| 18. | 0.91 | 0.51 |
| 19. | 0.72 | 0.56 |
| 20. | 0.82 | 0.68 |

| | | |
|---|---|---|
| 21. | 0.44 | 0.13 |
| 22. | 0.75 | 0.53 |
| 23. | 0.63 | 0.68 |
| 24. | 0.44 | 0.61 |
| 25. | 0.92 | 0.52 |

*Reference* : Christopher K.J. *Socio-psychological factors influencing the adoption of the innovation of starting a small industry units.* Hyderabad : SIET Institute.

31A1 ATTITUDE TOWARDS INDUSTRY

(The respondent has to check the following 25 statements on a 4-point scale of agreement).

1. What we need is a traditional type of society which is simpler than the industrial society.
2. A country's prestige is enhanced among the nations with its rapid industrialisation.
3. The country can become prosperous without industrialisation.
4. Establishing an industrial unit enhances the social status of a person.
5. Without all this industrialisation in the country, our fore-fathers were happier.
6. More emphasis should be given for the development of industry.
7. There is more security for an agriculturist than an industrialist.
8. Real progress lies in industrialisation.
9. In these days of cut-throat competition with so many controls on industry, it is wiser to take up a job than to start an industry.
10. Human values are appreciated more in an industrial society rather than in an agrarian society.
11. There is every danger that our cultural heritage will fade away with industrialisation.
12. An industrial community is more civilised than a farm community.
13. Industrialisation upsets our faith in God.
14. Industry makes men industrious.
15. People are happier in villages than in towns.
16. For the rapid development of a nation, industry must come first.
17. On the whole, industry creates unemployment.
18. There is always a certain amount of risk involved in starting an industry unit, but it is still definitely worthwhile taking this risk.
19. Industrialisation is mainly responsible for the rise of immorality.
20. The nation's progress today is mainly due to the industrialisation in the country.
21. The concept of the self-sufficient village economy has regained its importance in the context of the present state of our economy.
22. Compared to agriculture, industrialisation contributes more to national development.
23. Industrialisation leads to slums, congested towns and ill health.
24. For many years to come, we have to concentrate on agriculture rather

than on industry.

25. If given a fresh choice with regard to their occupation, the majority of industrialists choose to remain industrialised.

## 31A2 INTER-PERSONAL TRUST SCALE

*Author*: K.J. Christopher.

*Availability*: Author, SIET Institute, Yousufguda, Hyderabad.

*Level* : Small scale industrial entrepreneurs. Could also be used with other industrial managements.

*Uses* : To measure the inter-personal trust orientation.

*Main features* : This is a 25-item inventory requiring the respondent to describe himself or his thinking on the items. The respondent indicates this by indicating each item as true or as false.

*Reliability* : (By Rational Equivalence Method). Where K=Coefficient of alienation, E=Coefficient of forecasting efficiency of dependability and r=Correlation coefficient obtained from the conversion of reliability coefficient, a=Approximate formula, b=Direct formula.

*Validity*: The difficulty and validity indices of items are reproduced below:

| *Item No.* | *Difficulty Index* | *Validity Index* |
|---|---|---|
| 1. | 0.22 | 0.65 |
| 2. | 0.38 | 0.41 |
| 3. | 0.72 | 0.25 |
| 4. | 0.28 | 0.56 |
| 5. | 0.72 | 0.24 |
| 6. | 0.75 | 0.34 |
| 7. | 0.75 | 0.17 |
| 8. | 0.53 | 0.45 |
| 9. | 0.32 | 0.73 |
| 10. | 0.28 | 0.56 |
| 11. | 0.72 | 0.24 |
| 12. | 0.44 | 0.27 |
| 13. | 0.38 | 0.67 |
| 14. | 0.40 | 0.81 |
| 15. | 0.56 | 0.14 |
| 16. | 0.25 | 0.52 |
| 17. | 0.65 | 0.23 |
| 18. | 0.29 | 0.36 |
| 19. | 0.19 | 0.61 |
| 20. | 0.09 | 0.44 |
| 21. | 0.69 | 0.45 |
| 22. | 0.66 | 0.51 |
| 23. | 0.19 | 0.47 |
| 24. | 0.85 | 0.36 |

*Reference* : Christopher, K.J. *Socio-psychological factors influencing the adoption of the innovation of starting a small industry unit.* Hyderabad: SIET Institute.

## 31A2 INTER-PERSONAL TRUST SCALE

1. In important matters I never rely on others.
2. One should never confide in others as it makes matters worse for him.
3. Individuals should not hesitate to present genuine complaints to bosses.
4. People don't confide in me but I could not be careless because it's up to them to confide in me or not.
5. For people in an organisation to be creative, permissiveness is essential.
6. Listening to others with genuine interest encourages others to express themselves more freely.
7. Much of our tension and anxiety is reduced if we trust our fellow workers.
8. It is impossible to get accurate information from subordinates.
9. When changes are to be introduced, persons who will be affected by the change, should be consulted.
10. A good manager must make all the decisions himself.
11. To have good relations, one should conceal one's dislikes or disagreements with fellow workers.
12. Sometimes the best advice comes from the least of one's subordinates.
13. The moment you begin to treat the workers in a friendly way, they begin to take advantage of it.
14. "Treat others as you would like to be treated by others" may be a good maxim but in management, it never really works.
15. Discussion of personal matters should be kept out of one's professional relationship.
16. Most people like taking responsibility.
17. One's job is best done by oneself.
18. A co-operative decision leads to better implementation.
19. It is the superior's duty to see that the whole group is doing what he thinks is best.
20. In the practical world, most people cannot really be trusted.
21. If you don't watch out people will invariably take advantage of you.
22. I hesitate to give responsibility to others even if they are willing to take it, because it is difficult to trust them.
23. Human nature is fundamentally co-operative.
24. Unless there is constant and vigilant supervision, workers will avoid work.
25. Personal conveniences should not be allowed to interfere with one's job on hand.

## 31A3 ADOPTION PROPENSITY SCALE

*Author*: K.J. Christopher.
*Availability*: Author, SIET Institute, Yousufguda, Hyderabad.
*Uses*: To measure the adoption propensity of potential entrepreneurs.
*Level*: Small industrial entrepreneurs.
*Main features*: It is a 32-item inventory requiring the respondent to indicate his personal outlook on the items.

*Reliability* : Reliability coefficient and its forecasting efficiency of the test items at 5 per cent level. Where K=Coefficient of alienation, E=Coefficient of forecasting efficiency of dependability and 'r'=Correlation coefficient, obtained from the conversion of reliability coefficient, a=Approximate formula, b=Direct formula.

*Validity* : Difficulty indices and validity indices of the different items are as follows:

| *Item No.* | *Difficulty Index* | *Validity Index* |
|---|---|---|
| 1. | 0.25 | 0.16 |
| 2. | 0.91 | 0.17 |
| 3. | 0.63 | 0.54 |
| 4. | 0.47 | 0.18 |
| 5. | 0.19 | 0.17 |
| 6. | 0.75 | 0.53 |
| 7. | 0.56 | 0.52 |
| 8. | 0.22 | 0.11 |
| 9. | 0.38 | 0.26 |
| 10. | 0.91 | 0.51 |
| 11. | 0.69 | 0.21 |
| 12. | 0.75 | 0.16 |
| 13. | 0.38 | 0.52 |
| 14. | 0.63 | 0.17 |
| 15. | 0.88 | 0.26 |
| 16. | 0.79 | 0.26 |
| 17. | 0.75 | 0.16 |
| 18. | 0.72 | 0.41 |
| 19. | 0.69 | 0.45 |
| 20. | 0.29 | 0.36 |
| 21. | 0.69 | 0.21 |
| 22. | 0.69 | 0.21 |
| 23. | 0.69 | 0.21 |
| 24. | 0.35 | 0.20 |
| 25. | 0.38 | 0.26 |
| 26. | 0.72 | 0.40 |
| 27. | 0.82 | 0.40 |
| 28. | 0.41 | 0.47 |
| 29. | 0.88 | 0.26 |
| 30. | 0.85 | 0.36 |
| 31. | 0.72 | 0.16 |
| 32. | 0.85 | 0.36 |

*Reference* : Christopher, K.J. *Socio-psychological factors influencing the adoption of the innovation of starting a small industry unit.* SIET Institute, Hyderabad.

31A3 ADOPTION PROPENSITY SCALE

(The respondent has to check the following items as they are applicable to him).

1. I am completely satisfied with what I am doing in my profession.
2. I am always eager to know about new developments.
3. If I know that there is a risk in implementing a new practice, then I don't like to try the practice.
4. The traditional ways of our elders always contained a lot of good.
5. Caution is the most important thing when trying a new practice.
6. As soon as I hear something new from somebody, I like to try it.
7. Before I try out a new thing. I usually wait to see what results others have obtained.
8. Launching upon a new practice inevitably carries its own problems.
9. Trying out new methods is really a luxury and very few people can afford it.
10. I try to keep myself up-to-date on information pertaining to my professional field.
11. In these days of rapid progress all around us, we cannot afford to be slow to learn new ways of doing things.
12. If I hear about a new practice in my field, I feel restless till I try it.
13. These days, there is no end to new techniques, coming up. In the circumstances, the best policy is to wait and see.
14. I just do not have the time necessary to meet specialists in my field to discuss new ideas or improvements.
15. It is almost satisfying experience to try out a new idea or practice.
16. In a competitive market, one cannot survive for any length of time with applying new techniques and methods.
17. To accept new methods and techniques in a hurry is dangerous.
18. For sentimental reasons, I don't want to introduce any changes in my factory.
19. Old practices are generally more economical than the new ones.
20. I adopt those inventions which promise a high return.
21. I like to do anything which is new and out of the way.
22. The greater the prize, the greater the risk.
23. I think it is a waste of time to keep on trying new practices.
24. When it comes to adopting new techniques I prefer to be a follower than a leader.
25. I always rely on things that have been tried out successfully before.
26. To invent a new thing is certainly no mean achievement.
27. Any number of new techniques and methods are available for those who are prepared to accept them.
28. Generally, I prefer to be slow in accepting new ideas.
29. I always look out for new methods and techniques so that we can produce more in a shorter time.
30. In implementing new ideas I seek expert advice wherever necessary.
31. The older we grow, the more we realise how little we know.
32. In this fast-changing world, one should be able to adjust to changing conditions and ideas.

31A4 SUPERVISORY QUALITIES QUESTIONNAIRE

*Authors* : A. Hafeez and K.M. Gopalkrishna.

*Availability* : From the first author, Department of Industrial Management, Indian Institute of Science, Bangalore-12.

*Uses* : To study the orientation of supervisors and management to employees and to production.

*Time required* : No time limit. Generally it takes 10-12 minutes.

*Level* : Adult males working in factories.

*Main features* : It is a questionnaire, consisting of 34 items, covering areas such as motivation, formal and informal contact with the workers, control used over the workers, demands made on employees etc.

*Scoring* : Scoring through a key. The index of orientation is obtained by the following formula: Index of orientation=Employee Orientation Score — (minus) Production Orientation Score.

*Reliability* : Reliability was found to be 0.60, using Guttman's method.

*Norms* : Data on 42 supervisors is available.

*Reference* : Gopalkrishna, K.M. and Hafeez, A. A study of supervisors' attitude towards employees in relation to some personal factors. *Indian Journal of Applied Psychology*, 1964, 1(2), 78-83.

31A4 SUPERVISORY QUALITIES QUESTIONNAIRE

(The following items have to be checked on 'yes', 'no' alternatives).

1. Do you think supervisor should attend festivals and ceremonies conducted in his workers' house?
2. Should a supervisor maintain his official attitude with his workers always?
3. Should a supervisor try to promote recreation projects such as athletic teams, hobby clubs and social groups for his workers?
4. Is it necessary for a supervisor to delegate his work to some responsible person under him?
5. Should a supervisor take strict action against any worker who absents himself from work without leave?
6. Should a supervisor take some interest in washing out the misunderstanding between management and workers?
7. Can a supervisor deal with all his workers in one and the same way without considering them as individuals?
8. Is it necessary for a supervisor to take the opinion of the workers while making important decisions?
9. Should a supervisor take personal interest to explain the importance of the worker's job to the factory?
10. To keep a worker alert and do his work is it necessary to criticise him under some pretext or the other?
11. Should a supervisor take personal interest in the welfare of the workers?
12. Do you think a supervisor must be on watch to see that the workers quit their work at the schedule time every day?
13. Should a supervisor aspire for more responsibility in his work than he is assigned?
14. Should a supervisor expect all his workers to think and act exactly as he

does?

15. Should a supervisor strive to build team spirit amongst his workers?
16. Should a supervisor tolerate the worker who represents his grievances with higher authorities directly and without his permission?
17. Should the fear of "losing the job" be used in order to make workers work hard?
18. Though a supervisor is a representative of the management to the workers, should he in practice a representative of the workers to the management?
19. Should a supervisor make his men to overwork everyday in order to reach the target of production?
20. Should a supervisor treat his workers well even though he is not treated well by the management?
21. Do you think a supervisor can get better co-operation from his workers if he orders them to do things?
22. Does a supervisor have to be so straight forward as to publicly point out the mistake of a worker?
23. Does the appreciation of the worker affect him adversely?
24. Can the encouragement of a supervisor increase the amount of work of a low producing worker?
25. Should a supervisor pay more attention to increase production han to the welfare of the workers?
26. Should a supervisor have favourable attitude towards labour Union and its policies and practices?
27. Should a supervisor consciously try to attract the attention of others for the work he is doing?
28. Should only those workers who carry out all the orders given to them be considered as good?
29. Should a supervisor have high ambition?
30. Do you think, a good supervisor is one who forces his men to work hard and increase the rate of production?
31. Should a supervisor prohibit conversation between workers on routine jobs?
32. Should a supervisor be assertive with his workers in achieving his objectives?
33. Should a supervisor tell inefficient workers to "get busy or get out"?
34. Should a supervisor urge his employee to handle their own problems without seeking advise from anyone?

31A5 WORKERS' ATTITUDE QUESTIONNAIRE

*Authors* : A. Hafeez and S.V. Subbaraya.

*Availability* : First Author, Department of Industrial Management, Indian Institute of Science, Bangalore-12.

*Uses* : To measure the attitude of industrial workers, office personnel and supervisors and such others, to work, working conditions, management (employers) etc.

*Level* : Adult male and female workers, supervisors of middle management personnel.

*Main features* : It measures attitude to work, working conditions co-workers, supervisors, the company management, higher production, wages, working hours and cost consciousness.

*Scoring* : Scoring is done according to a prepared key indicating a positive or negative response. The algebraic sum of the scores for the items on each attribute, and the algebraic sum of the scores on the different attributes gave an indication of over all attitude.

31A5 WORKERS' ATTITUDE QUESTIONNAIRE

(The respondent has to check one of the alternatives given under each items).

**Work:**

1. The work here is very interesting:
   (a) I find real enjoyment in my work since it is very interesting.
   (b) My work is usually interesting enough to keep me from getting bored.
   (c) I feel that other jobs are more interesting than the work I am doing.
2. The work I am doing is ideal.
   (a) The work I am doing is the best and I would not change my job for another.
   (b) Most of the time I have to force myself to go to work.
   (c) I definitely dislike my work.
3. The work is creative.
   (a) This work gives me opportunity to express myself completely.
   (b) The work does not give many chances to improve myself.
   (c) This work does not require my creative ability at all.

**Working Conditions:**

4. The working conditions here are ideal.
   (a) Our working conditions are of a high order.
   (b) In our working conditions, there are many aspects that could be improved.
   (c) Working conditions here are not better than those in other places.
5. This place of my work is very satisfactory.
   (a) Our factory is the best possible place to work under the conditions.
   (b) Much thought should be given to place of work here.
   (c) Our factory is not at all suitable for working under the present conditions.

**Co-workers:**

6. The workers here are courteous to one another.
   (a) It is a pleasure to be courteous to the kind of employees we have.
   (b) Fellow employees are neither over bearing nor very courteous.
   (c) Little friendship exists amongst the workers here.
7. We are all co-operative.

(a) We always help in each other's work.
(b) Even though we are friendly each minds his own business.
(c) Even though we are friendly one need not help the other.

**Supervisors:**

8. Our supervisors know their job.
   (a) Our supervisors know their job very well.
   (b) Our supervisors need some more training.
   (c) The knowledge on the work is much less with our supervisors.
9. The supervisors give us advice and help all of us.
   (a) Our supervisors help us all impartially.
   (b) Our supervisors help only a few.
   (c) Our supervisors never help or advise us; they come only to remind us of our places.
10. In case of failure or loss the supervisor:
    (a) Shares responsibility with us.
    (b) Keeps himself unconcerned.
    (c) Tries to shift his responsibility.
11. Our supervisors are capable men.
    (a) Our supervisors have earned their positions by being good and capable.
    (b) Our supervisors could have been more capable.
    (c) Our supervisors pretend to be capable men.

**Company:**

12. I feel enthusiastic to be able to work for this company.
    (a) I feel enthusiastic to work for this company.
    (b) This company is a good enough company to work for.
    (c) I would get out of this company as soon as I can find some other work. (I don't like to work for this company).

**Management:**

13.. Do you feel the top management is interested in the Employees?
    (a) We are satisfied in our work through the assistance of the management.
    (b) The management is interested only in getting the work done.
    (c) Management treats workers as machines in the production process.
14. Do you fell the authorities are fair in their distribution of work.
    (a) Management is fair and will always be on the look out for the right person for the right job.
    (b) Management does not give the job according to the capacity and ability.
    (c) The work does not at all go to the right person here.
15. Do you feel you can work in the organisation as long as you do your work?
    (a) My job remains intact, I am sure, as long as I do my duty.

(b) Authorities can discharge me any time in their own interest.
(c) No man here can ever have feelings of security because of the authorities.

16. Management is making profits without taxing the workers.
(a) The profits are made without taxing the workers.
(b) The conditions should have been better with the present profits.
(c) The profits are made at the cost of the workers.

17. The present cost of materials do not permit the management to make profits.
(a) Making profits has become difficult due to the present day cost of materials.
(b) There is no relations between the cost of materials and profit making.
(c) No difficulty has been felt by the management in making profits.

18. Management is interested in higher production.
(a) Management is helpful to workers to increase production.
(b) Management is not enthusiastic about higher production.
(c) Management does not allow the workers to increase production.

**Cost Consciousness:**

19. Are you conscious of the cost of material you are producing.
(a) I am fully conscious of the cost of production of the product I am producing.
(b) There is necessity of being conscious of the cost of production.
(c) It is of no consequence to be conscious of the cost of production.

20. Does the product stand competition.
(a) The product will thrive in competition with this cost.
(b) There are chances of this product failing in competition due to this cost.
(c) The price of this product is not according to the product.

21. The cost of this product may bring in unemployment.
(a) The present cost is not so very high as to cause unemployment due to lessened sales.
(b) Unemployment has not resulted till now due to the cost.
(c) The present cost is very high.

31A6 JOB ATTITUDE INVENTORY

*Author* : J.S. Joseph.
*Availability* : Author.
*Time required* : 10 to 12 minutes.
*Level* : Skilled and semi-skilled workers.
*Main features* : It consists of sixteen job and situational factors based on Herzberg *et al.* findings. The 16 statements about job and job situation written separately on 5" × 3" size white cards and are numbered at random following a random digit table. Ratings of workers are obtained with these cards.
*Reliability* : Test-retest reliability of this ranking method in terms of composite

rank orders for all workers was found to be +.74 ($P > .005$).

*References* :

1. Joseph, J.S. Differential perception of factors in job attitude, *Psychology Annual*, 1970, 4, 22-24.
2. Joseph, J.S. A study of the rank ratings of industrial workers by rank comparison method. *Indian Journal of Applied Psychology*, 1968, 5(2), 66-77.

### 31A6 JOB ATTITUDE INVENTORY

(The following job factors written on cards have to be rank ordered by the respondent).

1. Being able to accomplish successfully a difficult task and to feel a sense of achievement.
2. Bring able to advance into a better job within a reasonable time.
3. Being able to take up responsibility in what you do in your work in the way you wish to take it up.
4. Being able to get praise and appreciation for the work done.
5. Being interested in the nature of work.
6. Having an adequate standard of cleanliness, heating, lighting and ventilation at the work place.
7. Being able to maintain personal relationship with your supervisor in the way you expect.
8. Being able to maintain personal relationship with your work mates in the way you want.
9. Feeling yourself to be an important part of the company you work for.
10. Being able to get help in your work from your supervisor in the way you expect.
11. Having better knowledge of company policy and administration.
12. Being able to earn enough according to your need.
13. Feeling yourself to be an important member of the group you work with.
14. Being able to get help in your work from the work mates in the way you expect.
15. Being able to learn what you want from the job and to increase your knowledge so that your prospects may be improved.
16. Being able to count on a steady employment.

### 31A7 JOB QUESTIONNAIRE

*Authors* : C.L. Nataraj and A. Hafeez.

*Availability* : A. Hafeez, Department of Industrial Management, Indian Institute of Science, Bangalore-12.

*Uses* : For finding satisfaction with jobs of industrial workers and as an indirect indicator of their morale.

*Time required* : No time limit.

*Level* : Adult males working in industry.

*Main features* : A questionnaire which takes into account a number of factors in the work situation such as physical and mental exertion, relations with workers and supervisor, security, advancement and other aspects.

*Scoring* : Using Guttman's formula

$$r = 2\left[1-\left(\frac{Sa^2+Sb^2}{St^2}\right)\right] = 0.80$$

which is highly significant.

*Norms* : Scores of 60 skilled workers are available.

*Reference* : Nataraj, C.L. and Hafeez, A. A study of job satisfaction among skilled workers. *Indian Journal of Social Work*, 1965, 26, 9-12.

31A7 JOB QUESTIONNAIRE

(The following items have to be answered on 'yes', 'no' alternatives).

1. Does your job tire you too much physically?
2. The working hours are so long that it seems that the work will never be over.
3. Do you feel that you cannot do full justice to your work as you have too much of work to do?
4. Do you become restless during working hours?
5. Does your work cause you mental strain?
6. Does your work have a bad effect on your health?
7. Do you feel that your co-workers regard you as their equals?
8. Do you generally get along with your co-workers?
9. Do you think that you are working with people whom you dislike?
10. Do you feel that others could make your work easier if they come to do?
11. Little friendship exists amongst the workers here.
12. Are you required to take more responsibility in your work than you can?
13. The supervisor treats workers as machine in the production process.
14. Even though we may be friendly one worker need not help the other.
15. Is your work approved by your supervisor?
16. We need others help in our work.
17. Do you move freely with the persons under whom you work?
18. Our supervisors never help us. They come only to remind us of our work.
19. Do you easily trust the authority under whom you work?
20. Do you feel that you are as efficient as your co-workers are?
21. Authorities can discharge me anytime in their own interest.
22. Are you afraid of losing your job?
23. The principle of the factory is to give less pay.
24. I only work because I have to earn my living.
25. Other jobs are more interesting than the work I am doing.
26. Are you actively trying for another job at present?
27. Do you often feel that your work is boring?
28. Do you come home with a feeling of satisfaction after your work?
29. Do you think that you have selected the wrong occupation?
30. I would get out of this factory as soon as I can find some other work.
31. I am really not interested in the present job.

32. Are you generally happy and cheerful when at work?
33. Do you feel sorry for accepting the job you have now?
34. Most of the time I have to force myself to go to work.
35. Did you really like the present job when you started on it?
36. Do you feel that you are really interested in your job?
37. Would your life seem to be empty without your present job?
38. If you have a choice would you choose a job in the present line of work or any other?
39. I do not worry a lot about my daily work.
40. Do you like to talk ill of your job?
41. Do you feel competent and able to handle your job?
42. Are you proud of your job and work you do?
43. Do you think that your work is important and worthwhile?
44. Do you think that your place in society as a worker is not so very respectable?
45. Our factory is not all suitable for working under the present conditions.
46. Do you feel that your work is too dirty and too noisy?
47. Do you feel that you have made a success of your job in your career?
48. Do you feel less satisfied with your work as time goes on?

31A8 SALES EXECUTIVE'S TROIKA CHECKLIST

*Author*: Udai Pareek.
*Availability*: Author, Indian Institute of Management, Ahmedabad.
*Uses* : To measure style of sales-persons and sales managers. Also used for training of sales persons and sales managers.
*Time required*: About 15 minutes.
*Main features* : It measures a combination of three orientations: concern for sales (product), concern for the sales person, and concern for the marketing strategy. Primary and secondary styles are obtained out of the 9 described below:

1,1,1 (Routine) My obligation to my company is to see that the salesmen carry on their working according to our plans.

1,9,1 (Friendly) My obligation is to the salesmen who are persons with feelings, and if they are satisfied the sales of products and business of the company will be high.

9,1,1 (Target-oriented) My obligation is to see the product, and this can be done by pushing salesmen who will eventually be happy if they sell the product, and the company will prosper.

9,9,1 (Friendly task master) My obligation is to see that salesmen are happy and satisfied and are able to sell the product. This will increase the business of the company.

1,1,9 (Marketing-oriented) My obligation is to develop an overall marketing policy of the company. If the company has a sound marketing policy, the sales will be high and the salesmen will be motivated.

1,9,9 (Friendly loyal) My obligation is to develop an overall effective marketing strategy of the company and to develop my sales people. The sales will take care of themselves.

9,1,9 (Target marketing-oriented) My obligation is to get good sales of my product and develop an appropriate marketing strategy. In such a situation salesmen will have job satisfaction.

9,9,9 (Creative) My obligation is to develop a sound marketing force and policy in my company, and I can do this by examining with my salesmen how the sales of our products can be increased and how new markets can be developed.

5,5,5 (Compromiser) My obligation is to balance emphasise on developing salesmen, marketing policy and sales of products.

*Scoring* : Scoring key is given below.

31A8 SALES TROIKA CHECKLIST

(For each of the five dimensions the statements (a to i) are to be ranked from 9 (describes the respondent) to 1 (describes him least accurately).

A. **Sales Goals**

(a) My main obligation is to inform the customer about our product.
(b) My main obligation is to please and personally relate to the customer.
(c) My main obligation is to sell the product.
(d) My main obligation is to help the customer solve his problem.
(e) My main obligation is to represent my company and its good name.
(f) My main obligation is to personally relate to the customer through the good name of my company.
(g) My main obligation is to sell the product of my company.
(h) My main obligation is to sell the company to the customer by helping him to take the best decision.
(i) My main obligation is to use tried techniques to sell my product.

B. **Decision-making**

(a) I directly influence and push for decisions in favour of my product.
(b) I work with the customer on agreed decisions.
(c) Decisions are made by the customer and my information about my company influences him.
(d) Decisions are made by the customer who is influenced by my good relations with him and the image of my company.
(e) Decisions are made by the customer on my making the information about my product available to him.
(f) Decisions are made by the customer and my good relations with him influence him.
(g) I work with the customer for reaching decisions that solve his problems and for continuing relationship with him.
(h) I influence the decision and also allow the customer to take his decisions.
(i) I influence the decisions by aggressively selling the product and the good name of my company.

C. **Anxiety Management**

(a) I try to stay unperturbed in the hope that some solution will emerge in due course.
(b) I try to locate the cause of anxiety, share the concern with the customer and my colleagues to work out a solution.
(c) I become more active in arguing for my product and my company.
(d) Under anxiety my arguments become more forceful and I become more active.
(e) I avoid anxiety provoking situations.
(f) I show and assure warmth and personal concern.
(g) I assure warmth and the support from the company.
(h) I try to recognise the cause of anxiety and share the concern with the customer.
(i) I avoid anxiety, but when confronted I report it to and get help from my superiors.

D. **Conflict Management**

(a) I avoid conflicts and remain neutral.
(b) I deal firmly with the situation through my ability and knowledge.
(c) I avoid conflicts but when faced seek the support of my company.
(d) I try to diagnose the conflict, and find solution which will help maintain mutually profitable relationship of my company with the customer.
(e) I work on personal relations and try to arouse friendly feelings.
(f) I try to resolve the conflict by finding out the causes.
(g) I work on personal relations and good relations with my company.
(h) I use my and my company's strength in winning it.
(i) I try to remain undisturbed and work for the resolution of the conflict.

E. **Self-management**

(a) I try to maintain good relations as well as sell my company's products.
(b) I try to win my arguments and take help of my company.
(c) I am concerned with my company's name and most of the time feel people do not understand us. I do not like such situations.
(d) I try to dominate others and rebuff them with my arguments.
(e) I try to adapt myself to the situation.
(f) I try to collect data and facts and find solutions to problems. I also enjoy relating to people and helping them search solutions to their problems.
(g) I try to appeal to others' feelings and also tell how my company can help them.
(h) I try to help others see what is good for them.
(i) I try to appeal to good relations and feelings of others.

31A9 S-D EMPLOYEES INVENTORY

*Authors* : D.M. Pestonjee and S. Sultan Akntar.

*Availability* : Authors, Department of Psychology, Banaras Hindu University, Varanasi.

*Uses* : To assess job satisfaction of blue collar workers.

*Time required* : 20 to 30 minutes (no time limit).

*Level* : Literate employee; blue collar.

*Main features* : Measures the extent of employees' satisfaction in four areas: (i) job, (ii) management (iii) social relations, (iv) personal adjustment. It is in Hindi.

*Scoring* : Scored by punched keys.

*Reliability* : Reliability coefficients calculated by the K.R. 20 formula are: (i) Job = .72, (ii) Management = .87, (iii) Social Relations = .61, (iv) Personal Adjustment = .66, (v) Overall = .67.

*Validity* : Item test score correlations (Point-Biserial *r*) computed and items found to be significant at .05 level were retained. Significance of difference between scores obtained by two *contrast groups* was determined by applying the Kolomogrov-Smirnov test.

*Norms* : Available on 400 textile mill workers, and 150 employees from light engineering units.

*Reference* : Pestonjee, D.M. A study of employees' morale and job satisfaction as related to organisational structure. Doctoral Thesis in Psychology, Aligarh Muslim University, 1967.

## 31A9 S-D EMPLOYEES INVENTORY

(The respondent has to check the following items on yes/no response system).

1. Do you work with good tools, material and equipment?
2. Do your supervisors reward good workers?
3. Do you think that good people are respected in society?
4. Does the thought of future mishaps make you worried?
5. Are most of your acquaintances reliable?
6. Do your supervisors sympathetically hear your difficulties?
7. Does this job provide good opportunities for promotion?
8. Do you feel that due to poor health you could not get ahead in your job?
9. Do your neighbours help you when you are in some difficulties?
10. Do you sometimes think that you do not have those qualities which others have?
11. Do you have to work with some such people whom you don't like much?
12. Do you often feel that you are alone in this wide world?
13. Do you feel satisfied with the overtime rule of your organisation?
14. Do your supervisors think that most of the people are hardworking?
15. Do you sometimes feel that there is none in whom you can confide?
16. Do you often get such ideas at the time of going to bed which make sleep difficult?
17. Do your supervisors behave well with the employees?
18. Do you think that the work you are doing is interesting?
19. Do you think that promotions to employees are given impartially?
20. Do you get upset for a long time when criticised by somebody?
21. Do you feel satisfied with the condition of the place where you work?

22. Do you believe that in case of emergency (such as illness or marriage) the management would help you?
23. Do you hesitate in accepting the responsibilities of social functions?
24. Are you frequently worried due to illness of your family members?
25. Are most of your neighbours gentle and worth mixing with?
26. Do your superiors invite suggestions from you for the welfare of your company?
27. Do you think that you have selected the right job for yourself ?
28. Do you sometimes think that your family members do not care for you sufficiently?
29. Do you sometimes think of changing your house due to the neighbours?
30. Are there any such members in your family whose presence causes you annoyance?
31. Do you sometimes think that you can earn more in some other job?
32. Do you think that bad people outnumber good people in the society?
33. Does your job allow you sufficient time for rest and creation?
34. Do your superiors respect your skills and abilities?
35. Do you think that most people exploit the weakness and shortcoming of others?
36. Do small things also hurt you?
37. Do your superiors harshly punish employees for simple mistakes?
38. Do your fellow workers help you?
39. Do you think that people get promotions due to personal pulls?
40. Do your relatives frequently bother or trouble you?
41. If you are offered elsewhere the same facilities which you are enjoying in your present job, would you like to change your job?
42. Are the employees dismissed from the job on simple and trivial matters?
43. Do you feel hesitation in talking to strangers?
44. Do you often have to leave tasks unfinished?
45. Do you think that your friends are sincere to you?
46. If you were an officer would you treat your subordinates the same way as your officers do?
47. Do you think that you have to work too much here?
48. Had there been some unpleasant experience in your childhood, which you cannot forget?
49. Do you believe that most of the social customs and traditions are troublesome?
50. Do you pass your time pleasantly in your home?
51. Do you think that your work is hard and difficult?
52. Are most of the people in society selfish?
53. Is your profession respected by others?
54. Do your superiors believe that the workers welfare is their own welfare?
55. Do you think that people do not make lasting friendship with you?
56. Do the members of your family often do things against your wishes?
57. Do most of your colleagues work under duress and fear?
58. Would you advise any of your close relatives to do the job which you are doing?
59. Do you think that the employees are treated here the way they should be treated?

60. Do you sometimes get worried without any apparent cause?
61. Do you sometimes feel like giving up this job and taking up some other job?
62. Do your superiors praise good workers?
63. Do most of the people misunderstand you?
64. Do you earn enough money so that you don't have to seek help from others?
65. Are you troubled by feelings of caste and creed in society?
66. Are you often given such orders by your superiors which are difficult to carry out?
67. Do you think that this work provides you opportunities to display your talent and skills?
68. Do you generally feel tired after doing ordinary jobs?
69. Do you think that your fellow workers generally avoid your company?
70. Do you think that things go wrong without any fault of yours?
71. Do you think that you need some more training on this job?
72. Do you feel hesitant in seeking advice from others?
73. Do you think that in spite of your lack of interest in this job, you work because you get good money?
74. Are you often asked to work at odd hours?
75. Do you easily make friends with new people?
76. Do the members of your family live cordially?
77. Do your superiors think that their employees are efficient?
78. Do you think that your present job is a respectable job for a person like you?
79. Do you think that you can place your problems before your superiors without any hesitations?
80. Do you get worried often thinking about the goal or purpose of life?

31A10 EMPLOYEES MORALE SCALE (EMS)

*Author*: D.M. Pestonjee.

*Availability* : Author, Department of Psychology, Banaras Hindu University, Varanasi.

*Time required*: 15-25 minutes. (No time limit).

*Level*: Literate blue-collar workers.

*Main features* : The E.M.S. is meant to assess moral in four areas: (i) Fairness of employer's policies and behaviour, (ii) Adequacy of immediate leadership, (iii) Sense of participation in the organisation, and (iv) Sense of worth of the organisation : Regard and identification. The scale was constructed using Thurstone's method. It is in Hindi.

*Scoring* : Scored by punched key.

*Norms* : Available on 400 textile mill workers.

*Reference* : Pestonjee, D.M. A study of employees' morale and job satisfaction as related to organisation structures. Ph.D. Thesis, Aligarh Muslim University, 1967.

31A10 EMPLOYEES MORALE SCALE

(The respondent has to check out three statements he agrees with from each of the I, II, III, & IV sections. In all he has to check out twelve statements).

SECTION I

1. Workers get a fair deal.
2. Workers' welfare is considered the most important thing here.
3. Workers' abilities are respected more here than in any other company.
4. Good work is praised sometimes and sometimes not.
5. Partiality is considered against the policy of the company.
6. Workers cannot raise their voice for their own welfare.
7. Ordinary workers are not considered as human beings.

SECTION II

1. Only able persons are appointed as officers here.
2. Officers here consider the welfare of workers as their own.
3. Some workers here are more capable than their officers.
4. Officers understand the difficulties of every body.
5. For officers here a good man is one who is a good worker.
6. Officers want their own welfare not that of workers.
7. There are no such qualities in the officers here for which they may be praised.

SECTION III

1. Everybody is consulted for the welfare of the company.
2. Workers are encouraged for suggesting new ideas about the work.
3. Workers are bound to work in particular way (order), so there is no enthusiasm for work.
4. Workers are free to apply new techniques (method) of work according their own will.
5. In other companies, workers are getting more chance to show their ability and to utilise their past experience.
6. Workers are never consulted about the work.
7. It is believed here that the progress of the company depends only on its officers.

SECTION IV

1. Workers are always willing to do everything for the company.
2. The future of the company and the future of workers is the same.
3. My company gets respect from every quarter.
4. Workers of this company are better off than workers of any other company.
5. I will not advise any of my relatives and friends to work here.
6. The progress of the company does not provide any benefit to the

workers.

7. Most of the people work here under conditions of helplessness or fear.

## B Instruments with technical information

### 31B1 ATTITUDE AND ADJUSTMENT INVENTORY

*Author* : S. Sultan Akhtar.
*Availability* : Author, Department of Psychology, Aligarh Muslim University, Aligarh.
*Uses* : For evaluating employees adjustment.
*Time required* : 15-20 minutes.
*Level* : Adult (employees).
*Scoring* : Scored by means of punched cardboard keys.
*Reliability* : Split-half reliability for various areas varies from .80 to .94.
*Validity* : Inter-correlations between the various areas range from .38 to .82. Correlations between area and total scores range from .77 to .94. Also validated against supervisors ratings.
*Norms* : Norms are available.
*References* :

1. Akhtar, S.S. and Pestonjee, D.M. A study of employee adjustment within and outside work situation. *Indian Journal of Social Work*, 1963, 23(4), 327-340.
2. Akhtar, S.S. and Pestonjee, D.M. Organisation structure and employees adjustment. *Indian Journal of Social Work*, 1968, 28(3).

### 31B2 ORGANISATIONAL CLIMATE QUESTIONNAIRE

*Authors* : T. Venkateswara Rao and S.N. Chattopadhyay.
*Availability* : First author, Indian Institute of Management, Ahmedabad.
*Uses* : To measure the organisational climate of an industry.
*Time required* : About half-an hour.
*Level* : Industrial workers, supervisors and managers.
*Main features* : It is 21-item Likert type questionnaire measuring different dimensions for the organisational environment of industries. Available in Telugu language.
*Reference* : Rao, T.V. and Chattopadhyay, S.N. *Perception of organisational climate, level of aspiration and productivity in small industries*. Hyderabad. SIET Institute, 1970.

### 31B3 JOB ATTITUDES SCALE

*Authors* : P.K. Chaudhury and Dilip K. Lahiri.
*Level* : Industrial workers.
*Main features* : It is a 49-item scale measuring different job variables related to satisfaction on a Likert type scale.

*Reference* : Chaudhury, P.K. and Lahiri, D.K. Perceived job characteristics as satisfiers and dissatisfiers by manual workers. *Indian Journal of Psychology*, 1968, 43, 41-61.

31B4 ATTITUDE TOWARDS FACTORY SCALE

*Author* : H.C. Ganguli.

*Availability* : Author, Department of Psychology, Delhi University.

*Main features* : It is a 41-item Likert scale measuring general satisfaction with the company, satisfaction with organisational technical aspects of supervision and supervisor as a person. Originally used on an electrical engineering company. Scales are based on factor analysis.

*Reference* : Ganguli, H.C. Attitude of union and non-union employees in a Calcutta Engineering Factory. *Journal of Applied Psychology*, 1966, 40, 78-87.

31B5 SUPERVISORY BEHAVIOUR QUESTIONNAIRE

*Authors* : K. Harigopal and S.N. Chattopadhyay.

*Availability* : First Author, Department of Psychology, Andhra University.

*Uses* : To measure supervisor behaviour as perceived by workers, managers and supervisors.

*Level* : Industrial workers, supervisors and managers.

*Main features* : It is available in English and Telugu. Covers various dimensions of supervisory behaviour. Five-point Likert scale type of items.

*Scoring* : Summated ratings.

*Reference* : Harigopal, K. and Chattopadhyay, S.N. *Job satisfaction and perceived supervisory behaviour in small industries*. Hyderabad : SIET studies, 1970.

31B6 JOB-SATISFACTION QUESTIONNAIRE

*Authors* : K. Harigopal, N.Y. Reddy and S.N. Chattopadhyay.

*Availability* : Authors, Department of Psychology, Andhra University, Waltair.

*Time required* : About 30 to 40 minutes.

*Level* : Workers, Supervisors and Managers.

*Main features* : It is a questionnaire consisting of 21 items. Each item is to be answered on a 5-point scale ranging from strongly agree to strongly disagree. The questionnaire measures attitude of an employee towards various aspects of the job such as (1) security, (2) pay, (3) working conditions, (4) interpersonal relations, (5) opportunity for advancement and (6) interest in job (in terms of change to show initiative, opportunity to learn tthe job, opportunity to use ones own ideas and interest in the company). It is available in Telugu.

*Scoring* : Five-point summated ratings.

*Reference* : Harigopal, K., Reddy, N.Y. and Chattopadhyay, S.N. Job satisfaction and productivity in small industries. *Research Bulletin*, 1969, 5, 15-23.

31B7 ATTITUDE TOWARDS LABOUR UNIONS

*Author* : P.S. Hundal.
*Availability* : Author.
*Time required* : About 5 minutes.
*Level* : Originally used with industrial entrepreneurs, could be used with others also.
*Main features* : Thurstone's technique of equal appearing intervals was used for selecting few statements out of forty statements.
*Scoring* : Key available with the weighted scores for each response.
*Reliability* : Split-half reliability coefficient was found to be .77 (corrected by S-B formula).
*Validity* : The face validity of the items indicated by the low Q-values of the statements (.19 to 1.74).
*Reference* : Hundal, P.S. A study of attitude of small scale entrepreneurs towards labour unions. *Indian Journal of Applied Psychology*, 1967, 4(1), 28-32.

31B8 BEHAVIOURAL FATIGUE INVENTORY (BFI)

*Author* : S. Narayanan.
*Availability* : Author.
*Uses* : To assess the behavioural manifestation of fatigue under an industrial condition.
*Time required* : 15 minutes.
*Level* : Industrial workers.
*Main features* : It consists of items relating to subjective aspects of fatigue in the industrial work situations. The symptoms of fatigue included in the inventory may be classified into (1) Decrement in responsiveness as related to productivity, (2) Physiological symptoms associated with energy expenditure, (3) Psychological symptoms of fatigue.
*Reliability* : Reliability coefficient was found out to be 0.57. Split-half method was used to measure the internal consistency which give a coefficient of .71.
*Validity* : Two approaches were made in assessing the validity of the BFI. The first approach was concerned with determining validity by way of computing reliability index. The reliability index was worked out from the correlation coefficient of the BFI arrived through the Kuder-Richardson formula. The validity of the BFI thus found out was 0.76. As a next method it was considered appropriate to validate the BFI against the battery of a number of objective behavioural tests that measure reactive inhabition. Hence the multiple correlation coefficient was found between the BFI scores and the scores on a battery of objective behavioural tests. The multiple correlation coefficient value of 0.7696 is sufficiently high showing the high validity of the BFI.
*Reference* : Narayanan, S. The Behavioural Fatigue Inventory (BFI). *Indian Journal of Applied Psychology*, 1971, 8(1), 41-45.

31B9 PALIWAL JOB DISSATISFACTION QUESTIONNAIRE

*Author* : T.R. Paliwal.

*Availability* : Author, Principal, Gandhi Maha-Vidyalaya, Orai.

*Uses* : To assess the degree of favourableness in attitudes and perceptions of employees concerning a number of job related factors.

*Level* : Industrial workers.

*Main features* : It is a questionnaire of an omnibus type consisting of 22 open ended items aimed at measuring the degree of dissatisfaction experienced by factory workers.

*Reliability* : Reliability of the test checked by odd-even split of items was found to be 0.97.

*Reference* : Mukherjee, B.N. and Menon, A.S. Personality characteristics and intra-individual variability in industrial output. *Indian Journal of Industrial Relations*, 1969, 4(4), 426-481.

31B10 JOB SATISFACTION QUESTIONNAIRE

*Authors* : G.V.S. Rao and T. Ganguli.

*Main features* : It is a questionnaire measuring job satisfaction- dissatisfaction with regard to 16 job factors, (7 motivators and 9 hygienes).

*Reliability* : Reliability coefficients for the satisfaction and dissatisfaction scales were 0.89 and 0.91 respectively.

*Reference* : Rao, G.V.S. and Ganguli, T. Job satisfaction of highly skilled personnel: a test of the generality of the two-factor theory. *Indian Journal of Applied Psychology*, 1972, 9(1), 26-31.

31B11 JOB ATTITUDE QUESTIONNAIRE

*Author* : S. Sinha.

*Availability* : Author.

*Uses* : To study the attitude of the workers towards different work situations and other factors connected with it.

*Level* : Industrial workers.

*Main features* : It contains 20 questions with four questions in each of the five areas viz. (1) job satisfaction, (2) satisfaction with wages, (3) satisfaction with supervisory practice, (4) company policy, (5) personal attitude. It is a Likert type scale.

*Scoring* : Likert type scoring. Summated ratings.

*Reliability* : Reliability of the questionnaire was found out by finding the inter-correlation between the scores in the 5 factors and also their correlation with total scores.

*Reference* : Sinha, S. A survey of some factors on the question of industrialisation in India. *Indian Journal of Psychology*, 1960, 35(1), 9-16.

## C Citations

31C1 ATTITUDE SCALE QUESTIONNAIRE

*Author*: R. Chatterjee.
*Reference* : Chatterjee, R. A study on the relationship between workers and their employers in two factories. *Indian Journal of Psychology*, 1954, 24(1-3).

31C2 BUREAUCRACY QUESTIONNAIRE

*Author*: S.K. Goyal.
*Reference* : Goyal, S.K. Bureaucracy : A sociological study of white-collar workers (clerks). *Social Science Review*, 1969, 2(2), 21-33.

31C3 JOB SATISFACTION QUESTIONNAIRE

*Author*: T.N. Guha.
*Reference* : Guha, T.N. Personality factors and job satisfaction among shoe factory workers. *Indian Psychological Review*, 1965, 2(1), 59-6.

31C4 JOB SATISFACTION SCALE

*Author*: A.K. Prasad.
*Reference* : Prasad, A.K. A study of personality and some personal factors in job-satisfaction. *Indian Journal of Psychology*, 1965, 4(4), 147-151.

31C5 JOB SATISFACTION QUESTIONNAIRE

31C6 FOUR-POINT RATING SCALE FOR JOB ANALYSIS

*Authors* : K.N. Sharma and P.N. Kalra.
*Reference* : Sharma, K.N. and Kalra, P.N. An empirical investigation of job analysis reliability method and results. *Journal of Psychological Researches*, 1959, 3(3), 102-114.

## D Adaptations

31D1 BRAYFIED AND ROTHE'S JOB SATISFACTION INDEX

*Author*: B.N. Mukherji.
*Language* : Marathi.

*Availability* : Author.

*Reference* : Mukherji, B.N. Inter-relationships among measures of job-satisfaction. *Indian Journal of Psychology*, 1969, 46, 21-32.

## 31D2 FREIDLANDER'S JOB SATISFACTION QUESTIONNAIRE

*Author* : B.N. Mukherjee.

*Language* : Marathi.

*Availability* : Author.

*Reference* : Mukherjee, B.N. Inter-relationships among measures of job-satisfaction and job involvement. *Indian Journal of Psychology*, 1969, 46, 21-32.

## 31D3 HUMAN RELATIONS INVENTORY

*Author* : U.P. Singh.

*Language* : Hindi.

*Availability* : Author.

*Main features* : It contains 33 items selected from the original 35.

*Reliability* : Split-half reliability coefficients were found to be .59 and .69 respectively for boys and girls (N=100 each).

*Reference* : Singh, U.P. Movement from one's own position towards group norm as a function of intellectual. *Psychological Studies*, 1969, 14(2), 88-93.

## 31D4 LODAHL AND KEFNER'S JOB INVOLVEMENT SCALE

*Author* : B.N. Mukherji.

*Language* : Marathi.

*Availability* : Author.

*Reference* : Mukherjee, B.N. Inter-relationships among measures of job satisfaction and job involvement. *Indian Journal of Psychology*, 1969, 46, 21-32.

## 31D5 YUZUK MORALE INVENTORY

*Author* : Prabhakar Singh.

*Reference* : Singh, Prabhakar. A factorial study of various morale factors of pro-union workers. *Indian Psychological Review*, 1959, 5(2), 202-206.

# 2. HOSPITALS

## A Complete instruments

32A1 WARD SOCIAL SYSTEM QUESTIONNAIRE

*Authors* : K.G. Agrawal and A. Timmappaya.
*Availability* : NIHAE, E-16, Greater Kailash, New Delhi-48.
*Uses* : For measuring social system of a hospital concerning its integration, adaptation, goal, conflict resolution etc.
*Time required* : About 60 minutes.
*Level* : Hospital employees.
*Main features* : It is a questionnaire based on Georgopouls model. Factor analysis revealed following 4 factors : (i) Goal attainment function; (ii) Tension management function; (iii) Integrative function; and (iv) Adaptation function.
*Scoring* : Four schemes of scoring are used based on 0 through 4 scores minus or plus; or 2, 1, 0, — 1, — 2 scheme.
*Validity* : Factor analysis revealed a factor structure, same as Parson's theoretical model.
*References* :


1. Timmappayya, A. *et al. Patient satisfaction and ward social system*, New Delhi, NIHAE, 1971.
2. Advani, M. Agrawal, K.G. and Timmappayya, A. Developing a hypothetical model for hospital ward social system, Delhi, NIHAE, 1971.


32A1 WARD SOCIAL SYSTEM QUESTIONNAIRE

(Respondent has to check one of the response alternatives given after each question).

1. How much satisfied do you feel with your present salary?
   (1) Completely satisfied; (2) Fairly satisfied; (3) A little satisfied; (4) Fairly dissatisfied; (5) Completely dissatisfied.
2. How much does your job give you a chance to do things you are best at?
   (1) An excellent chance; (2) A very good chance; (3) A fair chance; (4) Very little chance; (5) No chance at all.
3. How much satisfied do you feel about your chances of promotion in this hospital?
   (1) Completely satisfied; (2) Fairly satisfied; (3) A little satisfied; (4) Fairly dissatisfied; (5) Completely dissatisfied.

4. To what extent does your work here help you learn more about your profession or occupation?
   (1) To a very great extent; (2) To a great extent; (3) To some extent; (4) To a small extent; (5) Not at all.
5. On the whole, what do you think of this hospital as a place of work?
   (1) It is an excellent place of work; (2) A very good place; (3) A fair place; (4) A poor place; (5) It is a very poor place.
6. How easy is it for you to get together and exchange information and ideas about the work with people from other departments where jobs are related to yours?
   (1) It is very easy; (2) It is fairly easy; (3) It is not very easy; (4) It is rather difficult; (5) It is very difficult.
7. To what extent do the people from the various inter-related departments make an efforts to avoid creating problems or interference with each other's duties and responsibilities?
   (1) To a very great extent; (2) To a great extent; (3) To some extent; (4) To a small extent; (5) Not at all.
8. To what extent do you think people do their work according to rules and regulations set up by the hospital?
   (1) To a very great extent; (2) To a great extent; (3) To some extent; (4) To a small extent; (5) Not at all.
9. To what extent people in this ward do their work in the spirit of team work?
   (1) To a very great extent; (2) To a great extent; (3) To some extent; (4) To a small extent; (5) Not at all.
10. To what extent are all related things and activities well tip in the every day routine of the hospital?
    (1) To a very great extent; (2) To a great extent; (3) To some extent; (4) To a small extent; (5) Not at all.
11. In your opinion, how well is this hospital doing in making the patients comfortable?
    (1) Excellent; (2) Good; (3) Fair; (4) Rather poor; (5) Very poor.
12. In your opinion how well the *nursing* department is doing its job in this ward?
    (1) Excellent; (2) Good; (3) Fair; (4) Rather poor; (5) Very poor.
13. What would you like to say about the *medical care* (including surgical work) given to patients in this ward?
    (1) Excellent; (2) Good; (3) Fair; (4) Rather poor; (5) Very poor.
14. What would you like to say about the service rendered by the *nursing orderlies, ayiahs and sweepers*? How well are they doing in this ward?
    (1) Excellent; (2) Good; (3) Fair; (4) Rather poor; (5) Very poor.
15. How would you describe your *immediate superior?*
    (1) He is helpful and understanding; (2) He is personally likable person; (3) He is expert in his field.
16. On the whole, would you say that in this ward there is some tension or conflict (friction) between the two groups in each of the following pairs;
    (1) Nurses of one shift with another shift; (2) Staff nurses and student nurses; (3) Doctors and nurses; (4) Senior doctors and internees; (5) Orderlies and nurses; (6) Nurses and sweepers; (7) Sweepers and

orderlies; (8) Sister and nurses; (9) Sister and sweepers; (10) Sister and orderlies.

17. Check in the appropriate column below how often your *immediate superior* talks to you in the following way?
(1) Shows appreciation of your work; (2) Gives direction of orders; (3) Explains things or gives suggestions; (4) Asks for suggestions or opinions; (5) Asks for explanation or clarifications; (6) Criticises you or refuses to help you; (7) He is unnecessarily formal.
18. In general, how well established are the routines of the different departments in this hospital?
(1) Extremely well established; (2) very well established; (3) Fairly well established; (4) Not too well established; (5) Not well established.
19. Do you agree that the work assignments are well planned in this hospital?
(1) Extremely well planned; (2) Very well planned; (3) Fairly well planned; (4) Not too well planned; (5) Not well planned.
20. How clearly defined are the policies and the various rules and regulations of the hospital?
(1) They are defined as clearly as they should be defined; (2) They are defined almost as clearly as they should be defined; (3) They should be defined somewhat more clearly; (4) They should be defined more clearly; (5) They should be defined much more clearly.
21. To what extent do the members of staff here make an effort to avoid creating problems or interference?
(1) To a very great extent; (2) To a great extent; (3) To some extent; (4) To a small extent; (5) Not at all.
22. To what extent would you say, all persons in this ward do their jobs properly without getting in each other's way?
(1) To a very great extent; (2) To a great extent; (3) To some extent; (4) To a small extent; (5) Not at all.
23. To what extent, would you say, patients feel that the ward personnel around them work together smoothly and without conflict?
(1) They work completely smoothly; (2) They work very smoothly; (3) They work fairly smoothly; (4) They do not work smoothly; (5) They do not work smoothly at all.
24. Do you feel satisfied with mutual help or willingness of the members of staff to assist each other when it is needed?
(1) I feel very much satisfied; (2) I feel satisfied; (3) I feel somewhat satisfied; (4) I feel satisfied a little; (5) I do not feel satisfied.
25. Suppose you were having some sort of difficulty in your job. To what extent do you feel your *immediate superior* would be willing to go out of the way to help you if you asked for it?
(1) To a very great extent; (2) To a considerable extent; (3) To some extent; (4) To a small extent; (5) Not at all.
26. How do you feel about what your *immediate superior* expects you to do?
(1) He expects far too much; (2) It is too much; (3) It is a little too much; (4) It is all right; (5) I do not know what he expects.
27. How free do you feel to discuss your personal problems with your

*immediate superior?*
(1) I always feel free to discuss; (2) I usually feel free; (3) Sometimes I feel free; (4) Only once a while; (5) Never feel free.

28. What kind of reputation does this hospital have in the community?
(1) An excellent reputation; (2) A very good reputation; (3) A good reputation; (4) A fair reputation; (5) Rather poor reputation.
29. On the basis of your experience and information, how would you say patients feel about this ward?
(1) All patients without exception speak very well of this hospital; (2) Nearly all the patients speak very well of this hospital; (3) The large majority of the patients speak very well of this hospital; (4) Many of the patients speak well of this hospital; (5) Only a few of the patients speak high of this hospital.
30. How would you rate that quality of *patient care in this* hospital as compared to other hospitals?
(1) Outstanding; (2) Much better; (3) About the same; (4) Somewhat poorer; (5) Much poorer.

## 32A2 PATIENT SATISFACTION DOCTOR-NURSES QUESTIONNAIRE (PSDNQ)

*Authors* : K.G. Agrawal, M. Advani, Iqbal Akhtar, V.S. Chopra, S.N. Chattopadhyay, and A. Thimmappayya.
*Availability* : Authors, NIHAE, E-16, Greater Kailash-I, New Delhi-48.
*Uses* : For measuring doctors' and nurses' attitude regarding satisfaction of their patients.
*Time required* : 5 minutes.
*Level* : Nurses and Doctors.
*Main features* : Likert type scale.
*Scoring* : Five-point summated ratings.

## 32A2 PATIENT SATISFACTION DOCTOR-NURSES QUESTIONNAIRE (PSDNQ)

(The following items have to be rated on a 5-point scale).

1. How much do you think there is reasons for the patient to be dissatisfied?
2. How much do you think the service of this hospital could be improved if the interference by the politicians in the affairs of the hospital is stopped?
3. To what extent do you think patient satisfaction could be improved if you had more equipment?
4. If you had more medicines to what extent do you think the patients could be satisfied?
5. To what extent do you think additional beds can help in improving patient comfort?
6. How much do you think it is necessary to tell the patients about his treatment and illness for making him satisfied?

7. To what extent do you think your hospital requires public relation work to make the community conscious of your limitations?
8. To what extent do you think the community expectations are unreasonable in view of the resources of this hospital?
9. To what extent do you think lack of coordination between various people and departments in this hospital are responsible for the patient dissatisfaction?
10. To what extent would you say the inefficiency of the class IV employees is responsible for patient dissatisfaction from the hospital?

## 32A3 HOSPITAL FOOD QUESTIONNAIRE (HFQ)

*Authors* : A. Thimmappayya, U. Pareek, S.N. Chattopadhyay and K.G. Agrawal.
*Availability* : Authors, National Institute of Health Administration and Education, E-16, Greater Kailash-I, New Delhi-48.
*Uses* : For opinion survey regarding food among the indoor patients.
*Time required* : About 5 minutes.
*Level* : Adults.
*Scoring* : Qualitative, Percentages for patients likes/dislikes can be worked out.
*Reference* : Thimmappayya, A., Pareek, U., Chattopadhyay, S.N. and Agrawal, K.G. *Patient satisfaction and ward social system*, New Delhi, NIHAE, 1971.

## 32A3 HOSPITAL FOOD QUESTIONNAIRE (HFQ)

1. What do you think about food?
   (1) Tasty/tasteless, (2) Nice/useless, (3) Nourishing/not nourishing (4) on time/late.
2. Do you eat your food properly?
   (1) Yes, always, (2) Usually I take it, (3) Somehow I eat it, (4) I do not eat properly, (5) I eat with difficulty/I do not eat.
3. Reason for your not eating the food?
   (1) Manner of serving, (2) Untouchability, (3) Diet (4) Monotony, (5) Spicy, (6) Cold, (7) Loss of appetite, (8) Not well timed, (9) Supplied free.

## 32A4ORGANISATION ENVIRONMENT QUESTIONNAIRE (HOSPITAL)

*Authors* : Somnath Chattopadhyay; K.G. Agrawal and Mohan Advani.
*Availability* : National Institute of Health Administration and Education, E-16, Greater Kailash, New Delhi-48.
*Uses* : To study climates of and motivation to work in Hospital.
*Time required* : No limit.
*Level* : Senior Class I, Class I, Class II, Class III and Class IV employees of Hospitals.
*Main features* : Self-administered. Contains 70 questions covering following factors: bureaucratic orientation, individual involvement, dependence, boredom, sensitivity to others, role clarity, interdepartmental communication, authority, decision-making, security of job, team work, freedom of work, output orientation, freedom to express differences, organisational clarity,

grievance handling, trust and confidence, conformity, productivity, organisational structure, involvement, liberal versus conservatism, tension, red tapism, hostility, team spirit, personal loyalties, sense of time, conflict resolution, growth and involvement in work.

*Scoring* : Summated ratings.

*Reliability* : Item analysis was carried. Reliability coefficient was found to be .67.

*Validity* : Item validity, factorial validity and judges ratings were used to establish validity.

32A4 ORGANISATION ENVIRONMENT QUESTIONNAIRE (HOSPITAL)

(The following items have to be answered by the respondent by checking one of the alternatives provided below each item).

1. In some places people welcome differences in points of views, whereas in other places it is considered bad manners to express differences of opinion. How do Superior Officers in this organisation react to differences in opinion?
   (a) They almost always welcome them; (b) They usually welcome them; (c) They sometimes welcomes them; (d) They rarely welcome them; (e) They almost never welcome them.
2. How the objectives set in this organisation?
   (a) Orders are issued with no opportunity to raise questions or give comments; (b) Orders are issued and explained and then an opportunity is given to ask questions; (c) Orders are drawn up, but are discussed with subordinates and sometimes modified before being issued; (d) Specific alternative objectives are drawn up by supervisors, and subordinates are asked to discuss and choose the one they prefer; (e) Problems are presented to those persons who are involved and objectives are then set up by the subordinates and the supervisors jointly by group participation and discussion.
3. If somebody says the staff members in this organisation are so preoccupied with their duties that they can hardly spare time to participate in staff meetings". How far would you agree with it?
   (a) Strongly disagree; (2) Disagree; (3) Neither agree nor disagree; (4) Agree; (5) Strongly agree.
4. Whenever an important decision has to be taken regarding any work, the tendency here is to pass the file to somebody else for making the decision. How often does it happen here?
   (a) Almost always; (b) Usually; (c) Sometimes; (d) Rarely; (e) Almost never.
5. To what extent do the superiors and the knowledgeable colleagues take pains to help an employee who wants to learn more about his job?
   (a) To a great extent; (b) To a considerable extent; (c) To some extent; (d) To a little extent; (e) Not at all.
6. Disagreement among the staff about the best way to do things is encouraged in this hospital. How often does it happen here?
   (a) Almost never; (b) Rarely; (c) Sometimes; (d) Usually; (e) Almost always.

7. To what extent do people in your work group emphasise that work should be accomplished by individuals than as a team?
   (a) To a very great extent; (b) To a considerable extent; (c) To some extent; (d) To a little extent; (e) Not at all.
8. "Working as a group is no problem here". How often do people feel this here in this hospital?
   (a) Almost never; (b) Rarely; (c) Sometimes; (d) Usually; (e) Almost always.
9. Do people here get an opportunity to develop their skills further to do their jobs?
   (a) Almost all the people; (b) Most of the people; (c) Some of the people; (d) A few people; (e) Almost none.
10. How often does the staff here try to do things better than what they have done last time?
    (a) Almost never; (b) Rarely; (c) Sometimes; (d) Usually; (e) Almost always.
11. How much do you agree with the statement that this hospital is better than the other hospitals of the same size in the city, to work in?
    (a) Strongly agree; (b) Agree; (c) Neither agree nor disagree; (d) Disagree; (e) Strongly disagree.
12. How often are your ideas for change given a good hearing?
    (a) Never; (b) Sometimes; (c) Often; (d) Almost always; (e) Always.
13. Is it true that remaining busy is not enough in this hospital one has to show results?
    (a) Yes, it is true here to a very great extent; (b) Yes, it is true here to a great extent; (c) Well, it is true to a negligible extent; (d) No, it is not quite true; (e) Not, it is not true.
14. Do you agree that quite often a subordinate here has to attend to orders issued by more than one person at a time?
    (a) Strongly disagree; (b) Disagree; (c) Neither agree nor disagree; (d) Agree; (e) Strongly agree.
15. When decisions are being made about certain work that you are to do, are you asked for your ideas?
    (a) Almost never; (b) Rarely; (c) Sometimes; (d) Usually; (e) Almost always.
16. If somebody says, "there is so much work to do here everyday that I have to do it some how and I don't have the time to think about the quality of the work can be improved" how much would you agree with the statement?
    (a) Strongly disagree; (b) Disagree; (c) Neither agree nor disagree; (d) Agree; (e) Strongly agree
17. To what extent do you receive correct information about your work, duties etc.?
    (a) Not at all; (b) To a very little extent; (c) To some extent; (d) To a considerable extent (e) To a very great extent.
18. "There is a general feeling here that grievances of the employees are handled properly". To what extent do you agree with this statement?
    (a) Strongly agree; (b) Agree; (c) Neither agree nor disagree; (d) Disagree; (e) Strongly disagree.

19. Do you agree that almost every one here knows who is working under whom in this hospital?
(a) Strongly disagree; (b) Disagree; (c) Neither agree nor disagree; (d) Agree; (e) Strongly agree.
20. To what extent do people in your work group encourage each other in work?
(a) Not at all; (b) To a little extent; (c) To some extent; (d) To a considerable extent; (e) To a very great extent.
21. How frequently do you think it is true that in this hospital it is easier to deal with those things that have a precedence?
(a) No, it is not true in any case; (b) Yes, in some cases; (c) Yes, in many cases; (d) Yes, in most of the cases; (e) Yes, in almost all the cases.
22. Is this hospital receptive to new ideas?
(a) It is never receptive; (b) It is sometimes receptive; (c) It is often receptive; (d) Almost always receptive; (e) Always receptive.
23. "The general feeling here is that people do not get fair hearing from those who are higher up". How much do you agree with it?
(a) Strongly agree; (b) Agree; (c) Neither agree nor disagree; (d) Disagree; (e) Strongly disagree.
24. How adequate is the amount of information you get about what is going on in other departments and units of this hospital?
(a) Very inadequate; (b) inadequate; (c) Neither inadequate nor adequate; (d) Adequate; (e) Very adequate.
25. How often do superiors ask subordinates for new ideas?
(a) Almost always; (b) Usually; (c) Sometimes; (d) Rarely; (e) Almost never.
26. How often do you think that the members of staff here value friendship among their colleagues?
(a) Almost never; (b) Rarely; (c) Sometimes; (d) Usually; (e) Almost always.
27. To what extent do you feel that the employees here are allowed to make decisions to solve their problems without checking them with their superiors at each stage of the work.
(a) To a very great extent; (b) To a great extent; (c) To some extent; (d) To a little extent; (e) Not at all.
28. Is there a general feeling amongst the employees of your level that any body can be removed from his job at any time?
(a) Almost all the employees feel so; (b) Exists among most of the employees; (c) Among some of the employees; (d) Among a few employees; (e) Not exist at all.
29. How often are the rewards (such as raise in salary and promotions) given strictly on the basis of merit?
(a) Almost always; (b) Usually; (c) Sometimes; (d) Rarely; (e) Almost never.
30. In order to stay here, one just can't perform work somehow; work has to be well done. To what extent do you agree with it?
(a) Strongly agree; (b) Agree; (c) Neither agree nor disagree; (d) Disagree; (e) Strongly disagree.

31. To what extent there are facilities and opportunities for individual creative work in this hospital?
    (a) Not at all; (b) To a little extent; (c) To some extent; (d) To a considerable extent; (e) To a very great extent.
32. In your observation, how often does the staff in this hospital seem bored with their work?
    (a) On all occasions; (b) On most occasions; (c) On some occasions; (d) On a very few occasions; (e) Not at all.
33. "When there is appreciation the staff here tends to share it as an achievement of the whole work group than that of an individual." How much do you agree with this statement?
    (a) Strongly agree; (b) Agree; (c) Neither agree nor disagree; (d) Disagree; (e) Strongly disagree.
34. How do you get most of your information about your work and organisation? (Tick as many as possible).
    (a) Through Unions/Associations; (b) Through collegues/other persons/rumours; (c) Through talks with superiors; (d) Through meetings; (e) Through notices on boards.
35. "The nature of things that an employee is supposed to do in this organisation are so varied that it is logically difficult to put them together". How much do you agree with this statement?
    (a) Strongly Agree; (b) Agree; (c) Neither agree nor disagree; (d) Disagree; (e) Strongly disagree.
36. To what extent are people in the higher levels aware of the problems at lower levels in this hospital?
    (a) Not at all; (b) To a very little extent; (c) To some extent; (d) To a considerable extent; (e) To a very great extent.
37. How often do you have advance information of any changes which are planned?
    (a) Almost always; (b) Usually; (c) Sometimes; (d) Rarely; (e) Almost never.
38. To what extent is the information passed from one person to another in this organisation distorted or deliberately more inaccurate?
    (a) To a large extent; (b) To a considerable extent; (c) To some extent; (d) To a little extent; (e) Not at all.
39. Are discussions at meetings in this organisation very free and open?
    (a) Discussions are never free and open; (b) In a few meetings; (c) In some of the meetings; (d) In most of the meetings; (e) In all the meetings.
40. One can not simply go ahead and do a thing here unless one has discussed it with his superiors before. How often does it happen here?
    (a) Yes, it is almost always the case here; (b) Yes, it is usually the case here; (c) Yes, it is sometimes the case here; (d) No, it is rarely the case here; (e) No, it is almost never the case here.
41. If some one of your colleagues does his joy in improved way than it is usually done, does he get proper recognition for it?
    (a) Almost never gets recognition; (b) Usually gets recognition; (c) Surely gets recognition; (d) Sometimes gets recognition; (e) Almost always gets recognition.

42. Which of the following best describes the manner in which problems between departments are generally resolved?
(a) The problems are worked out at the level where they appear through mutual effort and understanding; (b) The higher authority in the college — and are usually resolved there; (c) The problems are appealed to a higher authority in the college — but often are still not resolved; (d) Little is done about these problems — they work themselves out with time; (e) Little is done about these problems — they continue to exist.
43. How often have your ideas for changing the way things are done here in this hospital been welcomed?
(a) Almost always; (b) Usually; (c) Sometimes; (d) Rarely; (e) Almost never.
44. "Grievances normally are not settled unless they are taken up by organised body of employees like employees' unions, associations etc". How often do you think it happens in this hospital?
(a) Almost never; (b) Rarely; (c) Sometimes; (d) Usually; (e) Almost always.
45. How often do you think the members of the senior staff patiently listen to complaints of the junior staff?
(a) They almost always listen; (b) They usually listen to; (c) They sometimes listen to; (d) They rarely listen to; (e) They almost never listen to.
46. How often is true that personal hostilities are usually resolved as quickly as possible?
(a) Almost never; (b) Rarely; (c) Sometimes; (d) Usually; (e) Almost always.
47. In some places employees are required to adhere strictly to the rules, policies, procedures and practices whereas in some other places they can deviate from these, what is generally required from people of your level here?
(a) Very strict adherence to rules, policies and procedures; (b) Strict adherence to rules policies and procedures; (c) Somewhat strict adherence to rules, policies and procedures; (d) A little adherence to rules, policies and procedures; (e) No adherence to.
48. How often do you think staff rules, procedures and policies members of different levels of hierarchy join together to work here as members of a team?
(a) Almost never; (b) Rarely; (c) Sometimes; (d) Usually; (e) Almost always.
49. To what extent do people in this hospital speak rather than write memo to each other?
(a) Almost always; (b) Usually; (c) Sometimes; (d) Rarely; (e) Almost never.
50. "If they have the alternative choice the staff in this hospital in general would feel happy to leave the hospital". To what extent do you think the statement is applicable to staff here?
(a) None of them feel happy to leave this hospital; (b) Very few of them feel happy to leave this hospital; (c) Some of them feel happy to leave this hospital; (d) Most of them feel happy to leave this hospital; (e) All of

them feel happy to leave this hospital.

51. How much do you think the top management of this hospital is aware of working conditions of its staff?
(a) Not at all aware; (b) Very little aware; (c) Somewhat aware; (d) Much aware; (e) Very much aware.
52. How often do you talk freely with your superiors?
(a) Almost never; (b) Rarely; (c) Sometimes; (d) Usually; (e) Almost always.
53. How often are the members of the staff in this hospital helpful to each other?
(a) Almost never; (b) Rarely; (c) Sometimes; (d) Usually; (e) Almost always.
54. How much do you think your hospital has interest in the welfare of the staff?
(a) They are not at all really interested; (b) They are not very much interested; (c) Only in certain ways they are interested; (d) They are somewhat interested; (e) They are very much interested.
55. In some places, anybody can go to anybody else to discuss any problem he faces. In your opinion, how offen does it happen here?
(a) Almost never; (b) Rarely; (c) Sometimes; (d) Usually; (e) Almost always.
56. Do you agree that in this hospital the capabilities of its staff members are fully utilised?
(a) Strongly agree; (b) Agree; (c) Neither agree nor disagree; (d) Disagree; (e) Strongly disagree.
57. How often do you think the professional jealousies obstruct the performance of duties in this hospital?
(a) Almost always; (b) Usually; (c) Sometimes; (d) Rarely; (e) Almost never.
58. Do the staff members here work with a team spirit?
(a) Team spirit does not exist at all; (b) A few members; (c) Most of the members; (d) Almost all the members; (e) All the members.
59. Are there things around your working environment (people, policies, conditions) that discourage you from working hard?
(a) Yes, practically everything around here discourage me from working hard; (b) Yes, a great many things around here discourage me from working hard; only a few do not discourage me; (c) About as many things discourage me as encourage me (d) No, most things around here encourage me to work hard; (e) No, practically everything around here encourages me to work hard.
60. Considering the busy schedules and work load here the employees seldom find time to share their concerns with each other. How much do you agree with it?
(a) Strongly agree; (b) Agree; (c) Neither agree nor disagree; (d) Disagree; (e) Strongly disagree.
61. How often do superiors ask subordinates for an informal discussion?
(a) Almost never; (b) Rarely; (c) Sometimes; (d) Usually; (e) Almost always.
62. How much influence do you think your colleagues have in deciding what

should be done in this hospital?
(a) Very much; (b) Much; (c) Some; (d) Little; (e) Not at all.

63. To what extent do you have confidence in the people you work with?
(a) Not at all; (b) To a very little extent; (c) To some extent; (d) To a considerable extent; (e) To a great extent.
64. How often do the members of the staff here trust one another?
(a) Almost always; (b) Usually; (c) Sometimes; (d) Rarely; (e) Almost never.
65. Are suggestions often solicited from employees here?
(a) Yes, from senior officers only; (b) Yes, from some officers only; (c) Yes, from all the officers only; (d) Yes, from all the employees except class IV employees; (e) Yes, from all the employees.
66. How often does a person in this organisation receive credit and appreciation if he finds out a different way of doing things which nobody has ever done before?
(a) Almost always; (b) Usually; (c) Sometimes; (d) Rarely; (e) Almost never.
67. How often are meetings held when needed?
(a) Almost never; (b) Rarely; (c) Sometimes; (d) Usually; (e) Almost always.
68. How much is your job important in this hospital?
(a) Very much; (b) Much; (c) Not much; (d) Little; (e) Not at all.
69. This hospital facilitates the self-improvement of its staff members. Do you agree with this statement?
(a) Strongly disagree; (b) Disagree; (c) Neither agree nor disagree; (d) Agree; (e) Strongly agree.
70. How often is conscientious attempt made to consider every one's views before a decision is made?
(a) Almost never; (b) Rarely; (c) Sometimes; (d) Usually; (e) Almost always.

## 32A5 PATIENT SATISFACTION INTERVIEW SCHEDULE

*Authors* : A. Thimmappayya, Udai Pareek and K.G. Agrawal.
*Availability* : Authors, NIHAE, E-16, Greater Kailash-1, New Delhi-48.
*Time required* : About 15 minutes.
*Level* : Adults.
*Scoring* : Positive score = 2, Mild dissatisfaction = 1, Negative = 0.
*Reliability* : Test-retest and inter-interviewer reliability were established, on each item.
*Validity* : Face validity and known 'good' and 'bad' comparison.
*References* :

1. Thimmappayya, A., Pareek, U. and Agrawal, K.G. *Patient satisfaction and ward social system*, New Delhi : National Institute of Health Administration and Education, 1971.
2. Timmappayya, A. and Agrawal, K.G. Patient satisfaction interview schedule for measuring patient satisfaction in general hospital, Manas, 1971, 18(2), 117-135.
3. Thimmappayya, A., Pareek, Udai and Agrawal, K.G. Measuring patient

satisfaction in a general hospital. *Indian Journal of Social Work*, 1971, 32(3), 295-304.

## 32A5 PATIENT SATISFACTION INTERVIEW SCHEDULE

1. How long have you been here?
2. What was your illness?
3. Who referred you to this hospital?
4. Where do you come from?
5. When you came to this hospital where did you go first?
6. This is a general feeling that admission in this hospital is rather difficult. Did you have any difficulty?
   (1) No; (2) Yes, not much; (3) Yes, much difficulty.
7. Some people think that doctors don't tell their patients about their illness. Do you feel that the doctor should have told you about it and he did not?
   (1) Yes, I was told; (2) Yes, But I knew, it (There was no need to ask); (3) No, I was not told.
8. In general how did you like this ward?
   (1) Good; (2) Alright; (3) Not good.
9. In the hospital were your linen clean?
   (1) Yes, were always clean; (2) Were not always clean; (3) Were dirty.
10. Some patients have a feeling that they are discharged even before they are cured. What do you think? Are you being discharged after being cured?
    (1) Yes; (2) Can't say; (3) No.
11. Sometimes you might need the help of the nurse. Was it difficult to call her?
    (1) No, not al all; (2) Yes, sometimes; (3) Yes, it was very difficult.
12. Whenever you called the nurse did she come?
    (1) Yes, she always came; (2) Yes, only sometimes she came; (3) She never came.
13. Every ward has nursing orderlies/ayahs to help the nurses in their work. How do you find their work?
    (1) They were prompt and helpful; (2) They were not prompt and helpful; (3) They were rude and unhelpful.
15. In fact the treatment is carried out by the doctors. What do you think about your doctors?
    (1) They were sympathetic; (2) They were careless; (3) They were rude.
16. Some people complain that the doctors do not look after them properly. How did your doctor look after you?
    (1) They cared a lot; (2) They cared inadequately; (3) They were careless.
17. Patients often complain about hospital food. Hospital food cannot be very tasteful but it should be good. How did you like the food here?
    (1) Good; (2) Tolerable; (3) Useless.
18. In large hospitals, as there are so many patients and departments, the treatment is delayed because the doctor has to consult other specialists and take help of several technicians. Your treatment might have also

been delayed for lack of co-operation between various people and departments e.g. your blood report, X-ray report etc. might have delayed your treatment — Was it so?
(1) No; (2) Can't say; (3) Yes.

19. Are you satisfied with the treatment and medical care you received here?
20. Are you satisfied with the concern, the doctors showed in your treatment here?
(1) Yes, completely satisfied; (2) Not completely satisfied; (3) Not satisfied.
21. Do you think you cold get better medical care and treatment here if you knew some people here?
(1) No; (2) Can't say; (3) Yes.
22. Will you give your opinion about the cleanliness in the ward? Were the floors, baths, etc. always kept clean?
(1) Yes, they were always clean; (2) No, they were not always clean; (3) No, they were always dirty.
23. On the whole, how did you find the hospital?
(1) An excellent hospital; (2) A good hospital; (3) An average hospital; (4) A poor hospital; (5) A very poor hospital.
24. Would you like to tell us any of good or bad experience during your stay in this hospital?
25. Did any body (a relative or a friend) stay with you to look after you?
(1) Yes, always stayed; (2) Yes, but only sometimes; (3) No.

32A6DOCTOR'S OPINION REGARDING PATIENT SATISFACTION (PSDQ)

(The following items have to be answered using yes, no, doubtful categories).

1. Do you think there is any reason to the patient for being dissatisfied.
2. Do you think the service could be better if interference by the politicians can be stopped?
3. Do you require more-equipment for improving the patient satisfaction?
4. If you had more medicines you could satisfy the patients much more?
5. Do you require more beds for improving hospital wards and patients comforts.
6. Is it necessary to tell the patients about their treatment and illness for making them more satisfied?
7. Do you think your hospital requires more of public relations work to make the community conscious of your limitations?
8. Do you think the community expects much more than what it should expect from this hospital?
9. Do you think there is a lack of co-ordination between various people and departments which reduces hospital efficiency to a great extent.
10. Do you think the behaviour of class IV employees is responsible for much of the dissatisfaction among the patients?

## 32A7 COMMUNITY IMAGE OF THE HOSPITAL QUESTIONNAIRE (CIHQ)

*Authors* : A. Thimmappayya, Udai Pareek, S.N. Chattopadhyay and K.G. Agrawal.

*Availability* : Authors, NIHAE, E-16, Greater Kailash-1, New Delhi-48.

*Uses* : For measuring visitors' perception of the hospitals.

*Time required* : 15 minutes.

*Level* : Adults.

*Scoring* : 2, 1, 0 scores : positive through negative responses; Also multiple choice and 5 through 1 items.

*Reference* : Thimmappayya, A., Pareek, U., and Agrawal, K.G. *Patient satisfaction and ward social system.* New Delhi : National Institute of Health Administration and Education, 1971.

## 32A7 COMMUNITY IMAGE OF THE HOSPITAL QUESTIONNAIRE (CIHQ)

1. How do you think about the time it takes for the patients to get admitted in this hospital?
   1. It takes very long; 2. It is reasonable; 3. I can't say.
2. How are the people of the Registration Counter?
   1. They are nice and helpful; 2. They are alright; 3. They are rude and unconcerned.
3. What do you think about the cleanliness in the ward?
   1. Wards are clean; 2. Wards are dirty; 3. I can't say.
4. How do you think about the garments and beds in this hospital?
   1. They are clean; 2. They are dirty; 3. I can't say.
5. Do you think that this hospital is well-equipped?
   1. Yes; 2. No; 3. Do not know.
6. In your opinion do the patients get all the necessary medicines, etc. in this hospital?
   1. Yes; 2. No; 3. Do not know.
7. How is the food served in this hospital?
   1. It is good; 2. It is so good; 3. It is not good.'
8. How are the Ayahs and Ward Boys or Nursing orderlies? (check as many as applicable).
   1. Nice and helpful; 2. Prompt; 3. Hard working; 4. Rude; 5. Inefficient; 8. Corrupt.
9. How are the Sweepers in this hospital? (check as many as applicable).
   1. Nice and helpful; 2. Prompt; 3. Hard working; 4. Rude; 5. Inefficient; 6. Corrupt.
10. How do you find the Nurses in this hospital? (check as many as applicable).
    1. Kind; 2. Sympathetic; 3. Rude; 4. Current; 5. Prompt; 6. Inefficient; 7. Hardworking.
11. How are the Doctors? (check as many as applicable).
    1. Kind; 2. Sympathetic; 3. Rude; 4. Ordinary; 5. Expert; 6. Mediocre; 7. Corrupt.
12. How are the visiting hours?
    1. Alright; 2. Should be longer; 3. Should be shorter.

13. How much do you think patients get attention from their Doctors here?
    1. Sufficient attention; 2. A little attention; 3. No attention.
14. Do you feel people with "right pull" get better attention in this hospital?
    1. Yes; 2. No; 3. Do not know.
15. Do they give proper *medical care* here?
    1. Yes; 2. No.
16. In comparison with other hospitals of Delhi is the recovery rate higher in this hospital?
17. What kind of reputation does this hospital has?
    1. An excellent hospital; 2. A good hospital; 3. An ordinary hospital; 4. Not so good a hospital; 5. Not a good hospital at all.
18. Can you give some suggestions for the improvement of this hospital?

## 32A8 OCCUPATIONAL DIFFERENTIAL FOR MEASURING INTER-ROLE PERCEPTIONS (ODIRP)

*Authors* : A. Thimmappayya, Udai Pareek, S.N. Chattopadhyay and K.G. Agrawal.

*Availability* : Authors, National Institute of Health, Administration and Education, E-16, Greater Kailash-I, New Delhi-48.

*Uses* : Perceptions of roles (occupational) in small groups.

*Time required* : 15 to 20 minutes.

*Level* : Adults.

*Main features* : It is a scale based on Singh's (1967, 1969) Occupational Differential.

*Scoring* : Same as Semantic Differential.

*Reference* : Thimmappayya, A., Pareek, U. and Agrawal, K.G. *Patient satisfaction and ward social system*, New Delhi, NIHAE, 1971.

## 32A8 OCCUPATIONAL DIFFERENTIAL FOR MEASURING INTER-ROLE PERCEPTIONS (ODIRP)

(The following bipolar adjectives have been used in rating different roles in the organisation).

1. Dull-intelligent;
2. Experienced-inexperienced;
3. Inefficient-efficient;
4. Unskilled-skilled;
5. Shirker-diligent;
6. Kind-cruel;
7. Lazy-smart;
8. Honest-dishonest;
9. Beautiful-ugly;
10. Glad-angry;
11. Poor-rich;
12. Clean-dirty.

## 32A9 SEMANTIC DIFFERENTIAL FOR MEASURING HOSPITAL IMAGE (SDMHI)

*Authors* : A. Thimmappayya, Udai Pareek, S.N. Chattopadhyay and K.G. Agrawal,

*Availability* : Authors, NIHAE, E-16, Greater Kailash-1, New Delhi-48.

*Uses* : For measuring hospital effectiveness.

*Time required*: About one hour.
*Level*: Adults.
*Main features* : It is a scale based on Semantic Differential technique. English and Hindi scales and concepts are simultaneously used.
*Scoring* : Summated ratings. +3, +2, +1, — 1, — 2, — 3.
*Reference* : Thimmappayya, A., Pareek, U. and Agrawal, K.G. *Patient satisfaction and ward social system.* New Delhi : National Institute of Health, Administration and Education, 1971.

## 32A9 SEMANTIC DIFFERENTIAL FOR MEASURING HOSPITAL IMAGE (SDMHI)

1. Good-bad;
2. Clean-dirty;
3. Happy-sad;
4. Dissatisfied-satisfied;
5. Dishonest-honest;
6. Hard-soft;
7. deligent-shirker;
8. Pleasure-seeking-self-restrained;
9. Humourous-serious;
10. Efficient-inefficient;
11. Kind-cruel;
12. Bitter-sweet;
13. Moral-immoral;
14. Dynamic-static;
15. Intelligent-dull;
16. Varied-repetitive;
17. Tense-relaxed;
18. Reputable-disreputable;
19. Proud-humble;
20. Active-passive.

# 3. Military and Others

## Complete instruments

A

### 33A1 MILITARY MORALE SCALE

*Authors* : S.K. Jain and S.K. Jain.
*Availability* : Authors.
*Time required* : No time limit.
*Levels* : Soldiers.
*Main features* : The scale has been developed to suit Indian conditions at the altitude of 12,000 ft. to 14,000 ft. above sea level. The MMS is self-administered consisting of 45 items to be checked on 5-point scale.
*Scoring* : Scores of 4 to 0 is given to the 5 points on each item (true to false for positive and false to true for negative items).
*Reliability* : Test-retest reliability (n=50) after an interest of 4 weeks was found to be .79 and the split-half reliability was found to be .83.
*Validity* : Correlation between the pooled subjective ratings by the senior officers and peers, and the total scores of the inventory was found to be .48.
*Reference* : Jain, Sarat K. and Jain, Suresh K. Morale in the army (scale for assessment). *Psychological Researches*, 1966 1(1-2), 40-45.

### 33A1 MILITARY MORALE SCALE

(The following items have to checked on a 5-point scale).

1. Indian soldiers can overcome every danger if they try hard.
2. In army one has hardly any time to help others in difficulty.
3. In Indian military brave deeds are rewarded handsomely.
4. Most soldiers feel confident that they can succeed in military through hard work.
5. I am not getting what I want out of my fellows.
6. One can rely on the ability of Indian military officers.
7. Soldiers' job is dignified and that explain his interest in it.
8. Authorities pay sufficient return for the hard work of the soldiers.
9. Indian soldiers are having the intelligent fighting plans.
10. War plans can't help the soldiers when they are actually fighting.
11. Sometimes enemy overcomes us with immoral tactics.
12. I am proud to say that the glory of Indian military is due to the efforts of the soldiers like me.
13. Generally war brings a lot of difficulties for soldiers.
14. The desire to fight for the glory of Indian is on increase among soldiers

day-by-day.
15. War is a change for soldiers to show their brave deeds.
16. Reversals in the war are sometimes the result of weak planning.
17. We fight to defend our country and not to offend others.
18. Under fighting situations killing enemy is not an act of immorality.
19. Soldiers feel responsible to do the work allotted to them.
20. I never mind the caste and creed of the fellow who is working with me in the operational areas.
21. My fellow soldiers respect me and encourage me.
22. Since I have confidence in Indian military system. I will encourage others to join army.
23. Justice and order regulates the Indian military system.
24. Merits count more than pull in the army.
25. Army line can't provide a bright future to the soldiers.
26. I am proud of corps services to the nation.
27. Sometimes Indian soldiers can't stand against the dangerous tactics of the enemy.
28. Sometimes the victory of offenders in the war has bad consequences.
29. It seems easy to me to keep up my courage in the war where so much happens.
30. I am not after salary to the neglect of or indifference to the aim of military.
31. Soldiers like their job because of the guidance of able military officers.
32. Although soldiers may sometimes feel unhappy, they try to do things collectively.
33. Indian soldiers are not jealous of the success and progress of their fellow workers.
34. My job as a soldiers is according to my taste so there is hope of prosperity in future life.
35. I am given clear orders as regards my work by my officers. So my work becomes easy.
36. I prefer to wear military dress rather than the civilian clothes.
37. Military discipline can be maintained with the help of military laws.
38. An Indian soldier will prefer to starve rather than to yield.
39. Supply of war material in an operational area is important to boost up the courage of the soldiers.
40. Most of the soldiers are doing all that can reasonably be expected from them.
41. My fellows are friendly towards me.
42. Indian soldiers have clearly defined goals before them to achieve.
43. Military laws are made for the benefit of soldiers.
44. Indian soldiers respect the military laws.
45. Usually soldiers enjoy good health.

## 33A2 JOB SATISFACTION SCALE

*Author*: O.S. Rathore.
*Availability*: Author, Department of Agricultural Extension, Rajasthan College of Agriculture, Udaipur.

*Time required* : About 7 minutes.
*Level* : Village level workers, Agricultural Extension Officers, and Block Development Officers.
*Main features* : Five-point Likert scale.
*Scoring* : Summated ratings.

33A2 JOB SATISFACTION SCALE

(The following items have to be checked on a 5-point scale of satisfaction).

1. Are you satisfied that you have been given enough authority to do your job?
2. How satisfied are you with your present position, when you compare it to similar positions elsewhere?
3. Are you satisfied with the progress you are making toward the goals which you had set for yourself in your present position?
4. Are you satisfied that the people in the area circle and in your department give proper recognition to your work as a specialist in your subject matter?
5. How satisfied are you with your department chairman or district supervisor?
6. How satisfied are you with your present salary?
7. How satisfied are you with your professional and clerical staff in your department or your area?
8. As a whole, are you satisfied that the clientele you serve accept you as a professional expert?
9. How satisfied are you with your present position in the light of your career expectations?
10. How satisfied are you with your present position when you consider expectation at the time you took the position?
11. How satisfied are you with the amount of time and energy you are devoting to your present position and the satisfaction you receive from your position?

33A3 ADMINISTRATIVE DECENTRALISATION QUESTIONNAIRE

*Author* : A. Adivi Reddy.
*Availability* : Author.
*Uses* : To measure the degree of decentralisation existing in an organisation and also to assess the degree of decentralisation needed by different function arises in an organisation.
*Time required* : 15-20 minutes. If used for other organisations, time required will depend on the number of job areas (or indicators).
*Level* : Employees in any organisation, having at least high school education.
*Main features* : It is a 6-point rating scale. The scale measures the degree of decentralisation in respect of 12 job areas in an agricultural extension organisation. However, the same scale can be used to measure the degree of decentralisation in any organisation, by merely substituting the indicators (i.e. job areas) given in this questionnaire with other indicators (or job areas)

relevant to that organisation.

*Scoring* : A = — 3, B = — 2, C = — 1, D = +1, E = +2, F = +3.

*Reliability* : Correlation between alternate forms = + 1.0 significant at .01. (Also Kendall's coefficient of agreement = 0.838; $\chi^2$ = 786.03; significant at .01).

*Reference* : Reddy, A.A. A study of perceptions about administrative decentralisation in Andhra Pradesh agricultural extension service. Doctoral Thesis in Agricultural Extension, Indian Agricultural Research Institute, 1969.

33A3 ADMINISTRATIVE DECENTRALISATION QUESTIONNAIRE

(The following items have to be checked on 6-point scales (A to F as shown below) on perceived and desired degrees of decentralisation).

(A) My superior makes the decisions and asks me simply to implement them.
(B) My superior makes the decisions and permits me to raise questions for clarification before implementing them.
(C) My superior calls for information and ideas from me and makes the decisions.
(D) I consult my superior and then I take decisions.
(E) I take decisions and then inform my superior.
(F) I am free to make decisions within the framework of departmental rules.

1. Programme planning — selection of schemes to be introduced in your jurisdiction.
2. Programme Planning — Fixation of targets for your jurisdiction under the schemes selected (who decides the following?).
   (a) Acreage to be covered under:
      (i) High yielding varieties.
      (ii) Other improved seeds.
   (b) Crops and acreage to be covered by plant protection measures.
3. Programme execution — Who decides?
   (a) The geographical units (in your jurisdiction) which are to be benefited by the selected schemes, (b) The number of demonstrations to be conducted, (c) The selection of demonstration farmers.
4. Programme review and/or evaluation (judging the achievements against the targets fixed for your jurisdiction).
5. Organising the distributing supplies, who decides about the distribution of the following in your jurisdiction?
   (a) Improved see, (b) Fertilisers, (c) Pesticides, (d) Improved implements, (e) Credit (i.e. loans) to farmers.
6. Fixing sale prices of the following in your jurisdiction:
   (a) Seeds, (b) Fertilisers, (c) Pesticides, (d) Implements.
7. Transfer of the stocks of the above inputs within your jurisdiction (when necessary).
8. Purchase of the following requirements for your jurisdiction.
   (a) Seeds, (b) Fertilisers, (c) Pesticides, (d) Implements.
9. Sanction of incidental charges connected with:

(a) the purchase and distribution of the above inputs.
(b) the conducting of demonstrations.

10. Appropriation of funds (i.e. budget allotments) for the schemes in your jurisdiction.
11. Reappropriation of funds from one head to another within the sanctioned budget amount.
12. The following aspects in respect of your immediate executive subordinates.(*)
(a) Recruitment, selection and appointment. (b) Postings within your jurisdiction, (c) Transfers within your jurisdiction, (d) Sanction of earned leave, (e) Sanction of casual leave, (f) Sanction of study leave or other extraordinary leave, (g) Selection of subordinates for inservice training, (h) Dismissal, (i) Suspension, (j) Awarding censure (k) Stopping increments, (l) Awarding red entries (for good work), (m) Reversion to lower cadre, (n) Sanctioning increments of pay, (o) Promoting to higher cadre, (p) Writing the confidential reports.

(*) AEOs to consider only VLWs as their immediate subordinates for the purpose.

## Instruments with technical information B

### 33B1 BANKING EMPLOYEES BELIEFS QUESTIONNAIRE

*Authors* : Ishwar Dayal and Baldev R. Sharma.
*Availability* : Authors.
*Uses* : To measure the beliefs of supervisors in banking industry in relation to (1) nature of man, (2) nature of bank employees', (3) out-put of bank employees, (4) personal goal of bank employees, (5) aims and activities of trade unions and the staff policies in banks.
*Reference* : Dayal, Ishwar, and Sharma, B.R. Beliefs of the supervisory staff in the banking industry. *Prajnan*, 1972, 1 (3), 230-238.

### 33B2 FORCED CHOICE LEADER BEHAVIOUR QUESTIONNAIRE

*Author* : R.C. Mehta.
*Availability* : R.C. Mehta, Reader, Extension Department, Rajasthan College of Agriculture, Udaipur.
*Uses* : To measure the initiating structure and consideration dimensions of Leader Behaviour of the incumbents of position in an organisation.
*Time* : 20 minutes.
*Level* : Extension Workers, Educational Administrators.
*Main features* : It is set of 16 totrads (statements) involving forced choice of the respondent in selecting the appropriate statement in self-appraisal.

### 33B3 JOB SATISFACTION QUESTIONNAIRE

*Author*: B.C. Muthayya.

*Availability*: Author, Director of Psychology, NICD, Rajendranagar, Hyderabad.

*Time required*: Half an hour.

*Level*: Block officials, Useful for officials in different organisations.

*Main features* : Contains 34 items of Agree, Not sure, Disagree. These are scaled 0-1-2.

*Norms* : Available for officials sample. BDO, Mukhya Sevika, Gramasevak and gramsevika of Southern state of Mysore, Kerala and Tamil Nadu.

# PART IV

# SOCIAL PHENOMENA

# Introduction

THIS PART of the Handbook reports instruments dealing with several social dimensions. These instruments are reported under six sections : (1) Values; (2) Stratification; (3) Social Distance and Group Attitudes; (4) Modernisation and Social Change; (5) Religion and Morality; and (6) Other Social Attitudes. As in earlier parts, classification in this part is also pragmatic rather than conceptual; it is based on the consideration of a number of instruments forming into a distinct category rather than on any theoretical basis. For example, the instruments under Social Distance and Group Attitudes, Modernisation and Social Change, Religion and Morality and Other Social Attitudes are, by and large, instruments dealing with social attitudes. As a group of them are specifically dealing with social preferences, they are grouped under such a heading. The section of Modernisation and Social Change includes a few important dimensions like Family Planning, Agricultural Innovations and general modernisation scales. Although the number of instruments available on each of these are sufficient to warrant separate divisions, all these have been grouped under Modernisation and Social Change to avoid any specific-issue- based classification. The instruments on other Social Attitudes include several dimensions of social issues like attitude towards society, government, widow remarriages, divorce, alienation, etc. In a way most of the miscellaneous categories of instruments dealing with social phenomena and social issues have been included in this section. In view of the broad based category system the reader is also suggested to refer to the subject index.

In all 148 instruments are reported in this part of the Handbook. Of these 65 have been reproduced here. Among these reproduced, a few happen to be indices like the Adoption Quotient, farm mechanisation index etc. information has been provided for another 47. About 28 are citations and 8 are adaptations. The break-up of the instruments of this part appears in Table 4.

TABLE 4: Details of the instruments related to social phenomena

| Area | Originals reproduced | Information only provided | Citations | Adaptations | Total |
|---|---|---|---|---|---|
| Values | 9 | 6 | 3 | 6 | 24 |
| Stratification | 4 | 3 | 2 | 0 | 9 |
| Social Distance and Group Attitudes | 5 | 2 | 5 | 2 | 14 |
| Modernisation and Social Change | 27 | 17 | 9 | 0 | 53 |
| Religion and Morality | 3 | 9 | 3 | 0 | 15 |
| Other Social Attitudes | 17 | 10 | 6 | 0 | 33 |
| Total | 65 | 47 | 28 | 8 | 148 |

**Values**

The instruments in this section cover value dimensions like: conservativism, fatalism, scienticism, authoritarianism, harmony, love, sympathy, tolerance, economic, security, independence, creativity, traditionalism, modernism, organic, aesthetic and religious values, domestic values, spiritual values, risk-preference, achievement orientation, democratic values like freedom, equality, national integration, character, dignity of labour, political values etc. Nine of the instruments measuring these values are reproduced here, information is provided for another 6, 3 more are cited and information about another 6 adaptations is provided here. These instruments cater to high school and college students, doctors, farmers, adult males and females. About 7 of these are meant for college students and another 5 for farmers, 2 are exclusively for women. Most of these scales use summated ratings method on a 3-point, 4-point or 5-point scales. One instrument uses paired comparison technique, another two are projective tests, and another is based on Thurstone's method of equal appearing intervals.

Eleven of the 15 instruments for which information is presented here report reliability. Split-half, parallel form and test-retest methods have been used, most of them using test-retest method. The reliability coefficients reported in most cases are fairly high (usually above .70). Eight of the scales also report validities. Validity by judges, item-validity (again by judges), validity against self-rankings or others' ratings and concurrent validity are the types of validities reported. Most of them report the use of judges.

In general, the constructors of value scales seem to have paid some attention to the standardisation of their scales. The first of the value scales reproduced here is by Ansari meant for college students. The second is a semi-projective test by Hafeez and Begum using a different methodology. This can be used in selections for jobs requiring social values. The next is a scale for farmers by Pareek and Chattopadhyay. The one on the work-values of doctors by Rao and Pareek uses paired comparison technique. The value scale by Reddy measures mainly the traditionalism and modernism dimensions. Ruhela's traditional Indian values checklist could be used with college students and adults, it measures organic, aesthetic and religious values. Singh and Sohal's value orientation scale and Supe's value scales measure several values dimensions related to progressive farming. Work-value inventory by Vasanta is meant for high school students. Most of the scales reproduced here are fairly well standardised. Six adaptations of value scales are reported here. Of these, 5 are adaptations of Allport-Vernon- Lindzey scale of values. Four of these adaptations are in Hindi and one is in English.

Instruments in this section reveal that besides some general value scales meant for all sectors of the population, some specific scales meant for sectors like agriculture have been developed. Professions like teaching, management, engineering, social-work, medicine etc. require specific scales, as some value dimensions required by these professions are different. There is need to develop more such instruments, emphasising some specific values of professions. The general value scales should also be extended to newer dimensions.

### Stratification

In all, 9 instruments are reported under this section. Four of them are reproduced here, and information is presented for another 2. Scales under this category deal with stratification by socio-economic status. The socio-economic stratification instruments are generally to be administered on adults and or grown up students for information about the parental income, material possessions, education etc. of the family members.

The first one to be reproduced in this section is by Aaron and his associates. While Kuppuswamy's scale is meant for the urban population, those by Pareek and Trivedi and Shirpukar are for rural population.

Most of the scales reported under this section have established reliabilities and validities. Test-retest reliabilities reported for most of the instruments are fairly high. Concurrent validities and validity against external criteria are mostly reported for these instruments. Weightages are given to possession of items, education etc. Besides socio-economic scales, scales for castes, social classes etc. are also needed in stratification area.

### Social Distance and Group Attitudes

This section was originally called a stereotypes and prejudices. However, in order to include a few broader instruments dealing with international attitudes, social integration etc. the present title has been used. Besides social distance scales, this section includes information about instruments measuring stereotypes, international attitudes, communal attitudes, social integration, ethnic attitudes, and prejudice. In all 14 instruments are included in this section of which only 5 could be reproduced, details have been provided for another 2. Of these 7 instruments 3 are meant for students and 4 could be used with all levels. Reliability coefficients have been reported only for 2 instruments, one of them split-half and another test-retest. For another scale it is reported to be in process. Validity is reported for only one of them, and for another one it is reported to be in process. Different methods have been used in the construction of these instruments. Summated ratings method is used in most of the group attitude scales. Bogardus social distance and semantic ratings are also used in some cases. One significant adaptation in this area is of the Minnesota inventory of social preference.

Communal and racial conflict is one important area of social problems in the country. Several researches have been done in the various geographical areas. However, because of the sensitive nature of the problem, no depth studies have been done. Researchers have used safer groups like students and only recently initiative has been taken by researchers like Prayag Mehta who studied the actual troubled areas in the field and administered communal attitudes scales. More such instruments and research studies are needed.

### Modernisation and Social Change

There are in all 53 instruments listed under this title. These instruments deal with several indicators of modernisation and social change. Variables like inter-state migration, position of women in the society, choice of mate, inter-caste marriage, social mobility, attitudes towards working women, social participation, family planning, small family norms, artificial insemination, commercialisation, communication skills, overall modernity, attitude towards nitrogenous fertilizers, attitudes towards high yielding varieties, traditional family ideology, adoption behaviour, change proneness, educational innovations, progressiveness, adoption of cotton practices, other farm practices, beliefs about health etc. have been covered by these instruments. Of the 53 instruments included in this section 27 have been reproduced here and information is provided for another 17. A large number of the instruments (17) deal exclusively with population and family planning; 8 of these are reproduced here and information is provided for another 9 of them. The instruments relating to agriculture and adoption behaviour also dominate this section. These two sectors (i.e. family planning and adoption behaviour) form two major chunks of instruments in this section.

The instruments reported here cater to adults both in rural and urban areas (a few of the instruments are exclusively meant for rural adults), farmers, college students, high school students and other workers associated with rural administration. About 50 per cent of the instruments are meant for farmers. The college students and high school students are covered under only two instruments. One instrument is meant for village level workers, extension officers etc. One is for medical students and the rest are for adults.

Different techniques have been used in the development of the instruments reported in this section. Thurstone and Likert's techniques have been most widely used. About 17 of them use Likert technique of self-rating, 6 use Thurstone method, 6 use weighted scores based on different methods, another 6 are based on projective technique methodology, 2 on Guttman scaling techniques and the others use all miscellaneous systems. Three of them are using indices formulae. The scoring systems used follow the technique of constructions of the instruments.

Regarding the reliability, 9 do not report any reliability coefficients. Among the rest different techniques of reliability have been used, the most frequently used being split-half reliability followed by test-retest reliability. Some reliability coefficients have been reported in a few cases without mentioning the type of reliability established. Parallel form reliability is also reported in a couple of cases. Coefficient of reproducibility is reported in two scales using Guttman's method. Interjudge reliability has been reported in one instrument. In general, wherever reliability coefficients have been reported they are at a fairly high level, and usually above .80 and around .90. This indicates a satisfactory level of attention given in standardising these instruments under this section.

Validities have also been reported for these instruments. These include item validity, concurrent validity, validity on the basis of extreme groups, construct validity, validity using self-ratings, face validity etc. About 11 of the 44 instruments do not report to have worked out any validity coefficients; 9 of them have worked out concurrent validity, 5 of them have worked out concurrent validity, 5 of them have worked out extreme group validity and the rest are spread over different types of validities mentioned above. By and large, sufficient attention has been paid to the standardisation of these instruments.

### Religion and Morality

There are 15 instruments reported under this section; 3 of them are reproduced here and information is provided for another 9. These instruments deal with dimensions like attitudes towards morality, religious, sexuality, religiousity, religious faith and untouchability, moral and religious instruction, religious practices, superstition and moral attitudes. The scales reproduced are mainly meant for adults. Two of them are for high school boys and girls, is meant for the teachers. Most of them are based on the Likert's method. Two of them use the checklist form, and uses a self-rating form. Reliabilities have been reported in 8 of the 12 instruments. Most of them have used split-half reliability technique; some have given test-retest reliability also. Not much attention has been given to validity. About half of the instruments do not report any validity coefficients. Most of the others report only face validity, using judges. This is one area where instruments are needed on various other aspects.

### Other Social Attitudes

There are in all 33 instruments included in this section. Instruments related to social phenomena, other than those covered earlier, are grouped in this section. Of the 33 instruments included in this, 17 are reproduced here, information has been given for another 10, and 6 are citations. The areas covered by these instruments include general attitudes of people, attitudes towards society, attitudes towards government, attitudes towards children, perceptions of leadership behaviour, perception of economic system, cooperation-competition proneness, attitudes towards divorce, widow remarriage, social economic policy, parental orientation, student activism, alienation, leadership preferences, attitudes towards retarded children, towards national plan, social awareness, nationalisation, nationality, image role activity etc. As this variety of dimensions indicate, instruments in social research are concerned with a variety of areas depending upon the emerging needs.

Most of the instruments reproduced here are meant for adults. In fact, about 12 of them serve this target group, about 5 of them deal with adolescent group also besides adults. A couple of them are meant for only pre-adolescents, and another two for college students; exclusively. These instruments reported in this section give different techniques like open-ended questionnaires, subinmated ratings, semi-projective techniques, equal appearing interval scales and so on. In general, most of them have reported test-retest reliabilities. Whenever reliabilities have been reported they are fairly high, as in the case of the other instruments. Split-half and other forms of internal consistency measures have also been used in a few of these instruments.

Attention does not seem to have been paid to the validity part of standardisation. Quite a few of them report face and content validities, while a few of them do not report any validity coefficients at all. Discriminant and concurrent validities have been reported in a few instruments.

Instruments on some new dimensions have been reported here. This scale of Anand and Dave measures general orientation of the person towards life. This has been tried out on students and was found to give excellent results. The instruments by Banerjee covering attitudes towards society and towards government are Likert type scales available in Bengali also. The leadership perception scale by Lokhande and Moulik is meant for farmers. The scale on the perception of economic system by Murthy measures farmers' perception of the socio- economic situation. The cooperation competition proneness instrument by Pareek and Dixit is an attempt to study these attitudes which are crucial in the personality development for adolescents. This has been included here because of its weightage on the social dimensions as compared to the personality dimension. The scales on widow remarriage and divorce by Kamala Gopal Rao are well standardised and measure some of the social problems of our society. Parental orientation inventory has been developed by Ravichandra and Parmeswaran in connection with a developmental norms project of the National Council of Educational Research and Training. The two scales on activism and alienation by Mall Reddy are two contributions in the area of student dynamics. There are several other areas of social phenomena that probably need attention of the researchers in this sector. Instruments need to be developed in areas of special significance like aggression, group conflicts, discrimination, group and national identity, alienation, work organisation, social commitment, power, poverty, deprivation etc.

# 1. Values

## Complete instruments A

### 41A1 VALUE ORIENTATION SCALE

*Author* : A. Ansari.
*Availability* : Department of Psychology, Aligarh Muslim University.
*Uses* : To measure: conservatism-liberalism, fatalism-scienticism, hereditarianism-environmentalism, authoritarianism-non-authoritarianism.
*Level* : College Students.
*Main features* : It is a 48-item inventory using a 6-point scale. Several items were borrowed from the item pools of Pareek and Chattopadhyay (See 41A3).
*Scoring* : Six-point summated ratings.
*Reliability* : Split-half reliability coefficients for the four value dimensions range from .70 to .83.
*Validity* : Items were selected on the basis of the judges ratings. Known group validity was also established.
*Reference* : Hasan, Q. A study of relationship between dogmatism, social attitudes, and certain personality characteristics. Ph.D. Thesis in Psychology, Aligarh Muslim University, 1972.

### 41A1 VALUE ORIENTATION SCALE

1. The good old days were golden.
2. A man's heredity determines his whole life.
3. With the help of knowledge and reasons a man may know and solve all the mysteries of the world.
4. The former pattern of education was necessarily better than the present schooling.
5. Obedience and respect for authority are the most important virtues that children must learn.
6. One cannot blot what is in lot.
7. Intercaste marriages are not desirable.
8. Equal status of women with men is neither possible nor desirable.
9. A basic human tragedy is that man proposes God disposes.
10. Justice must be tempered with mercy.
11. It is always advisable to go to a doctor than to a sadhu or a fakir for cure in case of illness.
12. Human beings are by nature aggressive and will always remain so.
13. One must always have unquestioning faith in one's leader.

14. Even those social customs for which we do not get proper explanation should be adhered to.
15. It is inhuman to be based on a competitive spirit.
16. Every event in a man's life has already been settled and determined by his fate.
17. It is better to persuade a person to do a certain thing than to compel him.
18. Everyone works in his own interest because human beings are by nature selfish.
19. In a dynamic community change is essential.
20. A new born baby is not a fullfledged human being, he is a candidate for humanity.
21. In any organisation the decisions of the leader should be final as too many cooks spoil the broth.
22. If a person believes in anything as really good, he is justified in imposing it on others.
23. He is a wise man indeed who listens carefully to the opposite views, weighs the pros and cons and then forms his own views.
24. Environmental influences are responsible both for the virtues and vices of the individuals.
25. The judgement of a tribunal is better than that of a single judge.
26. A true man of God can perform many a miracle which science can never explain.
27. In this changing world there is no advantage in clinging to one rigid viewpoint.
28. A child born among the lower strata of society is bound to have a low level of intelligence.
29. For any community development programme to be successful it is essential that people of the community sit together and decide what should be done.
30. One should pay proper attention to arguments forwarded by the young, and if convinced, be ready to accept them.
31. A country can progress only by utilising the scientific developments of the age.
32. Everyone can lead a decent and good life if brought up in desirable environments.
33. Science has benefited human society much more than the evil it has produced.
34. Students should be trained to form an attitude of superiority. It would bring in courage, determination and force to dominate others.
35. With the exception of born idiots anyone can benefit from a wisely conceived and properly planned education.
36. Even geniuses are indebted more to nurture than to nature.
37. A man's present life is determined by what he has done in his past life and his present activities will influence his life after death.
38. God thinks of everybody. He who is given life by Him will also be provided by Him.
39. A child born with a musical aptitude may remain ignorant of music in a culture which has no tradition of music and give no importance to it.

40. Children of immoral parents are bound to be immoral.
41 Woman should wear traditional, not ultra-modern dresses.
42. One may be right in refusing to accept dictum even if it has the authority of a great man.
43. In order to make real progress India should shake off the shackles of the past and not allow it to dominate the present.
44. There cannot be any relationship between the Chinese attack and the congregation of eight planets in the year, as some astrologers claim.
45. Co-operative effort is better than individual effort as it uses the talents of different people and helps to promote them.
46. If it is the demand of the situation, customs — however old and honorary they may be — should be unhesitatingly abandoned.
47. Happy is that home indeed where the wife follows the husband's wishes, sons obey their parents and daughters are always helpful in house work.
48. With the knowledge of history, we can understand and broadly predict the future course of events.

41A2 PROJECTIVE TEST OF INDIVIDUAL AND SOCIAL VALUES

*Authors* : A. Hafeez and S. Shakeela Begum.
*Availability* : Author, Department of Industrial Management, Indian Institute of Science, Bangalore-12.
*Uses* : In Vocational selection for jobs that require a person to be socially oriented.
*Time required* : No time limit.
*Levels* : Can be used on adult males.
*Main features* : The test is in the form of statements and words. The individual values measured include: ambition, courage, initiative, determination, fame, adventure, perseverance, power, wealth. The social values consist of: harmony, love, sympathy, tolerance, peace, service, cooperation and sincerity.
*Reliability* : Parallel form reliability coefficient was found to be $+0.89 \pm .034$ (N=350).
*Norms* : Available on a group of 192 boys and 91 girls.
*Reference* : Hafeez, A. and Begum Shakeela, S. A study of individual and social values. *Indian Journal of Psychology*, 1964, 39 (1), 35-46.

41A2 PROJECTIVE TEST OF INDIVIDUAL AND SOCIAL VALUES

PART I

(The following statements have to be rank ordered on preference).

1. Being broad-minded and tolerant i.e. live and let live attitude.
2. Having good deal of money and property.
3. Having a position of authority and power over others.
4. Living with understanding and adjustment with others.
5. Being affectionate and loving our relatives, friends and others.

6. Being persistent in your aim by facing all sorts of difficulties in order to reach the goal.
7. Being earnest and sincere.
8. Doing exciting or stimulating things by undertaking risk of the unknown.
9. Being kind and giving comfort to others.
10. Having a strong desire for something which you want.
11. Helping others (i.e. people, animals, etc.) without any selfish motive.
12. Starting some work spontaneously without being persuaded by others.
13. Having a strong will.
14. Living with peace: desire for mutual existence without quarrels.
15. Being well known to all.
16. Being cooperative: one with others in achieving a common goal.
17. Being brave and bold.

PART II

(Preference for one of the words in each of the following pairs have to be indicated).

1. Courage — harmony
2. Wealth — fame
3. Tolerance — co-operation
4. Power — determination
5. Love — peace
6. Perseverance — initiative
7. Sincerity — service
8. Adventure — ambition
9. Sympathy — courage
10. Harmony — wealth
11. Fame — tolerance
12. Co-operation — power
13. Determination — love
14. Peace — perseverance
15. Initiative — sincerity
16. Service — adventure
17. Ambition — sympathy
18. Courage — wealth
19. Tolerance — harmony
20. Power — fame
21. Love — co-operation
22. Perseverance—determination
23. Sincerity — peace
24. Adventure — initiative
25. Sympathy — service
26. Ambition — courage
27. Wealth — tolerance
28. Harmony — power
29. Co-operation — perseverance
30. Determination — sincerity
31. Peace — adventure
32. Initiative — sympathy
33. Service — ambition
34. Courage — tolerance
35. Power — wealth
36. Love — harmony
37. Perseverance — fame
38. Sincerity — co-operation
39. Adventure — determination
40. Sympathy — peace
41. Ambition — initiative
42. Service — courage
43. Tolerance — power
44. Wealth — love
45. Harmony — perseverance
46. Fame — sincerity
47. Co-operation — adventure
48. Determination — sympathy
49. Peace — ambition
50. Initiative — service
51. Courage — power
52. Love — tolerance
53. Perseverance — wealth
54. Sincerity — harmony
55. Adventure — fame
56. Sympathy — co-operation
57. Ambition — determination
58. Service — peace
59. Initiative — courage
60. Power — love

61. Tolerance — perseverance
62. Wealth — sincerity
63. Harmony — adventure
64. Fame — sympathy
65. Co-operation — ambition
66. Determination — service
67. Peace — initiative
68. Courage — love
69. Perseverance — power
70. Sincerity — tolerance
71. Adventure — wealth
72. Sympathy — harmony
73. Service — co-operation
74. Ambition — fame
75. Initiative — determination
76. Peace — courage
77. Love — perseverance
78. Power — sincerity
79. Tolerance — adventure
80. Wealth — sympathy
81. Harmony — adventure
82. Fame — service
83. Co-operation — initiative
84. Determination — peace
85. Courage — perseverance
86. Sincerity — love
87. Adventure — power
88. Sympathy — tolerance
89. Ambition — wealth
90. Service — harmony
91. Initiative — fame
92. Peace — co-operation
93. Determination — courage
94. Perseverance — sincerity
95. Love — adventure
96. Power — sympathy
97. Tolerance — ambition
98. Wealth — service
99. Harmony — initiative
100. Fame — peace
101. Co-operation—determination
102. Courage — sincerity
103. Adventure — perseverance
104. Sympathy — love
105. Ambition — power
106. Service — tolerance
107. Initiative — wealth
108. Peace — harmony
109. Determination — fame
110. Co-operation — courage
111. Sincerity — adventure
112. Perseverance — sympathy
113. Love — ambition
114. Power — service
115. Tolerance — initiative
116. Wealth — peace
117. Harmony — determination
118. Fame — co-operation
119. Courage — adventure
120. Sympathy — sincerity
121. Ambition — perseverance
122. Service — love
123. Initiative — power
124. Peace — tolerance
125. Determination — wealth
126. Co-operation — harmony
127. Fame — courage
128. Adventure — sympathy
129. Sincerity — ambition
130. Perseverance — service
131. Love — initiative
132. Power — peace
133. Tolerance — determination
134. Wealth — co-operation
135. Harmony — fame

41A3 FARMERS VALUE ORIENTATION SCALE

*Authors* : Udai Pareek and S.N. Chattopadhyay.

*Availability* : First author, Indian Institute of Management, Ahmedabad or second author, NIHAE, E-16, Greater Kailash-I, New Delhi-48.

*Level* : Farmers.

*Scoring* : 4-point scale having 4 categories of responses: 'strongly agree', 'agree', 'disagree', 'strongly disagree' for each item.

*Validity* : Validity by judges.

*Reference* : Pareek, Udai and Chattopadhyay, S.N. Farmers Value Orientation

Scale, *Manas*, 1965, 12, 5-34.

## 41A3 FARMERS VALUE ORIENTATION SCALE

(The following items are to be checked on 4-point scale).

1. 'Mantras' have far-reaching effects. If one can chant and recite accurately right 'Mantras' on right occasion, he can produce miraculous effects.
2. If one believes in anything as truly good, he is justified if he ruthlessly imposes it on others.
3. Every event in a man's life has already been settled and determined by his fate.
4. The good old days were golden.
5. The caste system has more virtues than vice.
6. One should not have any faith in meetings, committees or corporate bodies; since there the members indulge in wranglings only and no effective work is ever-done.
7. There cannot be any real relationship between massive Chinese attack and congregation of eight planets in the same year though some astrologers claim it to be so.
8. All kinship relations should be maintained as they have been so far.
9. In any organisation, the decisions of the head should be final as too many cooks spoil the broth.
10. The present pattern of education is better than the former.
11. A basic human tragedy is that man proposes but God disposes.
12. People should be forced to contribute to National Defence Fund.
13. It is better to disbelieve in what is not proved or tested; but when proved it is to be relied on.
14. To deny our past and break with it is to uproot the people and sapless dry up.
15. It is better to rule in Hell than to serve in Heaven.
16. Marriage within one's own caste should not be strictly pursued; intercaste marriage should be favoured.
17. The judgement of tribunal of judges is better than that of a single judge.
18. Those who say that they have been ghosts, either distort the truth or tell a lie.

## 41A4 PHYSICIANS' WORK VALUES INVENTORY

*Author* : T. Venkateswara Rao and U. Pareek.
*Availability* : Author, Indian Institute of Management, Ahmedabad.
*Time required* : About 35 minutes.
*Level* : Medical Doctors.
*Main features* : It uses paired comparison method in scaling ten values: Economic, Security, Work conditions, Status, Humanistic, Co-workers, Independence, Creativity, Social, Rural and Academic. Three points have to be distributed in each pair of statements depending on the preferred work value. In all 45 pairs of statements are used each value having to be

compared with 9 other values.

*Scoring* : Total of the scores assigned for statements reflecting each value.

*Reliability* : Test-retest reliability coefficients range from .29 to .81 for the ten values.

*Validity* : Content and face validities were established by using judges. Validity coefficients using self-rankings on the ten values range from .35 to .86.

*Norms* : Means and SDS of final year medical students from 7 colleges are available.

*Reference* : Rao, T.V. and Pareek, U. Developing a work value scale for medical professions. *Interdiscipline*, 1973, 1-15.

41A4 PHYSICIANS' WORK VALUES INVENTORY

(The following 45 pairs of items have to be answered by the respondent by distributing 3 marks in each of the pair depending on the item he prefers and the amount of preference he has in each item of the pair).

1. (a) Work in which you develop new ideas.
   (b) Work in which you get good pay.
2. (a) Work in which you do not need to depend on others for help.
   (b) Work in a job with a good designation.
3. (a) Work in which you solve others problems.
   (b) Work which gives you an opportunity to teach others what you know.
4. (a) Work that pays you enough so that you can have all the things you want.
   (b) Work in a job which you are sure to have at all times.
5. (a) Work in which people respect you.
   (b) Work in which you teach and do research.
6. (a) Work which gives you sense of achievement.
   (b) Work in which you and your fellow workers all get along well together.
7. (a) Work in which you have enough freedom and independence.
   (b) Work in which you solve other peoples' problems.
8. (a) Work which gives you an opportunity to invent new things.
   (b) Work in a job where you do not have the fear of loosing your job.
9. (a) Work in which you do things the way you like.
   (b) Work in which you do research.
10. (a) Work which makes others happy.
    (b) Work in which you have all the physical facilities you like.
11. (a) Work which provides you a high financial reward.
    (b) Work in which the physical surroundings are good.
12. (a) Work which gives you a high status.
    (b) Work in which the physical surroundings are good.
13. (a) Work in which you help other people.
    (b) Work in a regular job.
14. (a) Work in a job with a high salary.
    (b) Work in a job of which you are respected by people.
15. (a) Work in which you will be an influential person.

(b) Work where nothing can threaten your job.
16. (a) Work in which you do unique things.
(b) Work in which you do not need to depend on others for help.
17. (a) Work in which you do things almost entirely by yourself.
(b) Work in which you do not fear that you will loose your job.
18. (a) Work in which you solve the health problems of others.
(b) Work in which you have good associates to work with.
19. (a) Work in which provides you an adequate income.
(b) Work in pleasant surroundings.
20. (a) Work in which you are respected by many.
(b) Work in which your fellow workers are the people you like.
21. (a) Work in which you invent new things and find out new ways of doing things.
(b) Work where the surroundings are pleasant.
22. (a) Work in which you have the freedom to do things the way you want.
(b) Work which pays you enough money.
23. (a) Work in which you will have the satisfaction of helping a number of people.
(b) Work where there is a good opportunity for salary increase.
24. (a) Work in which you have good company of your colleagues.
(b) Work in which you save enough money.
25. (a) Work which makes you important.
(b) Work in a village where you are treated as big man.
26. (a) Work that requires the use of your great potential.
(b) Work in which you have an influential position.
27. (a) Work in which you do things independently.
(b) Work in which your fellow-workers are your friends.
28. (a) Work in which others have the benefit of your services.
(b) Work in a village where you can serve a number of people.
29. (a) Work which gives you adequately high income.
(b) Work in a village where you can earn lot of money.
30. (a) Work in which you can be creative and use your brains.
(b) Work in which you have an opportunity to teach.
31. (a) Work in which you have the freedom to do things the way you want to.
(b) Work in which the physical surroundings are likable.
32. (a) Work in which you service to others.
(b) Work in a job that gives you good status.
33. (a) Work in a job which you are sure to have at all times.
(b) Work where superiors and subordinates get along well with each other.
34. (a) Work where you teach and do research.
(b) Work where you have enough facilities.
35. (a) Work that gives you the feeling of job well done.
(b) Work in which you satisfy a number of patients.
36. (a) Work in which you do things independently.
(b) Work in a village where you are the master of your own.
37. (a) Work where your job is secure.
(b) Work in which you have adequate physical facilities.

38. (a) Work where people with whom you work are good to you.
    (b) Work in a village you have good team of friends to work with you.
39. (a) Work where you can be a good teacher and a researcher.
    (b) Work in a village where you can do lot of research and contribute to theory of medicine.
40. (a) Work which you feel is challenging.
    (b) Work in a village where you can do remarkable things.
41. (a) Work which provides you a regular job.
    (b) Work in which you can be an academician.
42. (a) Work in which you get along well with others without any problems.
    (b) Work in which you can explore the theory of medical sciences further.
43. (a) Work in which you will not be forced to search for a new job.
    (b) Work in a village where you can be sure of your job any time.
44. (a) Work in which ycur superiors and subordinates are people you like.
    (b) Work in which you have all the facilities you like.
45. (a) Work where the work facilities are good.
    (b) Work in a village which has all good work facilities.

41A5 VALUES SCALE (TRADITIONALISM-MODERNISM)

*Author* : Malla Reddy.
*Availability* : Author, College of Education, Osmania University, Hyderabad.
*Level* : College students.
*Main features* : It is a 56-item scale measuring traditional and modern values.
*Scoring* : Five-point summated ratings.
*Reliability* : Test-retest reliability coefficient was .78.
*Validity* : Concurrent validity with traditionalism-modernism dimension of Reddy's social attitude scale.

41A5 VALUES SCALE (TRADITIONALISM-MODERNISM)

(The following items have to be checked on a 5-point scale of agreement).

1. Self-realisation is an empty ideal.
2. There can be no greater evil than allowing a Harijan to marry a Brahmin.
3. Accumulated property is a hindrance to man's salvation.
4. What is predestined must have its course.
5. The way the times are changing today do not promise anything but destruction.
6. The material world is nothing but Maya.
7. Our religious beliefs are the major obstacles in the way of our material progress.
8. Marriage is a sacrament not a contract.
9. The legalisation of abortion is nothing short of sin.
10. Man out of ignorance is trying to interfere in the plans of God in the name of family planning.
11. The Guru cult of India is nothing but 'blind leading the blind'.
12. Why take the world so seriously after all we are birds of passage?

13. It is more important to strive for a better rebirth than to waste one's energy on a temporary social problem.
14. We should live like water drops on lotus leaves-attached yet unattached to the materials of the world.
15. Religion is not a subject of intellectual discourse, it is an unquestionable reality.
16. In the interest of communal unity inter-religious marriages should be encouraged.
17. All the evils of the present day are due to the deterioration of the caste system.
18. The only way to abolish caste system is to banish economic inequalities.
19. All men are born equal.
20. In choosing a wife man need not pay attention to whether she will get on well with his parents.
21. Adjustment is the only way to happy wedded life divorce can never be a solution.
22. Scientific knowledge can never be equal to Vedas.
23. While society must change, towards established Dharama is the real progress.
24. It is a disgrace for Indian women to go in for divorce.
25. The free access to contraceptives is dangerous to standards of morality.
26. All children including girls must equally share the property of parents.
27. Society is deteriorating because our 'Acharas' are being ignored.
28. Science is important for human progress, religion is a poor substitute for science.
29. Religion is the only source of peace and harmony in this restless world of today.
30. Some people are innately inferior to some other people.
31. Purity and pollution are mere prejudice.
32. The evils of joint family outweigh the benefits.
33. The present trend of equality between husband and wife is not desirable.
34. Young people should seek advice from elders on all vital matters.
35. Once the sons are married parents should claim no authority over them.
36. Social and economic status of a person is not the criteria to judge his one's action.
37. 'Papa' and 'Punya', 'Heaven' and 'Hell' are mere superstitions.
38. If the young and old live separately each is more free to do what each likes.
39. Children should obey their parents without question or arguments.
40. An ideal person cares more for his family prestige than for his personal ends.
41. To a woman chastity should be as dear to her as her own life.
42. One should have a small family to find more peace and less problems.
43. Inter-caste marriage will reduce many social tensions in the country.
44. Come what may caste system will not disappear.
45. Marriage is essentially a personal affair, even parents should not interfere.
46. One of the causes for student unrest is the lack of training for

self-restraint.
47. The ideal of 'Brahmacharya' is an unrealistic expectation from the young people.
48. Introduction of widow remarriage is nothing but down fall of our morals.
49. Equality of opportunity is a costly game for a country with limited opportunities.
50. The traditional ways of life should be the guiding lines of our behaviour.
51. In selecting a marriage partner family status must count more then individual competence.
52. In selecting a person to a public office, family status is more important than personal qualities.
53. A woman's vision is enlarged only when she is given sufficient social and economic freedom.
54. Many of man's problems are the results of undue social restrictions.
55. Government must impose a legal.
56. Social and economic status of a person is not the criterion to judge his real achievement.

41A6 TRADITIONAL INDIAN VALUES CHECKLIST

*Author*: Satya Pal Ruhela.
*Availability*: Author, Teachers College, Jamia Millia Islamia, New Delhi-25.
*Time required*: One hour.
*Level*: College students, other educated people.
*Main features* : A checklist of traditional Indian values. The basic values of the different religions of India have been identified and presented in this checklist. Measures organic, aesthetic and religious values.
*Scoring*: Simple totalling and percentages.
*Reference* : Ruhela, S.P. Traditional values of the Indian society and college students. *Indian Educational Review*, 1969, 4(1), 135-162.

41A6 TRADITIONAL VALUES CHECKLIST

(The following items have to be checked on a 3-point scale of belief and 2-point scale of practice).

1. One should eat to live and not live to eat.
2. One should learn to control hunger by fasts.
3. One should eat meat.
4. One should not eat beaf.
5. One may die of hunger but he should not accept food from a member of a low caste/tribe.
6. Sex should be enjoyed only with one's married partner.
7. One should remain a bachelor/virgin till his studies are finished up.
8. Child marriage should be allowed.
9. One should have only one living wife/husband.
10. One should be free to marry any person of his liking.
11. One should marry a person selected by his/her parents.
12. A man should not marry a woman of a higher caste.

13. A woman should not marry a man of a higher caste.
14. One should marry within his caste only.
15. Sexual enjoyment is a dirty thing.
16. The first duty of a person is to keep himself healthy.
17. A person should try to live a very old age.
18. One should earn as much wealth as possible in his married life.
19. One should follow his family occupation.
20. One should accumulate wealth for his children.
21. Every profession is noble.
22. One should try to make profit any how in business.
23. A wife should bring dowry with her for the husband.
24. One should be honest in his profession.
25. One should save for future.
26. One should not run after wealth.
27. As a form of amusement gambling may be allowed.
28. As a form of amusement hunting may be allowed.
29. One should play games for his recreation.
30. One should have social relationship mostly with his own caste people.
31. One should have kinship feelings for the people of his sect or panth.
32. It is one's duty to favour his caste/sect persons.
33. All members of a faith/sect should observe equality.
34. One should have many friends.
35. One should contribute to his joint family.
36. One should have most of the social relationship with one's kin.
37. One should do everything for his friends.
38. One should live in peace within his group or society.
39. One should obey his parents and teachers uncritically.
40. Service to others should be one's ideal.
41. The untouchables have lower levels of intelligence and character.
42. Like a king a husband should have full control over his family.
43. A wife should faithfully carry out her husband's commands.
44. It is parent's duty to provide good education and training to their children.
45. A person should contribute to the welfare of the society in cash or kind.
46. One should be very hospitable to his guests at all cost.
47. One should be sympathetic to others.
48. The Brahmans should be worshipped as a god or respected most of all.
49. We should be prepared to undergo any sacrifice for the sake of one who seeks our shelter.
50. We should have something like the old ashram system of India even now. (25 years for Brahmacharya stage, 25-50 years Grahstha stage, 50-75 for Vanprastha Ashram 75-100 for Sanyas Ashram).
51. We should give cooperation to others in good things.
52. All mankind is one, so one should try to seek unity with others.
53. One must have restricted relations with people of other castes.
54. Women are not to be believed for they have unstable nature.
55. Action is one's duty, reward is not his concern.
56. One should be good to everyone, even to his enemies.
57. One should be thoroughly honest under all circumstances.

58. One should be humble before his elders.
59. One should be industrious in his work.
60. One should be loyal to all others.
61. Truth should be the ideal of one's life.
62. A loyal wife should silently bear all sorts of atrocities or vices of her husband.
63. One should keep his old parents with him and serve them.
64. One must sacrifice his wealth for the welfare of his younger brothers or sisters.
65. One should have pity for others in trouble.
66. One should be very obedient to his elders.
67. One should have amicable relations with all others.
68. One should have very high ideals in life.
69. One should study under a good teacher.
70. One shouid have absolute faith in his teachers.
71. One should have curiosity for all new things.
72. Life without gaining knowledge is worthless.
73. One should have full faith in the written word.
74. Cramming as a method of acquiring knowledge is good.
75. A learned man will gladly like to have discussions with others.
76. One must not believe what he has not seen.
77. Learning comes with reverence and humbleness.
78. Beauty is to be admired and enjoyed.
79. One who does not love others is not a good person.
80. For a beautiful thing, one should not hesitate to sacrifice anything.
81. For fulfilling his/her beloved's desire, one should not hesitate in sacrificing anything.
82. One must have affection for all his younger ones.
83. One should observe ancestor worship (Shradh).
84. One should worship the prophet or leader of his religion.
85. One should have attitudes of faith and help towards hermits and saints.
86. Every soul passes through the endless cycle of birth and rebirth.
87. One should not believe idol working.
88. Non-believers in the prophet should be killed.
89. Heathens and barbarians should be converted into christianity.
90. One should give charity to the needy.
91. One should give food/corn to animals and birds.
92. One should worship cows.
93. Those who do good actions in their worldly life get in heaven after death.
94. One gets only what lies in his fate.
95. Those who do bad actions in this worldly life go to hell after death.
96. Idol worship is the best kind of worship.
97. It is a man's foremost duty to try for the propagation of his religion.
98. One should care more for improving his life after death rather than this worldly life.
99. This worldly life is worthless afterall.
100. Eat, drink and be marry for tomorrow we die.
101. One must eat, dress and behave strictly according to what is

traditionally prescribed in his religion, sect or panth.

102. One should not eat, drink and marry with a person of other religion.
103. Whenever there is a great threat to religion, an incarnation (*Avatar*) is born in this world.
104. Miracles (like *Akashvani*, sudden changes, magical happenings etc.), do happen at the command of gods, saints and other religious people.
105. Ghosts and evil spirits do exist.
106. One must believe in means.
107. All what is written in our religious books is good for us even today.
108. There is only one God, not many Gods.
109. God certainly exists.
110. One should observe rituals pertaining to dead relatives.
111. Non-violence must be practised by every one.
112. A person professing non-violence must not eat meat.
113. One should believe in nature if he is religious.
114. One must worship God every day.
115. One should observe religious fasts.
116. One should give charity to religious people and sadhus.
117. A food touched by a lower caste person or that of another religion becomes polluted.
118. A man should be prepared to sacrifice every thing for the sake of high spiritual attainments.
119. All religions must be respected.
120. One must work for the salvation of his soul.
121. Killing animals is a sin.
122. Mother should be respected above all.
123. A man's worldly miseries are due to his bad actions in his past life.

**Other Values:**

124. One must do the work allotted to him sincerely.
125. It is the moral duty of every person to help the poor people.
126. It is immoral to exploit persons in difficulty.
127. Real knowledge is that which leads to self-realisation.
128. Real knowledge is that which enables a man to earn his living.
129. Real knowledge is that which helps a man to act effectively according his status in the society.
130. Real knowledge is something unworldly; it is really spiritual.
131. It is good to have ideas, but one should not hesitate to abandon these and act differently if the circumstances so warrant.

## 41A7 VALUE ORIENTATION SCALE

*Author*: Ranjit Singh and T.S. Sohal.

*Availability* : Author, Department of Agricultural Extension, Punjab Agricultural University, Ludhiana.

*Time required*: 30 minutes.

*Level*: Farmers.

*Main features* : Five-value orientations are included: (1) progressive outlook, (2) economic fain, (3) dignity of labour, (4) willingness to take risk, (5) achievement of goals. It consists of 25 items with five for each value.

*Scoring* : Three-point scale in which a score of 3 for 'agree', 2 for 'undecided' and 1 for 'disagree' are assigned. Method of summated ratings is used.

*Reliability* : Test-retest reliability coefficient was found to be .796. Alternate form method gave reliability coefficient as high as .967.

*Validity* : Validity of the scale was tested with "jury's opinion" and 'known group' technique.

*References* :

1. Singh, R. and Sohal, T.S. Value orientations of adopters and non-adopters of hybrid maze. *Journal of Research*, Punjab Agricultural University, 1969, 6(2), 5-7.
2. Singh, R. and Sohal, T.S. Intensity of farmers values orientation. *Indian Journal of Extension Education*, 1970, 6(3-4), 77-79.

41A7 VALUE ORIENTATION SCALE

(The following statements have to be rated on a 3-point scale of agreement).

1. If one does not have sufficient finances, he should not hesitate in borrowing for making permanent improvements on the farm.
2. One should not feel satisfied with his present way of farming.
3. One must adopt modern methods of cultivation, if he wants to increase his yield.
4. There is no end to improving one's yield/farm.
5. Whatever new practice is recommended by the extension service, a farmer should readily adopt it.
6. Farmers should change their cropping programme on the basis of market prices and necessarily adhere to the cropping pattern which has been followed year after year by their forefathers.
7. A farmer must know when to sell his crops and live stock in order to make the most money.
8. Farmers should select varieties for their farms according to the needs of the market.
9. A farmer should produce only those commodities at his farm which can give him maximum cash profits.
10. A farm plan, prepared in consultation with an extension worker, which will give maximum return's should be acceptable to all the farmers.
11. A farmer should not hesitate in doing his farm operations with his own hands.
12. A farmer has no facility for irrigation, and the canal is at a distance of two furlongs from his farm. Canal authorities informed him that he will be provided water if he digs the channel himself. He should not dig the channel.
13. A farmer should gladly work along with his farm labour so that they show better output.
14. The difference between the successful farmer and the non-successful one is more in how hard they work than in how much time they spend in planning their farming operations.

15. Compost should be kept in pits even if it involves carrying the cowdung by the members of the family.
16. If a farmer has no money to purchase chemical fertiliser, he should get taccavi even if he knows that his crop can sometime be destroyed by natural calamities.
17. If there is a possibility of making good profit a farmer should not mind taking a risk on a farming enterprise.
18. A chemical (2-4D) is very effective to control weeds of wheat crop. Farmers should use it even when they know that it can some time give reverse results with slight negligence in the desired time of its application.
19. As farming is a gamble on the rains and on nature, therefore, one should not invest much in farming.
20. Innovation always involves some risk. A good cultivator should not hesitate to take that.
21. A farmer must encourage his son who wishes to attend young farmers courses for three months at Punjab Agricultural University even if he has to do more work in his absence.
22. One must provide good education to his children instead of buying more cattle for farm even if he has surplus feed and labour.
23. A farmer has not all the farm machinery he needs but has enough to get alongwith. He preferred to buy machinery even when the family like some new furniture in the house.
24. "Nature plays a vital role in successful harvest of the crops so it is useless to put extra efforts" say a few farmers.
25. I feel like working very hard on the farm and use improved practices so that I shall be rich man.

## 41A8 VALUE SCALES

*Author*: S.V. Supe.

*Availability*: Author, College of Agriculture, Nagpur.

*Time required*: 20 minutes.

*Level*: Farmers.

*Scoring* : The scoring scheme for positive items is as followers negative items are scored in the reverse order. Strongly agree 7, Agree 5, Undecided 4, Disagree 3, Strongly disagree 1.

*Main features* : The value scales measure economic motivation, scientific orientation, mental activity, independence and risk preference. They are developed using Thurstone-cum-Likert methods. Each scale has six statements which are rated on the basis of a 5-point continuous as per Likert Method.

*References* :

1. Supe, S.V. Factors related to different degrees of rationality in decision-making among farmers. Doctoral Dissertation in Agricultural Extension, IARI, 1969.
2. Supe, S.V. and Kolte, N.V. Values and adoption of farm innovations. *Indian Journal of Social Work*, 1971, 32(1), 9-16.

41A8 VALUE SCALES

(Under each value scale, all items are to be checked on a 5-point scale of agreement).

(a) **Economic Motivation Scale**

1. A farmer should work toward larger yields and economics profits.
2. The most successful farmer is one who makes the most profit.
3. A farmer should try any new farming idea which may earn him more money.
4. A farmer should grow cash crops to increase monetary profits in comparison to growing of food crops for home consumption.
5. It is difficult for the farmer's children to make good start unless he provides them with economic assistance.
6. A farmer must earn his living but the most important thing in life cannot be defined in economic terms.

Items 1, 2, 3, 4 and 5 are positive and item 6 is negative.

(b) **Scientific Orientation Scale**

1. New methods of farming give better results to a farmer than the old methods.
2. The way a farmer's forefathers farmed is still the best way to farm today.
3. Even a farmer with lots of experience should use new methods of farming.
4. Though it takes time for a farmer to learn new methods in farming it is worth the efforts.
5. A good farmer experiments with new ideas in farming.
6. Traditional methods of farming have to be changed in order to raise the level of living of a farmer.

Items 1, 3, 4, 5 and 6 are positive and item 2 is negative.

(c) **Independence Scale**

1. If a farmer wants a thing done right he must do it himself.
2. Independence in decision-making is the most important quality of a successful farmer.
3. A farmer is at his best when he is free, self-reliant and avoids all outside help.
4. A financially successful farmer is one who stands on his own feet.
5. A farmer should teach his children to be able to make their decisions independently.
6. Now-a-days a farmer can no longer afford to be independent.

Items 1, 2, 3, 4 and 5 are positive and item 6 is negative.

(d) **Mental Activity Scale**

1. Every farmer should devote some time on planning his daily farm work.
2. A farmer's thinking and planning counts far more in farming today than does his routine work.
3. A farmer should attend Farmers' Training Camp where new ideas are presented.
4. A farmer should not spend much time in thinking and planning but should go ahead and do the job the way he already knows.
5. A farmer should prefer to work with his hands rather than reading a farm magazine.
6. The time spent by a farmer in planning and evaluating is well spent than time spend in physical work.

Items 1, 2, 3 and 6 are positive and its 4 and 5 are negative.

(e) **Risk Preference Scale**

1. A farmer should grow large number of crops to avoid greater risks involved in growing one or two crops.
2. A farmer should rather take more of a chance in making a big profit than to be content with a smaller, but less risky profits.
3. A farmer who is willing to take greater risks than the average farmer usually does better financially.
4. It is better for a farmer not to try new farming methods unless most other farmers have used them with success.
5. Trying an entirely new method in farming by a farmer involves risk but it is worth it.

Items 2, 3 and 5 are positive and items 1 and 4 are negative score as earlier.

41A9 WORK VALUE INVENTORY

*Author* : A. Vasantha.
*Availability* : Author, Central Institute of Education, Delhi University, Delhi.
*Time required* : No time limit.
*Level* : High school students.
*Main features* : It is an inventory consisting of 71 items (15 values) to be rated by the subject on a 5-point scale.
*Scoring* : Separate scoring for each value area can be obtained by summation of weighted responses for 4, 3, 2, 1 and 0 on the 5-point scale.
*Reliability* : Test-retest correlations ranged from .19 to .68, one significant at .05 and others at .01 level.
*Validity* : Correlations of the long form (71 items) with the short form (15 items) ranged from .33 to .56, all significant at .01 level.
*Reference* : Vasantha, A. A study of work-values of higher secondary students of Delhi in relation to their intelligence, achievement and socio-economic status. Doctoral Dissertation in Education, University of Delhi, 1971.

41A9 WORK VALUE INVENTORY

(The following items are to checked on a 5-point scale of importance).

1. Work in which you plan, organise and direct the activities of others.
2. Work in which there is certainty of continued employment.
3. Work in which you tackle unexpected or novel situations.
4. Work in which the fellow workers are the kind of people you would like to work with.
5. Work in which you work under conditions you like; not too hot or not too cold, quick, clear etc.
6. Work in which you have hours that enables you to pursue your hobbies and interests.
7. Work in which you do many different things on the job.
8. Work in which you can express your ideas, talents and skills.
9. Work in which you invent new things, design new products and develop new ideas.
10. Work in which you have a feeling of personal satisfaction.
11. Work in which you have the satisfaction of having helped people.
12. Work in which there is opportunity to improve skills and move further on the job.
13. Work in which you can combine a career and good family life.
14. Work in which you win the respect and admiration of people.

## Instruments with technical information B

41B1 TRADITIONAL VALUE SCALE

*Author* : B. Rama Devi.
*Availability* : Author.
*Level* : Indian women.
*Main features* : It consists of 65 items out of which 5 are check items. The values covered include: moral-spiritical, economic, social and family.
*Scoring* : Five-point rating scale was used, the answers ranging from strong agreement through neutral to strong disagreement. The rating scale values ranged from 1 to 5, 3 being the neutral score. Low scores indicate positive attitudes towards traditional value, while high scores indicate negative attitude. The total score range of TV Scale is 60 to 300; the neutral 180.
*Reliability* : Test-retest reliability coefficient was found to be .66 (N=20).
*Reference* : Rama Devi, B. Indian women and her attitude to traditional values. *Journal of Psychological Researches*, 1963, 6(1), 72-78.

41B2 ISB TECHNIQUE

*Authors* : H.K. Kapil and S. Aggarwal.
*Availability* : Authors.

*Uses* : To find out the change in orthodox system of values in Hindu society due to forces of social change.

*Level* : Adult women.

*Main features* : Questionnaire and schedule.

*Reliability* : Reliability of the tool was obtained through parallel form method. A correlation of .63 between the scores obtained by the questionnaire method and ISB was found in the present study.

*Validity* : Validity of the instrument was ascertained through expert opinion.

*Reference* : Kapil, H.K. and Aggrawal, S. Changing patterns of value amongst women in modern Hindu society. *Psychological Researches*, 1966, 1(1-2), 29-32.

41B3 SOCIAL VALUES SCALE

*Authors* : P. Mohinder Kaushal and B.S. Saraon.

*Availability* : Authors, Punjab Agricultural University, Ludhiana.

*Level* : Farmers.

*Main features* : A 22-item inventory developed through Thurstone method of Equal Appearing Intervals.

*Scoring* : Scale values are available.

*Reliability* : Reliability coefficient was found to be .81.

*Reference* : Kaushal, M.P. and Saraon, B.S. A scale to measure change in social value under the impact of mechanisation of agriculture. *Interdiscipline*, 1971, 8(2), 86-96.

41B4 TEST OF DEMOCRATIC VALUES (HINDI)

*Author* : S.P. Kulshrestha.

*Availability* : Commercially available from M/s. Indian Psychological Corporation, 'Shanti Sadan' Rai Behari Lal Road, Lucknow-7, U.P.

*Uses* : The test measures the democratic values of students, teachers and other groups. It also measures seven democratic values viz. freedom, equality, national integration, character, health, intellectual ability and dignity of labour.

*Time required* : No time limit, but takes about 30 to 40 minutes.

*Level* : Higher secondary students and above, including adults.

*Main features* : There are 140 items, 20 each referring to each of 7 values.

*Scoring* : Seven scoring key stencils are available for the seven values.

*Reliability* : Split-half reliability using SMC formula was found to be .82, .87, .91, .85, .90 and .19 for the value of character freedom, equality, intellectual ability, national integration dignity of labour and health.

*Validity* : Concept and construct validity were established. Validity coefficient with teachers rating were .79, .81, .85, .78, .78, .82 and .83 respectively for C, F, E, I, N, D and H values.

*Norms* : Norms have been developed on 680 students of Delhi. Classifications of value scores are provided for each value.

*References* :

1. Kulshrestha, S.P. A study of democratic values of Delhi students, ***Manika***, 1969, 5(3).

2. Kulshrestha, S.P. The impact of teacher training programme on democratic values of the teacher trainees. *Haryana Journal of Education*, 1972, Jan.

41B5 STUDY OF VALUE INVENTORY

*Authors* : P.M. Patel, M.M. Patel, D.S. Parikh, M.N. Palsane, M.B. Buch and Jamanaji Parikh.
*Availability* : P.M. Patel, National Institute of Education, Sri Aurobindo Marg, New Delhi-16.
*Time required*: 15 minutes.
*Level*: 13+ to 18+ (teenagers).
*Main features* : Standardised inventory multiple-choice questions measuring six values—interests, social, theoretical, political, economic, aesthetic and religious.
*Scoring* : Objective.
*Norms* : Available.
*Reference* : Bhatt, L.J., Patel, P.M., Patel M.M., and Parikh, D.S. *Inquiry into Psychological factors related to adolescent adjustment.* Report of the Indian Council of Medical Research Project. Baroda: Faculty of Education and Psychology, 1960.

41B6 SCALE OF INTENSITY OF THE VALUES IN THE ADOPTION OF IMPROVED FARM PRACTICES

*Authors* : Y.P. Singh and V.K. Babu.
*Availability* : Available on request from the authors.
*Time required*: One hour.
*Level*: Farmers.
*Scoring* : Ranking scores from 1 to 10 were assigned to each statement about a particular farm practice.
*Reliability* : Reliability of the scale was measured on the basis of the calculated Q value of each statement only those statements were included in the scale where the scale value of each statement was higher than the calculated 'Q' value.
*Reference* : Singh, Y.P. and Babu, V.K. A study of adoption of improved farm practices as a function of positive values. *Indian Journal of Extension Education*, 1968, 4(3-4) 71-77.

## Citations C

41C1 WORK VALUES INVENTORY

*Author* : C. Dhar.
*Reference* : Dhar, C. Work values of adolescent boys. *Guidance Review*, 3 (1), 12-21.

41C2 SOCIAL VALUES CHECKLIST

*Author* : S.P. Ruhela.

41C3 VALUE SCALE

*Author* : Durganand Sinha.
*Availability* : Author, Department of Psychology, Allahabad University, Allahabad.
*Reference* : Sinha, D. A study of the conflict of generations. *ICSSR Research Abstracts*, 1971, 1(1), 34-43.

## D Adaptations

41D1 ALLPORT-VERNON STUDY OF VALUES

*Author* : R.P. Bhatnagar.
*Language* : Hindi.
*Availability* : Author.
*Reliability* : Split-half reliabilities were found to be as follows: Theoretical = 71; Aesthetic = 64; Economic = .718; Social = .61; Political = .76 Religious = .65.
*Validity* : Validity has been computed by correlating individual items with the total score on each respective value scale.
*References* :

1. Dixit, R.C. and Sharma, D.D. Incorporation by students of teachers' values: A study of student-teacher relationship. *Indian Education Review*, 1969, 4(2), 89-96.
2. Dixit, R.C. and Sharma, D.D. Transformation of social and religious values of different castes. *Psychologia*, 1970, 13, 117-119.
3. Dixit, R.C. and Sharma, D.D. Differential values of high school and university students and their teachers. *Journal of Psychological Researches*, 1971, 15(1), 12-17.
4. Dixit R.C. and Sharma, D.D. A Study of student-teacher relationship in terms of value incorporation. *Journal of Psychological Researches*, 1970, 14(2), 57-63.

41D2 ALLPORT-VERNON LINDZEY STUDY OF VALUES

*Author* : V. George Mathew.
*Language* : English.
*Availability* : Department of Psychology, Kariavattom, P.O. Kerala University, Trivendrum.
*Level* : College students with at least two years of college education in Kerala. Applicable to English knowing adults all over India, though norms have been prepared on college students in Kerala.

*Reliability* : Odd-even reliabilities range from 0.55 to 0.70.

*Validity* : Correlation coefficients upto .59 were obtained with scales of vocational interest inventory. All six scales showed a significant difference between college students in Kerala specialising in nine fields of study.

*Norms* : T-score norms.

41 D3 ALLPORT-VERNON LINDZEY STUDY OF VALUES

*Author* : M.P. Jaiswal.

*Language* : Hindi.

*Availability* : Author, Department of Psychology, R.D.S. College, Bihar University, Muzaffarpur.

41 D4 ALLPORT-VERNON LINDZEY STUDY OF VALUES

*Author* : S.P. Kulshrestha.

*Language* : Hindi.

*Availability* : Author, Commercially available from Rupa Psychological Corporation, Sora Kuan, Varanasi.

*Reliability* :

| | T | E | A | S | P | R |
|---|---|---|---|---|---|---|
| Split-half | .87 | .85 | .83 | .89 | .80 | .89 |
| Stability | .92 | .90 | .88 | .99 | .91 | .92 |

*Validity* : Validity coefficients with Allports english adaptation of Chaudhary were .90, .89, .90, .94, .91 and .92 respectively for Theoretical, Economic, Aesthetic, Social, Political and Religious values.

*Norms* : Available for students, teachers, engineers, doctors, artists and other professions.

*References* :

1. Kulshrestha, S.P. A study of value patterns of in-service and preservice teachers. *Educational Trends*, Ajmer, July, 1970.
2. Kulshrestha, S.P. Manual of directions for revised and modified Hindi. Adaptation of the study of values. Rupa Psychological Corporation, 1971.

41 D5 ALLPORT-VERNON STUDY OF VALUES

*Author* : K. Raychoudhury.

*Reference* : Raychoudhury, K. Allport-Vernon Study of values (1958 modification), in Indian situation. *Indian Psychological Bulletin*, 1959, 4(2), 67-74.

41 D6 KLUKHON VALUE QUESTIONNAIRE

*Author* : Binod C. Agrawal.

*Availability* : Author.

*Reference* : Agrawal, B.C. Family organisation and authoritarian personality: Comparative study of U.P. and Madras, Hindu and Muslim. *Journal of Social Research*, 1967, 11(2), 7-26.

# 2. Stratification

## A Instruments with technical information

### 42A1 A COMMON SOCIO-ECONOMIC SCALE FOR RURAL AND URBAN AREAS

*Authors* : P.G. Aaron, M.G. Marihal and R.N. Maltesha.
*Availability* : Authors, Department of Education, Karnatak University, Dharwar.
*Time required* : No time limit.
*Level* : Adults.
*Main features* : Consists of five variables. Occupation of father, fathers education material possession, house, shirts or blouses, and 50 items divided into 7 categories.
*Scoring* : Total of the weightages of items possessed in different categories.
*Reliability* : Retest reliability coefficient was found to 0.77.
*Validity* : Concurrent validity coefficient was found to be .61.
*Reference* : Aaron, P.G., Marihal, V.G. and Maltesha, R.N. A common *socio-economic* status scale for rural and urban areas. *Research Monograph*, 1969, 3, Karnataka University, Dharwar.

### 42A1 A COMMON SOCIO-ECONOMIC STATUS SCALE FOR RURAL AND URBAN AREAS

1. **Occupation of Father :** 1. Unemployed. 2. Labour. 3. Cast-occupation. 4. Small business/cultivation. 5. Business/clerk/elementary school teacher, etc. 6. High school teacher; technician. 7. Landlord, high government officials, professions.
2. **Father's Education :** 1. Illiterate. 2. Can read only. 3. Can read and write well. 4. Middle or high school education. 5. College graduate. 6. Post-graduate. Professional (M.Sc., M.B.B.S., Law, etc.). 7. Advanced education (Ph.D., M.D.).
3. **Material Possession :** 1. None. 2. Cycle/1 farm animal (cow, buffalo, bull). 3. Radio/2 farm animals. 4. News paper/3 farm animals. 5. Wrist watch (own)/4 farm animals. 6. Motor cycle/scooter/pump set/5-10 farm animals. 7. Car/truck/tractor/more than 10 farm animals.
4. **House :** 1. 1 room. 2. 2 rooms. 3. 3 rooms. 4. 4 to 6 rooms. 5. 7 to 8 rooms. 6. 9 to 10 rooms. 7. More than 10 rooms.
5. **Shirts or Blouses :** 1. One only. 2. Two. 3. Three. 4. Four to six. 5. Seven to eight. 6. Nine to ten 7. More than ten.

42A2 SOCIO-ECONOMIC STATUS SCALE (URBAN)

*Author*: B. Kuppuswamy.
*Availability* : Published by Manasayan and available commercially from Manasayan, 32, Netaji Subhash Marg, Delhi-6.
*Time required*: Maximum 10 minutes.
*Level*: Form-A for adults only. Form-B for students only.
*Main features* : Scales consist of three parts; (a) Education, (b) occupation and (c) Income. Each of these categories have 7 sub-categories.
*Scoring* : Total score of the sub-categories checked in each criteria shows the socio-economic status of the subject.
*Validity* : Various methods were used to test the validity: (a) matching against outside criterion, (b) distribution patterns, (c) comparison of dichotomous groups.
*Reference* : Kuppuswamy, B. *Manual of Socio-economic Status Scale*. Delhi: Manasayan, 1962.

42A2 SOCIO-ECONOMIC STATUS SCALE (URBAN)

(Weightages for items appear in parentheses).

A. **Education**

1. Professional degree or Hons. M.A. and above (7)
2. B.A. or B.Sc. degree (6)
3. Intermediate or post high school diplomas (5)
4. High school certificate (4)
5. Middle school completion (3)
6. Primary school or literate (2)
7. Illiterate (1)

B. **Occupation**

1. Profession (10)
2. Semi-profession (6)
3. Clerical, shop owners, farm owners etc. (5)
4. Skilled worker (4)
5. Semi-skilled worker (3)
6. Unskilled worker (2)
7. Unemployed (1)

C. **Income**

1. Above Rs. 1,000 per month (10)
2. Between Rs. 750 and Rs. 999 (7)
3. Between Rs. 500 and Rs. 749 (6)
4. Between Rs. 300 and Rs. 499 (5)
5. Between Rs. 101 and Rs. 299 (4)
6. Between Rs. 51 and As. 100 (2)
7. Below Rs. 50 (1)

| | Total Score | SESS Class |
|---|---|---|
| S | 26 — 29 | I |
| C | 16 — 25 | II |
| A | 11 — 15 | III |
| L | 5 — 10 | IV |
| E | Below 5 | V |

42A3 SOCIO-ECONOMIC STATUS SCALE (RURAL)

*Authors* : U. Pareek and G. Trivedi.
*Availability* : Manasayan, 32 Subhash Marg, Delhi-6.
*Uses* : For measuring socio-economic status of rural families.
*Levels* : Rural population.
*Main features* : It consists of nine main items relating to land, education, occupation, house, caste, farm powers, material possessions, family and social participations. Each item contains sub-items.
*Scoring* : Weighted scores for different categories.
*Reliability* : Test-retest reliability (two months) .87. Inter-judge reliability .93.
*References* :

1. Pareek, Udai and Trivedi, G. Norms for Delhi area of a socio-economic status scale (rural). *Buniyadi Talim*, 1963, 6, 120-124.
2. Trivedi, G. and Pareek, Udai. Categorisation of rural socio-economic groups. *Indian Journal of Social Work*, 1964, 24, 297-303.
3. Pareek, Udai and Trivedi, G. *Socio-economic Status Scale (Rural)*. Form and Manual, 32 p. Delhi: Manasayan, 1964.
4. Pareek, Udai and Trivedi, G. Factor analysis of socio-economic status of farmers in India. *Rural Sociology*, 1965, 30, 311-321.

42A3 SOCIO-ECONOMIC STATUS SCALE (RURAL)

(Weightages appear in parantheses).

1. **Caste :** a. Schedule caste (1). b. Lower caste (2). c. Artisan caste (3). d. Agricultural caste (4). e. Prestige caste (5). f. Dominant caste (6).
2. **Occupation :** a. Labour (1). b. Caste occupation (2). c. Business (3). d. Independent profession (4). e. Cultivation (5). f. Service (6).
3. **Education :** a. Illiterate (0). b. Can read only (1). c. Can read and write (2). d. Primary (3). e. Middle (4). f. High school (5). g. Graduate (6).
4. **Social Participation :** a. Member of one organisation (1). b. Member of more than one organisation (2). c. Office holder (3). d. Wider public leader (6).
5. **Land :** a. No land (0). b. Less than 1 acre (1). c. 1-5 acres (2). d. 5-10 acres (3). e. 10-15 acres (4). f. 15-20 acres (5). g. More than 20 acres (6).
6. **House :** a. No home (0). b. Hut (1). c. Katcha house (2). d. Mixed house (3). e. Pucca house (4). f. Mansion (6).
7. **Farm Powers :** a. No drought animal (0). b. 1-2 drought animals (2). c. 3-4 drought animals or 1 or more prestige animal (4). d. 5-6 drought animal or tractor (6).

8. **Material Possession :** a. Bullock-cart (1). b. Cycle (1). c. Radio (1). d. Chairs (1) e. Improved agricultural implements (2).
9. **Family :** Type: a. Single (1). b. Joint (2).
   Size: c. Upto 5 (1). d. Above 5 (2) e. Distinctive features (2).

42A4 SOCIO-ECONOMIC STATUS SCALE

*Author* : G.R. Shirpurkar.
*Availability* : Author, Superintending Agricultural Officer, Nasik Division, Nasik.
*Time required* : 5 minutes.
*Level* : Farmers.
*Reliability* : Split-half reliability was found to be r=0.21.
*Validity* : The box and card system of estimating validity was adopted. The coefficient of correlation between the scores of family heads obtained by this method and those obtained by the scale was .519.
*Reference* : Shirpurkar, G.R. Construction and standardisation of a scale for measuring socio-economic status of farm families. *Indian Journal of Extension Education*, 1967, 3(1-2), 16-24.

42A4 SOCIO-ECONOMIC STATUS SCALE

1. **Land :** a. No land, b. Upto 1 acre, c. Upto 5 acres, d. Upto 10 acres, c. Upto 15 acres, f. Upto 20 acres, g. Above 20 acres.
2. **Education :** a. Illiterate, b. Can read only, c. Can read and write, d. Primary, e. Middle, f. High school, g. Graduate.
3. **House :** a. Numbers — One, two, Three; b. Type — Kachha, Mixed, Pucca.
4. **Occupation :** a. Labour, b. Caste occupation, c. Business, d. Independent, e. Profession, f. Cultivation, g. Service.
5. **Caste :** a. Chamar, Bhangi, Dom, b. Jhimar, Khati, Dhobi, Badi, c. Lohar, Khumhar, Tailor, Nai, Baniya, Sonar, Ahir, Jolaha, d. Saini, Brahmin, e. Jat.
6. **Farm Power :** a. Bullocks — Nil, one to two, three to four, five to six, b. Camel one, c. Tractor.
7. **Material Prossession :** a. Bullock cart, b. Cycle, c. Radio, d. Chairs, e. Improved agricultural implements.
8. **Family :** a. Type: single, Joint, b. Size : Upto 5, above 5, c. Distinctive features.
9. **Social Participation :** a. Members of one organization, b. Members, of more than one, organization, c. Office holders, d. Distinctive features.

1. **Occupation :** (The term occupation refers to the occupation of head of family). No occupation (0), Agricultural Labour (1), New-Agricultural Labour (1).
2. **Saldar :** (Saldar is a person who is appointed on one year contract). Farmer or a Shopkeeper (2), Part-time or whole-time Government (3), Servant or a servant in any important firm (4).
3. **Total Land Owned :** (Includes uncultivated and follow land and the land owned by the respondent in the village of his residence and other villages far or near). No land (0), 0.1 to 5.00 Acres (1) 5.1 to 10.00

Acres (2), 10.1 to 15.00 Acres (3).
Additional weight at the rate of 1 for every additional 5.0 Acres.

4. **Gona** : (A crude carpet made of thick fibre is used for filling cotton, grain etc. in the cart while carrying it to a distant market). Non-possession (0), Possession (1).

## B Instruments with technical information

42B1 SOCIO-ECONOMIC STATUS SCALE (SESS)

*Authors* : S.P. Kulshrestha and Priya De.
*Availability* : Commercially available. The Institute for Studies in Psychological Testing, L.O. 35/166, Navbasta, Agra-2, U.P.
*Time required* : 10 minutes.
*Level* : School, College and adult population.
*Main features* : Seven factors are included in this test. Each factor is supplemented by two to five questions. Rural and urban forms are separately available.
*Reliability* : Test-retest reliability was found to be .90 and inter-item correlations vary from .42 to .70.
*Scoring* : Stencil scoring key.
*Validity* : Correlation coefficients with Kuppuswami's Scale was .52, with Pandey, Jalota and Kapoor's Scale .62.
*Norms* : Norms are provided for college level. Cutting scores are given.
*Reference* : Kulshrestha, S.P. and De, Priya. *S.E.S.S.* Institute for studies in Psychological Testing, Agra.

42B2 SOCIO-ECONOMIC SCORE BOARD

*Author* : Indera P. Singh.
*Availability* : Author, Department of Anthropology, Delhi University.
*Uses* : For scaling and placement of households in terms of economic position.
*Time required* : 10 to 15 minutes.
*Level* : Socio-economic/cultural investigators and/or research workers.
*Main features* : It is a scale based on observation and interview and has to be administered by a trained worker. The results can then be even computerised in the absence of which manual treatment is possible.
*Scoring* : Numerical scoring after observation and questionnaire.
*Reference* : Biswas, P.C. and Singh, I.P. *The Ex-criminal Tribes of Delhi State*, Department of Anthropology, Delhi University.

42B3 SOCIO-ECONOMIC STATUS SCHEDULE

*Author* : R.M. Verma.
*Availability* : Author.
*Main features* : It is a 5-point scale. Contains three parts.

*Reliability* : Correlation coefficients between the different parts and the total test range from .47 to .64.
*Validity* : Concurrent validity was worked out.
*Reference* : Verma, R.M. Development of a tool to appraise socio-economic status. *Journal of Psychological Research,* 1962, 6(1), 35-38.

## Citations C

42C1 BIOGRAPHICAL QUESTIONNAIRE

*Authors* : S. Chatterjee and M. Mukherjee.
*Reference* : Chatterjee, S. and Mukherjee, M. Relation between interest and achievement. *Indian Journal of Psychology,* 1963, 38(4), 117-192.

42C2 HOME BACKGROUND SURVEY QUESTIONNAIRE

*Author* : N.Y. Reddy.
*Reference* : Reddy, N.Y. A study of the relationship between ordinal position of adolescents and their adjustment. *Psychological Studies,* 1967, 12(2), 91-100.

# 3. Social Distance and Group Attitudes

## A Complete instruments

43A1 STEREOTYPES TEST

*Authors* : A.P. Arifunnisa and A. Hafeez.
*Availability* : Authors, College of Arts and Science, N.R. Colony, Bangalore, and Indian Institute of Science, Bangalore-12.
*Level* : Adult men and women or college students.
*Main features* : It is a combination of different features.
*Scoring* : S = P — N (Score is equal to the sum of positive attributes minus the sum of negative attributes).
*Norms* : Scores of college boys and girls available.

43A1 STEREOTYPES TEST

(The caste-group or the community studied has to be checked for the presence or absence of the following traits).

PART I

1. Hard-working; 2. Unity-loving; 3. Cunning; 4. Refined; 5. Vulgar; 6. Cruel; 7. Poor; 8. Progressive; 9. Faithful; 10. Conservative; 11. Ugly; 12. Intelligent; 13. Friendly; 14. Selfish; 15. Pleasure-seeking; 16. Unreliable; 17. Self-controlled; 18. Cultured; 19. Sociable; 20. Harmonious; 21. Arrogant; 22. Illiterate; 23. Altruistic; 24. Learned; 25. Materialistic; 26. Boastful; 27. Brave; 28. Clean; 29. Economical; 30. Practical; 31. Orthodox; 32. Greedy; 33. Miserly; 34. Educated; 35. Inhospitable; 36. Fanatic; 37. Dirty; 38. Kind; 39. Artistic; 40. Religious; 41. Patriotic; 42. Quarrelsome; 43. Domineering; 44. Cowardly; 45. Backward; 46. Industrious; 47. Tolerant; 48. Disciplined; 49. Generous; 50. Peace-loving.

PART II

The communities or caste groups rated in part I have to be ranked in this part as for the preference by the subject.

PART III

In this part the subject has to indicate the desirability or undesirability of the 50 characteristics rated by him in part 1.

PART IV

In this part the subject has to indicate the categories into which he will admit the persons from each of the communities rated by him earlier.

1. To kinship by marriage; 2. To take food in my dining room; 3. As my intimate personal friend; 4. As my neighbour; 5. To employment in my occupation; 6. As an acquaintance; 7. No relationship.

43A2 INTERNATIONAL ATTITUDE SCALE

*Authors* : Satyapal Duggal.

*Uses* : To measure the international attitudes [attitude towards international (cross national) relations].

*Time required* : 15 minutes.

*Levels* : Anyone having high school education.

*Main features* : It consists of eleven items.

*Scoring* : In order to obtain numerical scores, items are assigned points as follows:

| Item No. | 1 | 2 | 3 | 4 | 5 | 6 | 7 | 8 | 9 | 10 | 11 |
|---|---|---|---|---|---|---|---|---|---|---|---|
| Points: | –5 | –4 | –3 | –2 | –1 | 0 | +1 | +2 | +3 | +4 | +5 |

Positive or negative credit was given for each circled item number. thus, maximum score could be +15 and minimum score could be –15. This score could be converted into positive score on eleven-point scale — zero extreme negative international attitude and ten extreme positive international attitude by applying the formula: international attitude score = 5+ Score/3 Mean I.A.S. for students = 8.67.

43A2 INTERNATIONAL ATTITUDE SCALE

(Each item to be checked for agreement).

1. One should have nothing to do with other races.
2. People using backward economic methods are stupid.
3. For world peace different nations should mind their own business.
4. Our nation need not spend its resources for the development of other countries.
5. Every nation should carry its own burden.
6. Security of U.S.A. depends upon her nuclear weapons.
7. One should evaluate one's customs and values as seen by others.
8. I like to join a picnic with the foreigners.
9. A house is necessary for all human beings but it is made out of the material which happens to be available.
10. One should have a deep concern for the well being of humanity.
11. One should understand why people in other lands live as they do.

43A3 COMMUNAL ATTITUDE SCALE (INGROUP AND OUTGROUP)

*Authors* : Prayag Mehta, B.P. Sinha and P.P. Gokulnathan.

*Availability* : Author, Department of Psychology, University of Udaipur, Udaipur (Raj.).

*Uses* : To study ingroup — outgroup attitudes.

*Time required* : 15 minutes.

*Level* : Upper primary level.

*Main features* : The scale consists of 10 adjectives each for Hindu, Muslims, Christian and Harijans. Respondents are asked to rate their own and other communities on each of the bipolar adjectives ranged from 1 to 7. The scale is developed under a project "A Communication study of national integration and secularism" of the Ministry of I & B and has been used in the riot affected sites of Ahmedabad, Ranchi and Bhiwandi. The scale is particularly useful to study inter-communal stereotypes and in relevant educational programmes.

*Scoring* : Seven-point scoring method was used.

*Reliability* : in process.

*Validity* : in process.

*Norms* : in process.

43A3 COMMUNAL ATTITUDE SCALE INGROUP AND OUTGROUP

(The following bipolar adjectives have been used in rating one's own and other communities on a 7-point semantic differential scale).

1. Kind-cruel. 2. Reliable-Unreliable. 3. Honest-Dishonest. 4. Good-Bad. 5. Happy-Sad. 6. Healthy-Unhealthy. 7. Patriot-Traitor. 8. Fair-Ugly. 9. Loyal-Unfaithful. 10. Own-others.

(Hindi equivalents available).

43A4 SOCIAL INTEGRATION ATTITUDE SCALE (SIAS)

*Author* : Biswanth Roy.

*Availability* : Author, Department of Educational Psychology, National Institute of Education (NCERT), Sri Aurobindo Marg, New Delhi-16.

*Uses* : To measure the integrative capacity of the students, towards certain westerners. But it can also be used or employed on any sample on population.

*Level* : Students.

*Time required* : Average 30 minutes.

*Main features* : The SIAS consists of 24 social relations or items. The items were prepared by incorporating the basic assumption developed by Bogardus to construct the social distance scale.

*Scoring* : The scoring weights are 4, 3, 2, 1 and 0 for responses checked.

*Reliability* : Split-half reliability was found to be .901 (First Half Vs. Second Half) and .904 (Odd Vs. Even).

*References* :

1. Roy, B. Social integration attitude of the post-graduate students towards certain westerners. *Psychological Studies,* 1967, 12(1) 39-45.
2. Roy, B. A cross cultural study of the persons residing within the industrial belt of Calcutta. *Journal of Social Psychology,* 1963, 195-201.

3. Roy, B. Industrialisation and the development of social integration attitude. *Bulletin, Council of Social and Psychological Researches,* 1965, 5, 17-24.
4. Roy, B. Cross-cultural SIA of the P.G. students towards fellow Indian sub-groups. *Journal of Social Research,* (in press).
5. Roy, B. On the social integration of the ethic groups in India. *Calcutta Review,* (in press).
6. Roy, B. Do individuals differ? *Naya Sikshak, (Teacher Today),* 1970, 13(2), 32-38.
7. Roy, B. Education and the problem of humanism. *Quest in Education,* (in press).
8. Roy, B. On values — A social-psychological analysis of the adolescent point of view. *Quest in Education,* 1972, 9(1) 21-30.

43A4 SOCIAL INTEGRATION ATTITUDE SCALE (SIAS)

(The following items are to be checked on a 5-point scale).

1. Would like to live with him if he be the landlord.
2. Would contact him to develop a capital for business.
3. Would he be the teacher the subject of study will be clearly comprehended.
4. Would accept him a partner in business.
5. Would like him as an employment officer.
6. Would accept him as a stranger guest in home.
7. Would like him as colleague.
8. Would establish friendship with him.
9. Would be able to mix him freely in respect of manners.
10. Would discuss with him about culture.
11. Would like him as an university examiner.
12. Would vote his candidature in UNO elections.
13. Would accept him as a neighbour.
14. Would participate with him in sports and games.
15. Would take loan from him when in need.
16. Would accept him as a leader.
17. Would like as a principal of educational institutions.
18. Would support his UNO presidency.
19. Would like him as a co-traveller.
20. Would keep him as an assistant.
21. Would like him as associate of the children of self-home.
22. Would establish relationship through marriage.
23. Would like him as a co-worker.
24. Would like him as a co-tenant.

43A5 A SCALE OF SOCIAL DISTANCE

*Authors* : H.D. Vasantharapaiah and A. Hafeez.

*Availability* : Authors, Maharaja's College, Mysore University, Mysore, and Deptt. of Industrial Management, Indian Inst. of Science, Bangalore-12.

*Uses* : To measure social distance which is a form of prejudice.

*Level* : Adult men and women.

*Main features* : It is a scale consisting of 8 statements depicting intimacy of relationship, the highest degree being given a weight of 8, and the lowest degree being given a weight of 1. The group's (of subjects') score is given by multiplying the responses of the group with their weight and adding them together.

*Norms* : Scores of a group of engineering students (N=90) and another of science and humanities students (N=140) are available.

43A5 A SCALE OF SOCIAL DISTANCE

(The following scale has to be used in rating each of the different groups mentioned below it).

1. I will not admit him to my country.
2. I will not allow him to reside in the same street.
3. I will not admit him to work in the same office, factory, or field.
4. I will not permit him to live as co-tenant.
5. I will not admit him to my club.
6. Prepared to share my house as a co-tenant.
7. I have no objection to marry my sister or daughter to a member of that group.

A. **Linguistic Groups**

1. Bengalies; 2. Gujaraties; 3. Malayalies; 4. Madrasies; 5. Maharashtrian; 6. Mysorians; 7. Punjabies; 8. Pakistanies.

B. **Linguistic Groups**

People whose mother tongue is: 1. English; 2. Hindi; 3. Kannada; 4. Malayalam; 5. Marathi; 6. Tamil; 7. Telugu; 8. Urdu.

C. **Religious Groups**

1. Animists; 2. Atheists; 3. Buddhists; 4. Christians; 5. Hindu; 6. Muslims; 7. Parsis; 8. Sikhs.

D. **Economic Groups**

1. Millionaire; 2. Very rich; 3. Rich; 4. Upper middle class; 5. Lower middle class; 6. Poor; 7. Refugees; 8. Beggars.

E. **Communal Groups**

1. Bedas (a); 2. Brahmins; 3. Harijans; 4. Jains; 5. Lingayats (a) 7. Vokkaligas (a); 8. Vysyas. (a) These caste groups live in South India, mostly in Mysore Distt.

F. **Political Groups**

1. Anarchists; 2. Congress; 3. Communists; 4. Hindu Mahasabha; 5. Imperialists; 6. Independents; 7. Prajapaksha; 8. Socialists.

G. **Racial Groups**

1. Aborigines; 2. Anglo-Indian; 3. Anglo-Saxon; 4. Arabic-Semetie; 5. Dravidian; 6. Indo-Aryan; 7. Mongoloin; 8. Negroid.

H. **Professional Groups**

1. Administrators; 2. Clerks and Teachers; 3. Doctors, Engineers and Lawyers; 4. Moneylenders; 5. Merchants; 6. Menials; 7. Skilled labourers. 8. Unemployees.

## Instruments with technical information B

43B1 PICTURE TEST OF SOCIAL DISTANCE

*Authors* : Pratibha Deo and A. Arora.
*Availability* : From first Author, Department of Education, Panjab University, Chandigarh.
*Uses* : To measure social distance between Indian University students and members of two adjoining countries Pakistan and China.
*Time Required* : 10 to 15 minutes.
*Level* : Post-Graduate students.
*Main features* : Twelve levels of ascending order of social nearness were chosen. Instead of choosing one level as is done in the Bogardus Distance Scale, the subject is asked to respond to each picture and each response is indicating acceptance, neutrality or rejection.
*Scoring* : Each response is scored +1, 0 or —1 depending on whether the response is indicating acceptance, neutrality or rejection.
*Reliability* : Test-retest reliability of the scores was found to be 0.89 (with an interval of month).
*Validity* : Cross validated against an adaptation of the 7-point Bogardus Scale. Coefficients of correlation obtained were 0.69 and 0.72 for Pakistanis and Chinese series respectively.
*Norms*: Percentile norms are available.
*Reference* : Deo, P. and Arora, A. Measurement of social distance and its change with a new projective test. *Journal of Psychological Research*, 1966 10(2), 68-7.

43B2 ETHNIC ATTITUDE INVENTORY

*Authors* : Asghari Mohiuddin and N.Y. Reddy.
*Availability* : Authors, Department of Psychology, Osmania University,

Hyderabad-7.

*Reference* : Mohiuddin, A. and Reddy, N.Y. Development of social concepts and ethnic attitudes in orphan and normal children. Paper presented at the First Annual Convention of the Indian Psychological Association, University, Hyderabad, Feb. 1973.

## C Citations

43C1 SOCIAL DISTANCE SCALE FOR SCHOOL CHILDREN

*Author* : C.S. Bennur.

43C2 SOCIAL DISTANCE PROJECTION TEST

*Authors* : Pratibha Deo and A. Arora.

*Reference* : Deo, P. and Arora, A. Measurement of social distance and its change with a new projective test. *Journal of Psychological Researches*, 1966, 10, 63-71.

43C3 BIPOLAR STEREOTYPE SCALES

*Author* : J. Mullick.

*Reference* : Mullick, J. A study of discriminating power of stereotypes. *Indian Journal of Psychology*, 1967, 42, 68-73.

43C4 SOCIAL DISTANCE SCALE

*Author* : B.G. Reddy.

*Reference* : Reddy, B.G. Development of social distance scale for use with Indian college students. *Research Bulletin*, 1967, 3, 31-35.

43C5 SOCIAL DISTANCE SCALE

*Author* : Prem Shanker.

*Level* : Students.

*Scoring* : The score of a person was the sum of scale values corresponding to the scale items endorsed by him. The attitude score obtained for three castes by the two techniques were correlated by the rank difference method.

*Reference* : Shankar, P. A simple method of scoring a social distance scale. *Journal of Psychological Researches*, 1964, 8(1), 7-12.

## Adaptations D

43D1 BOGARDUS SOCIAL DISTANCE

*Authors* : T. Narayan Rao and E.G. Parameswaran.
*Availability* : Authors, Department of Psychology, Osmania University, Hyderabad (A.P.).
*Main features* : Final scale consists of 7 items.
*Scoring* : Weighted scores are assigned to items.
*Reliability* : Test-retest reliability based on 30 Ss. was found to be .97.
*Reference* : Rao, T.N. and Parameswaran, E.G. The effect of duration of hostel stay on social distance patterns. *Research Bulletin,* 1965, 1, 25-34.

43D2 THE MINNESOTA INVENTORY OF SOCIAL PREFERENCE

*Authors* : M.C. Joshi and J. Pandey.
*Language* : Hindi.
*Availability* : Commercially available from Rupa Psychological Corporation, Varanasi.
*Reliability* : Test-retest reliability coefficients ranged from .795 to .845. Split-half reliability coefficients ranged from .685.
*Validity* : Very high based on different external criterion.
*Norms* : Under process.
*Reference* : Pandey, J. A psychological study of the adjustment problems of adolescents in relation to their personality variables. Unpublished Ph.D. thesis, Banaras Hindu University.

# 4. Modernisation and Social Change

## A Complete instruments

44A1 MODERNISATION ATTITUDE SCALE

*Authors* : P.G. Aaron, V.G. Marihal and R.N. Maltesha.
*Availability* : Authors, Department of Education, Karnatak University, Dharwar.
*Level* : Adults.
*Main features* : The scale is divided into the following parts (i) inter-State migration, (2) position of women, (3) free choice of mate, (4) family planning, (5) inter-caste marriage, and (6) social mobility. In all there are 95 statements for these dimensions reflecting extreme positive to negative values.
*Reference* : Aaron, P.G., Marihal, V.G. and Maltesha, R.N. Scale to measure the attitude of modernisation (English). Department of Education Research Monograph, Karnatak University, 1969.

44A1 MODERNISATION ATTITUDE SCALE

(The following items are to be checked by the respondent).

I. **Inter-state Migration**

1. Laws should be increased to stop inter-state migration.
2. Only the inefficient would try to migrate.
3. Migration would bring people of different cultures to our state and they would become undesirable neighbours.
4. Migration should be left to the wish of the individual.
5. Migration would lead to confusion due to language difficulty and hence should not be encouraged.
6. Migration would be the only method to know each other and their cultures well.
7. Migrants should be encouraged because they could be placed in better houses than they ever were.
8. Migration from one place to another arouses a sense of civic responsibility and should be encouraged.
9. Migration is desirable since it may bring out equal distribution of skill and competition.
10. State Government should pass laws in order to stop inter-state migration .
11. Migration of other people to our state would increase competition;

therefore it is not desirable.

12. Migration from one place to another should be encouraged as it would solve the problems of the poor.
13. The public standards could be improved by migration.
14. It does not matter much whether there is any migration within our country or not.
15. Everyone owes a debt to his native soil and should not, therefore, migrate to other states.

II. **Position of Women**

1. Women are not fit to be political leaders.
2. The present position of women in India is satisfactory.
3. Home is the place of women and it is not desirable to have them in offices and factories.
4. From time immemorial woman was the pillar of strength; hence more opportunities should be open to her.
5. The present discontentment could be solved only by making women stay inside the four walls.
6. Women are intellectually inferior to men and could not therefore claim equality.
7. When woman finds her marriage intolerable she should be free to dissolve it.
8. Employing women would only lead to deterioration of efficiency.
9. Women should not be allowed to compete in public events like the olympics; it is repulsive.
10. Woman should be given complete freedom in deciding her future.
11. The timing and number with respect to children should be based on the wish of the woman.
12. Woman should not have the right to vote as it is in some countries.
13. Government should encourage women's community activities.
14. High School education is enough for women.
15. It is absolutely immaterial whether the position of women is improved or not.

III. **Free Choice of Mate**

1. Opportunities for both the sexes to know each other should be created.
2. One should be free to choose his future wife since this is a fundamental right.
3. The so-called 'free marriage' is preferable because the economic burden of arranged marriages is too heavy for most parents to bear.
4. Free choice of mate would be frowned upon by elders and therefore should not be encouraged.
5. Both bad and good results would arise if one is free to choose one's own mate.
6. Free choice of mate should not be encouraged because it would results in social revolution.
7. Free choice of mate would be the only solution to the evil of 'dowry

system'.

8. Freedom in the choice of mate would lead to mass immorality.
9. It is absolutely immaterial whether we have arranged marriages or free marriages.
10. A growing number of Indians will accept the principle of free choice of mate, if sincere and effective attempts are made to teach them.
11. Freedom in the choice of mate is of vital importance and should be encouraged.
12. Since it is the duty of the Government to preserve the national culture and tradition, it should take steps to abolish freedom in the choice of mate.
13. People who freely select their own mates should be severely punished.
14. Only the disobedient would go for free choice of mate.
15. Freedom in the choice of mate would bring in desirable social change.

IV. **Family Planning**

1. Family planning should be encouraged because it is very useful.
2. Individuals who adopt family planning should be rewarded by the Government.
3. The concept of small family has gained wider acceptance and hence family planning should be encouraged.
4. Family planning is good in principal but it would do more harm than good.
5. Family planning should come from one's own accord: otherwise it would be undesirable.
6. Family planning has been tried and has proved a failure.
7. Family planning should be encouraged as science is advancing very fast on that subject.
8. Family planning is not acceptable to the culture mores of the country.
9. Family planning is a curse to the human family. Therefore, it should not be practised.
10. Family planning would encourage immorality and therefore is undesirable for India.
11. Laws should be increased to encourage family planning.
12. The practice on family planning might be of some value and hence worth trying.
13. Every medical student should be made to do his internship in the field of family planning in rural areas.
14. It does not matter much whether family planning is implemented in India or not.
15. Family planning is not desirable now because there may not be a sufficiently large majority in favour of it.
16. The subject of family planning is elastic and hence the Government may leave things alone.
17. Family planning would be harmful to the prosperity of the nation.
18. People should be allowed to take whatever method of choosing to limit their family that they want.
19. States which implement family planning should be rewarded.

20. Family planning should be adopted as a nation wide programme.

V. **Intercaste Marriage**

1. Intercaste marriage should be a matter to be decided by the individual and not by the Government.
2. Intercaste marriage increase the unity of society and should be encouraged.
3. Intercaste marriage would not be durable as both partners have grown up in different cultures.
4. Government should discourage severally intercaste marriage.
5. People who encourage and promote intercaste marriage should be punished by the Government.
6. Intercaste marriage is useful to the society and hence should be encouraged.
7. Financial assistance should be given to children who are born to parents of different castes.
8. Agencies which promote intercaste marriages should be penalised.
9. Co-educational institutions should be closed in order to reduce the incidence of intercaste marriage.
10. Enough freedom should be given to women so that they would come to know men of other castes.
11. It does not matter much whether we have intercaste marriage or not.
12. Intercaste marriage would be undesirable as it comes in the way of the nation's traditions.
13. Agencies to promote intercaste marriage should be supported by the Government.
14. Children born out of intercaste marriage are a social burden.
15. More co-educational institutions should be opened since they may promote intercaste marriage.

VI. **Social Mobility**

1. There is no harm if one aspires to become a Governor or even a Central Government Minister, for after all, they are also people like us.
2. Opportunities for job should be increased for the poor so that they also would become wealthy.
3. Untouchability imposes a barrier and therefore should be removed.
4. Children should be told that material wealth brings comfort and that one should strive for it.
5. Schools and hostels that are opened based on caste and economic status are more desirable.
6. It is desirable not to aspire for positions like Governorship because we can't even imagine ourselves in that position.
7. Since low economic status and low caste go hand in hand we should not tamper with them.
8. Caste system restricts social mobility and should be discouraged.
9. Caste is part of our culture and should be retained.
10. A casteless society increases unity and should be encouraged.

11. Now-a-days labourers think they are equal to us. Such a tendency is not good for national growth.
12. Caste system has come from the vedic age and should be maintained as such.
13. The present social and economic situation of the country is satisfactory and should be continued as such.
14. God has put every man in his position and it is no use trying to change it.
15. Caste system is undesirable because it keeps man in a fixed position.

## 44A2 SCALE TO MEASURE ATTITUDE TOWARDS WORKING WOMEN

*Author*: S. Sultan Akhtar.

*Availability* : Author, Department of Psychology, Aligarh Muslim University, Aligarh.

*Time required*: 8-10 minutes.

*Level*: Adults (men and women).

*Scoring* : Punched scoring-keys are available.

*Reliability*: Spilt-half reliability varies from .72 to .89 (N = 100).

*Validity* : Tetrachoric coefficients of correlation were calculated between items and total scores and only those items were included which yielded values of it significant at 1 per cent level. Also discriminative value of each item was computed.

*Norms* : Available.

## 44A2 SCALE TO MEASURE ATTITUDE TOWARDS WORKING WOMEN

(The respondent is to indicate high agreement, disagreement or indecisiveness for each of these items).

1. Woman was made by God to be a custodian of home and not a wage-earner.
2. A working wife can give the desired love and affection to her husband.
3. Working women are neglectful of their social obligations.
4. Women, in our country, should be encouraged to think seriously in terms of having a vocation.
5. Working women do not find time to attend to their domestic duties.
6. Working women develop suspicious and jealousies.
7. Working women hold high social position in society.
8. Women should stay at home to take care of their family.
9. Women impress as efficient workers.
10. Working women generally lead a happy married life.
11. Working women are suspected to have a doubtful morality.
12. Working women who have children feel guilty of neglecting them.
13. Working women enjoy as much prestige in our society as do the non-working women.
14. It is not possible for women to work with full devotion.
15. Working women are deprived of the freedom which they have as a housewife.

16. Working women develop a realistic approach towards life.
17. Employment of women creates many problems for the employer.
18. It is not difficult for a working woman to divide her time between home and work.
19. I think that most of the employed women are frustrated in life.

## 44A3 SOCIAL PARTICIPATION SCALE

*Authors* : S.N. Choudhari and S.N. Singh.
*Availability* : Authors, Indian Agricultural Research Institute, New Delhi.
*Level* : Farmers.
*Scoring* : Summation of weighted scores of the items checked. Maximum score is 28.88 and the minimum is 0.
*Reliability* : Test-retest (1 month) reliability coefficient was .96 and split-half = .71.
*Validity* : Correlation between participation scores and households identified for status was .799. Correlation with Chopin Participation Scale was .779.
*Reference* : Singh, K.N., Singh S.N. and Lokhande, M.R. *Measurement in extension research: instruments developed at IARI* New Delhi, Division of Agricultural Research, IARI, 1972, pp. 36-48.

## 44A3 SOCIAL PARTICIPATION SCALE

1. Member in one organisation.
2. Member in more than one organisation.
3. Attending information group activities.
4. Attendance in meetings of organisation.
5. Membership in committee.
6. Participation in affairs of meetings.
7. Organising informal groups activities.
8. Helping fixation of agenda of meetings.
9. Financial contribution for common work.
10. Participation in raising fund for common work.
11. Attending implementation of programme of work as supervisors.
12. Office bearers in formal organisation.
13. Organising common village work.
14. Direct active participation in execution of common village work.

## 44A4 SCALE FOR MEASURING ATTITUDE TOWARDS SMALL FAMILY

*Author* : E. Govindachari.
*Availability* : Author, Institute of Rural Health and Family Planning, Gandhigram, Tamil Nadu.
*Level* : Rural People.
*Main features* : It contains 10 statements developed using Thurstone and Likert's techniques.
*Reliability* : Computed by the method of consistency between parallel sub-samples.
*Validity* : Interior group validity was established by comparing adopters and

non-adopters.

*Reference* : Govindachari, E. A scale for measuring attitude towards small family in a rural community. *Action Research Monographs*, No. 3 Institute of Rural Health and Family Planning, Gandhigram, 1966.

## 44A4 SCALE FOR MEASURING ATTITUDE TOWARDS SMALL FAMILY

(The following items are to be checked for agreement. Scale values of the items appear in parentheses).

1. As children are the joy of life, there is no need to restrict their number. (1.39)
2. As the Creator will take care of the created, one need not worry about the family size. (1.40)
3. There is lesser chance of children in small families realising parents' difficulties than in large families. (1.92)
4. Since in a small family the number of children is less, the family income also decreases. (1.67)
5. One cannot say whether a small family is advantageous or disdvantageous. (2.72)
6. Whether a family is small or big it matters little. (2.96).
7. Proper food and clothing are provided for the members of the small family rather than in large ones. (4.48)
8. Parents will be able to bestow more love and care on children only if the family is small. (4.49)
9. Since the number of births in a small family is less, the health of the mother and the child is not affected adversely. (4.59)
10. Whether rich or poor, a planned family with two or three children will be ideal. (4.67)

## 44A5 FAMILY PLANNING ATTITUDE SCALE

*Author* : L.L. Katakwar.
*Availability* : Author.
*Level* : Adults.
*Main features* : Likert-type 5-point scale.
*Scoring* : As in Likert scale.
*Reliability* : Spilt-half = .91, and test-retest =.90.
*Validity* : Two contrasting groups (medical doctors and uneducated villagers) were used. Point-biserial correlation was found to be .565, significant beyond .01 level.
*Reference* : Katakwar, L.L. A comparative study of attitude towards family planning and birth control a Likert type scale. Ph.D. Thesis in Education, Jabalpur University, 1972.

## 44A5 FAMILY PLANNING ATTITUDE SCALE

(The following statements are to be checked on a 5-point scale of agreement item 1 to 11 are favourable, and from 12 to 24 unfavourable).

1. Family planning and birth control is a boon to the welfare of the nation.
2. Family planning and birth control is the easiest and the most appropriate method to check the growth of population.
3. Family planning and birth control should be popularised extensively for the economic development of the country.
4. Scientists should ceaselessly develop some easier and more suitable contraceptives.
5. Extensive and free-of-cost distribution of contraceptives should be provided.
6. Family planning and birth control provides equal opportunity to every member of the family.
7. For the proper upbringing of children, their number should be limited.
8. Family planning and birth control is very essential for the happiness of the family.
9. In the larger interest of the nation, family planning and birth control programme must be implemented even with force.
10. Success of family planning and birth control programme will lead to higher standard of life.
11. To make family planning and birth control successful, extensive sterilisation facilities should be made available.
12. Family planning and birth control is against nature.
13. Family planning and birth control will demoralise people and will lead to sexual extravagance.
14. Family planning and birth control will ruin Indian culture and civilisation.
15. Legalising abortion will lead to encouragement of immoral and anti-social tendencies.
16. Sterilisation being irreversible, is not a suitable method of family planning and birth control.
17. Family planning and birth control is one of the most selfish doctrines of modern times.
18. The use of artificial contraceptives leads to psychological troubles.
19. Moral restraint should be popularised in place of artificial methods of family planning and birth control.
20. Artificial methods to prevent pregnancy are harmful to the health of the parents.
21. Family planning and birth control propaganda, being hasty, has unfavourable and injurious effects.
22. The use of artificial contraceptives interferes with sexual pleasure.
23. More and more hands are needed for all-round economic development therefore family planning and birth control should be abandoned without any delay.
24. Human interference is undesirable as children are created by God.

## 44A6 ATTITUDE TOWARDS ARTIFICIAL INSEMINATION

*Authors* : M.S. Khoura and Y.P. Singh.
*Availability* : Second Author, Department of Extension, Punjab Agricultural

University, Hissar.

*Level*: Farmers.

*Scoring* : Masked window stencil. Scores assigned for the favourable statements were: strongly agree-4, agree-3, undecided-2, disagree-1 and strongly disagree-0. For unfavourable statements, the scoring system is reversed.

*Reliability* : Spilt-half reliability was found to be .87, test-retest reliability .89 and inter-judge reliability was found to be .86.

*Validity* : Content, concurrent and construct validity of the scale was found to be .93.

44A6 ATTITUDE TOWARDS ARTIFICIAL INSEMINATION

(The following items are to be checked on a 5-point scale of agreement).

1. Artificial insemination means to torture cow.
2. Road to prosperity is artificial insemination.
3. Artificial insemination is the best gift of the Government to the farmers.
4. Artificial insemination is inhumane.
5. Money spent on artificial insemination is a waste.
6. Reluctance to accept artificial insemination is a blunder.
7. Should artificial insemination progress, the milk will overflow our drains once again.
8. Why talk of artificial insemination our old ways are best.
9. Once conceived artificially cow does not conceive by natural service.
10. Artificial insemination can conceive a cow only once.
11. Government is spoiling the progeny of cattle by artificial insemination.
12. Artificial insemination produces life long patients.
13. Artificial insemination pregnants abort after pregnancy test.
14. Artificial insemination is a sin.
15. Artificial insemination born calf brings misfortune to the family.
16. One should go for artificial insemination even against the fee of Rs. 10- service.
17. Staunch supporter of artificial insemination should be elected as M.L.A.
18. Artificial insemination born calf is underdeveloped.
19. Artificial insemination should be made compulsory by law.
20. Artificial insemination makes cow a repeater.
21. Artificial insemination is the only answer to our milk problem.
22. Better to keep the cow uncovered than try artificial insemination.
23. Today's famine is the result of artificial insemination.
24. A worst bull is better than a '*pitchkari*'.
25. Adoption of artificial insemination is worship of cow.
26. Americans are wealthy because they follow artificial insemination for their cattle.
27. Artificial insemination will make people immoral.
28. Artificial insemination increases milk of the cow two times.
29. A man who adopts artificial insemination should be outcasted.
30. '*Pitchkari*' can conceive even a sterile cow.

## 44A7 COMMUNICATION SKILL RATING SCALE

*Authors* : Udai Pareek and Y.P. Singh.
*Availability* : Author, Indian Institute of Management, Ahmedabad-15.
*Level* : Farmers.
*Scoring* : Each item is placed against a 5-point scale ranging from always to never.
*Validity* : Extreme group validity was found to be significant at .01 level.
*Reference* : Pareek, Udai and Singh, Y.P. A scale for rating communication skill of farmers. *Indian Journal of Applied Psychology,* 1966, 3(1), 10-14.

## 44A7 COMMUNICATION SKILL RATING SCALE

(The following items are to be rated on a 5-point scale from always to never).

1. Listens patiently to what others say.
2. Encourages others to raise questions.
3. Initiates discussion.
4. Illustrates a point by example and anecdote.
5. Summarises points made.
6. Analyses and evaluates the problem.
7. Takes in pervasive tone with moderate pitch and with proper gesture.

## 44A8 OVERALL MODERNITY SCALE

*Authors* : Prayag Mehta, B.P. Sinha and P.P. Gokulnathan.
*Availability* : Authors, Deptt. of Psychology, University of Udaipur, Udaipur.
*Uses* : To study modernisation.
*Time required* : 15 minutes.
*Level* : Above upper primary level.
*Main features* : This scale is an adaptation of the short derivation of the OM scale developed by Inkeles *et al.* for a cross cultural study in six developing countries — India, Israel, Chile, Nigeria, Pakistan and Argentina. It consisted on 13 items. Except three questions, all the replies are given in alternative responses. The scale has potential not only in research but could serve in practical personnel screening service and selection of individuals for training or employment and particularly helpful for the selection of personnel for programmes like community development and family planning.
*Scoring* : Scoring is done separately for each item ranging from 1 to 5 score.
*Reliability* : In process.
*Validity* : In process.
*Norms* : In process.

## 44A8 OVERALL MODERNITY SCALE

1. Have you got highly concerned any time regarding some social problems such as communal riots?
   (a) Frequently; (b) Sometimes; (c) Never.
2. If schooling is freely available how much schooling do you think children

of people like yourself should have?

3. Two twelve years boys took time out from their work in the rice field. They were trying to figure out a way to grow some amount of rice with fewer hours of work.
   (1) The father of one boy said: "That is a good thing to think about. Tell me your thoughts about how we should change our ways of growing rice".
   (2) The father of other boy said: "The way to grow rice is the way we have always done it. Talk about change will waste the time but not help.

   Which father said the wise words?
4. What quality should a man have to hold high office?
   (1) Coming from high family background.
   (2) Devotion to the old and time-honoured ways.
   (3) Being the most popular among the people.
   (4) High education and special knowledge.
5. Which is most important for the future of this country?
   (1) The hard work of the people; (2) Good planning on the part of the government; (3) God's help; (4) Good luck.
6. Scientists in the universities are studying such things as what determines whether a baby is a boy or a girl and how is it that a seed turns into a plant. Do you think that these investigations are:
   (1) all very good; (2) all somewhat good; (3) all somewhat harmful; (4) all very harmful?
7. Which of these opinions do you agree with more?
   (1) Some people say that it is necessary for a man and his wife to limit the number of children to be born so that they can take better care of those they have.
   (2) Others say that it is wrong for a man and wife voluntarily to limit the number of children to be born.
8. Which of these kinds of news interest you most?
   (1) World events. (2) The nation. (3) Your home town or village. (4) Sports. (5) Religious events or festivals.
9. If you were to meet a person who lives in another country a long way off. Could you like his ways of thinking?
   (1) Yes. (2) No.
10. Do you think a man can be good without having an religion at all?
   (1) Yes. (2) No.
11. Do you belong to any organisation for example, social clubs, union, church organisations, political groups or other groups? If "yes" what are the names of these organisations you belong to?
12. What are the biggest problems facing the country?
13. How often do you get news and information from newspapers?
   (1) Everyday. (2) Few times a week. (3) Occasionally. (4) Never.

## 44A9 ATTITUDE TOWARDS NITROGENOUS FERTILISERS

*Authors* : T.K. Moulik and C.S.S. Rao.
*Availability* : Authors, Indian Agricultural Research Institute, New Delhi.

*Level*: Farmers.

*Main features* : Likert type scale with scoring done as suggested by Eyseck and Crown using Thurstone weightage.

*Scoring* : Weightage of each item is multiplied by the Likert weightage (5, 4, 3, 2, 1). The sum of the products gives the total score.

*Reliability* : Test-retest .89 and split-half .96.

*Validity* : Correlation with general opinion was .92 (concurrent validity) and with adoption scores was .76 (construct validity).

*Reference* : Singh, K.N., Singh, S.N. and Lokhande, M.R. *Measurement in extension research: instruments developed at I.A.R.I.*, New Delhi. Division of Agricultural Research, I.A.R.I., 1972, pp. 49-58.

44A4 ATTITUDE TOWARDS NITROGENOUS FERTILISERS

(Responses are to be given on a 5-point scale; Thurstone weightage appear in parentheses).

1. The food problem of the country can be solved by using nitrogenous fertilisers for the crops (6.5).
2. The use of nitrogenous fertilisers might be a good practice, but the results shown are not always encouraging (5.5).
3. If my neighbour seeks my opinion as to which practice he would adopt for increasing his farm-income I will definitely advise him to adopt the practice of use of nitrogenous fertilisers (8.5).
4. The use of nitrogenous fertilisers is a time consuming practice (5.0).
5. The use of nitrogenous fertilisers is not the only practice to increase farm-income (3.5).
6. If the neighbouring farmers want to form a co-operative society to utilise the practice of nitrogenous fertiliser use in the village effectively, I would be the first man to join the co-operative society (6.0).
7. Most farmers in this area should use the nitrogenous fertilisers (7.5).
8. Though the use of nitrogenous fertilisers is a good practice, the economic situation of most farmers do not permit the use of it (4.0).
9. The use of nitrogenous fertilisers is said to be a good practice but trials have to be made to prove its worth before its adoption (4.5).
10. The use of nitrogenous fertilisers is a practically useful practice, (8.0).
11. The use of nitrogenous fertilisers is a new practice and so I am reluctant to adopt it (3.0).
12. The use of nitrogenous fertilisers results in further improvement in farming (7.0).

44A10 SELF-RATING PERSONALITY SCALE FOR FARMERS

*Authors* : T.K. Moulik and C.S.S. Rao.

*Availability* : Authors, Indian Agricultural Research Institute, New Delhi.

*Uses* : Measuring innovation proneness, adoption leadership, closeness with extension agents, rural life preference.

*Level*: Farmers.

*Main features* : Forced choice of indicating 'most like' and 'least like' in 3 statements.

*Scoring* : Sum of the ratios of the weights of the 'most like' statements to the weights of the 'least like' statements.

*Validity* : Correlation coefficients with independent self-rating ranged from .69 to .68.

*Reference* : Singh, K.N., Singh, S.N. and Lokhande, M.R. *Measurement in extension research: instruments developed at I.A.R.I.*, New Delhi. Division of Agricultural Research, I.A.R.I., 1972, pp. 69-80.

44A10 SELF-RATING PERSONALITY SCALE FOR FARMERS

(Weightages appear in parentheses).

**Innovation Proneness**

1. a. I try to keep myself up-to-date with information on new farm practice, but that does not mean that I try out all the new methods on my farm (2).
   b. I feel restless till I try out a new farm practice, I have heard about (3).
   c. They talk of many new farm practices these days but who knows if they are better than the old ones (1).
2. a. From time to time I have heard of several new farm practices and I have tried out most of them in the last few years (3).
   b. I usually wait to see the results my neighbours obtain before I try out the new farm practice (2).
   c. Some how I believe that the traditional ways of farming are the best (1).
3. a. I am cautious about trying a new practice (2).
   b. After all our forefathers were wise is their farming practices and I do not see any reason for changing these old methods (1).
   c. Often new farm practices are not successful, however, if they are promising I would surely like to adopt them (3).

**Economic Motivation**

1. a. All I want from my farm is to make just a reasonable living for the family (1).
   b. In addition to making reasonable amount of profit, the enjoyment in farming life is also important for me (2).
   c. I would invest in farming to the maximum to gain large profits (3).
2. a. I do not hesitate to borrow any amount of money in order to run the farm properly (3).
   b. Instead of growing new cash crops which cost more money, I follow the routine farming practices (1).
   c. It is not only monetary profit but the enjoyment of work well done which gives me satisfaction for my hard work on the farming (2).
3. a. I hate to borrow money, on principle, even when it is necessary for running the farm (1).

b. My main aim is maximising by growing cash crops in comparison to growing of crops which are simply consumed by my family (3).
c. I avoid excessive borrowing of money for farm-investment (2).

**Adoption Leadership**

1. a. I try to participate as much as possible in discussions on new farm practices in the group meetings we hold in the village from time to time (2).
   b. I expect as part of my civic duty to convince my neighbours of the advantages of the new farm practices which I adopted (3).
2. a. Whenever I see a new farm practice, usually I initiate discussions about it with my villagers (3).
   b. I do not see any reason why I should go on influencing others about new farm practices (1).
   c. Some villagers often ask my advice about new farm practices and I try to convince them about my ideas on these practices (2).
3. a. I have no time to waste in discussing new farm practices with the village people (1).
   b. I am usually a listener in group meetings, but I give my opinion about the new farmings practices, when asked for (2).
   c. I think, the village people who come to me for advice, regard me as a good source of information on new farm practices (3).

**Closeness with Extension Agents**

1. a. I know that I can get all the possible help from the local extension agents if I ask, but I don't want to bother them too often with my farming problems (2).
   b. Whenever I get a new idea from some other source, I talk it over personally with the local extension agent who always advises me properly (3).
   c. I am more aware of the existence of new farm practices than the extension agents and so I never feel like discussing my farming problems with them (1).
2. a. May be I do not get to see the extension agents often enough and that is why I am missing possible helps from them (2).
   b. To be honest, I don't have much personal interest in the extension agents (1).
   c. I avail myself of all the opportunities in meeting the Agricultural Extension Agents and discuss my farm problems with them (3).
3. a. For me, it is sheer wastage of time to discuss my farming problems with the extension agents and as such I try to avoid them (1).
   b. Extension agents are fine people and I am glad to ask help from them (3).
   c. I find I don't have time to see the extension agents and that is why I can't always discuss my farming problems with them (2).

**Rural Life Preference**

1. a. City life offer a variety of attractive amenities. Surely there are more interesting experiences in a city life than in a village (1).
   b. I am happy and contented with the free air and quietness in my village which keep me healthy (3).
   c. So long my family is provided with a reasonable standard of living out of farm-income, I am not keen on living in a city (2).
2. a. I like to watch and enjoy the gradual growth of the crops cultivated by myself and I know that this is not possible anywhere else except in village life (3).
   b. No doubt there are various advantages in urban living but I don't like the inevitable bossing involved in urban professions (2).
   c. Farming is a non-profit and hardworking enterprise and I think it is useless to stick to it and stay in the village. It is far better to go into a city occupation (1).
3. a. One of the important attractions in farming for me is that I am independent and do not have to follow other people's order (3).
   b. Rural life is very difficult and boring, but in the city I can have a good time (1).
   c. I may shift to city life when I am assured of a fairly good income (2).

## 44A11 FAMILY NORMS SCALE

*Author* : Suryanarayan A. Murthy.
*Availability* : Author, Extension Education Institute, Rajendra Nagar, Hyderabad-30.
*Uses* : Useful in studies of social change.
*Time required* : About 5 minutes.
*Levels* : Farmers.
*Main features* : Family norms have been selected on eight facets of traditional modern continuum viz. concentration of authority, pooling family resources, family prestige, orientation of credit, empathy, orientation towards agricultural innovations, group conformity, and information seeking habits. The scalable statements were obtained by item analysis. There are eight items in the final scale with a maximum possible score of 32 on a 4-point continuum of the Likert model.
*Scoring* : Summated ratings method.
*Reliability* : The reliability coefficient by Kerlinger formula was found to be 0.94.
*Validity* : Content validity by judges opinion was found.
*Reference* : Murthy, A. Suryanarayan. Social and psychological correlates in predicting communication behaviour farmers. Doctoral thesis in Agricultural Extension, I.A.R.I., 1969.

## 44A11 FAMILY NORMS SCALE

(The following statements are to be rated on a 4-point scale of agreement).

1. A farmer should invest all his money in land which increase his power

and prestige in the village.

2. Elders say that one should rely more on the experience of elder or aged members of the family and should not have ties with outsiders as they tend to exploit the ignorance.
3. Younger members are as capable in making decisions as the older ones.
4. A nuclear family provides greater satisfaction, freedom and individual growth to its members than a joint family.
5. A farmer should not hesitate to borrow capital from others in order to earn more from land.
6. A farmer should not try an innovation which comes in conflict with the existing belief system.
7. An innovation which has group approval is definitely better than one which has no group approval.
8. A farmer should believe the agricultural scientists' recommendations even if they are not tested in his village conditions.

44A12 ATTITUDE TOWARDS IR-8 PADDY (HIGH YIELDING VARIETY)

*Author*: A. Suryanarayan Murthy.
*Availability* : Author, Extension Education Institute, Rajendra Nagar, Hyderabad-30.
*Time required*: About 5 minutes.
*Level*: Farmers.
*Main features* : A 4-point scale.
*Scoring*: Four-point summated ratings.
*Reliability*: Reliability coefficient by Kerlinger formula was found to be 0.88.
*Reference* : Murthy A. Suryanarayan. Social and psychological correlates in predicting communication behaviour of farmers. Doctoral thesis in Agricultural Extension, I.A.R.I., 1969.

44A12 ATTITUDE TOWARDS IR-8 PADDY (HIGH YIELDING VARIETY)

(The following items are to be rated on a 4-point scale of agreement).

1. New varieties like IR-8 should be released only if their susceptibility to pests and diseases is known to be low.
2. It is risky to depend on VLWs for high yielding varieties information.
3. It is wrong to use high doses of fertilisers for IR-8.
4. IR-8 is no better than local varieties as it is also subject to lodging and losses in yield.
5. It is not possible to grow IR-8 as its cultivation involves line planting.
6. Demonstration plots have proved the usefulness of IR-8.
7. One can grow IR-8 as he is assured of fertiliser supply.
8. There is no need to introduce IR-8 as we have good local varieties.
9. Farmers training programmes are necessary to provide adequate information on high yielding varieties to the farmers (especially IR-8).
10. There is no need for the delta farmer to care for additional production through use of IR-8.

11. Cultivation of IR-8 has highlighted existing problems of improper drainage in the delta areas.
12. I am not sure that IR-8 will be successful in this area.
13. IR-8 is good in places where rains do not occur. During harvesting season.
14. It is wrong to say that buyers are offering lower prices for IR-8 than what they should.

## 44A13 TRADITIONAL FAMILY IDEOLOGY SCALE

*Author*: B.C. Muthayya.
*Availability*: Author, Director of Psychology, NICD, Rajendra Nagar, Hyderabad.
*Uses* : To assess autocratic-democratic attitudes.
*Time required*: Half an hour.
*Level*: College students.
*Main features* : Contains 40 items. Each item is to be answered on a 5-point scale. Items pertain to male roles of husband and father, females roles of wife and mother, husband-wife and parent child relationship, and general values.
*Scoring* : Scored for autocratic tendency.
*Reliability*: Split-half and also test-retest reliabilities have been worked out.
*Validity*: Established.
*Norms* : Available on college students.
*References* :

1. Muthayya, B.C. A study of autocratic-democratic attitudes. *Journal of Psychological Researches*, 1958, 2(1), 9-11.
2. Muthayya, B.C. Autocratic-democratic attitudes and achievement motive. *Journal of Psychological Researches*, 1967, 11(1), 32-35.

## 44A13 TRADITIONAL FAMILY IDEOLOGY SCALE

(The respondent has to rate the following items on a 5-point scale of agreement).

1. In bringing up their children, parents must follow the traditions of their ancestors rather than follow their (parents) personal opinions.
2. If the children are told much about sex, they are likely to go too far in experimenting with it.
3. Some equality in marriage is a good thing but by and large the husband should have the final decisions in family matters.
4. Woman who does not care to be submissive to her husband during married life, has not understood the meaning and duties of a wife.
5. Parents in providing comforts to their children should consider male children first and then female children.
6. A woman who engages herself in social activities cannot be expected to become a good wife.
7. It is better for a wife to vote for whatever her husband does because he knows more about such things.
8. A youth should not marry a girl whom he loves, if his father objects to it.

9. The unmarried mother is morally a greater failure than the unmarried father.
10. It is the man rather than the woman who should take part in outdoor sports and games and women should confine themselves to indoor games.
11. Women should not be more intelligent for their own good.
12. It is a disgrace to his manliness for a man who can't go ahead in the world.
13. One of the worst problems in our society today would be "the introduction of divorce" because it mars the true value of marriage since marriage is something sacred.
14. Even today women live under unfair restrictions that should be removed immediately.
15. It does not seem quite right for a man to be visionary, dreaming should be left to women.
16. We will have to be very strict towards young people to save our moral standards as the facts on crime and sexual immorality are more.
17. One must marry a woman who is less educated than himself, otherwise she will boss over him.
18. A wife has no right to question her husband about where he goes or why he came home late.
19. The future of the child must be planned by the father, and mother should not have any say in it.
20. She is the ideal wife who never disagrees with her husband in family matters.
21. It is the duty of the wife to serve food to her husband and children first and serve herself the remaining food in the last.
22. Parents should see that their children should mix with only those whom they approve.
23. Women have as much right as men to lead a reckless life.
24. Talking with a boy in privacy is something a nice girl would not want to do.
25. Woman should not participate in men's talks and keep herself confined to her home work (domestic).
26. A man can scarcely maintain respect for his girl, whom he is to marry, (fiancee) if they have sexual before they are married.
27. In order to have a control over wives, men should be reserved in their expressions of love and affection towards their wives.
28. It is wise for men, not to take their wives to certain foreign movies, otherwise they learn many vices from such pictures.
29. Women think less clearly than men and are more emotional.
30. Women should take active interest in politics and community problems as well as in their families.
31. One must consider the family as a sacred institution bestowed by God and must conform to the traditions of his family.
32. Smoking before elders should be discouraged as it indicates disrespectful attitude towards them.
33. It is right for each person to think that his family and caste are superior to any others.

34. The most important qualities of a real man are strength of will, assertiveness and driving ambition.
35. It goes against nature to place woman in position of authority over men.
36. Women should not compete with men in business and professional work to display their superiority.
37. Boys rather than girls should be taught to be self-assertive and autonomous in their behaviour.
38. Woman should not be allowed to re-marry if her husband dies. As it brings down the value of womanhood.
39. No marriage should be conducted unless the couple is prepared to have children.
40. A good child is one who implicitly obeys his parents and does not criticise their mistakes.

44A14 ADOPTION QUOTIENT SCALE

*Authors* : Udai Pareek and S.N. Chattopadhyay.
*Availability* : Author, Indian Institute of Management, Ahmedabad.
*Uses* : To measure multipractice adoption behaviour.
*Level* : Farmers.
*Main features* : Main factor is the applicability of the practice available or recommended. For each of these practices the factors considered are potentiality, extent, time, consistency and weights.
*Scoring* :

$$AQ = \frac{\sum_{J=1}^{N} Y_j W_j}{\sum_{J=1}^{N} W_j} \times 100$$

where $$Y_j = \frac{\sum_{t_p - t_1}^{J=1} (e_j / p_j)}{t_p - t_1}$$

where $N$ = Number of practices which the individual has the potential to adopt.

$\sum_{J=1}^{N}$ = Summation over each of the $N$ practices, of which $J$=1 any one is the $j$th practice.

$W_j$ = Weight to be given to a $j$th practice based on its difficulty of adoption determined from a list of differential weights of practices.

$\sum_{t_p - t_1}^{J=1}$ = Summation over each from $t_1$ to $t_p$

$e_j$ = Extent of adoption of any particular ($j$th) practice in a particular year.

$p_j$ = Potential of any particular ($j$th) practice from $e_j$ is calculated in that particular year.

$t_p$ = Time of investigation (year).

$t_1$ = Time of first introduction of $j$th practice in a community (year).

*Validity* : Validity from judges' rating *rho* = .80. Agreement among judges Kendall's Tax = .766.

*Reference* : Pareek, Udai and Chattopadhyay, S.N. Adoption quotient: A measure of multipractice adoption behaviour. *Journal of Applied Behavioural Science*, 1966, 2(1), 95-108.

44A15 CHANGE PRONENESS SCALE

*Authors* : Udai Pareek and S.N. Chattopadhyay.
*Availability* : Authors, Indian Institute of Management, Ahmedabad.
*Uses* : To measure change proneness of farmers.
*Level* : Farmers.
*Main features* : Projective test. Consists of 5 pictures.
*Scoring* : Content analysis.
*Reliability* : Inter-judge reliability: percentage of agreement = .86.
*Validity* : Validity coefficient (Rank order correlation between scale score and ratings on change proneness = .577).
*Norms* : Distribution of change proneness score in a North Indian village are given.
*Reference* : Pareek, Udai and Chattopadhyay, S.N. A projective technique to measure change proneness of farmers. *Journal of Social Sciences*, 1965, 4 (1), 1-14.

44A16 ATTITUDE TOWARDS EDUCATIONAL INNOVATIONS

*Author* : O.S. Rathore.
*Availability* : Author, Department of Agricultural Extension, Rajasthan College of Agriculture, Udaipur.
*Time required* : About 5 minutes.
*Level* : Village Level Workers, Agricultural Extension Officers and Block Development Officers.
*Main features* : Five-point Likert Scale.
*Scoring* : Summated ratings.

44A16 ATTITUDE TOWARDS EDUCATIONAL INNOVATIONS

(The following items are to be checked on a 5-point scale of agreement).

1. The use of super 8 mm film is a threat to the teacher's position.
2. Para-professionals spare the professional from routine tasks.
3. All specialists and area agents should engage in some team teaching.
4. Teaching with the help of the overhead projector leads to "teaching over the heads of the learner".
5. Audio-visual aids like Super 8 mm film make learning more effective.
6. Emphasis upon interdisciplinary programme and teaching can help solve rural people's problems.
7. Para-professionals are highly incompetent to perform any technical and professional work.
8. A synchronised slide and tape presentation brings the learn closer to reality than through the use of words alone.
9. A teacher can cover more subject matter in less time by the use of an

overhead projector.

10. If a specialist has something to offer, people will be pounding on his door; than there is no need for interdisciplinary planning.
11. Team teaching is time consuming and should not be encouraged.
12. A synchronised slide and tape presentation is an excellent teaching tool.
13. The use of an overhead projector eliminates monotony and provides variety in teaching.
14. Interdisciplinary programme development leads to sound planning.
15. Team teaching improves the quality of instruction.
16. Teaching lay people with slides and tape is folly.
17. Super 8 mm film is a toy, not a tool for the teacher.
18. Para-professional are a threat to professional job security.

## 44A17 PROGRESSIVENESS SCALE

*Authors* : A.G. Venkataramana Reddy, K.A.L.N. Sarma and A.S Murthy.

*Availability* : Authors, Extension Education Institute, Rajendra Nagar, Hyderabad-30.

*Uses* : Useful in studies of social change and communication.

*Time required* : About 5 minutes.

*Level* : Farmers.

*Main features* : It is a Guttman scale type of scale with seven statements incorporating items regarding adoption of improvements, agricultural leadership, use of communication media and institutional agencies.

*Scoring* : Weightages are given to items. Total is obtained by summing the weightages of the items checked.

*Reliability* : Coefficient of reproducibility was found to be 0.88. Minimal marginal reproducibility was found to be 0.88.

*Validity* : Content validity was established by judges opinion, and concurrent by known group technique was found to be 0.97.

## 44A17 PROGRESSIVENESS SCALE

(The following items are to be answered for agreement by 'Yes' or 'No').

1. A progressive farmer should be up-to-date in knowledge of latest technology.
   Do you keep yourself up-to-date in latest technology?
2. A progressive farmer should be receptive to change resulting in better income.
   (a) Do you generally try to adopt any improvements recommended?
   (b) Are you changing to new varieties as and when they are recommended?
3. A progressive farmer should be helpful to other farmers in adopting improvements.
   (a) Did you tell others about the benefit of adoption of improvements (Agril. leader)?
   (b) Did you help any farmers to follow improved practices?
4. A progressive farmer should be an innovator or at least an early

adopter.

(a) Are you the first to adopt any improved practice in your village? OR

(b) If not, have you adopted any of the practices recommended in the past 2 years? If so, what are they?

5. A progressive farmer should have more contacts with extension workers.

   Do you meet extension workers (BLEO, AEO, VLW, etc.) for advice?

6. A progressive farmer should use improved or other high yielding varieties.

   Did you grow any improved or high yielding variety last year?

   T.N. 1 paddy, Chinau-2 paddy, T.N. 65 paddy, I.R. 8 paddy, Jaya paddy, Padma paddy, Hamsa paddy, Hybrid Jowar, Hybrid Bajra, Hybrid Maize, Mexican wheat, Hybrid pulses, Co-997 sugarcane.

7. A progressive farmer should adopt plant protection measures (in full).

   (a) Did you dress the seed with chemical? 1

   (b) Did you take up PP measures for nursery? 2

   (c) Did you take up PP measures for mainfield? 4

44A18 FAMILY SIZE THEMATIC REACTION TEST (TRT)

*Author* : K. Ramachandra Sastry.

*Availability* : Author, Institute of Rural Health and Family Planning Gandhigram, Tamil Nadu.

*Uses* : To measure the attitude towards family size norm.

*Validity* : Validated on adopters and non-adopters.

*Reference* : Sastry, K.R. Instruments for measuring small family size norms in a rural community. *Action Research Monograph No. 3.* Institute of Rural Health and Family Planning, Gandhigram, 1966.

44A18 FAMILY SIZE THEMATIC REACTION TEST (TRT)

(The following two stories are used in the Thematic Reaction Test).

**Story 1**

Melur is one of the progressive villages. It was due to the enthusiastic panchayat members it had. Whenever a new idea or scheme was introduced by Government, they used to immediately ask for the same. They used to discuss freely and frankly on many issues and developmental schemes. One day, they had a discussion of family limitation. A very interesting discussion followed. One of the members said that it was not necessary to think of limiting the number of children as everything would follow a natural course. Another pointed out that there are a number of poor families with large number of children, hence they have to limit the size. One of the members expressed the feeling that one should have a large number of children so that some of them will survive when the parents grow old. Another said that infant mortality is not so great today due to advancement of medical science and as such there was no need to have this fear. So this fear should not deter them from having a planned family which is for their own good.

*Probes* : 1. What is your opinion about this? 2. (a) Do you agree with the member who said that we should have large families to cover the risk of loss of children? (b) If you agree, how big should a family be? 3. One of the members said that we should not worry about the number of children as everything will following nature. What is your opinion about this? 4. (a) It is necessary to pre-plan as to how many children one should have? (b) If 'yes' what is the number beyond which one should not add to the family size on any account?

**Story 2**

Venkataswamy and his wife Chellammal were a happy couple. They belonged to an average middle class agricultural family. Their village, Pandupatti, was one of the progressive villages. Venkataswamy was very quick in adopting new ideas and progressive measures. His wife was equally progressive in outlook. Both husband and wife used to talk freely on many issues. As time went on, they had three children. Chellammal had seen some of her relatives suffering on account of too many children. So she wanted to limit the children in her own family. For some time she was thinking on this subject and waiting for an opportunity to express her feelings on the subject to her husband. One day, Venkataswamy was in very good mood, she raised this point. She expressed the view that they should limit with the present number so that they may be happy and look after these children well. Venkataswamy also liked this idea, but he was worried that all the three children he had were females and that they should have at least one male child. For him an ideal family should have representation of both sexes. When he expressed these ideas, Chellammal argued that it would be impossible to get a child of the desired sex. Who knew, she said, they may be adding further numbers to the female sex if they did not try to stop at that stage. As husband and wife did not come to any decision on this point, they did not take any action. As time went on, they had another child. Unfortunately it was also a female. At this stage, Venkataswamy started thinking seriously about the subject. He consulted some of his intimate friends in the village and outside.

*Probes* : 5. If you were a friend of Venkataswamy, what advice would you given him? 6. (a) Venkataswamy said that an ideal family should have children of both sexes. Do you agree with him? (b) If 'yes' what should be the number of male and female children in an ideal family? 7. (a) Should he go on until he gets a male child? (b) If 'No' when should he stop? 8. (a) Was Chellammal right in saying that an ideal family should consist of only three children? (b) If 'no' what in your opinion, is the ideal size for a family? 9. (a) If they were rich, do you think they should still limit the number of children in the family? (b) If 'yes' when?

44A19 FAMILY SIZE PICTORIAL CHOICE TEST (PCT)

*Author* : K. Ramachandra Sastry.
*Availability* : Author, Institute of Rural Health and Family Planning, Gandhigram, Tamil Nadu.
*Uses* : To measure the attitude towards family size norm.
*Level* : Rural adults.

*Main features* : Contains human pictures of families of different size, and equal sex ratio of children (odd number being a baby whose sex was concealed). A person in the picture is posed as a friend of the respondent.

*Validity* : Validated on adopters and non-adopters.

*Reference* : Sastry, K.R. Instruments for measuring small family size norm in a rural community. *Action Research Monographs, No. 3.* Institute of Rural Health and Family Planning, Gandhigram, 1966.

44A19 FAMILY SIZE PICTORIAL CHOICE TEST (PCT)

(The following probes are used after presenting the pictures. The pictures are not reproduced here).

1. (a) Do you find any difference among these pictures?
   If 'yes' what is the difference?
   (b) What do these pictures relate to?
2. In your opinion, which of these pictures represent small families and which ones large families?
3. (a) Which of these is an ideal family size?
   (b) Why do you consider it as an ideal size?
4. With how many children do you think this person should have limited?
5. (a) Supposing he was rich, should this person have limited the size of his family?
   (b) If 'yes' after how many children should he have stopped?
6. Probably this person is afraid of love of children and so he has allowed the number to increase.
   (a) Do you agree with him?
   (b) If 'no' after how many children should he have stopped?
7. Supposing he did not get proper sex combination among the children, should he still limit the size?

44A20 FAMILY PLANNING ATTITUDE SCALE

*Author* : A. Sengupta.

*Availability* : Author, Indian Statistical Institute, Calcutta-35.

*Main features* : A 39-item scale of which 17 items deal with attitude towards family planning and 22 with family size. Scale was constructed using Thurstone's method of equal appearing intervals.

*Scoring* : Scale values.

*Reference* : Sengupta, A. Constructing a scale for measuring attitude towards family planning: an experiment with Thurstone. *Journal of Family Welfare*, 1966, 13(2).

44A20 FAMILY PLANNING ATTITUDE SCALE

**Group A: Statements of Family Planning in General**

1. If the number of children is limited through the application of birth control techniques then the natural sex relations between the spouses

will be hampered.

2. By adopting family planning husband and wife experience conjugal differences.
3. Social and moral ruin will be inevitable as a consequence of introduction of birth control.
4. Family planning is a bad idea imported to India from abroad.
5. It is difficult for husbands and wives to talk together freely about sex, and so family planning is not possible.
6. Family planning is important and should be used by everyone.
7. Family planning is important and should be used whenever it is reasonably possible to do so.
8. Family planning is of some value and more people should use it.
9. Family planning has qualities which are distasteful.
10. Family planning is harmful, dangerous and contrary to religious.
    (a) If 'no', up to what number should he go?
    (b) What is the number beyond which a family should not have further teaching.
11. Mothers of few children maintain better health than mothers of many children.
12. Parents having few children can provide proper facilities for their children's education.
13. Every citizen of the country must practise birth control.
14. For a healthier nation family planning is essential.
15. Emphasis on family planning is the correct measure to have healthier children.
16. When family planning ideas spread throughout the country, they will increase the divorce rate.
17. Planned families maintain a good standard of living.

**Group B: Statements on Family Size**

1. If I could live my life again, I would choose to have fewer children than I have now.
2. Unless a man has a small family, he finds himself going from bad to worse.
3. People with many children are usually unhappy.
4. However rich a mother is, bearing many children can bring her many troubles.
5. The fewer children a man has, the better he will do financially.
6. The fewer children one has, the better on can look after each child.
7. More than four children means too much expense for the parents.
8. The fewer children a family has the happier it is.
9. Everything considered it is better to have few children.
10. If I could only have either two children or four children I would prefer to have only two.
11. A large family enhances the prestige of the parents.
12. A father of a large family cannot fulfil his duties adequately.
13. Too many children are sure to wreck the mother's health.
14. A large family means a lot of work for the mother.

15. A large family ruins the health of other children.
16. I am a career woman, I cannot fulfil this desire if I have many children.
17. With exorbitant rents and intolerable housing conditions it is not possible to accommodate a large family.
18. A large family means illiteracy, poverty and misery.
19. A large family means going down the economic ladder and downward mobility.
20. Good health is maintained by having a small family.
21. The quality of population tends to deteriorate with the curtailment of family size.
22. Most religious people favour large families so they are against family planning.

44A21 ATTITUDE TOWARDS COMMUNITY DEVELOPMENT PROGRAMME

*Authors* : R.P. Singh and K.N. Singh.
*Availability* : Authors, Indian Agricultural Research Institute, New Delhi.
*Level* : Farmers.
*Main features* : Likert type 5-point scale.
*Reliability* : High split-half test-retest reliability.
*Validity* : High discriminating value.
*Reference* : Singh, K.N., Singh, S.N. and Lokhande, M.R. *Measurement in extension research: instruments developed at I.A.R.I.*, New Delhi, Division of Agricultural Research, I.A.R.I., 1972, pp.118-136.

44A21 ATTITUDE TOWARDS COMMUNITY DEVELOPMENT PROGRAMME

(Items are to be checked on a 5-point scale).

**Scale 1: Community Development Block in General**

1. The work of the Block is done mostly on paper and very little in the villages.
2. The small and big, poor and rich, all the village people alike derive benefits from the Block.
3. The village people will be benefited more if the money the government spends on the Block is distributed among them.
4. In the wake of the Block the economic conditions of the village people and their standard of living have improved.
5. There is a little work and more of its propaganda done in the Block.
6. Quite good job is being done through the Block for the betterment of the villages.
7. The Block is nothing but the source of livelihood for the government personnel.
8. The problems of the village people can be solved only through the Block.

**Scale 2: Agricultural Development Programme**

9. It is only because of the Block that the facilities of fertilisers, improved seeds, improved agricultural implements etc. are available to the farmers.
10. The profit earned from farming by following the recommendations of the Block is less in relation to the cost involved.
11. Because of the Block, agricultural production has considerably increased during the last few years.
12. Agricultural facilities from the Block are not available to the farmers in time.
13. The Block has brought about the quite good changes in methods of agriculture.
14. For any help from the Block in agricultural matters, the farmers have to undergo a lot of trouble.
15. The Block has very much added to the farmers knowledge about new and improved methods of farming.
16. Agricultural facilities from the Block are available only to the selected few of the farmers in the village.
17. Because of the facilities provided by the Block, the farmers, farm income has increased.
18. The farmers do not get agricultural facilities from the Block in required amount.
19. The farmers get all sorts of help from the Block in agricultural matters.
20. The farmers will not be adversely effected if the Block is closed.

**Scale 3: Block Personnel**

21. The Block personnel are quite sympathetic to the village people and help them a great deal.
22. The Block personnel have only culture and no experience of practical agriculture.
23. For the sake of convenience of the villagers, the Block personnel themselves often meet the people in the villages itself.
24. The Block personnel help only the selected few in the village and have no consideration for the general mass.
25. The Block personnel always give useful advice to the farmers in agricultural matters.
26. The Block personnel make commitments very easily but do not keep them.
27. The Block personnel pay due respect to the village superiors and elders and their views.
28. The Block personnel do nothing in the village except completing papers.

**Scale 4: Village Panchayats**

29. The village panchayat has created factions and aggravated conflicts in the village.
30. The village panchayat helps a great deal in the betterment of the village.

31. The funds of the village panchayat are misutilised.
32. Because of the village panchayat, much facilities are available to the farmers in agricultural matters.
33. The village panchayat has done more harm than good to the village.
34. The village people in general are benefited bv the village panchayat.

**Scale 5: Village Cooperatives**

35. There is much advantage in becoming a member of the cooperative society.
36. The rules and regulations of the cooperative society are quite complicated and not easily understandable.
37. Because of the cooperative society, necessary supplies like fertilisers, seeds, sugar, etc., become easily available to the village people.
38. For taking loans from the cooperative society, the members have to undergo a lot of trouble.
39. There is more advantage in taking loans from the cooperative society than from the village moneylenders.
40. Only the selected few and not the members in general are benefited by the cooperative society.

**Scale 6: Chemical Fertilisers**

41. The use of chemical fertilisers make the soil poor.
42. The use of chemical fertilisers is the easiest way to increase the crop yield.
43. The use of chemical fertilisers in food crops is harmful for health.
44. The use of chemical fertilisers improves the quality of grains which fetch more price in the market.
45. The use of chemical fertilisers is less profitable in relation to the cost involved.
46. As no adequate farm yard manure is available the use of chemical fertilisers is essential.
47. The use of chemical fertilisers deteriorates the taste of food.
48. The yield of crops is very much increased by the use of chemical fertilisers.
49. The crops fertilised become more susceptible to diseases and insect pests.
50. It is good to use chemical fertilisers, because as compared to farm yard manure, they act more quickly.
51. Chemical fertilisers are useless because their effects are confined to the crop to which they are applied.
52. The use of chemical fertilisers is essential for better crop yields.

**Scale 7: Improved Farm Implements**

53. Improved implements save much time and labour.
54. The mould-board plough renders the soil poor because it turns over the fertile surface soil to the sub-surface soil under the unfertile sub-surface

soil to the surface.

55. Improved farm implements are not costly as compared to their benefits.
56. It is more difficult for the ploughman to handle improved farm implements.
57. The mould-board plough cuts the weeds and turns them under the soil making the field quite clear.
58. Improved farm implements are beneficial only to big cultivators, not to small ones.
59. Improved farm implements make a good tilth.
60. Improved farm implements require very high draft and make the bullocks too weak.
61. The crop yield is increased by ploughing the land with improved farm implements.
62. The mould-board plough is useful only for the weed-infested fields, not for the clean ones.

**Scale 8: Green Manuring**

63. Green manuring is the best way of increasing the yield of wheat crop.
64. Green manuring in a fallow land allows which weeds to grow.
65. Green manuring improves fertility status of the soil.
66. Green manuring involves more cost in relation to profit.
67. It is better to take green manuring crop in a field than to leave it fallow.
68. Green manuring involves much trouble and botheration.
69. Next to farm yard manure, green manure is the best.
70. It is more profitable to take any other crop instead of a green manure crop.
71. Green manuring is very good because it has residual effects on several subsequent crops.
72. Green manuring is profitable only to big cultivators who have enough land.

## 44A22 ATTITUDE TOWARD HIGH YIELDING VARIETIES PROGRAMME

*Author*: S.N. Singh.

*Availability* : Author, Training Officer, Bayer (India) Limited, Express Towers, 19th Floor, Bombay-400 001.

*Level*: Farmers.

*Uses* : To study the attitudes towards high yielding varieties programmes.

*Time required*: About 10-15 minutes.

*Main features* : A 14-item Likert scale requiring respondent to indicate the extent of agreement on each item on a 5-point scale.

*Scoring* : Summated ratings.

*Reliability* : Split-half reliability coefficient = 0.86. Test-retest reliability coefficient = 0.83.

*Validity* : Construct validity was established. Known groups were differentiated by the scale significantly at .01 level.

## 44A22 ATTITUDE TOWARD HIGH YIELDING VARIETIES PROGRAMME

(The following statements are to be checked on a 5-point scale of agreement).

1. People talk much of High Yielding Varieties Programme but actually no work is done.
2. Fertilisers recommended in the package of High Yielding Varieties are too costly and an ordinary farmer cannot dare spend so much.
3. After the start of High Yielding Varieties Programme there had been a significant improvement in the economic condition of ordinary farmers.
4. High Yielding Varieties Programme has helped farmers increase their knowledge about improved methods of farming.
5. High Yielding Varieties Programme will make rich people richer and poor people poorer.
6. High Yielding Varieties Programme is the only hope for solving India's food problems.
7. High Yielding Varieties Programme will create regional inequality and social disparity.
8. High Yielding Varieties Programme has created more problems rather than solving the problems.
9. All types of farmers, small or big, rich or poor will equally be benefited by the programme.
10. High Yielding Varieties are not profitable as they are prone to discuss and pests which cannot be controlled easily.
11. It is worthwhile to invest much in the cultivation of High Yielding Varieties.
12. Income from the cultivation of High Yielding Varieties compensates the trouble taken in their cultivation.
13. Farmers should not hesitate to participate in High Yielding Varieties Programme.
14. High Yielding Varieties are not better than local varieties.

## 44A23 FARM MECHANISATION INDEX

*Authors* : S.N. Singh and K.N. Singh.
*Availability* : Authors, Indian Agricultural Research Institute, New Delhi.
*Level* : Farmers.
*Main features* : $FMI = \sum_{i=1}^{N} W_j \times n_j \times t_j$

Where: *FMI* = Farm Mechanisation Index. $W_j$ = Weightage of the *j*th item. $n_j$ = The number of the *j*th item possessed by the individual. $t_j$ = The total period in years the *j*th item has been possessed. *N* = Total number of items selected. The items used are as following (with weightages in parentheses): Tractor (7), Pumping set (6), Trailor or haulage (2), Disc harrow (4), Cultivator (3), Levellor (2), Seed drill (3), Winnower (3).

*Reference* : Singh, K.N., Singh, S.N., and Lokhande, M.R. *Measurement in extension research: instruments developed at I.A.R.I.*, New Delhi. Division of Agricultural Research, I.A.R.I., 1972, pp. 178-181.

## 44A24 AGRICULTURAL PROGRESSIVENESS SCALE

*Authors* : K.N. Singh, S.N. Singh, K. Pal and J. Singh.
*Availability* : Authors, Indian Agricultural Research Institute, New Delhi.
*Level* : Farmers.
*Validity* : Villages independently chosen as progressive and non-progressive were found to be significantly discriminated on the scores.
*Reference* : Singh, K.N., Singh, S.N. and Lokhande, M.R. *Measurement in extension research: instruments development at I.A.R.I.,* New Delhi. Division of Agricultural Research, I.A.R.I., 1972, pp. 187-198.

## 44A24 AGRICULTURAL PROGRESSIVENESS SCALE

(Weightages appear in parentheses).

1. Extent of the Cultivation of High Yielding Varieties (30).
   (a) Percentage coverage with H.Y. Varieties.
   (i) Upto 10%; (ii) Upto 25%; (iii) Upto 50%; (iv) Upto 75%; (v) Cent per cent.
   (b) Percentage farm families cultivating H.Y. Varieties.
   (i) Upto 10%; (ii) Upto 25%; (iii) Upto 50%; (iv) Upto 75%; (v) Cent per cent.
2. Extent of the use of plant nutrients (30).
   (a) Percentage of farm families applying plant nutrients.
   (i.) Upto 10%; (ii) Upto 25%; (iii) Upto 50%; (iv) Upto 75%; (v) Cent per cent
   (b) Annual consumption of the fertilisers per irrigated area.
   (i) Upto 15 kg/acre; (ii) Upto 25 kg/acre; (iii) Upto 35 kg/acre; (iv) Upto 40 kg/acre; (v) More than 40 kg/acre.
3. Intensity of land use (20).
   (i) Upto 100%; (ii) Upto 150%; (iii) Upto 200%; (iv) 250%; (v) Upto 300% and more.
4. Extent of area under assured irrigation (20).
   (i) Upto 25%; (ii) Upto 50%; (iii) Upto 70%; (iv) Upto 85%; (v) Upto cent per cent.
5. Extent of the use of plant protection chemicals (20).
   Percentage of farm families using the plant protection chemicals.
   (i) Upto 10%; (ii) Upto 25%; (iii) Upto 50%; (iv) Upto 75%; (v) Cent per cent.
6. Extent of the use of improved agricultural implements (20).
   Number of improved farm implements per farm family.
   (i) Upto 2; (ii) Upto 3; (iii) Upto 4; (iv) Upto 5; (v) More than 5.
7. Contact with the extension agency (20).
   Frequency of contact with such categories of extension personnel as B.D.O., Pusa workers, A.E.O., V.L.Ws. etc.
   (i) Never; (ii) Rarely; (iii) Often; (iv) Most often.
8. Extent of the small farmers as adopters of improved practices (20).
   Percentage coverage of the area of the H.Y. Varieties with the small farmers.

(i) Upto 10%; (ii) Upto 25%; (iii) Upto 50%; (iv) Upto 75%; (v) Cent per cent.

9. An effective Cooperative Society (20).
   (a) Percentage of the farm families member of the cooperative society.
   (i) Upto 10%; (ii) Upto 20%; (iii) Upto 30%; (iv) Upto 40%; (v) 50% and above.
   (b) Amount of annual turn over of the business.
   (i) Upto Rs. 10,000; (ii) Upto Rs. 25.000; (iii) Upto Rs. 50,000; (iv) Upto Rs. 75,000 (v) Upto Rs. 1,00,000 and above.
10. Consumption of electricity for agricultural purposes (10).
   Number of units consumed per farm family per year.
   (i) Upto 100 units; (ii) Upto 150 units; (iii) Upto 200 units; (iv) Upto 250 units.
11. Transport facilities (10).
   (a) Nearness to the highway.
   (i) Upto 1.6 km; (ii) Upto 3.2 km; (iii) Upto 4.8 km; (iv) Upto 6.4 km; (v) Upto 8 km and above.
   (b) Existence of feeder road (10).
   (i) Track; (ii) Kucha Road; (iii) Pucca Road.
12. Educational status. (10).
   Percentage of literate farmers.
   (i) Upto 25%; (ii) Upto 40%; (iii) Upto 55%; (iv) Upto 70%; (v) More than 70%.
13. Extent of Farmers' Participation (10).
   (i) Upto 5%; (ii) Upto 10%; (iii) Upto 15%; (iv) Upto 20%; (v) More than 20%.
14. Percentage of farmers cultivating their own land (10).
   (i) Upto 50%; (ii) Upto 70%; (iii) Cent per cent.
15. Consolidation of land holdings (10).
   (i) Land consolidated; (ii) Lands partially consolidated; (iii) Lands not consolidated.
16. Means of Mass Communication (10).
   (a) Number of radio sets, newspapers, farm magazines, journal etc. per farm family.
   (i) Upto 0.10; (ii) Upto 0.25; (iii) Upto 0.50; (iv) Upto 0.75; (v) More than 0.75.

44A25 COMMERCIALISATION INDEX

*Authors* : S.N. Singh and K.N. Singh.
*Availability* : Authors, Indian Agricultural Research Institute, New Delhi.

*Main features* :
$$CI = \frac{F_1 \times W_1 + F_2 \times W_2 + F_3 \times W_3}{W_1 + W_2 + W_3} \times 100$$

Where: $CI$ = Commercialisation Index. $F_1$ = Fraction of the total farm produce marketed annually. This was calculated by dividing the value of the produce marketed with the gross values of total produce raised in a year. $F_2$ = Fraction of the purchased inputs used annually. This was calculated by dividing the values of the purchased inputs used with the total values of the inputs used. $F_3$ = Fraction of hired labour used in a year. This was calculated by dividing the values of hired labour (both animal and human) used on the farm in a particular year.

$W_1$, $W_2$ and $W_3$ are the weightages of the first, second and third items respectively.

*Reference* : Singh, K.N., Singh, S.N., and Lokhande, M.R. *Measurement in extension research : instruments developed at I.A.R.I.*, New Delhi, Division of Agricultural Research, I.A.R.I., 1972, pp. 182-186.

44A26 ATTITUDE OF FARM PEOPLE TOWARDS FERTILISERS

*Authors* : R.P. Singh and K.N. Singh.

*Availability* : Authors, Department of Extension, Haryana Agriculture University, Hissar.

*Time required* : 20 to 30 minutes.

*Level* : Farmers.

*Main features* : The instrument is a scale developed according to the Likert method of summated ratings.

*Scoring* : Likert method of scoring.

*Reliability* : Split-half and test-retest reliability coefficients were found to be 0.83 and 0.96.

*Norms* : Percentile norms are available.

*Validity* : Content validity has been established.

44A26 ATTITUDE OF FARM PEOPLE TOWARDS FERTILISERS

(The following items are to be checked on a 5-point scale of agreement).

1. The use of chemical fertilisers, makes the soil poor.
2. The use of chemical fertilisers is the easiest way to increase the crop yield.
3. The use of chemical fertilisers in food crop is harmful for the health.
4. The use of chemical fertilisers improves the quality of grains which fetch more price in the market.
5. The use of chemical fertilizers is less profitable in relation to the cost involved.
6. As no adequate farm term measure is available, the use of chemical fertilisers is essential.
7. The use of chemical fertilisers deteriorates the taste of food.
8. The yield of crops is very much increased by the use of chemical fertilisers.
9. The crops fertilised become more susceptible to diseases and insect pests.
10. It is good to use chemical fertilisers because as compared to farm yard manure, they act more quickly.
11. Chemical fertilisers are useless because their effects are confined to the crop to which they are applied.

12. The use of chemical fertilisers is essential for better crop yield.

## 44A27 COTTON PRACTICES ADOPTION INDEX

*Author*: S.V. Supe.
*Availability*: Author, College of Agriculture, Nagpur.
*Time required*: 15 minutes.
*Level*: Farmers.
*Main features* : The instruments has 10 items representing each practice. It is a scale meant for measuring the adoption behaviour of cotton growers.
*Scoring* : Each item is given a maximum score of six. The actual scores obtained by respondents on each items are totalled and it represents their adoption behaviour.
*Reference* : Supe, S.V. Factors related to different degrees of rationality in decision-making among farmers. Doctoral Dissertation in Agricultural Extension, I.A.R.I., 1969.

## 44A27 COTTON PRACTICES ADOPTION INDEX

1. Using improved cotton seed (6)
2. Disinfection cotton seed with fungicide (6)
3. Use of sowing method for cotton
   Not using square method (0)
   Using square method on less than half area of his cotton (2)
   Using square method on about half area (4)
   Using square method on more than half area (6)
4. Using four cotton seeds per hill (6)
5. Thinning cotton stand and keeping two plants per hill (6)
6. Use of fertiliser on cotton
   Not using fertiliser on cotton (0)
   Using fertiliser on less than half area of his cotton (1)
   Using fertiliser on about half area (2)
   Using fertiliser on more than half area (3)
   Using less than 20 lbs. N per acre (1)
   Using 20 lbs. N per acre (2)
   Using more than 20 1b. N per acre (3)
7. Use of insecticides on cotton
   Not using insecticides on cotton (0)
   Using insecticides on less than half area of his crop (1)
   Using insecticides on about half area (2)
   Using insecticides on more than half area (3)
   One spraying of endrin (1)
   Two to three sprayings of endrin (2)
   More than three sprayings of endrin (3)
8. Plants other crops with cotton (6)
9. Rouging practices followed (6)
10. Picking of the bolls when fully riped (6)

# B Instruments with technical information

## 44B1 ATTITUDE TOWARDS CHEMICAL FERTILISERS

*Authors* : B.N. Choudhary and C. Prasad.
*Availability* : Authors.
*Level* : Farmers.
*Main features* : A 15-item scale developed using 50 judges through Thurstone's method of equal appearing intervals. Scale is given in Likert type. The statements are used for three chemical fertilisers.
*Scoring* : Rating on the 5-point scale multiplied by the scale value of the item gives the item score. Total of the item scores give attitude score.
*Reliability* : Split-half reliabilities for 3 fertilisers were .81, .87 and .89. Test retest reliability coefficients were .72, .73 and .78.
*Validity* : Construct validity established.
*Reference* : Choudhary, B.N. and Prasad, C. A scale to measure the attitude of farmers towards the use of chemical fertilisers. *Interdiscipline*, 1971, 8(2), 72-79.

## 44B2 FAMILY PLANNING ATTITUDE SCALE

*Author* : Ahmed S. Fareed.
*Availability* : Author, Lady Harding Medical College, New Delhi.
*Level* : Medical students.
*Main features* : Contains 10 statements on a Guttman scale.
*Reliability* : Items having a coefficient of reproducibility .89 and marginal reproducibility .86 have been retained.
*Reference* : Fareed, A.S. A study of attitude of medical students towards family planning as potential service givers. Paper presented at the Third Family Planning Communication—Action Research Workshop, April, 1965.

## 44B3 DAS GUPTA ATTITUDE SCALE OF FARMERS

*Author* : D. Das Gupta.
*Availability* : Author, University of Kalyani.
*Uses* : To measure the general attitudes of farmers towards farming practices.
*Level* : Farmers.
*Main features* : The scale revealed high loadings on two factors: first dealing with education, block personnel, use of improved implements, and improved agricultural operations, the second composed for extension methods, irrigation and marketing, use of seeds, use of fertilisers, and use of plant protection chemicals.
*Reliability* : Test-retest reliability coefficient was .861.
*Validity* : Validity coefficient with judges ratings was .5.
*Reference* : Das Gupta, D. and Majumdar, A.K. Factor analytic aspects of an

attitude scale of farmers. *Indian Journal of Applied Psychology*, 1971, 8(2), 56.60.

44B4 ATTITUDE TOWARDS A SMALL FAMILY (FORM T)

*Authors* : E.I. George, V. George Mathew and B. Dharamangadan.
*Availability* : Authors, Department of Psychology, Kariavattom Trivendrum.
*Uses* : For the measurement of family size norms (attitudes and ideals).
*Time required* : Ten minutes.
*Level* : Malayalam speaking adults.
*Main features* : It is an attitude scale of Thurstone type and has a supplementary scale measuring family size ideals.
*Scoring* : Usual Thurstone method. The supplementary scale also yields a summated attitude score.
*Reliability* : Split-half reliability was 0.84.
*Validity* : Correlations were above 0.5 with other instruments measuring family size norms.
*Norms* : Percentile norms are available for both scales.

44B5 PICTURE RESPONSE TEST: ATTITUDE TOWARDS A SMALL FAMILY

*Authors* : E.I. George, V. George Mathew and B. Dharamangadan.
*Availability* : Authors, Department of Psychology, Kariavattom, Trivendrum.
*Uses* : For the measurement of family size norms (attitudes and ideals).
*Time required* : Ten minutes.
*Level* : Malayalam speaking adults. The 7 questions can be easily translated to any other language and used anywhere in India with reservations.
*Main features* : Seven pictures are shown and seven question are asked, one for each picture. Questions have multiple choice alternative answers which yield a summated attitude score. There is a supplementary scale of family size ideals.
*Scoring* : Summated score.
*Reliability* : Odd-even reliability coefficient was 0.90.
*Validity* : Correlations above 0.5 were obtained with various other measures of family size norms.
*Norms* : Percentile norms are available.

44B6 ATTITUDE TOWARD A SMALL FAMILY

(Parallel forms TL 1 and TL 2).

*Authors* : E.I. George, V. George Mathew and B. Dharamangadan.
*Availability* : Authors, Department of Psychology, Kariavattom, Trivendrum.
*Uses* : For the measurement of family Size norms (attitudes and ideals).
*Time required* : Ten minutes.
*Level* : Malayalam speaking adults.
*Main features* : Items were selected for the two forms after matching items in pairs on scale value, Q value, point biserial item total correlation, and *p*

value. There is a supplementary scale measuring family size ideals.

*Scoring* : Summated scoring method for both scales.

*Reliability* : Parallel form reliability was .81.

*Validity* : Correlations were above 0.6 with various other measures of family size norms.

*Norms* : Percentile norms are available.

## 44B7 STORY RESPONSE TEST — ATTITUDE TOWARDS A SMALL FAMILY

*Authors* : E.I. George, V. George Mathew and B. Dharamangadan.

*Availability* : Authors, Department of Psychology, Kariavattom, Trivendrum.

*Uses* : Measurement of family size norms (attitudes and ideals).

*Time required* : Ten minutes.

*Level* : Malayalam speaking adults. The study can be easily translated to any other language and so with some caution used anywhere in India.

*Main features* : A story is told and seven questions leading from the story are asked. Each question has multiple choice alternative answers. There is a supplementary scale on family size ideals.

*Scoring* : Summated scores.

*Reliability* : Odd-even reliability coefficient was 0.77.

*Validity* : Correlations were above 0.55 with other measures of family size norms.

*Norms* : Percentile norms are available.

## 44B8 CIRCULAR SCALE

*Authors* : C. Lakshmanna and V. Subrahmaniam.

*Availability* : Authors, Department of Sociology, Extension Education Institute, Rajendra Nagar, Hyderabad-30.

*Uses* : For assigning values on each of the statements of reasons for success or failure of package of practices.

*Level* : Used only for analysis of reasons put forth at the level of farmers.

*Main features* : The scale is a circular continuum of individual to external factors viz. (i) Individual, (ii) Local and (iii) External. Each of these factors in the scale represents 3 value spaces, the spaces in the scale continuum ranging from 1 to 9. One of the values on the continuum is to be assigned to each statement of reason. This scale helps in determining the role played by any of these factors is the final acceptance of the particular practice.

*Scoring* : A list of various statements of reasons for adoption and non-adoption of practices along with a self-explanatory instruction-sheet were distributed to thirty judges in the field of extension education. On collection of data, the appropriate factor was fixed through modal analysis, by determining the mode by grouping method. Subsequently tables were prepared and conclusions and inferences were drawn.

## 44B9 ATTITUDE SCALE

*Authors* : A.K. Majumdar and P.K. Majumdar.

*Availability* : Author.
*Uses* : To study the attitude of farmers to adoption of improved methods.
*Time required* : No time limit.
*Level* : Farmers.
*Main features* : The scale contains the following categories: Knowledge of Block Development and Panchayat Personnel, improved seeds, fertilisers and manures, disease and plant protection, chemicals and improved implements.
*Reliability* : Test-retest reliability was found to be 0.69.
*Reference* : Majumdar, A.K. and Majumdar, P.K. Adoption of some psychological characteristics of farmers. *Indian Journal of Extension Education*, 1967, 3(3), 138-142.

44B10 SMALL FAMILY SIZE ATTITUDE SCALE

*Author* : S.P. Mohanty.
*Availability* : Author, Demographic Research and Training Centre, Bombay.
*Main features* : Contains 14 questions: Likert scale.
*Reference* : Mohanty, S.P. Measurement of favourableness to a small family size by the summated rating scale technique, Paper presented at the Third Family Planning Communication. Research Workshop, April, 1965.

44B11 ATTITUDE SCALE

*Author* : J.M. Ojha and C.N. Mathur.
*Availability* : Author. Behavioural Science Centre, 32, Netaji Subhash Marg, Delhi-6.
*Uses* : To measure attitude towards hospital and medicine.
*Level* : Adults.
*Main features* : The scale is based on the method of summated ratings. 50 statements on the basis of interviews were prepared showing positive and negative attitude. The scale consists of 14 statements for hospital and 14 for medicine.
*Scoring* : The five points were given scores of 1, 2, 3, 4 and 5 where 1 was the most favourable and 5 the most unfavourable response.
*Reliability* : Split-half reliability coefficients after correction by Spearman-Brown prophecy formula were found to be. Attitude Towards Hospital $r$ = .64; and Attitude Towards Medicine $r$ = .51
*Reference* : Ojha, J.M. and Mathur, C.N. Attitude towards and beliefs about major diseases in urban and rural groups. ICMR Research Reports, Behavioural Sciences Centre, Delhi-6, 1971.

44B12 ATTITUDE TOWARDS FAMILY PLANNING SCALE

*Authors* : K.C. Panda and R. Kanungo.
*Availability* : Author.
*Main features* : A 20-item scale developed using Thurstone's method of equal appearing intervals.
*Scoring* : Adding the scale values of items checked.

*Reliability*: Split-half reliability coefficient was .74.

*Reference* : Panda, K.C. and Kanungo, R. A scale of measurement of attitude towards family planning. *Indian Journal of Social Work*, 1964, 25(2).

44B13 ATTITUDE TOWARDS PLANNED PARENTHOOD

*Author*: K.C. Pandey.

*Availability*: Author.

*Levels*: Married males and females between the age 20 to 55 years.

*Main features*: Thurstone's method was used in developing it.

*Reliability*: Reliability of the test was found to be .74.

*Reference* : Pandey, K.C. A study of measurement of attitudes towards planned parenthood. *Journal of Indian Academy of Applied Psychology*, 1967, 4(3), 77-84.

44B14 ADOPTION OF INNOVATIONS SCALES

*Author*: T. Sengupta.

*Availability*: Author.

*Uses* : (i) For developing a measure for innovativeness of farmers or an adoption scale, (ii) to find out the position of farmers belonging to different levels of innovativeness with regard to adoption of Formoson peddy varieties, and (iii) to indicate a method for selection of farmers for the high yielding programmes on rice.

*Level*: Farmers (N=279).

*Main features* : In this schedule 5 improved practices e.g. improved seed, chemical fertiliser plant protection and line cultivation were chosen against each of the important crops viz. paddy, jute, wheat, potato and sugarcane.

*Scoring*: The stages from 'ignorance' to 'adoption' were assigned scores from 0 to 50; 5 for negative, 5 for positive.

*Reliability*: The test-retest reliability of the scale was found to be:

*Coefficient of Correlation between*

| Village | Adoption Quotient & Adoption Score | Adoption Quotient & State of adoption |
|---|---|---|
| 1st Village (N=279) | 0.6012 | 0.4769 |
| 2nd Village (N=142) | 0.6489 | 0.4845 |

*Validity* : Concurrent validity of the new adoption scale was tested by correlating the adoption quotient of the farmers with their adoption scores as determined from the number of years over which the 4 practices had been followed by them. Coefficient of correlation worked out at 0.6012, which was found to be significant even at one per cent level. The scale possesses concurrent validity. The predictive validity of the scale was tested by correlating the adoption quotient of the farmers with their state of adoption on the hypothesis the high adopting farmers will also be at a higher stage of adoption in relation to the adoption of a new innovation, like Farmosan paddy. The coefficient of correlation scores and the adoption quotient came to 0.4769, significant at one per cent level. The scale possesses the predictive validity for using for selection.

*Reference* : Sengupta, T. A simple adoption scale for selection of farmers for high yielding varieties programme on rice. *Indian Journal of Extension Education*, 1967, III (3), 107-35.

44B15 ATTITUDE TOWARDS PACKAGE PROGRAMME

*Authors* : B.N. Singh, N.K. Jaiswal and R.S. Thakur.
*Availability* : Authors.
*Main features* : These are three scales developed according to the method of equal appearing intervals. The number of statements arrived at were 38 for package programme in general, 39 for its personal and 28 for farm production plan.
*Scoring* : The theoretical attitude score ranged from 1 to 7. A score of less than 3.5 indicated unfavourable attitude and more than 4.5 favourable attitude. A score between 3.5 to 4.5 showed that the individual had neither favourable nor unfavourable attitude towards the items studied.
*Reliability* : Reliability coefficients for package programme in general, its personnel and farm production plan by split half method were found to be + 0.68, + 0.59 + 0.63 respectively and by test-retest method were found to be + 0.74, + 0.68 and + 0.61 respectively.
*Reference* : Singh, B.N. Jaiswal, N.K. and Thakur, R.S. Attitude of farmers towards intensive agriculture district programme. *Indian Journal of Extension Education*, 1966, 11(3-4), 156-162.

44B16 ATTITUDE TOWARDS FAMILY PLANNING

*Authars* : G.P. Thakur and M. Thakur.
*Availability* : Authors, Ministry of R.D.S.O., Lucknow.
*Main features* : A Likert type scale.
*Scoring* : Summated ratings.
*Reliability* : Split-half reliability coefficient was found to be .72.
*Reference* : Thakur, G.P. and Thakur, M. A study of the effect of economic status on students attitudes towards family planning. *Indian Journal of Applied Psychology*, 1972, 9(2), 83-85.

44B17 BELIEF ABOUT HEALTH

*Author* : C.V. Venkatachalam and K. Kulandaivel.
*Availability* : Second author, S.R.K. Vidyalaya Teacher Training College, S.R.K. Vidyalaya, P.O. Coimbatore.
*Level* : High school students.
*Main features* : It is a questionnaire and attitude scale. The scale consists of 20 statements and is Likert type.
*Scoring* : Summated ratings.
*Reliability* : Reliability for this test was calculated and found to be +0.63.
*Validity* : Face validity is high in the questionnaire because identical situation type of testing is adopted.
*Reference* : Venkatachalam, C.V. and Kulandaivel, K. A study of health concepts and health habits of pupils in some secondary schools in Coimbatore. *Journal of Educational Research and Extension*, 1965, 1(3), 25-38.

## C Citations

44C1 FAMILY PLANNING ATTITUDE SCALE

*Author*: P.K. Dhillon.
*Reference* : Dhillon, P.K. A study on the attitudinal differences on family planning of two cultural groups. *Manas*, 15(1), 25-36.

44C2 LIBERALISATION OF ABORTION QUESTIONNAIRE

*Author*: I.Z. Husain.
*Reference* : Husain, I.Z. Liberalisation of abortion law: a survey of opinions. *Economic and Political Weekly*, 1969, 4(45-46), 1777-1780.

44C3 QUESTIONNAIRE (WITH DOGMATISM SCALE)

*Author*: Brij Behari Khare.
*Reference* : Khare, Brij Behari, Political modernisation and social change: a paradigm and its application to the Indian situation. Doctoral dissertation, 1969.

44C4 ATTITUDE TOWARDS EDUCATIONAL CHANGE

*Author*: H.N. Majoo.
*Availability*: Author, Department of Education, Lucknow University, Lucknow.

44C5 FAMILY PLANNING ATTITUDE SCALE

*Author*: A.S.K. Menon.
*Reference* : Menon, A.S.K. Some correlates of attitude towards family planning in India. *Journal of Family Welfare*, 1967, 13(4), 12-4.

44C6 AWARENESS OF SOURCES OF INFORMATION SCALE

*Author*: A. Suryanarayan Murthy.
*Reference* : Murthy A. Suryanarayan. Social and psychological correlates in predicting communication behaviour of farmers. Doctoral thesis in Agricultural Extension, I.A.R.I., 1969.

44C7 CONCEPT OF GRAMSEVAK QUESTIONNAIRE

*Author*: B.S. Singh.

44C9 OCCUPATIONAL INVENTORY

*Author*: T.S. Sodhi.

*Reference* : Sodhi, T.S. A comparative study of the personality patterns of students of religious and secular institutions. Ph.D. Thesis in Psychology, Agra University, 1970.

# 5. Religion and Morality

## A Complete instruments

### 45A1 ATTITUDE TOWARDS MORALITY

*Author* : D. Banerjee.
*Availability* : Author.
*Time required* : No time limit.
*Level* : Adults.
*Main features* : Five-point Likert type scale. Available in Bengali also.
*Scoring* : Summated ratings.
*Reliability* : Split-half reliability coefficients were found to be .80 and .85 respectively by odd-even and first versus second halves respectively using Spearman-Browns correction formula.
*Validity* : Face validity and Jury validity have been established.
*Norms* : Scores on 200 adults are available.
*Reference* : Banerjee, D. Development of scales for measuring attitude towards government, morality, religion and society. *Indian Journal of Psychology*, 1962, 37(3), 137-142.

### 45A1 ATTITUDE TOWARDS MORALITY SCALE

(The following items are to be checked on a 5-point scale of agreement).

1. Moral character has no value in the way to be established in life.
2. There is no fault in giving indulgence to unfairness on special occasions.
3. Honesty alone is the ladder to success in life.
4. Under no circumstances should one defy the orders of one's parents.
5. It is improper to have sexual relations with other women, even if one does not get sexual gratification from one's wife.
6. Honesty is not always the best policy.
7. One should not take shelter in a lie even to perform any noble deed.
8. One's happiness rests only in helping the neighbourers in their woes.
9. In order to get at any ideal one cannot depend upon sincerity alone.
10. Under no hostile circumstances should one slay others.
11. Sincerity is not the stepping stone to success in all spheres.
12. Under special circumstances one can take resort to a lie for the progress of the society.
13. It is not improper for a married woman to enjoy sexual relations with another person in case her husband is incapable of sexual intercourse.

14. It is bad to lie in any occasion.
15. It is better to steal than to die of starvation.
16. Under special cases harsh comments even towards superiors may be allowed.
17. By cheating others one cheats oneself.
18. Better not tell the truths in order to avoid a danger.
19. Without true thinking and true speaking there is no progress of society.
20. Under any circumstances all males are bound to maintain sincerity with their wives.

45A2 ATTITUDE TOWARDS RELIGION

*Author* : D. Banerjee.
*Availability* : Author.
*Time required* : No time limit.
*Level* : Adults.
*Main features* : Five-point Likert scale. Available in Bengali also.
*Scoring* : Summated ratings.
*Reliability* : Split-half reliabilities. Coefficients using Spearman Brown's correction formula were found to be .87 for odd-even items and .89 for the first and second halves.
*Validity* : Face validity and validation by expert ratings have been established.
*Norms* : Scores on 200 subjects available.
*Reference* : Banerjee, D. Development scales for measuring attitude towards government, morality, religion and society. *Indian Journal of Psychology*, 1962, 37(3), 137-142.

45A2 ATTITUDE TOWARDS RELIGION SCALE

(The following items are to be checked on a 5-point scale of agreement).

1. Religious faith alone leads man to right path.
2. Religion alone helps man to control his animality.
3. Faith in religion makes man accept factual truth and scientific truth.
4. Religion alone makes man tolerant and his life decent.
5. Religion alone helps man keep himself under restraint.
6. Faith in religion is absolutely obsolete to this age to science.
7. Faith in religion makes man averse to domestic duties.
8. Faith in religion makes man philanthropic.
9. Religion alone can give man what science can never give.
10. Religious faith cripples man's power of free thinking.
11. There is no way out than to take shelter in religion in order to enjoy the gusto of life.
12. Faith in religion makes man cowardly.
13. Faith in religion is a superstition.
14. Religion alone shows us the path to lead a healthy life individually as well as socially.
15. Religion alone is capable of inspiring the mind in the midst of frustration and basement.

16. Religious faith takes man away from the reality.
17. Religion has no room for developing a better society.
18. It is very difficult for a God fearing man to accept scientific truths.
19. Religious faith dwarts the free thinking of man.
20. Religious faith testified the religious backwardness.

45A3 OVERALL SECULARITY SCALE

*Authors* : Prayag Mehta in collaboration with B.P. Sinha and P.P. Gokulnathan.
*Availability* : Author, Department of Psychology, University of Udaipur, Udaipur, Rajasthan.
*Uses* : For the study of secular attitudes.
*Level* : Upper primary level.
*Main features* : The scale consists of 17 items. The items are based on the following dimensions — fundamental right of citizens, respect for religion of own and others, tolerance attitudes towards material cultural and social improvement of people of India, patriotism and nationalism and, scientific attitudes. The scale is developed under project "A communication study of national integration and secularism" of the Ministry of I & B and has been used at the respective places of study e.g. Ahmedabad, Bhiwandi and Ranchi. The scale is particularly useful for the sensitive services of the government and elsewhere and for training programmes for school children and others.
*Scoring* : Separate scoring was done for each item ranging from 1 to 5 score.
*Reliability* : In process.
*Validity* : In process.
*Norms* : In process.

45A3 OVERALL SECULARITY SCALE

(Each item is to be checked for one of the alternatives provided under it).

1. Each person should get equal opportunity in getting employment irrespective of caste and religion.
   (a) Strongly agree; (b) Agree; (c) Indefinite; (d) Disagree; (e) Strongly disagree.
2. Two students live in one room.
   (a) Some of the neighbours thought that they will quarrel shortly, since one is Hindu and another Muslim; (b) Some other persons thought, they can live together in spite of different religions.
   Which particular thought is right according to you?
3. There are following thoughts about religion. Which one do you feel more adequate.
   (a) Modern society is not progressing because it is getting away from religion; (b) Religion should change according to time, otherwise society can not be blamed for becoming a religionless society; (c) Religion is not of much significance in the modern society.
4. One Hindu house owner gave his house on rent to some Muslim family. Some of his neighbours commented in the following ways. Which

appeals more to you.

(a) House owner is being unfaithful to his religion; (b) House owner is concerned with rent and not religion.

5. We have other more important work to do than national duties. Do you agree with this?

   (a) Yes; (b) No.
6. What do you think if a Hindu girl marries a Muslim boy.

   (a) They must be liking each other; (b) Boy must have persuaded the girl; (c) Girl's parents must have persuaded the boy.
7. Which one of the following is more important for the development of villages.

   (a) Police chowki; (b) Government office; (c) Small market; (d) Cooperative society.
8. Some of the Muslim families established themselves in the colony of Hindus. Some of the reactions were as follows:

   (a) Hindu and Muslims can not live together in one locality and they should establish themselves separately; (b) Hindu and Muslim both should live together in one locality.
9. Each person of either caste and religion should feel secure about his money and belongings.

   (a) Strongly agree; (b) Agree; (c) Indefinite; (d) Disagree; (e) Strongly disagree.
10. What is more important for the progress of our country.

    (a) There should be religion only; (b) Each religion should get equal opportunity and freedom to develop.
11. There is one famous temple in the city. Harijans wants to go and worship. What steps should be taken by management according to you:

    (a) Harijans should not be allowed to enter in the temple; (b) They should be allowed to go on special occasions; (c) Temple should be for all the castes.
12. Which is more appropriate:

    (a) We should love our country even at the cost hating other country; (b) Humanity is more important for the love of our country. It is not good to hate others.
13. It is said that majority should give protection to the minority. How far do you agree with this statement.

    (a) Strongly agree; (b) Agree; (c) Indefinite; (d) Disagree; (e) Strongly disagree.
14. How far do you agree with "Ladies should be given an equal opportunity in every field".

    (a) Strongly agree; (b) Agree; (c) Indefinite; (d) Disagree; (e) Strongly Disagree.
15. If any Hindu boy marries a Muslim girl, how parent should behave with him.

    (a) Girl should be accepted as "bahu" (daughter-in-law); (b) Boy should be forced to break relationship with that girl; (c) Parents of the girl should have no relationship with boy's family; (d) Boy should be asked to get out from house.
16. What can be the chief cause of struggle between two castes.

(a) Some persons try to create misunderstanding; (b) Majority class perplexes minority caste which as the ultimate cause of struggle; (c) Mischiefs by the minority class give rise to conflict.

17. If some one says that some theft has taken place in the night in your locality. Will you believe?
    (a) Hearing at once; (b) After confirming from others; (c) After confirming from the house where theft took place.

## B Instruments with technical information

### 45B1 RELIGIOSITY SCALE

*Author*: Dr. L.I. Bhushan.
*Availability* : Author, Reader in Psychology, Bhagalpur University, Bhagalpur or from Psychological Testing Centre, Raja Mandi, Agra-2.
*Time required*: About 20 minutes.
*Level*: Adults.
*Main features*: It is a 36 item Likert type scale. Available in Hindi.
*Reliability* : Internal consistency coefficient was .82 and temporal stability coefficient was .78.
*Validity*: Content predictive and concurrent validities ensured.
*Norms* : In process.
*Reference* :

1. Bhushan, L.I. Religiosity scale. *Indian Journal of Psychology*, 1970, 45(4), 335-342.
2. Bhushan, L.I. and Sinha, N.P. Religiosity as a function of age, education and sex. *Indian Psychological Review*, 1971, 8(1), 104.

### 45B2 RELIGIOUS FAITH AND UNTOUCHABILITY QUESTIONNAIRE

*Author*: M. Broacha and H.M. Singh.
*Availability*: Authors.
*Level*: Students and educated adults.
*Main features* : It contains six sections including items on religious faith, methods of worship, religious belief, belief in the methods of sacrifice and system of untouchability.
*Reference* : Broacha, M. and Singh, H.M. An examination of religious faith and sense of untouchability amongst girls of 12 to 16 years. *Psychological Researches*, 1969, 3(1 & 2) 11-17.

### 45B3 QUESTIONNAIRE ON SUPERSTITION

*Author*: Ved Prakash Gupta.
*Availability*: Author.
*Uses* : To study superstitious beliefs in people.
*Main features* : It is a questionnaire containing about 90 questions on all

possible types of prevalent superstition. Each question has three responses i.e. agree, partially agree and disagree.

*Reference* : Gupta, Ved Pradesh. A study of some correlates of superstition. *Journal of Psychological Researches*, 1969, 13(1), 16-20.

45B4 MORAL ATTITUDE INQUIRY FORM

*Authors* : J.N. Joshi and H. Sharma.

*Availability* : Authors, Deptt. of Education, Panjab University, Chandigarh.

*Time required* : About 40 minutes.

*Level* : High/Higher secondary boys and girls.

*Main features* : Six problem situations are given in the first four parts, and to each poblematic situation three responses are provided — positive, negative and doubtful. In the fifth part attitude towards morality is judged on the basis of the liking of the students for different groups of reformers, politicians, singers, rich persons, scientists, writers, dacoits. In each group seven persons of prominence from past and present are included. In the sixth part wicked actions are classified into (i) beating, abusing, teasing, cruelty, towards animals, cruelty towards human beings, killing, (ii) lying, swearing, (iii) making surroundings dirty, (v) cheating etc. (v) raping, black mailing, (vi) black marketing, (vii) cold war etc.

*Scoring* : Simple counting of responses under different categories of responses.

*Reference* : Joshi, J.N. and Sharma, H. Moral attitudes among the secondary school students in relation to their intelligence and achievement. *Education and Psychology Review*, 1969, 9(1), 42-45.

45B5 ATTITUDE TOWARDS MORAL AND RELIGIOUS INSTRUCTION SCALE

*Authors* : B. Kuppuswamy and P.C. Eapen.

*Availability* : Second author, Regional College of Education, Mysore-6.

*Level* : Teachers.

*Main features* : It is a Likert type scale with 40 items.

*Reliability* : Split-half reliability was found to be 0.89.

*Reference* : Kuppuswamy, B. and Eapen, P.C. The attitude of teachers towards moral and religious instruction in schools. *Journal of Educational Research and Extension*, 1968, V(1), 91-6.

45B6 RELIGIOUS PRACTICES SCALE

*Authors* : Uma Dutta Pandey and Ranjit Prasad Singh.

*Availability* : First author, Senior Scientific Officer, Directorate of Psychological Researches, Ministry of Defence, 'M' Block, New Delhi-1.

*Uses* : To assess the degree of religious (Hindu) practices of the students of college.

*Time required* : No time limit. Roughly it takes 25 minutes.

*Level* : For college students and farmers as well.

*Main features* : It consists of 15 items (forced choice) based on rituals and values of orthodox Hindu families.

*Scoring* : One score for each 'yes' answers of the positive items and one score for each 'no' of the negative ones. The range of scores is 0 to 15.

### 45B7 RELIGIOUS BELIEFS SCALE

*Authors* : Uma Dutta Pandey and Ranjit Prasad Singh.

*Availability* : Author, Senior Scientific Officer, Directorate of Psychological Researches, Ministry of Defence, 'M' Block, New Delhi-1.

*Uses* : To measure the degree of beliefs in Hindu religion. It measures the extrinsic religious beliefs.

*Time required* : No time limit. Takes roughly 30 minutes.

*Level* : For college students and farmers as well.

*Main features* : It is a 5-point Likert type scale, with 20 items based on rituals, values, beliefs etc. which prevail in orthodox Hindu family.

*Scoring* : As in Likert type scale.

*Reliability* : Test-retest reliability was found to be .92.

*Validity* : Items were judged by 10 psychologists and 80 per cent agreement on each item was the criterion for selecting the items.

*Reference* : Pandey, U.D. and Singh, R.P. The effect of sex and culture on achievement motivation religious beliefs and religious practices. *Journal of Psychological Researches*, 1971, 15(2), 49-52.

### 45B8 RELIGIOUS ATTITUDE SCALE

*Author* : M. Rajamanickam.

*Availability* : Author, Department of Psychology, Annamalai University, Tamil Nadu.

*Time required* : 15 to 20 minutes.

*Level* : Adults (both sexes).

*Scoring* : Self-rating.

*Reliability* : Reliability coefficient was found to be 0.98 significant at .001.

*Validity* : Validity coefficient was found to be 0.86 significant at .001 level.

### 45B9 ADOLESCENT RELIGIOUS ATTITUDE SCALE

*Author* : T.S. Rao.

*Availability* : Author.

*Level* : Adolescents.

*Main features* : 60 items, some favourable to religion and some unfavourable were selected for inclusion in the scale. It is a Likert type scale.

*Scoring* : Summated ratings.

*Reliability* : Split-half reliability coefficient was found to be 0.88.

*Reference* : Rao, T.S. A study of attitudes of adolescents towards religion. *Journal of Psychological Researches*, 1963, 7(3), 135-141.

## Citations

45C1 ATTITUDE TOWARDS RELIGION QUESTIONNAIRE

*Authors* : K. Kulandaivel and P.K. Jacob.
*Reference* : Kulandaivel, K. and Jacob, P.K. Attitude towards religion in some high schools of Kottayam district. *Journal of Educational Research and Extension*, 1964, 1(1), 15-25.

45C2 MORAL IDEOLOGY TEST

*Author* : S. Rajnagam.
*Reference* : Rajnagam, S. Personality structure of some inmates of Madras vigilance and rescue homes. *Journal of Psychological Researches*, 1957, 1(1), 47-48.

45C3 ATTITUDE INVENTORY FOR ADOLESCENTS

*Author* : T.S. Rao.
*Availability* : Author.
*Level* : Boys and girls of 13-18 years of age.
*Reference* : Rao, T.S. A study of adolescents towards religion. *Journal of Psychological Researches*, 1963, 7(3), 136-141.

# 6. Other Social Attitudes

## A Complete instruments

46A1 GENERAL ATTITUDE SCALE (GAS)

*Authors* : C.L. Anand and Prafulla N. Dave.
*Availability* : Authors, Regional College of Education, Mysore-6.
*Time required* : 10-20 minutes.
*Level* : To any group, although tried out on B.Ed. applicants.
*Main features* : It is in the format of an open-ended questionnaire. A certain action situation is described and the subject is asked to give his reaction to it.
*Scoring* : The responses were categorised on a 9-point scale, maximum and minimum values being 8 and 0 respectively.
*Reliability* : Inter-scorer reliability ranged from .8 to .9.
*Validity* : Validity has been worked out by comparing the means of the students selected and rejected for the courses (M=92.2 and M=77.8) which were significantly different.
*Reference* : Anand, C.L. and Dave, Prafulla, N. Validation of a general attitude scale. *Research Report in Education and Psychology*, 1969, 8-11.

46A1 GENERAL ATTITUDE SCALE (GAS)

(The following open-ended items have to be answered).

1. You are standing in a queue to get into the bus. Someone tries to push ahead of you. What do you usually do?
2. A drama is to be staged in your college and the selection of various characters is being made from a group. Nobody comes forward for a particular role. You think that you are capable of accepting that role. What would you do?
3. You have given your cycle for repair. You call for it at the time appointed, but the man informs you that he has "only just begun work on it". What will be your normal reaction?
4. You are one among the audience listening to a talk from a public speaker. The speaker makes a statement hurting your religious feelings. How will you react in that situation?
5. The shopkeeper to whom you go for purchases overlooks you and waits on a customer who has come after you. What do you normally do?
6. A friend of yours talks too much and never gives you a chance to express your views. How do you treat him?

7. You meet a person whom you think you have met or known before in, the market, railway station or any other crowded place. What would be your reaction?
8. Your are fined for retaining library books for more than the period prescribed. You are not in a position to pay the fine. How will you react?
9. You undertake a journey by train. All of a sudden you find your ticket missing. What will be your normal reaction?
10. Every suggestion that you put forward in a group discussion is turned down. How do you feel?
11. You are very hungry. You are seated and the food has been served. You are about to start eating. You realise that you have not washed your hands. What will you do?
12. You have invited your best friends for dinner. They arrive one hour later than the scheduled time. What will be your usual reaction?
13. One of your best friends is expelled from the institution because of insulting the teacher. How will you act?
14. In conversing with a person older than yourself whom you respect, on an issue you happen to disagree, how would do you express your disagreement?
15. In a practice session you are playing tennis singles with a friend who had won a tournament match against you the previous week. Nobody is watching you both play. A stroke by your opponent just reaches one of the boundary lines. You fail to return the ball. You do not really know whether the ball was 'in' or 'out'. If you declare that the ball was 'out' you win the game, and thereby feel satisfied that you have avenged your defeat the previous week. If you declare it was 'in' then there is a possibility of your losing to him again. What will be your decision?
16. You are the captain of your college cricket team. Your team is playing a vital tournament match. At crucial stage of the match, the umpire gives a decision which makes you lose the match. How do you react?
17. You come to the class late a number of times. Your classmates make insulting remarks. What kind of remarks do you pass on them?
18. Your father is 46. He works at a desk throughout the day. In his younger years he was active in his various sports but in recent years he has had no physical activity beyond a little work at home. You are concerned because he seems short of breath and appears flabby and unfit. What would you do?
19. You go out with a group of people for hiking. One of the members of the party proves incapable of coping with the speed and efficiency of others. What would you normally do?
20. You are witnessing a hockey or football match between your college team and some other team. Your college team seems to be losing. What will be your reaction?

## 46A2 ATTITUDE TOWARDS SOCIETY

*Author* : D. Banerjee.
*Availability* : Author.
*Time required* : No time limits.

*Level* : Adults.
*Main features* : Five-point Likert scale. Available in Bengali also.
*Scoring* : Summated ratings.
*Reliability* : Split-half reliability after using Spearman-Brown's correction formula were found to be .58 and .68 respectively for the odd-even halves and first and second halves of the scale.
*Validity* : Face validity and judges ratings.
*Norms* : Scores on 200 subjects are available.
*Reference* : Banerjee, D. Development of scales for measuring attitude towards government, morality, religion and society. *Indian Journal of Psychology*, 1962, 37(3), 137-142.

## 46A2 ATTITUDE TOWARDS SOCIETY SCALE

(The following items are to be checked on a 5-point scale of agreement).

1. Any sort of marriage others than sacramental should be highly pursuable.
2. Early marriage has done harm to the society.
3. It is necessary for the males and females to have equal rights and opportunities in the sphere of service.
4. Sex education during student-life is not at all desirable.
5. Wide publicity of planned parenthood is necessary for the development of society.
6. The opportunity for free mixing between boys and girls is detrimental to society.
7. It is necessary to marry early for having peace in domestic life.
8. It is necessary to impose proper physical punishment on students for violating discipline.
9. It is highly necessary to minimise the grandeur of religious right for the progress of society.
10. Registration marriage has brought no evil effects in the society.
11. It is necessary before marriage to have the right of mixing between the sexes.
12. It is necessary to establish socialism by abolishing the system of individual profit making.
13. It is necessary to impart sex-education to the school students.
14. So much deterioration of the society is due to the abolition of casteism.
15. Love marriage never ends in happiness.
16. Introduction of marriage among different tribes will advance the society.
17. Widow-marriage in a large scale should be introduced in the society.
18. Introduction of love marriage is necessary for a happy marriage life.
19. The rich in the society always enjoy happiness.
20. Caste system is necessary for keeping the social structure in force.

## 46A3 ATTITUDE TOWARDS GOVERNMENT SCALE

*Author* : D.Banerjee.
*Availability* : Author.

*Time required* : No time limit.
*Level* : Adults.
*Main features* : Five-point Likert scale. Available in Bengali also.
*Scoring* : Summated Ratings.
*Reliability* : Split-half reliability using Spearman-Brown's correction were found to be .84 and .78 respectively for odd-even halves and first and second halves.
*Validity* : Validated by judges ratings and face validity established.
*Norms* : Scores available on 200 subjects.
*Reference* : Banerjee, D. Development scales for measuring attitude towards government, morality, religion and society. *Indian Journal of Psychology*, 1962, 37(3), 137-142.

46A3 ATTITUDE TOWARDS GOVERNMENT SCALE

(The following items are to be checked on a 5-point scale of agreement).

1. All the Government laws are constituted/framed for the benefit of the rich.
2. The Government has no clear-cut policy for interest of the labourer.
3. The educational institutions of our country are not thriving because of negligence of the present Government.
4. The Government policy regarding foreign affairs is quite firm.
5. The Government policy requires radical change for the progress in the educational fields.
6. Thanks to the Government enough progress in science and industry is taking place in the country.
7. The five-year plans are really the steps to national progress.
8. The present Government has given evidence of enough efficiency in internal administration.
9. The public has to court humiliations at the hands of the Government on many occasions even after the independence.
10. On the whole the country is progressing as a result of the Government policies.
11. For the propagation of education the Government policies can claim appreciation.
12. The blackmarketeers are being pampered by the Government policies.
13. The present Government is a resort for the weak characters and worthless people.
14. The allegation against the Government about its malpractices in internal administration is not baseless.
15. Enough endeavours of the Government are evident for the unliftment of agriculture in the country.
16. The Government scheme for refugee rehabilitation cannot be supported.
17. The Government policy alone is responsible for not becoming self-sufficient in food production.
18. The present Government has shown evidence of enough patience as to the refugee rehabilitation.

19. All the Government laws are framed for the good purpose.
20. The present Government is taking proper measures for the solution of unemployment problems.

## 46A4 QUESTIONNAIRE OF INTER-PERSONAL CONFLICTS ON ATTITUDE TOWARDS CHILDREN

*Author* : S.B. Kakkar.

*Availability* : Author, Department of Psychology, State College of Education, Patiala.

*Uses* : For assessing inter-personal conflicts on a attitude towards children.

*Time required* : No time limit. Takes about 20 minutes.

*Scoring* : A score value of one is given to each item on which the responses of father and mother differ.

*Reference* : Kakkar, S.B. Family conflicts and scholastic achievement. *Indian Journal of Psychology*, 1970, 45(6), 159-164.

## 46A4 QUESTIONNAIRE OF INTER-PERSONAL CONFLICT ON ATTITUDE TOWARDS CHILDREN

(The following statements are to be checked for agreement).

1. Parents should punish the child when he does any wrong.
2. Expressions of love between the two parents should not be made in the child's presence.
3. When the child criticises his parents, they should stop him from doing so.
4. A child should not be coerced to wear clothes he does not like.
5. Differences or conflicts between parents should be concealed from the child.
6. Parents should indulge in fondling and loving their children openly.
7. A child should not accompany his parents when they visit their friends.
8. Parents should answer every question that a child asks.
9. Parents should not allow their child to kiss or hug them or fuss with them at the time they are entertaining guests.
10. Parents should not eulogize their children before others.
11. A child should not be stopped from doing anything.
12. Parents should not discuss serious problems in the presence of their child.
13. Parents should solve their child's problems.
14. When a child is fussy, his parents should not bother.
15. A child's needs should be satisfied as soon as they arise.
16. A child should be allowed to express all his emotions.
17. Parents should not let a child who disobeys go unpunished.
18. A child should be allowed to enjoy the company of everyone he comes across.
19. A child showing rude behaviour in the presence of outsiders in the home should be rebuked there and then.
20. A child should be allowed complete freedom.

21. Parents should make their child do whatever they want.
22. When a child is attempting to solve a problem, parents should jump in to help him.
23. Parents should not force their child to respect their wishes.
24. Child should not be expected to own the prides and prejudices of his parents.
25. In a child's dispute with others parents should take the side of their own child.
26. A child should not be forced to talk to persons he does not like
27. Parents in the home should stop quarrelling with each other if their child comes in.
28. Parents should defend each other when the child finds fault with one of them.
29. A child should not be asked to exhibit his talents or baby pranks before guests.
30. Parents should not mind if their child interferes in the problems they discuss.

46A5 LEADERSHIP BEHAVIOUR PERCEPTION SCALE

*Authors* : M.R. Lokhande and T.K. Moulik.
*Level*: Farmers.
*Main features* : One of the 5 statements is to be checked.
*Scoring* : Median of the scale values checked give the attitude score.
*Reliability* : Average discrepancy showing internal consistency ranged from .041 to .071. Coefficients of agreement ranged from .061 to .32, all significant at .01 level.
*Reference* : Singh, K.N.; Singh, S.N. and Lokhande, M.R. *Measurement in extension research: instruments developed at I.A.R.I.*, New Delhi. Division of Agricultural Research, I.A.R.I., 1972, pp.137-147.

46A5 A RATING SCALE OF RURAL LEADERSHIP BEHAVIOUR

(Under each behavioural characteristic the statement most closely expressing the views is to be checked. Weightages appear in parentheses).

A. Possess the personal characteristics?
   1. He does not care for personal gain in fulfilling obligations. (0)
   2. He practices before he preaches. (4.5)
   3. He spends or donates money material resources and effort in the welfare work of the village. (5.0)
   4. He accepts and practices new ideas in farming readily. (5.5)
   5. He is impartial and gives correct evidence. (7.0)
B. Perform the social function?
   1. He does not discriminate (say in offering hukka) aiming people on account of caste, creed or rank. (0)
   2. He identifies himself with others in times of sorrows. (4.0)
   3. He helps people, especially those with little resources in hours of their (e.g., medical facilities) even at his own inconvenience. (11.0)

4. He warns and chastises potential delinquents. (10.5)
5. He writes favourable reports as a refree. (11.0)

C. Perform the functions to facilitate the achievement of the task of the group?
1. He educates people in adoption of improved technology and in skills to improve their employment potential. (0)
2. He raises contributions and mobilises people through work like 'Shramdan' for developing facilities in the village. (6.0)
3. He invests panchayat money profitable sources and expedite development projects by advancing required funds. (7.0)
4. He follows rules and carried out action according to rules. (8.6)
5. He boldly implements the decision of the panchayats. (9.0)

D. Performs the functions which helps/maintaining the group/in integrity and solidarity?
1. He encourages those who fail to try again. (0)
2. He brings order in the meeting by appealing in the name of village prestige. (1.0)
3. He helps in settlement disputes within the ramily or in the village impartially by consulting responsible and concerned person of age. (1.0)
4. He settles baffled elements when unforeseen mishaps occur. (1.5)
5. He presents several alternatives in settling disputes in order to evolve a commonly agree solution. (5.5)

## 46A6 PERCEPTION OF THE ECONOMIC SYSTEM

*Author*: A. Suryanarayan Murthy.

*Availability* : Author, Extension Education Institute, Rajendra Nagar, Hyderabad-30.

*Uses* : Useful for studies in connection with Social Change.

*Time required*: About 5 minutes.

*Level*: Farmers.

*Main features* : A 13 itemed four point scale to determine the perception of economic system: demand-supply, credit, cooperatives, processing of paddy farm surpluses, prices and profit, marketing etc.

*Scoring* : Four-point summated ratings.

*Reliability* : Reliability by Kerlinger Formula was found to be 0.62.

*Validity* : Content validity was established by using Judges opinion.

*References* :

1. Singh, S.N. and Murthy, A.S. A scale to measure farmers' perception of the economic system. *Manas*, 1970, 17(1), 49-56.
2. Murthy, A. Suryanarayan. Social and Psychological correlates in predicting communication behaviour of farmers. Doctoral thesis in Agricultural Extension, I.A.R.I., 1969.

## 46A6 PERCEPTION OF THE ECONOMIC SYSTEM

(The following statements are to be rated on a 4-point scale: extremely true, very true, fairly true, not at all true).

1. The middle men profit greatly by the seasonal price rise at the expense of the small farmers.
2. Demand for agricultural products is rising rapidly due to increase in population and incomes of people. Therefore, demand for paddy increased recently.
3. Mortgaging land for obtaining cooperative credit may raise questions of risk to the farmer which he is not willing to face and collateral signer may be difficult to obtain.
4. Farmers are encouraged to adopt high yielding varieties as credit facilities for purchase of seeds, fertilisers etc., are assured through the cooperatives.
5. With increase in modernisation of agriculture-credit needs of medium and high income farmers increase greatly.
6. Local millers who by produce ~~from the~~ farmers pay less due to lower extraction and breakage of grains which results from the inefficient machinery owned by them.
7. Farmers sell very small portion of what they produce.
8. High investment required for cultivation of high yielding varieties opened up greater opportunities to richer farmers than the small farmers.
9. Cooperative societies have a bureaucratic organisation which reduces their flexibility and creates costs while marketing agencies like merchants operate on relatively narrow margins such as cost of establishment etc.
10. Technological development requires development and refinement of a whole host of institutions.
11. Uncertainty of prices and want of local demand for coarse grain varieties like IR-8 paddy have always been important considerations for the farmer not to grow them.
12. A reduction in real prices of what farmers buy like fertiliser and consumer goods is as valuable an incentive as an increase in the real prices of what they sell.
13. Improvement in marketing, include improved milling methods of paddy resulting in greater extraction and greater savings to the consumers. This indirectly benefits the farmers by ensuring better prices as more demand is ceritified his produce.

46A7 COOPERATION-COMPETITION PRONENESS INSTRUMENT

*Author* : Udai Pareek and Narendra Dixit.

*Availability* : Authors, Indian Institute of Management, Ahmedabad-15.

*Level* : Pre-adolescents and adolescents.

*Main features* : Scale consisting of 5 items each item having 3 alternate responses. Semi-projective test.

*Reliability* : Test-retest reliability = .496 (N=19) with two weeks difference.

*Validity* : Content validity through ratings of judges.

*Reference* : Pareek, Udai and Dixit, Narendra. An analysis of cooperation and competition amongst preadolescents. *Indian Journal of Social Work*, 1974, 35(1), 73-85.

## 46A7 COOPERATION-COMPETITION DISPOSITION INVENTORY

1. Shyam went to play with his two friends in the games period. Teacher gave them some wooden blocks to make designs. The teacher only told them that today we will make designs with these blocks. Then what shyam will do?
   (a) Shyam will try quickly to make those designs alone without his friends.
   (b) Shyam will like to finish those designs with his friends.
   (c) He will ask the teacher to distribute equal amount of work to them.
2. Sohan and Pran were given a game to play, at the end of which they were supposed to get a toffee for each 20 marks. They could be played in three ways (1) more marks, but distributed equally to both. (2) either of them may get. (3) neither of them may get. What will Sohan think in this situation.
   (a) Sohan will like to score as much number as possible even if his friend gets equal marks.
   (b) Sohan will like to score as much as possible but not let other partner get any.
   (c) He will go on play without any understanding.
3. Ram and Shyam are studying in the same class. Ram is good at science and Shyam at mathematics. Shyam always helps Ram in mathematics but Ram never helps him willingly. What will Ram Do?
   (a) In future, he will not give any help to Ram and would like to get more marks in science than Ram.
   (b) Even when Ram is not helping. Shyam will help Ram.
   (c) Both will try to study by themselves.
4. On the occasion of School's annual function, the school was being decorated. All classes were distributed the work of preparing garlands. What Suresh of class VIII will think before starting the work.
   (a) I will work along with other boys of my class so that we can decorate the best.
   (b) I will do my work nicely and will not help others no matter the reputation of my class goes down.
   (c) I will ask my monitor what I should do?
5. Five boys of the class were asked to write slogans to be used in the election. They were told to make interesting and small slogans. What will they do?
   (a) All will write some slogans together and those like by all will be given to the teacher.
   (b) All the boys will write the slogans separately and will try that his slogans should be interesting and shorter than others.
   (c) They will ask the teacher what is the minimum number of slogan, one has to write.

## 46A8 COOPERATION-COMPETITION DISPOSITION INVENTORY

*Authors* : Udai Pareek and Narendra Dixit.
*Availability* : Authors, Indian Institute of Management, Ahmedabad-15.

*Level*: Pre-adolescents and adolescents.

*Main features* : Self-checking inventory, subject is required to respond on a 4-point scale (applicable to not-applicable).

*Reliability*: Test retest reliability was .59 (N=19) with a difference of two weeks.

*Validity*: Content validity through ratings of judges.

*Reference* : Pareek, Udai and Dixit, Narendra. An analysis of cooperation and competition amongst pre-adolescents. *Indian Journal of Social Work*, 1974, 35(1), 73-85.

46A8 COOPERATION-COMPETITION DISPOSITION INVENTORY

1. Being given any work on the class, I always help others to that they can also finish that with me.
2. In the class when two of us have solved the problem simultaneously, even then I wish that the teacher should see mine first and praise me.
3. Whenever there is a problem in the class, I want to solve it jointly.
4. I enjoy accomplishing a work, if I feel that others also have done equally good.
5. I want that there should be competition in the class and I must get the highest mark.
6. Whenever there is a problem in the class, I want to solve it myself.
7. Generally, I like to work with those whom I think that they are better than me in two or three things.
8. While playing, I want to play the best and win.
9. I like to do better than others on any task.
10. At the time of examination I want to help my friends alongwith me.
11. While playing, I wish that my team-mates should win the game.
12. Sometimes when I see that other boys are fairing equally good, I feel depressed.
13. I wish that others should also get reward, along with me on my rewarding task.
14. At the time of examination, I what to study alone, so that I can stand first.
15. Being given any work in the class I want to finish it by joining others.
16. I want to top the class in studies.
17. I always think how to surpass others.
18. I like playing after making team.
19. I like to take parts in competitions and also wish that I must do better than others.

46A9 ATTITUDE TOWARDS WIDOW REMARRIAGE

*Author*: Kamala Gopal Rao.

*Availability* : Sample copy only with the author. Professor of Social Sciences, National Institute of Health Administration and Education, E-16, Greater Kailash, New Delhi-110048.

*Uses* : To assess overall liberal conservative orientation towards social problems.

*Time required*: About 15 minutes.

*Level* : Older adolescents, adult males and females.

*Main features* : This is a summated ratings scale (Likert scale) covering a wide range of opinions .38 items initially culled out from various sources were tried out to select items with suitable discriminatory power. Discriminatory power was ascertained by comparing mean scores of the upper lower 27 per cent scorer 20 items were selected to form the final scale.

*Scoring* : Usual procedure followed for Likert type of scales-assigning arbitrary weightage to the responses on the 5-point scale ranging from strong agreement to strong disagreement.

*Reliability* : Split-half reliability was found to be $r$ = .80, reliability for the whole test by Spearman-Brown Formula 0.88, $Z/\sigma Z$ = 1.20.

*Validity* : Validated through correlating it with the equal appearing intervals scale on widow-remarriage prepared by the author. A Pearsonian of .85 was obtained with $N$ = 13.8 which was found to be very significant.

46A9 ATTITUDE TOWARDS WIDOW REMARRIAGE

(The respondent has to check the following items on a 5-point scale of agreement).

1. Society must strongly support widow remarriage.
2. Increase in the number of widow remarriages reduces many tensions in the joint family and hence desirable.
3. When widows can remarry, widows too can do so.
4. Virgin widows can re-marry.
5. Law should enforce that all widows below 30 years should remarry.
6. Widow remarriage is a curse on ideal Indian womanhood.
7. Widow remarriage degrades the sacred bond of marriage to the status of a contract.
8. It is inauspicious even to see a remarried widow.
9. Objecting to widow remarriage increases immorality in society.
10. Widow remarriage will be a blot on Hinduism, known for its high principles.
11. Widows without children can remarry.
12. Special agencies must be established to arrange proper alliances for widows to remarry.
13. Widow remarriages create many social problems.
14. Widows should lead a life of self-restraint and never think of remarriage.
15. It is a sin for a widow to remarry.
16. The State should install funds to aid widow remarriages.
17. A widow who remarries should be treated as an outcaste in her community.
18. Young, and charming widows may remarry.
19. It is inauspicious for a young man to marry a widow.
20. A widower can marry as many times as he likes, but a widow should never remarry.

## 46A10 ATTITUDE TOWARDS WIDOW REMARRIAGE

*Author* :Kamala Gopal Rao.

*Availability* : Sample copy only with author, Professor of Social Sciences, National Institute of Health Administration and Education, E-16, Greater Kailash-I, New Delhi-110048.

*Uses* : To assess general liberal-conservative orientation to social problems.

*Time required* : About 15 minutes.

*Level* : Older adolescents, adult males and females.

*Main features* : It is an equal-appearing intervals scale consisting of a seven point attitude continuum ranging from 'reactionary' to 'radical'. 96 statements on 'widow marriage' collected from various sources, edited and protected were submitted to 56 adult judges (Senior professionals of various categories like engineers, doctors, authors, socio-political workers etc.) who sorted out the statements on the 7-point attitude continuum. The objectivity of the scoring of statements on different scale positions along the continuum was ascertained by submitting the same statements to a group of student judges. (Postgraduate students in a liberal arts college.) A high correlation between the ratings of the two groups of judges was obtained. Scale-values and ambiguity indices of statements sorted out by judges were ascertained through plotting of gives and ambiguous statements were weded out. A final scale consisting of 42 statements was formulated based on the criteria of least ambiguity and representativeness of scale values along the 7-point attitude continuum. Attitude statements of almost similar scale-values were assigned to alternate forms C and D which constitute the parallel forms for testing the reliability of the scale.

*Scoring* : The attitude score of an individual is the mean scale value of all items endorsed by the subject.

*Reliability* : Derived by administering the parallel forms of the scale (Forms C and D) to the same subjects after sufficient time interval to obviate the influence of memory, $r$ = 0.69, corrected by Spearman-Brown formula = 0.816 $Z/\sigma z = 9.24$, which is well over twice the standard error indicating that the scale is very reliable. Reliability of the scale-values assigned by judges was ascertained by computing the S.E. and P.E. of the scale value which gave a value of 0.0959 which is very satisfactory.

*Validity* : Self-rating by subjects on the attitude continuum was matched with actual scores on the attitude scale, and chi-square was worked out to test the null hypothesis. There was a very significant association between actual scores on the attitude scale and the self-ratings. Self-rating by subjects was matched against friends' ratings which also yielded significant association between the two.

## 46A10 ATTITUDE TOWARDS WIDOW REMARRIAGE—FORM C

1. No widow should be allowed to remain unmarried.
2. When widowers are allowed to marry again, there is no reason why widows should not do so.
3. Widow remarriage is an issue that depends entirely on the emotional state of the widow.

4. Introduction of widow-remarriage means injustice to maidens, whose marriage problem has already become a complex one.
5. A widow had better burn along with her dead husband, than survive to marry again.
6. It should be enforced by law that all widows below 30 years should remarry.
7. Widows who inherit their dead husband's property with full rights can marry again, if they want.
8. It is wrong to force those widows who are unwilling to marry, to get married.
9. Widow-remarriage should be prevented, as "Kanyadanam" means that she has been given away and no gift of the samething can be done twice over.
10. In recruitment for jobs, first preference should be given to men who have married widows.
11. Many tensions in the joint family can be resolved, by permitting widow remarriages.
12. Though widow remarriage gives security to the woman concerned, it creates a number of other social problems.
13. Widow remarriage must be opposed as it is against the Shastras.
14. Failure to legalise widow remarriage demoralises society.
15. Society should not look down upon a man, who remarries a widow.
16. A widow by remarriage, displays her lack of self-control.
17. Allowing widow remarriage is disastrous, as it affects the moral standards of society as a whole.
18. Young, educated and rich men, should come forward to marry widows.
19. Widows who are young and charming may marry, if they want.
20. The increased number of widow remarriages in modern times are undermining respect for our cultural heritage.
21. A remarried widow should be treated as an outcaste in her community.

46A10 ATTITUDE TOWARDS WIDOW REMARRIAGE—FORM D

(The respondent checks the items he agrees with).

1. Even widows with children should be compelled to remarry.
2. It would solve a number of our economic problems, if widow remarriage gets common sanction.
3. Only widowers may marry widows.
4. A remarried widow should have the same disabilities in religious ceremonies, as a widow.
5. Widows who intend remarrying should be kept under custody.
6. Youths should make a sacred resolve, that they would willingly marry a girl who is a widow.
7. It will relieve the anxiety of parents if their widowed daughters are remarried.
8. Widows of the age of 15 years and below can be allowed to marry again.
9. Widow remarriage is bad, as it spoils the basic sanctity of the marriage

bond.

10. The state should install proper funds to see that all widows are remarried.
11. Some of our social problems can be resolved, if widow remarriages take place.
12. Widow remarriage is not the key to the solution of many of our problems.
13. Widow remarriage is a curse on ideal Indian womanhood.
14. Every child-widow must be remarried.
15. If the widows think that they cannot lead a life of pure widowhood, they have as much right to remarry as a widower in the same condition.
16. Widow remarriage is undesirable, as it results in the negligence of the children by the first marriage.
17. A widower can remarry as many times as he likes, but a widow should never remarry.
18. Continued objection to widow remarriage ultimately increases the rate of prostitution.
19. Widows without encumbrances and children can remarry.
20. Our conventions are most sensible in opposing widow remarriage.
21. All widow remarriages should be declared illegal.

### 46A11 ATTITUDE TOWARDS DIVORCE

*Author* : Kamala Gopal Rao.

*Availability* : Sample copy only with author — Professor of Social Science, National Institute of Health Administration and Education, E-16, Greater Kailash-I, New Delhi-110048.

*Uses* : To assess general liberal-conservative orientation to social problems, to assess even attitude to divorce as such, may also be utilised assess marital adjustment — potential as well as actual, particularly in terms of perceived solutions for marital discord.

*Time required* : About 15 minutes.

*Level* : Adult males and females.

*Main features* : It is an equal appearing intervals scale running on a 7-point attitude continuum ranging from reactionary to radical. 98 statements on "Divorce" collected from various sources particularly in the light of the Hindu Marriage Act of 1955 edited and pretested were submitted to 56 judges (senior professionals of various categories) who sorted out the statements on the 7-point attitude continuum. The dependability of the statements sorting done by the judges was cross-checked by submitting the same statements to a group of student judges. The mean ratings of the two groups yielded a *F* value of 0.16 indicating objectivity in the ratings. After working out the scale values and *Q* values of statements by calculating the mean and *Q* values on the Ogive, ambiguous statements were ruled out. For the final scale 42 statements were selected based on criteria of least ambiguity and representatives of scale values along with 7-point attitude continuum. Attitude statements of almost identical scale values were assigned to alternate forms A and B, which constituted the parallel Forms for testing reliability.

*Scoring* : Mean scale value of all items endorsed by the subject forms the attitude score of an individual.

*Reliability* : Derived by testing the same subjects on parallel forms (*A* and *B*) $r$ = 0.69, corrected by Spearman-Brown formula, 0.816. $Z/\sigma z$ = 9.24, which is much more than twice the standard error, indicates that the scale is very reliable.

Reliability of scale values was ascertained by computing the standard error and probable error of the scale value which gave a value of 0.10318 which is very satisfactory.

*Validity* : Self-rating by subjects on the attitude continuum was matched with actual scores on the attitude scale, and chi-square was worked out to test the null hypothesis. There was a very significant association between actual scores on the attitude scale and the self-ratings.

Self-rating by subjects was matched against friends' ratings also yielded significant association between the two.

46A11 ATTITUDE TOWARDS DIVORCE—FORM A

(The respondent has to check the items he agrees with).

1. One must not hesitate to break the bond of marriage, if necessary, even though the society objects.
2. Instead of leading a life of constant misery, it is better to use for divorce.
3. The problem of divorce among Hindus is a crucial one to be decided with discrimination.
4. Divorce brings catastrophe in the lives of children and therefore must be avoided.
5. A woman must tolerate ill-treatment from her husband, rater than seek divorce.
6. Marriage must become a contract, so that divorce can be obtained whenever needed.
7. As a wife is not bound to be an accomplice in her husband's crimes, she can get divorce, if he does not mend his ways.
8. Social pressure must be exerted, to compel the mismated couple to readjust and not divorce their partner.
9. Divorce disintegrates the family, individual and society.
10. If divorce is not legalised in our society, death is the only way for the suffering partner, to get rid of the tie.
11. In cases of moral breach, divorce is desirable.
12. Divorce is not the correct solution for marital difficulties.
13. The legalisation of divorce has been the greatest blot on Hinduism.
14. Divorce is extremely desirable for it permits the correction of mistakes and happy readjustment.
15. It marital difficulties are serious enough, divorce may be obtained.
16. Divorce is bad, as it leads to suffering for the emotionally-dependent partner.
17. It is better not to exist, if one cannot adjust, rather than to seek divorce.
18. In cases where the temperaments of the husband and wife do not agree, divorce is inevitable.

19. Divorce is more of a personal problem than a social one.
20. As our ethical background emphasises tolerance rather than selfishness, it is wrong to seek divorce.
21. Society should look down upon a woman who has divorced her husband.

46A11 ATTITUDE TOWARDS DIVORCE—FORM B

(The respondent checks the items he agrees with).

1. To oppose divorce is to uphold organised hypocrisy.
2. Women should have equal rights with men in the matter of divorce.
3. As our society is in a transitional stage, it is better to wait before we accept or reject divorce system.
4. The possibility of divorce, reduces the sanctity of the marriage bond.
5. The wife should submit to the authority of the husband, however, cruel he may be.
6. Divorce should be encouraged, as it is the only way out of a mistaken-choice.
7. Divorce is a method of rearranging the family if the marriage is a failure.
8. The husband and wife must patch up their differences for the sake of the children and should not seek divorce.
9. Introduction of divorce among Hindus, has been a blind and harmful imitation of the west.
10. In our society, divorce must continue to be a legally recognised termination of the status of marriage.
11. A man can claim divorce, only when he provides for the maintenance of his wife.
12. The possibility of divorce, lessens the capacity for adjustment on the part of the couple.
13. As marriages are made in heaven, it is deadly sin to dissolve them.
14. Instead of pretending happiness, it is better to seek divorce boldly.
15. If the husband or wife is mad, the other can seek divorce.
16. The legalisation of divorce has created economic insecurity in the woman.
17. Under no circumstances should a wife try to get free from the marriage bond.
18. Since marriage was made for man, and not man for marriage, divorce must be permitted when desired.
19. It is for the court of law to decide whether divorce is desirable or not in particular cases.
20. In marriage, duty is more important than pleasure and therefore divorce undesirable.
21. The religious institutions should forcibly inflict a ban on divorce.

46A12 ATTITUDE TOWARDS DIVORCE

*Author* : Kamala Gopal Rao.
*Availability* : Sample copy only with the author. Professor of Social Science,

National Institute of Health Administration and Education, E-16, Greater Kailash-I, New Delhi-110048.

*Uses* : To assess liberal-conservative orientation towards Social problems.

*Time required*: About 20 minutes.

*Level*: Older adolescents, adult males and females.

*Main features* : This is a Likert scale (summated ratings) covering a wide range of opinions on the issue of "Divorce". 40 items initially culled out from various sources were submitted to preliminary try out the discriminatory power of items was ascertained by comparing mean scores on the scale of the upper and lower 27 per cent scorers, 20 items were selected for the final scale.

*Scoring* : Usual procedure followed for Likert type of scales — assigning arbitrary weightage to the responses on the 5-point rating scale ranging from strong agreement to strong disagreement.

*Reliability* : Split-half reliability was found to be $r = 0.87$, reliability for the whole test by Spearman-Brown formula was 0.93, $Z/\sigma z = 14.40$.

*Validity* : Validated through correlation with the Thurstone scale on Divorce, prepared by the author. A pearsonian $r$ of 0.77 was obtained between the equal appearing scale and the Likert scale on Divorce, $z$ was 1.02 and was 11.08 which was found to be very significant.

46A12 ATTITUDE TOWARDS DIVORCE

(The respondent has to check each of the following statements on a 5-point scale of agreement).

1. Acute differences in the temperaments of the husband and wife may be a reasonable ground for seeking divorce.
2. As marriage is a sacred tie and not a contract, divorce should not be allowed.
3. Divorce is undesirable, as it creates emotional insecurity in the children.
4. Divorce is the only way of relieving the constantly suffering partner in marriage.
5. Divorce should be discouraged, as it spoils the spiritual values of the younger generation.
6. One can divorce if one so feels, regardless of the reactions of society.
7. Divorce should never be thought of, as it leads to suffering for the emotionally dependent partner.
8. Divorce should be prevented in the interests of conserving the family.
9. Divorce is the only means of escaping from a cruel husband.
10. Divorce is justified in cases of acute domestic disharmony.
11. Divorce may be sought, when the personal happiness of the couple is at stake.
12. Divorce for Indian couples is a blind and harmful imitation of the west.
13. As marriage is a sacred oath, divorce is a sin.
14. Divorce should never be legalised, as it sets a bad example for the younger generation.
15. Divorce is the only way out of a mistaken choice of partner.
16. Divorce is necessary for happy readjustment to life.

17. Divorce is not desirable as it creates many other social problems.
18. As disharmony among growth of children, divorce is the only resort in such cases.
19. Once married, the couple should live together till the end.
20. Divorce is a constructive method of rearranging the family institution, if the marriage is a failure.

## 46A13 ATTITUDE TOWARDS SOCIALISTIC ECONOMIC POLICY

*Author*: Kamala Gopal Rao.

*Availability* : Sample copy only with the author. Professor of Secial Sciences, National Institute of Health Administration and Education, E-16, Greater Kailash-I, New Delhi-110048.

*Uses* : To assess liberal-conservative orientation towards socialistic economic policy.

*Time required*: About 20 minutes.

*Level*: Older adolescents, adult males and females.

*Main features* : It is a summated ratings scale, covering five major areas of economic policy — namely (1) Land problem, (2) Private property, (3) Income distribution, (4) Labour and labour unions, and (5) Nationalisation. An initial set of 85 items on these different areas of economic policy was subjected to editing and pretesting, which resulted in 65 statements. These were administered on different groups of subjects to ascertain the discriminatory power of items. Significance of difference between the mean scores of upper 27 per cent and lower 27 per cent of scorers and the critical ratio were worked out to retain only such items in the final scale that would discriminate between those having entirely different attitudes towards the issue 20 items were finally retained, four items on each of the five areas of economic policy.

*Scoring* : Usual procedure of assigning arbitrary weights to the responses on the 5-point rating scale ranging from strong agreement to strong disagreement.

*Reliability* : Split-half reliability was found to be 0.66 estimated reliability of the whole test was 0.79, $Z/\sigma z = 8.5$.

*Validity* : Analysis of variance of mean scores of subjects with different political party affiliations indicated significant differences, indicating that the scale is valid and does measure politico-economic liberalism conservatism.

*Reference* : Rao, K.G. A study of the attitudes of the different political parties towards some aspects of the socialistic economic policy. *Indian Journal of Applied Psychology*, 1964, 1(2), 101-105.

## 46A13 ATTITUDE TOWARDS SOCIALISTIC ECONOMIC POLICIES

(The respondent has to indicate his agreement on a 5-point scale for the following items).

1. Labour unions must grow stronger by gaining political influence.
2. No individual should be allowed to earn more than 1,000 Rupees per month.
3. Confiscation of extra land from land-owners, will kill all incentives in the

present owners.

4. It is wrong to prevent private investment and enterprise in industries.
5. Private property has succeeded in making nations economically prosperous as in U.S.A.
6. Labour unions are a source of trouble to the managements and the society.
7. It is impossible to achieve equality of wages even under the best economic system.
8. Government must distribute land freely among people, on the basis of the size of the family and redistribute as the family changes.
9. State-ownership of all means of production (land, capital, rewanterials) is desirable, as it ends profiteering.
10. Private ownership of property leads to aggression by the rich.
11. Labour unions must not merely be tolerated, but actively encouraged.
12. The difference in salaries between the labour and other professional people must be minimised.
13. Abolition of landlordism is a hasty measure.
14. Government ownership of industries and factories, fails to provide the necessary incentive to efficiency.
15. It is essential to abolish all private property, so as to reduce inequities of wealth.
16. Participation of labour in the management of industry is not possible at all.
17. Lessening the disparity in income between various occupations will weaken all incentives among people of higher professions.
18. The tenant must have the full right of ownership of the land, he is cultivating.
19. State-ownership of industries will render the objects we need in our lives, cheap.
20. Complete abolition of private property is impracticable.

## 46A14 PARENTAL ORIENTATION INVENTORY OF CHILDREN

*Author*: K. Ravichandra and E.G. Parameswaran.
*Availability*: Authors, Department of Psychology, Osmania University.
*Level*: Parents of children.
*Main features*: It has 20 pairs of items dealing with achievement orientation and development orientation.
*Reliability*: Test-retest reliability was found to be .80 (N = 20, one month gap).
*Validity*: Validity coefficient of .85 was found with another projective test.
*Reference*: Ravichandra, K. and Parameswaran, E.G. Construction of a parental orientation inventory. *Research Bulletin*, 1972, 7, 65-70.

## 46A14 PARENTAL ORIENTATION INVENTORY OF CHILDREN

(The respondent has to choose one statement with which he agrees in each pair).

1. (a) It disturbs me when my child is not superior to other children in

studies.

(b) I do not expect my child to be a book-warm just to get high marks in examination.

2. (a) A child's success in life depends mostly on school grades.
   (b) Success in life depends on healthy and all-round development in studies, sports, etc., and not largely on school marks.
3. (a) I am satisfied if my child can play some games well.
   (b) Thee is no point in playing games without winning.
4. (a) I want my child to be the best actor in his school.
   (b) I am happy if my child can participate in school cultural programme.
5. (a) I insist on my child repeating certain thing until he masters it.
   (b) I encourage my child to try out new things on his own accord.
6. (a) I am of the view that failure is often a stepping stone to success.
   (b) I am perturbed if my child fails in an examination.
7. (a) Activities other than studies are not going to help in the long future.
   (b) Child should also take an interest in art, music and other co-curricular activities besides studies.
8. (a) I do not encourage my child to make many friends as it will affect his studies.
   (b) A child should have many friends as it will help to broaden his out look.
9. (a) Children should be encouraged to cultivate a hobby as it is educative by itself.
   (b) I think that cultivating a hobby is a waste of time for the child, instead he can concentrate on his studies.
10. (a) Participation in sports is very helpful irrespective of the child's attainment in sports.
    (b) A child should not waste time on sports unless he can achieve distinction in sports.
11. (a) If my child is unwilling to do his school work I do not force him.
    (b) I usually override the feeling of my child if it comes in the way of his achievement.
12. (a) I am happy if he is a member of his school team.
    (b) I expect nothing short of excellent performance from my child in games or sports.
13. (a) I want my child to guide the activities of his class.
    (b) I am happy if my child can participate in class activities satisfactorily.
14. (a) It does not worry me if my child does not get along well with others provided he is good at studies.
    (b) Even if the child is not good at studies, I worry if he does not get along well with others.
15. (a) Competition is the best way to make a child do better.
    (b) Free give and take with his peers will help him to greater achievement in his task.
16. (a) I am satisfied if my child is popular among friends.
    (b) I want my child to be the class representative.
17. (a) Child should be made to do small tasks which will make him a responsible person.

(b) A child should not be given any responsibility as it will affect his studies.

18. (a) I always tell my child that studies alone are not enough.
    (b) I always instil in my child the necessity for studies.
19. (a) I accept only first grade from my child.
    (b) I am satisfied if my child is above average in his studies.
20. (a) I prefer my child to be disciplined and well mannered rather than having only excellent academic achievement.
    (b) Doing well in studies is the only important thing for a child.

## 46A15 ACTIVISM SCALE

*Author*: Malla Reddy.
*Availability*: Author, College of Education, Osmania University, Hyderabad-7.
*Level*: College students.
*Main features*: It is a 30 situational item scale with three response alternatives. Weightages are given to the alternative chosen.
*Scoring*: Summation of the scores of response alternatives chosen.
*Reliability*: Test-retest reliability coefficient was found to be 0.87.
*Validity*: Was found to discriminate known groups of activists and non-activists.
*Reference*: Reddy, M. Alienation and activism, paper presented on the First National Conference of the Indian Psychological Association, Department of Psychologies, Osmania University, Hyderabad, 2, 1973.

## 46A15 ACTIVISM SCALE

(The respondent has to check one of the response alternatives given under each item).

1. If a teacher, in the classroom makes a statement that what you think is offensive, what is your usual reaction?
   (i) To be indifferent;
   (ii) To enter into argument with the teacher;
   (iii) To organise a collective protest against the teacher.
2. When you are in a demonstration to oppose the Government on an issue the police resorts to lathi-charge without warning and threatens with firing. Will you then:
   (i) Disperse immediately;
   (ii) Continue to demonstrate by pelting stones;
   (iii) Violently attack the police.
3. At a reception or a big social gathering, when you want to meet the important person present, somebody prevents you from meeting. What is your customary reaction?
   (i) To do nothing;
   (ii) To enter into argument;
   (iii) To create a scene.
4. At a lecture or an entertainment when you take the front seats available, the organisers object saying 'they are meant for special invitees'. What would be your reaction?

(i) Accept the objection;
(ii) Enter into an argument with the organiser;
(iii) Take the seats with a challenge.

5. When you approach a rich man for donations for a genuine cause in which you are interested, the man mistrusts you and insults you. What is your reaction?
   (i) To leave gently;
   (ii) To give him a bit of your mind;
   (iii) To carryout an active campaign against him.
6. You have heard indirectly that your friend has been spreading rumours about you which are likely to be serious and unjustified. Do you usually:
   (i) Let it pass without noticing it;
   (ii) When your friend;
   (iii) Expose him to other friends and isolate him.
7. Someone tries to push in ahead of you in line for cinema tickets, you have been waiting for sometime, and in spite of your objection he does not move out of the line. Do you usually:
   (i) Feel for a while and forget about it;
   (ii) Call the attention of the police man on duty;
   (iii) Push the intruder out of the line.
8. A photographic camera which you want to use for your college day programme is given for an urgent repair. You call for it at the repair shop at the time appointed but the repair man informs you that he has only "just begun work on it". Is your customary reaction:
   (i) To wait patiently till he repairs;
   (ii) To show your annoyance and get back the camera;
   (iii) To pick up a quarrel and create a scene.
9. If a teacher does not complete the syllabus, and questions in the examination appear from the portion which is not covered, what is your customary reaction?
   (i) Keep quiet because the problem is common to all;
   (ii) Take the initiative to appeal for special marks;
   (iii) Organise a walk-out from the examination hall.
10. If one of your best teachers of your college is dismissed from service on certain allegations which according to you are baseless, what would be your reaction?
    (i) To be indifferent;
    (ii) Give moral support to the teacher;
    (iii) Yourself initiate a protest and go on strike.
11. If the authorities do not agree for the postponement of the examination in spite of just demand from the students, whether your reaction would be —
    (i) To feel helpless;
    (ii) Take initiative to gherao the authorities;
    (iii) Unite the students to boycott the examination.
12. If you are not allowed to enter the examination hall for coming slightly late than the scheduled time, due to some unavoidable reasons, what will be your reaction?
    (i) To leave the place gently;

(ii) To persuade to permit you;
(iii) To enter the hall forcibly creating a scene.

13. If the office bearers of your union misuse the Union Funds, will your reaction be:
(i) To be indifferent;
(ii) To ask for the accounts;
(iii) To organise a 'no confidence motion' against the union.

14. When you find that the food in the hostels or a restaurant is not worth the charges that are paid, what would be your customary reaction?
(i) To accept it without questioning;
(ii) To call the attention of the management;
(iii) Refuse to pay the charges.

15. When the college authorities decide to increase tuition fees ignoring the financial difficulties of the students; will your reaction be:
(i) To agree with the decision;
(ii) To represent the case to the authorities;
(iii) To do 'Dharna' till the fee is reduced.

16. You are travelling by bus during night time. You find that a woman passenger is trying to get into the bus and the conductor does not allow her. Will you usually:
(i) Be indifferent;
(ii) Persuade the conductor to take the passenger;
(iii) Bring pressure of your co-passengers on the conductor to allow her.

17. When you find a cinema proprietor indulging in black marketing the tickets and you do not get the ticket for the normal rate. What would you generally do?
(i) Not mind buying your ticket at the black rates;
(ii) Lodge a protest with the police;
(iii) Organise people to damage cinema property.

18. If you come across situations where you find that appointments and promotions are made by favouritism and persons with merit are deprived of their rightful chances. Do you usually:
(i) Accept this to avoid conflict;
(ii) Organise public opinion;
(iii) Organise a mass protest.

19. You are interested in participating in a legitimate agitation and your parents oppose you. Do you usually:
(i) Obey your parents;
(ii) Persuade them and give up the idea if they still oppose you;
(iii) Join the agitation in spite of their disapproval.

20. If the elections in your college are cancelled to avoid clashes and your group was sure to win, will your customary reaction be:
(i) To be indifferent;
(ii) Insist on having elections;
(iii) Organise a collective demonstration for having elections.

21. If the leader of your group becomes a tool in the hands of the authorities and betrays the cause for which he is elected, what would be your reaction?
(i) Not be bothered about it;

(ii) Warn the leader with serious consequences;
(iii) Organise a no confidence motion against him.

22. If the authorities do not give you an interview to represent your important problem even after a few attempts, whether your customary reaction would be:
    (i) To give up the idea;
    (ii) To protest individually;
    (iii) To prevent the institution from functioning.
23. If the authorities keep the colleges closed when the students feel that there is no such need, is your customary reaction:
    (i) To be indifferent;
    (ii) To take the initiative to appeal for reopening;
    (iii) To gherao the authorities.
24. If your neighbour comes home drunk and starts disturbing the people in the locality, do you usually:
    (i) Tolerate it;
    (ii) Close him in a room;
    (iii) Hand over him to the police.
25. If some members of your family constantly refer to you as 'useless' and 'good-for-nothing', do you usually:
    (i) Resign yourself to it;
    (ii) Burst out emotionally;
    (iii) Leave the family for good.
26. When the officer in an office where you were awaiting for some time to see him, overlooks you and attends to another person who has come into the office after you. Do you usually:
    (i) Do noting;
    (ii) Give him a bit of your mind;
    (iii) Pick up a quarrel and cerate a scene.
27. If the authorities cancel the examinations held on the ground that there was mass copying and you have done well in the examination without resorting to any malpractice, what would be your reaction?
    (i) To feel helpless;
    (ii) To make an appeal for investigation and give it up;
    (iii) To organise a violent protest.
28. If a teacher not competent enough to teach a subject is appointed in your college, is your normal reaction:
    (i) To be indifferent;
    (ii) To prevent the teacher from functioning;
    (iii) To organise a protest against the appointment of the teacher.
29. If the buses from your place to the University Campus do not run as per the schedule timings causing inconvenience to a number of people. What is your reaction?
    (i) To ignore it;
    (ii) To lodge a protest with the authorities;
    (iii) Try to damage the buses to show your severe concern.
30. If one of the groups violates the rules of the union election and the college does not take any action to stop this will your reaction be —
    (i) To be indifferent;

(ii) To force the authorities to take action;
(iii) To directly attack the group.

## 46A17 ALIENATION SCALE

*Author*: Malla Reddy.
*Availability*: Author, College of Education, Osmania University, Hyderabad-7.
*Level*: College students.
*Main features* : A 14-item inventory developed on the basis of Seeman's multidimensional framework for alienation. It is a Likert scale.
*Scoring* : Five-point summated ratings.
*Reliability*: Test-retest reliability coefficient was 0.82.
*Validity* : Item validity on the basis of discriminating power of items. Concurrent validity with Leosrole scale = 0.43.
*Reference* : Reddy, M. Alienation and activism. Paper presented at the First National Convention of the Indian Psychological Association, Osmania University, Hyderabad-7.

## 46A17 ALIENATION SCALE

(The following items have to be checked on a 5-point scale of agreement).

1. We should be extra careful in life, lest we would be exploited by others.
2. These days elders never consult youngsters on many matters which affect the youngsters.
3. It is difficult to trust any one in our dealings because human nature is fundamentally selfish.
4. We are not really sure whether the present education is of any value to us in our actual life.
5. We often feel as strangers in our own surroundings.
6. It is hard for any one to get a job these days, unless one can influence or bribe.
7. We do not know how to set right things which are going worst in our society.
8. The man with morale and scruples is better able to get ahead in this world.
9. It is hard to train the children now-a-days because what is right today may not be the same tomorrow.
10. One is confused about what one should do when he faces a new situation in this disorderly world of today.
11. We do a number of things in life mechanically to please others but honestly they are not meaningful to us.
12. These days colleges are indifferent on many matters which offset the students.
13. I do not know where the world is really going.
14. What is good for me today may not be the same for tomorrow.

# Instruments with technical information B

## 46B1 LEADERSHIP PREFERENCE SCALE

*Author* : L.I. Bhushan.
*Availability* : Author, Reader in Psychology, Bhagalpur University, Bhagalpur-4.
*Uses* : To assess degree of preference for authoritarian or democratic leadership.
*Time required* : About 15 to 20 minutes.
*Level* : Adults.
*Main features* : It is a 30-item Likert type scale. Available in Hindi.
*Reliability* : Internal consistency coefficient was 0.74 and temporal stability coefficient was .79.
*Validity* : Content and construct validities ensured.
*Norms* : In process.
*References* :


1. Bhushan, L.I. Leadership preference as related to age, education, residence and sex. *Indian Journal of Social Work*, 1968, 29, 193-196. Bhushan, L.I. A scale of leadership preference. *Psychological Studies*, 1969, 14, 28-34.
2. Bhushan, L.I. An investigation of certain personality correlates of leadership preference. *Psychological Studies*, 1970, 15, 15.
3. Bhushan, L.I. Leadership preference as a function of authoritarianism and intolerance of ambiguity. *Journal of Indian Academy of Applied Psychology*, 1970.
4. Singh, A.P. Certain background factors of leadership preference. Unpublished report submitted to Banaras Hindu University, 1967.
5. Bhushan, L.I. A study of leadership preference in relation to dependence proneness and parental attitudes. Manuscript unpublished, 1971.


## 46B2 ATTITUDE QUESTIONNAIRE

*Authors* : J.S. Gandhi and K.G. Agrawal.
*Availability* : Authors.
*Uses* : For measuring public attitude towards the mentally retarded.
*Time required* : About 45 minutes.
*Level* : Adults.
*Main features* : A questionnaire to measure public attitude towards the retarded regarding following areas: (a) abilities, (b) Social aspects, (c) Family and sexuality, (d) Societal attitude in general, (e) Personal characteristics.
*Scoring* : A 3-point scale of "yes/no?" type is used. Total number of items is fifty.
*Reference* : Gandhi, J.S. and Agrawal, K.G. Attitude of public towards the mentally retarded. *Indian Journal of Mental Retardation*, 1969, 2(1), 21-26.

## 46B3 QUESTIONNAIRE FOR ASSESSMENT OF OPINION ABOUT NATIONAL PLAN

*Author* : Amal Kumar Mallick.
*Availability* : Author, 227, A.H.L.R. Road, Calcutta-28.
*Uses* : To find out the attitude of the people towards the development plans of India.
*Time required* : About one hour.
*Level* : Adult male population with some knowledge about five-year plans.
*Main features* : A summated questionnaire consisting of a series of integrated poll-type questions. The questions (twenty in number) are concerned with the hopes and aspirations, fears and anxieties, expectations, fears and anxieties, expectations and ambitions of people regarding national planning. It is of Likert type and the extent of one's favourableness or unfavourableness of opinion is expressed on a 5-point scale.
*Scoring* : Likert's principle of summated ratings.
*Reliability* : Items of the questionnaire were selected on the basis of internal consistency.
*Validity* : Validity was checked by the method of contrasted groups and concurrent validity was determined. Correlation with a direct question about attitude towards the issue was found to be as high as .85.
*Reference* : Mallick, Amal Kumar. A study on the relative importance of some determinants of opinion about national planning in India. *Psychological Studies*, 1969, 14(2), 125-131.

## 46B4 SEMANTIC DIFFERENTIAL FORMS (TWO)

*Authors* : H.N. Majoo and S.K. Shukla.
*Availability* : First Author, Department of Education, Lucknow University.
*Uses* : For evaluating peoples, reactions towards the mentally retarded and mental retardation.
*Time required* : About 25 minutes.
*Level* : Can be used at all levels.
*Scoring* : Same procedure as in all good's Semantic Differential scales.
*Validity* : Cross validated.
*Reference* : Majoo, H.N. and Shukla, S.K. Evaluation of the terms 'mental retardation' and 'mentally retarded people' by a sample of University students. *Indian Journal of Mental Retardation*, 1970, 3(2), 62-68.

## 46B5 SOCIAL AWARENESS INVENTORY

*Authors* : Asghari Mohiuddin and N.Y. Reddy.
*Availability* : Authors, Department of Psychology, Osmania University, Hyderabad-7.
*Level* : Children 5-$^1/_2$ to 10-$^1/_2$ years.
*Reference* : Mohiuddin, A. and Reddy, N.Y. Development of social concepts and ethnic attitudes in orphan and normal children. Paper presented at the First Annual convention of the Indian Psychological Association, Osmania University, February 1973.

## 46B6 NATIONALISATION SCALE

*Author* : S.M. Mohsin.
*Reliability* : Split-half reliability coefficient was found to be .85.
*Validity* : Construct validity established by Yousuf, (1972).
*Reference* : Yousuf, S.M. An investigation into the construct validity of the nationalisation scale. *Psychological Studies*, 1972, 16(2).

## 46B7 NATIONALITY IMAGE QUESTIONNAIRE (NIQ)

*Author* : A.B. Ojha.
*Availability* : Author.
*Uses* : Originally designed to elicit images formed by other and rich nationalities.
*Time required* : 5-7 minutes.
*Level* : Boys, girls and adults beyond 12-13 years age.
*Main features* : Two sets of responses are taken one word and three words descriptions.
*Scoring* : For stereotypes the words provide the information for perceptual categories four categories could be descriphered attitude the minor fiddling with probability give 5-point rating.
*Reference* : Ojha, A.B. A study of cross-national semantic confusion and nationality images. *Journal of Indian Academy of Applied Psychology*, 1969, 6(2), 61-69.

## 46B8 INVENTORY TO STUDY ROLE ACTIVITY

*Author* : P.V. Ramamurti.
*Availability* : Author, Department of Psychology, S.V. University, Tirupati, A.P.
*Time required* : 30 minutes.
*Level* : Men and women.
*Main features* : It contains rating scales to study degree of role activity in fifteen major role areas.
*Scoring* : Rating scale 0 to 8 in steps 2.
*Norms* : Available on a sample of 1040 (men and women, urban, semi-urban, rural).
*References* :

1. Ramamurti, P.V. Unpublished report of ICSSR Project on A Study of Roles and Problems of middle-aged and older people (under preparation).
2. Ramamurti, P.V. A study of roles and problems of middle-aged and older people. ICSSR project, S.V. University, Tirupati.

## 46B10 FAMILY AND PARENTS ATTITUDE SCALE

*Author* : Udai Pratap Singh.
*Availability* : Author, Bhagalpur University.
*Uses* : Used to measure the attitudes of criminals towards parents and family.
*Main features* : A 40-item Likert type scale.
*Reference* : Singh, U.P. A comparative study of attitude of male and female

criminals towards their family, parents and authority. *Journal of the Indian Academy of Applied Psychology*, 1972, 9(1) 18-21.

## C Citations

46C1 PARENT CHILD RELATIONS QUESTIONNAIRE

*Author* : Anjali Choudhuri.
*Reference* : Choudhuri, A. Emotionality and parent-child relationship. *Indian Journal of Psychology*, 1967, 42, 89-92.

46C2 ATTITUDE TOWARDS SOCIAL REFORMS QUESTIONNAIRE

*Authors* : S. Jalota and S. Tewari.
*Reference* : Jalota, S. and Tewari, S. A study of attitude towards social reforms. *Indian Psychological Review*, 1965, 2(1), 65-68.

46C3 ATTITUDE TOWARDS DRUG USER

*Author* : H.N. Majoo.
*Availability* : Author, Department of Education, Lucknow University, Lucknow.

46C4 ATTITUDE TOWARDS MENTALLY RETARDED (ABS-MR)

*Author* : H.N. Majoo.
*Availability* : Author, Department of Education, Lucknow University, Lucknow.

46C5 QUESTIONNAIRE TO STUDY SMOKERS' BEHAVIOUR AND THEIR IMAGE OF THE CHARMINAR BRAND CIGARETTE

*Author* : K.K.A.P. Rao.
*Reference* : Rao, K.K.A.P. Smokers speak — a case study of the consumer behaviour. *Indian Journal of Commerce*, 1969, 22(78), 17-28.

46C6 TEST TO IDENTIFY THE DELINQUENTS

*Author* : A.B. Ray.
*Reference* : Ray, A.B. Comparison of two different methods of item analysis. *Psychological Studies*, 1965, 10(1), 66-69.

# INSTRUMENT INDEX

# AUTHOR INDEX

# SUBJECT INDEX

# CICIL LIST

## CONCEPTS IN COMMUNICATION, INFORMATICS & LIBRARIANSHIP (CICIL)

*General Editor:* S.P. AGRAWAL

CICIL-1 Development of Library Services in India: Social Science Information
**S.P. Agrawal** Rs. 150

CICIL-2 Development of Documentation in India: Social Science Information
**S.P. Agrawal** Rs. 250

CICIL-3 UNESCO and Social Sciences: Retrospect and Prospect
**S.P. Agrawal** and **J.C. Aggarwal** Rs. 250

CICIL-4 INDIANA : A Bibliography of Bibliographical Sources
**M.K. Jain** Rs. 200

CICIL-5 Dimensions of Library and Information Science: Kaula Festschrift
**V. Venkatappaiah** (Eds.) Rs. 600

CICIL-6 Book Numbers: Some Indian Methods
**M.P. Satija** and **S.P. Agrawal** Rs. 100

CICIL-7 National Policy for University Libraries in India: Problems and Perspectives
**N.B. Inamdar** and **L.S. Ramaiah** (Ed.) Rs. 250

CICIL-8 Media Utilisation for the Development of Women and Children
**B.S. Thakur** and **Binod C. Agrawal** Rs. 150

CICIL-9 Terrorism: An Annotated Bibliography
**Susheela Bhan** (Ed.) Rs. 275

CICIL-10 Transnational Library Relations: The Indo-American Experience
**M.B. Konnur** Rs. 175

CICIL-11 Geography of Marketing and Commercial Activities in India (Documentation on Research Information)
**R.S. Dixit** Rs. 130

CICIL-12 Information India 1988: Global View
**S.P. Agrawal** and **J.C. Aggarwal** Rs. 200

CICIL-13 Women's Education in India: Historical Review, Present Status and Perspective Plan
**S.P. Agrawal** and **J.C. Aggarwal** Rs. 360

CICIL-14 Cultural Communication in India: Role and Impact of Phonograms
**J.M. Ojha** (in press)

CICIL-15 Second Historical Survey of Educational Development in India: Select Documents 1985-1989
**S.P. Agrawal** and **J.C. Aggarwal** Rs. 490

CICIL-16 Documentation Encyclopaedia of UNESCO and Education
**J.C. Aggarwal** and **S.P. Agrawal** Rs. 800 (set of 2 parts)

CICIL-17 Attitude Towards Information: A Study of Post-Graduate Teachers and Researchers in Social Sciences
**N.G. Satish** (in press)

CICIL-18 Librarianship and Bureaucratic Organisation: A Study in the Sociology of Library Profession in India
**P.K. Jayaswal** Rs. 175

CICIL-19 Literature Search
**K.A. Isaac** Rs. 150

CICIL-20 Child Education in India: Index to Scholarly Writings in Indian Educational Journals and Newspapers since independence
**S.P. Agrawal** and **Naresh Kanta** Rs. 100

CICIL-21 Lok Sabha and Vidhan Sabha Elections in India 1989 & 1990: Process and Results with Comparative Study of Manifestos
**S.P. Agrawal** and **J.C. Aggarwal** Rs. 250

CICIL-22 Islamic Studies in India: A Survey of Human, Institutional and Documentary Sources
**Mohamed Taher** Rs. 180

CICIL-23 Panchayati Raj: An Annotated Bibliography
**N.B. Inamdar, N.G. Satish** and **Anil Takalkar** 290

CICIL-24 Information India 1989-90: Global View
**S.P. Agrawal** and **J.C. Aggarwal** Rs. 500

CICIL-25 First Handbook of Psychological and Social Instruments
**Udai Pareek** and **T. Venkateswara Rao** Rs. 500

CICIL-26 Educational and Social Uplift of Backward Classes: At What Cost and How? Mandal Commission and After
**S.P. Agrawal** and **J.C. Aggarwal** Rs. 275

CICIL-27 Mass Media and New Horizons: Impact of TV & Video an Urban Milieu **H.R. Trivedi** Rs. 180

CICIL-28 Indian Writings on Education : An Indicator to Indian Educational Journals Grouped by Subject Deseriptors 1979 to 1986 (in two parts) **S.P. Agarwal** Rs. 900 (per set)

CICIL-29 Nation in Crisis
**S.P. Agrawal** and **J.C. Aggarwal** Rs. 200

CICIL-30 Information India 1990-91: Global View
**S.P. Agrawal** and **J.C. Aggarwal** Rs. 500

CICIL-31 Development of University Libraries in India After Independence
**O.P. Gupta** Rs. 270

CICIL-32 Handbook on Child : With Historical Background
**Pramila Pandit Barooah** Rs. 320

CICIL-33 Weaker Section in Indian Society : Undiscovered Past, Uncertain Present and Unpredictable Future Index to Writings in Indian Scholarly Journals and 10 National Newspapers Classified under 1500 Descriptors 1886-1990
**S.P. Agrawal** and **Rajeev Kumar Sharma** Rs. 600

CICIL-34 Communication Informatics and Librarianship in India : An Introductory Guide to Publications Based on a Survey of Libraries in Capital of City India
**S.P. Agrawal** and **Pushpa Rani Sharma** Rs. 720